CONTENTS

FOREWORD

By SAM HAMMAM

Sometimes you can describe a person's character in few words. For Annis Abraham there is only one word - FAMILY - Annis equals family and family equals Annis and anything else is incidental.

My first encounter with Annis was in 2000 when I was looking to buy a club. Having been bombarded with many communications by Cardiff fans and local media a meeting was set at the Friendly Inn Hotel. My request was for two or three fans because I was curious. I had only asked to meet an hour and a half before. When I reached the two fans were not there. Instead there were about fifty and they kept coming. This showed me passion and it hit me clear and strong.

Every person has their first moment with a club. Annis's was in November 1973. The Watergate scandal was breaking, Princess Anne was marrying a commoner, Ryan Giggs was busy being born and Annis would have been on the terraces of Ninian Park watching Gil Reece put in a goal that won Cardiff City the game. Everyone has their moment. For me it was at the Friendly Inn Hotel Saturday 1st July 2000.

Amongst those fans was a tall man who introduced himself as Annis. I told him that this is an Arabic name and asked him whether he knew what it meant - he didn't or at least pretended not to. So I told him - amiable, sociable, and friendly but mainly, CHERISHED FRIEND.

What I heard that day had a major effect on the future on the club and that of my own. Someone called out that if Cardiff were successful in the Premier League there would be over 50,000 supporters in the stands! It was Annis who said that. It was him who started that line, and he was supported by a host of other passionate Bluebirds. That day was the birth of the modern day Cardiff City.

What I saw and felt from those loyal fans that day, I took to heart and it made me a believer in THE DREAM.

Cardiff can, and should, be as big as any club in the world. We have the base to do it, because we have the catchment area and very significantly we have the natural Welsh passion which other cities do not have - at least not in the same intensity. We are a club for a whole nation, The Welsh Nation. The only thing stopping us is if we let our heads drop, it is an inner thing. It is Belief. In Annis (and others) you get that belief in the Cardiff City family. Cardiff will be in a league with Barcelona there may be no terraces when it happens, and Gil Reece not to be the one slipping in the winning goal, but its there.

This is how my friendship with Annis began, with that first awe-inspiring feeling at the Cardiff City family. They do say a club chooses you. That friendship has continued throughout my time as chairman and into my forced temporary exile to this day.

From this time, I have had the pleasure of meeting his flesh and blood family, Joanne his wife and his three daughters Annaise, Alexandra and Tilly. His father, who was once a feared self-made man from an immigrant Egyptian family, was at that time a semi invalid having suffered a stroke and in the main stayed at home. His mother Dawn was renowned for her work in saving, caring and rehabilitating greyhound dogs. Annis adored both his parents. He loved them in different ways because they were different people to each other - they completed each other.

It seemed to me that his father represented the power, achievement and discipline and his mother the values, principle and guidance.

These are the things he brings to his own children. He is an active and doting father, and has fought and continues to fight many battles in order to give them the best possible education, upbringing and values.

One Christmas when I visited his home he had a room full of a zillion presents. I told him that this was too much and that he should not spoil his children so, (but he was having none of that) what are you trying to get at here?

We have faced many moments together. These are not for now. There were three distinct changes that I saw in is personality. The first was after the death of his both parents, the second was the disappointment of the betrayal after the shamefully biased BBC Panorama programme which portrayed him as a hooligan and the third was after his marriage to Joanne. Through these, he has been standing by Cardiff City F.C. through the ups and downs, and sometimes the all rounds.

It is commonly claimed that, "Football is a business". Wrong! Football is never a business, never was and never will be! A football club is a passion, a continuous love affair and part of a person's soul. It is a sense of belonging to a bigger family. For those who get the privilege of running a club - be the owner, executives or managers - making business decisions is part of the deal, but that is no different than when parents are making business decisions (like what house to buy). A football club is not a club - it is a clan. It is a family.

Just as Annis cares for his immediate family he cares passionately for the Bluebirds family and gets involved in its positivity, actively and passionately. He was amongst other things, pivotal in getting me involved in the first place and in setting up and implementing our goals; he continues to be totally committed, involved and opinionated on anything and everything that is CITY.

Along with Annis, and a few of the lads, a strategy was set to reach our first goal by 2015 in the Premier League (after that it is consolidating and real growth). The ingredients to achieve THE DREAM were: STADIUM - YOUTH POLICY - STRONG - ADMINISTRATION - COMBATING HOOLIGANISM - EXCELLENT COMMUNICATION with fans and media - keeping good control of our FINANCES - excellent relationship with our local COUNCIL - effective SCOUTING SYSTEM and of course THE TEAM.

Annis was involved in working on all these things. He had strong views and gave advice. Some I took on board, some I didn't. In hindsight, I should have listened to some of the key advice he and others gave.

What I have learned from him as well is a Cardiff City of the past, nostalgia, and of roots. His mind is for the future, but his heart is for the past. It is Ninian Park that he longs for, the new logo which was designed to promote our Welshness he hated and lobbied successfully to get the previous one back, he wants standing not seats for the hardcore and younger fans, he is fixated with enmity to Swansea, and loathes Rugby and their people who are jealous of the massive superiority of football.

Over a year ago he was considering getting involved in buying Merthyr in order to save them because it reminds him of old Cardiff City ie of a human nature and dimension. I told him fine but only if he is willing to do all four things. Give it a hell of a lot of time, be ready to augment his plan with money, give it a lot of his love and attention - like his own child - and be ready to get abuse no matter how much he succeeds and at the very outset of a backward step. He capitulated and never got involved.

There are many stories, anecdotes and memories we shared together. Some were hilarious, others practical and some painful (very painful). Through it all I can say that in him I have a FRIEND.

I hope that he can now share with you some of his family's experiences and I hope that you all KEEP THE FAITH in THE DREAM and in this WELSH FAMILY.

One day we will succeed and THE DREAM will be achieved. If we fail to do it in our own time our children will and they will remember the Friendly Inn and those who came before. And when THE DREAM is a reality a new era will begin and it will be THE AWAKENING.

God Bless,
As Always
Much Love,
Sam

Sam Hammam, celebrating after Cardiff beat QPR 1 nil on the 25th May 2003 at the Millenium Stadium and therefore winning promotion to the Championship

ACKNOWLEDGEMENTS

A special thanks to my loving wife, Joanne, for putting up with me and always being there for me and to my three beautiful daughters, Annaise, Alexandra, and Tilly Annis for singing Bluebirds and doing the Ayatollah every day to me which kept me going.

I could not have written this book without the help of Carl Curtis (Neath Blues).

My Godsons Connor Sullivan and Daniel Evans.

My Uncle Garth for returning, Uncle Tony and Aunty Pauline Vile.

My good friend Sam Hammam who dared to let us Cardiff City fans dream and we would today not be where we are without him.

Owain Davies (front cover of the book and administrator to www.cardiffcityforum.co.uk and www.annisabraham.co.uk)

I owe a big thank you to George Calder, a Kilmarnock Football Fan, because when I was on holiday in Mallorca, we started chatting and, after listening to my many endless tales about Cardiff City, he convinced me to write a book, Shattered Dreams and from there I have now written 6, Well, here we are again, thanks again George.

Jamie Sullivan, Anna Stewart, Dave Bennett, Geraint Handley (Cheggers), Jonathan Evans, Nils Anderson, Colin Howells (Little Colin), Pat Dollan (Chelsea), Mikey Dye (Dio), Warren Feeney (Northern Ireland international) and George Feeney (Warren's son), Bobby and Billy McCluskie (Scotch Corner Santa Ponsa), Jonathan Owen (BBC), Conrad Pheasant, Simon and Charles Williams, Vince Alm (Cardiff City Supporters Club), Gwyn Davies (Founder of the Valley Rams), Julian Jenkins (Cardiff City), Paul Corkrey, Sam Murphy (Big Sam), Neil MacNamara (Mac), Simon Neads (Neath Punk), Peter Mannings, Malcolm McCann (Mallo), Wayne Anderson (Dibs), Steve Day (Daya), Lyndon Cushing for changing from egg head to the round ball.

All the following fans and persons have all helped in one way or another Stuart and Pat Muff, Dai Noble (Nobby), Ian Shepheard (Shep), Nash Snr and George Nash (Goldsmith's), Gareth Davies (Gazza), Terry Phillips, Paul Abbandonato and Tim Gordon (South Wales Echo), Ian Butterworth, George Wood, Jason Turner, Jason Perry, Phil Dwyer, Steve and Christine Borley, Peter Ridsdale, Lee and Nicky Beames, Wayne Critchon (photographer), Dave, Angie and Rob of Express Imaging, Mike Morris of the CCFC unofficial website, Frankie Dimodica, Lorrie Guppy, Olly Clifford, Derek Holmes (Queen of the South), Jamie DeCruz, Alun Griffiths (Jaffa), Steve Evans (Wolf), Peter Morgan (Mogs), Kevin Milward (Kettie), Dai Thomas, Ian Charles, Matthew Alm, Leon Phipps, Linda Sullivan, Victoria Sullivan, Jason Eaton,

Ray Phipps, Jason Burrows, Kenny, John (Simmo), Pam, Jermaine, and Lee Simmonds, Sian, Bradley Ashford for giving up Man United for the Bluebirds, Peter Crawford (Jock), Tonto, Johnny Bywater, Ben and Chris Griffiths, Gareth Rogers, Brian Harris, Naveed Khan, Nigel Harris, Sticky, Spike and Mr Williams for having to spend seven seasons with me, sitting behind me listening to me always moaning, Tony Rees (ex-News of the World reporter), Alan Kersleg, Simon Insole, Mario, Wayne Palmer, Craig McGowen, Elizabeth Jenkins, Sheila & Brian Hollin, Neil & Pauline Davey, Tony and Lyn Roblin, Mark & Jane Crowley, Peter & Samantha Lamb, Ali - The one and only DJ, Gary Lee, Dan James, Richard England, Steven & Joanna Hamilton, John Doel. Thanks to my three great postmen, Glyn Pattern, Phil Fry & Alun Thomas all loyal Bluebirds. Tony Clemo (ex-Cardiff City chairman), Mona and all the girls in the City Ticket Office, Suzanne Twamley (Welsh FA) and Richard Twamley, Alyson, Bradley and Caitlyn Bennett, Alison Curtis and Angharad Curtis, Laura Cushing, Debbie and Kate Murphy.

Glenn Villis, Steven Kajed, Alan Rawlins, Stan, Dexy, Anthony Lewis (Bomber), Neil Macinnes, Adam Brown, Jason McAuley, Paul Blackburn, Gareth Gardner, Stud, Pricey, Nigel Lancastle, Paul Mohammed (Mojo), Wilburs, Jamo, Brian Edge, Skeeny, Glen Waithe, Chris Snibs, Mark Gardner, Roy Jones, Wally, Kersleg, Marksy, Gonk, Gary Tyre, Leighton & Thomas Rees, Billy (Badge seller), Joey Mullins, Gareth Davies, Paul Morgan, Lee Bratcher, Emlyn Richards, Alex Mannings, Pete Lintern, Anton (Taffy Anton), Knowles (Chunky), Lee Atkinson (Ackers) and anyone else from Section A of the grandstand.

Tony Ridgeway (Guff), Steve Wilson, Ginger Jones, Frankie Humphries, Liam Tresilian, Joff Lee, H (Thailand), Darren Williams (Bridgend), Steve Williams (Suggs), Kev Ederle (Holyhead), Bev Dale, Paul Williams (Canton), Bobby Hawker, Valley Commandos, Tosh, Little Natalie, Kenny Collins, Steve Pritchard, Aaron Morgan, Rob Hutchinson, Jeff Evans, Robert Maggs, Kevin Evans, Andrew Jones, Gary Summerfield, Dai Hunt, Lawrence Riel (Rusty), Jellyhead, Paul Grexson, Ivor, Amour Mear (Bear), Dave Allen (Top man), Mark Watkins, Clive Francis, Dilwyn, Simon Beddis (Ely Valley Blue), Andrew (The Blueline Fanzine), John (from Swansea), Alan Swain, Anthony Rivers (Lakey), Alan Williams (Hafren Roofing), Dave Hayman, Sam (Dinas Powys), Dai Taxi, Mike Flynn, Michael Harvey, Daryl Lewis, Dibble, Glen Price, Jeff Lloyd, Nigel Raphes, Roy Williams, Clayton Smith, Jeff Marsh, Kersie, Chris Beer, Dafydd May, Adam O'Shea, Steven Parker, Mark Jeffries, Mark Bloom, Mark Todd, Steven Byrne, Les Beckett, Timothy Wood, Mike and Decklyn Joyce, Paul Drummond, Big Tom, Neck, Bonker, Skull, Ritchie Jones, Taylor, Terry Lewis, Dessey, Donald Barry, Big Karl Stillman, Edgey, Robbie Bounds, Falarty, Carlton, Pip, Pie Face, Dido, Robert Harry, Anthony Gee, Cissy, Earnie, Chris & Jamie Dye, Adrian Beer (Zub), Dulla, Derym, Mexi, Joker, Nicky Randall, Dai H, Robert Penny, Robert Moore, Carl Newel (fruit machines), Richard Sandam (Skewen), Helen Thomas, June & Liam Coulthard, Julian Kelly, Stefan Davies and Phil Newman (Merthyr), Tarki Micallef, Peg (Denmark Bluebird) and all the London based 1927 members. Mike Lambert, Mike Pearce, Phil Southall (Port

Talbot), Gwilym Rees, Mark & Mary Jeremy (Section B Grandstand), John Cross, Eric Botchett, Steve Perry, John Lancy, Phil Lathey, Les Hayes, Martin Knott, Ian Allaway, Ian Mitchard, Matthew Jones (Matty), Richard Cordle, Paul Santos, Steve Davies, Chrissy and James Dye, Terry Lownes, Clem brothers(Bridgend), Marksy, Dave Jones, Craig Hughes (Guppi), Skeeny.

Claire Mallon, Nathan (Milly) and Adam (Chippy) Millichip, Robert Barrett (Baz), Tony Iacobucci (Top Cat), Adam Brown, Claire (Jez), Steve Thomas (Nuclearblue), Adam Soper and Cheri Price, Mark Davies, Nugent, Dave Roberts (Conwy Bluebird), Paul Cummings (Clydebank Bluebird), Gareth Hughes (Wiltshire Blue), Cameron Curtis and Aaron Curtis (Neath Blues), Marc Broadbent, Neil Macdonald , Dominic Towell and The Ant Hill Mob, Phil Roberts, Gareth Thomas (Gaffa), Martyn Tobin (Port Talbot Blues), Neil Owen (Earnieblue), Julian Richards, Bill Tandy, Jim (Jimbo), Rob (Bluebird 23), Ricardo (Rick) and Antonio Garcia, Richard (Fairwater Youth), Peter Jennings (Worcester Blue), Tim Wegener (Lawnmower), Steve O'Mara (Uncle Fester), Jules (Luton Bluebird), Luke Coakley, Ieuan Bisatt; Jamie Curtis, Joshua Curtis, Brioni Curtis (Neath Blues), Steve Barnett, Nigel (Rotters) and Andrew Williams, Gareth Tarent, Neil Guest (Cwm Bluebirds), Darren Stevens (Ebbw Vale), Woody, Boulton, Quinny (Tredegar Blues), Ian Hallam (Derby Bluebird), Berwyn Jay, Gary Field (Castleblue), Robert Shopland (Nobber), Damien Evans, Richard Huish (Gabbs), Dean Gover, Dean Potter, Andrew Parsells (Premier 1), Andy, Morgan and Llwyd French-Simonds, Thomas Fish, Tony Williams, Neil (earnieblue), Chris CCFC, Jonathan Smith, Adam Price, Clive Sedgebeer, Vince Gulley (Hereford Blue), Craig Green (Merlin), Jeff Deere (Caesars DJ), Lewis 91, Roy and Lewis Jones, Tony Jeffries, Jerry Waddel, Cath, Gareth and Thomas Seville, Jarred and Aaron Weaver, Gareth Jenkins, Elliot Lugg, Gerwyn Teague, Greg Davies, Richard Hopkins, John Smith (Merthyr), Roy Colley, Liam (Glammy 74), Morgan Anderson, Nathan Freeman, Peely, Blakey, Blain and Daniel (Port Talbot Blues), Paul, George and Jack (Yiacoumi Bro's, Barbers), Mike (NI Bluebird), Nick Fish, Paul (Sludge).

Chongo, Mucky, Paul O'Connell, Lugg, Dobbo, Wilo, Gabby, Jacko, Big Tec, Little Tec, Chris Price, Christian, Steven Deacon, Hugh Boy, Jesse, Blond Simmo, Beachy, Gethin and Chris(Original Soul Crew), the Baker Brothers, Steven Breads, Pricey, Lez Millward, Jammo, Dowie, Shoulders, Mike Pederic, Joe Mullins, Dicky Donut, Rhys, Joseph and Sarah Mackay, Jonah (Brighton Bluebird), Newt, Ducky, Pocock, Spud, Richie (Blackwood), Foster, Keith, Mark, Ganville, Ginger John, David Stanley, Beefy, Bevan, Chris (Caerphilly), Pigeon and Ching.

To all the lads from Sunderland (Seaburn Casuals): Brookie, Daz, Jason, Locky, The Twins, Joe and the many more that I've met who have always made me and my friends welcome and shown us great hospitality.

Nicky Muff (Leeds Utd), Tony Rheardon (Bolton Wanderers), Dave and Daniel Roberts, Pricket, Ian Woodward and Adams (Newport County), Dave Chappell

(Crystal Palace), Stefan (Offenbach FC), Mark Gregor and Ricky Dee (QPR), Big Al, Bones, Jason (Sooty) and Cuddles (Birmingham), Gilly Shaw (Wolves), Mark Forrester and Fowler (Villa), Karl (Hereford), Paul Wright and Paul (Millwall), Alex, Marilyn, Ben and Lee Watson (Kilmarnock), Danny Robinson and Mike (Plymouth Argyle), Murco (Stoke C), Mike (Wigan), Paul (Reading FC), John Newey (WBA), Diddy and Dave (Boro), Sam Salim and Mandy McCann (Sheff Wed), Alan Swain, Jamie Eddolls, Angus, Neil, Marc Parcell (Bristol C), Terry Last, Steve Hickmont and Stuart Glass (Chelsea), Neil, Scoots and Ponch (Wrexham), Simon and Ian (AFC Wimbledon), Rowland (Pompey), Chris Anderson and Paul (Burnley FC),Christopher Peter and Cass Pennant (West Ham Utd), Ginger Bob (Millwall), Chris Gilly (Newcastle Utd), Barry Bedford (Swansea), Jon Newey (WBA).

RIP Derek Ford, Mike Rayer, Budgie, Ginger Jason, Jeff Richards, Gareth Tarent (Cardiff City), Manny (Bradford City), Lemmy (Newport County).

To the following persons and book shops, who have helped me and have sold my books Mark Dudden Newsagents, 80 Albany Road Cardiff. John Bassett (Ninian Park Pub), Matthew, Stern Clothing (Pontypridd). Sam Jones, A2 Clothing, Victoria Street, Merthyr. Here's Newsagents, 32 Albany Road, Cardiff. Billy (Billy Badge), Sean (Sports shop, Cardiff indoor Market), Paul (Mojo King, Wellfield Arcade, Roath, Cardiff).

www.cardiffcityforum.co.uk & www.annisabraham.co.uk

MY STORY

Introduction

As soon as I began thinking about putting this book together I knew I'd get heavily criticised if I went ahead with it but that's a risk I'm willing to take. I've been told often enough that mine is a story worth telling so I've finally decided to go for it.

This book is not just about my life at football, far from it, you could say I have had rather an eventful life, I have worked in nightclubs/pubs/hotels the length and breadth of Wales and England, I've seen people at deaths door, gang warfare, racial hatred, throughout running many successful businesses, I will tell how I have met many and dealt with showbiz stars, sports stars, musical legends and politicians. I will tell how Tom Jones asked my father to be his manager, plus many other people like Peter Stringfellow who have tried to come in to business with us.

My father and I would buy failed or bankrupt night clubs/hotels and then turn them around and then move on to the next one.

I am very proud to have come from a working class background, whose father rose from the Docks of Tiger Bay to become the first nightclub owner and casino owner in Wales and a mother who came from a working class family who became one of Europe's leading trumpet players and the founder member of Greyhound Welfare. I was taught the true values of life, which stood me in good stead in my working life from the age of 12.

I have had some unforgettable relationships with some of the biggest names in recent British football history of Chairman. My love for Cardiff City led me to kicking boardroom doors open, to threatening to blow up the club all because we lost a game.

Warts and all accounts of the highs and lows including my brushes with the law, my two well documented Panorama specials.

Also how I have become a changed man and how different life is now.

The game of football has been a huge part of my life ever since I first watched Cardiff City play in November 1973. I was a seven year-old schoolboy at the time. During the subsequent thirty eight years I've supported the Bluebirds at almost every ground in the Football League, at numerous non-league venues and in a variety of other countries. I've sponsored Cardiff's players, their kits, their vehicles, match balls and programmes.

I've become friendly with hundreds of other City fans and a number of ex-players, directors and chairmen. I've tried to buy a major shareholding in the club on two occasions and have even written a book about it. Nevertheless, the fact remains that whenever my name is mentioned in connection with Cardiff City it is most commonly associated with hooliganism.

The simple truth is that the club has had a large and active hooligan following for the majority of the time that I've been supporting it. Right the way throughout the Seventies, Eighties and Nineties, an unusually high percentage of Cardiff's fans were lads of various ages who enjoyed getting involved in trouble on match days and for almost twenty years I was one of them. My experiences during that time form the basis of the book you are about to read.

While I'm not expecting anyone to approve of the way that I and the lads I mixed with behaved in the past, I'm not going to start issuing any apologies either. For some of us it's just the way things were at the football back then. A lot of people might not be comfortable with that fact but I want to be as honest about the situation as I can. I'll be explaining to the best of my knowledge how life was for those of us who were involved in football hooliganism but I won't be apologising for anything. I want to make that clear from the beginning. Don't misunderstand me though, I do have some regrets. No doubt about that. However, as far as I'm concerned the need for apologies disappeared when my parents passed away.

Generally speaking, the atmosphere at football matches when I started travelling around the country with Cardiff back in the late-Seventies was totally different to how things are nowadays. It was much more hostile by comparison but it was also very exciting for lads like me who were in our teens and early-twenties. It was really easy to get carried away by the thrill that trouble at the football provided and thousands of youngsters from all over South Wales did. Some would get involved regularly, others just occasionally, but for a few of us football violence developed into much more than a bit of entertainment on a Saturday afternoon. It became a way of life.

The kind of excitement that could be generated when it kicked off before, during or after a game is something that's very difficult to describe to anyone who never experienced it for themselves. The adrenalin rush was incredible. It was the sort of feeling money couldn't buy. Regardless of their circumstances, most people never encounter anything even remotely close to that kind of buzz in their everyday lives, and that's one of the main reasons why I believe so many young men who were growing up during the same era as me were drawn towards hooliganism.

Having said that, the prospect of violent disorder and the excitement it produced certainly wasn't the only factor involved in the formation of hooligan gangs such as

Cardiff City's Soul Crew. It was never just about fighting. There was a lot more to it than that. As strange as it may sound, there was a definite sense of identity that came with belonging to a football firm and that was very important to a lot of the lads. Then there were the fashions that many of us followed, particularly during the Eighties and Nineties. Clothes became an obsession for some of the boys, me included. The friendships that would be forged whenever a group of lads got together for the football were also very significant. That's demonstrated by the fact that many of us who first met on football trips became friends for life as a result of the time we spent together supporting our teams and battling with rival mobs. In my case, almost all of the close friendships I've developed since my early teens have come about as a direct result of football. In fact, such was the weird world within the football casuals' culture that I even became friendly with a number of lads who supported different clubs and belonged to different firms.

Something that's always irritated me is the way in which the British media has portrayed those of us who got involved in football violence. There were times during the last three decades when known hooligans were demonized by the press to such an extent that the general public must have thought the lads concerned were among the most evil men in the country. It's as if the media wanted the public to believe we were in the same category as murderers, rapists and paedophiles, and I'm speaking from bitter personal experience when I say that. The producers of Panorama's June 2000 program 'England's Shame' made the events I was caught up in at the European Championships in Belgium look far worse than they actually were, but that's the way a lot of journalists appear to work. Why bother with truth if it doesn't make for such a good story? That seems to be their attitude. The BBC dragged my name through the mud during the summer of 2000 and they attempted to do so again in 2002. Life became very difficult for me for a few months after the first of those two Panorama programmes was screened, particularly in terms of my business activities. I expect there are plenty of people who will say I deserved it and considering my history I suppose they might be right. Nevertheless, something I definitely learned from that episode was how those who work within the British media industry can occasionally twist the facts to suit themselves.

The manner in which the press has usually depicted football hooligans over the years has resulted in the common misconception that we were all mindless thugs with low levels of intelligence. Now obviously there were a reasonable percentage of boys who did fit that stereotype. Nobody can deny that and I won't even try. However, I reckon many people would be shocked if they knew the backgrounds of some of the lads who regularly played their part in football-related disorder, particularly when hooliganism was as its peak in the Eighties. For example, Cardiff City's mob during that period included businessmen, civil servants, company directors, local government officers, bank clerks and servicemen, while a few of the lads who used to run with the Soul Crew later became police officers and solicitors. People might find that hard to believe but it's the honest truth. If nothing was known of their antics at football matches, then all of those boys would have been considered respectable members of society.

However, if they were caught misbehaving on a match day, then the whole picture would suddenly change. They would immediately be labelled the scum of the earth by the media and the public alike. To me, that's just ridiculous.

The actual levels of violence that were involved when rival hooligan gangs clashed were something that was often greatly exaggerated by the press. Yes, of course there were times when things got really nasty. I won't attempt to pretend otherwise, although in my experience genuinely violent encounters which resulted in anything other than minor injuries were the exception rather than the rule. In all honesty, I witnessed much more serious examples of violence during my years working in the bars and nightclubs than I ever saw on the terraces, as I'll demonstrate later.

I'm always amazed when I hear people suggest that those of us who got involved in trouble at matches were not proper supporters. To me, such stupid comments indicate a complete lack of understanding about football hooliganism. During my time following Cardiff I've seen the team play league games in front of crowds of less than 2,000 at Ninian Park and I've been among tiny numbers of away fans at places like Hartlepool, Darlington and Scarborough. The truth is that almost all of the lads who were considered trouble makers would usually be there supporting City home and away regardless of how bad the team was, who the opposition were and whether there was any likelihood of trouble or not. In fact, at various times during the Seventies, Eighties and Nineties, some of the club's so-called hooligans were among its most loyal supporters. There are plenty of Cardiff fans today who will deny that was ever the case but I didn't see too many of them on our travels when the team were getting beaten regularly in the Football League's bottom divisions. Where were they all hiding when City were rubbish, I wonder?

Due to my numerous contacts in football and business, I've watched games from directors' boxes on a few occasions but I've turned down invitations to do so many more times as the experience has always left me cold. The atmosphere is totally different and it doesn't suit me at all. I'm a vocal kind of supporter and I find you just can't enjoy a game to the same degree in a directors' box as you can when you're stood on the terraces or sat in the stands with your mates. There's no shouting, no chanting and no winding up the opposition supporters when you're alongside the directors and their guests. That scene is not for me and it never will be. I'd much rather be in among the lads, which is where I've been since 1973 and where I expect to be until I'm no longer able to go to the football.

I'm a family man these days with a wife and three young daughters. It's been many years since I was last involved in hooligan activities of any sort, but although that's all in the past now I'm still as proud to be a Cardiff City fan as I was when I first started supporting the team in the early-Seventies. The game of football in this country has changed considerably in recent times, and not necessarily for the better as far as I'm concerned, but nevertheless I remain a Bluebirds fanatic and I always will be. That's one thing I know will never change. This is my story; I hope you enjoy reading it.

CHAPTER ONE

GROWING UP IN THE SEVENTIES

Before I start talking about the various events during the many years I've spent following Cardiff City and the 22 years I spent working in nightclubs, hotels, shops and any business that would make money, I thought I'd give you a little bit of information about my family background as it's an unusual one to say the least.

My Egyptian grandfather settled in Cardiff's famous Tiger Bay docks area shortly before the outbreak of the First World War. He arrived in South Wales without any money and he couldn't read or write but he spoke eight different languages so was able to get a decent job working in the law courts as an interpreter. Unfortunately though, he was a heavy gambler and not a particularly clever one. Therefore, the family often struggled for money and my father, Annis Snr, had a fairly tough upbringing as a result. I reckon his life story is worthy of a book all of its own.

Like many young men of his generation from the Tiger Bay docklands he signed up for the Merchant Navy shortly after leaving school. However, he quickly discovered that life as a seafarer wasn't to his liking so he enlisted in the Royal Air Force instead. During his five years of service with them he developed a talent for boxing and he eventually became the RAF middleweight champion – an achievement he was always very proud of. He only gave the sport up after breaking his hand during a fight and years on it would swell up if ever he hit anyone. My father was never a drinker or a smoker, so he managed to save a lot of the cash he earned in the Air Force and he used it wisely after he was demobbed.

Following brief spells as a taxi driver and a bookie's runner, he made his first mark in the world of business by travelling around Cardiff selling candyfloss and other confectionery from the back of a van. The money he made from that venture enabled him to buy two small garages, where he traded in used cars whilst also operating a backstreet bookmaker's office. In 1958 he invested in a place he called El Cuba, which became Cardiff's first coffee bar. Within the space of a year he'd bought himself another establishment which he named Mayfields. That one became the city's first fully-licensed nightclub.

It was an immediate success and my father soon became renowned as one of the leading names in the nightclub business. He went on to own no less than forty four different clubs in various towns and cities across the country, as well as four more overseas. Among the numerous show business acts he gave a helping hand to during his many years as a nightclub owner was a young up-and-coming singer from

Treforest called Tommy Woodward. He was later to find fame and fortune after moving to London and changing his name to Tom Jones. I had the pleasure of meeting Tom in Las Vegas in 1980 and he told me then how grateful he was for the way in which my father had backed him during the early stages of his career. My father had an eye for talent and during the late 1950's there were street parties down Tiger Bay, as they were all partying away, my father went and got a small sound system out with a microphone and asked a young Shirley Bassey to sing for everyone. She was an instant hit; my father a few years later took her around all the local clubs in South Wales and got her booked in to them.

My mother, Dawn, was originally from Bury in Lancashire. She worked as a professional trumpet player in Ivy Benson's popular All Girl Band and met my father in 1963 while playing at one of his clubs. He was forty two at the time and she was just eighteen, but despite their considerable age difference it was apparently a case of love at first sight and they were married soon afterwards.

I was born in the Roath area of Cardiff in November 1965 and I'd say my childhood was generally a happy one apart from a two-year period when the family moved over to Spain. We lived in a small place called San Augustin, which is a few miles away from Palma de Mallorca where my father had bought a nightclub. I was only five years old at the time and just couldn't settle down there at all, particularly as I hated the infants' school I attended. As a result, I was sent back to Britain to live with my grandparents after eighteen months or so, which was about six months before my parents returned to this country. It's ironic as I love Spain now and spend most of my holidays over there.

My father was a strict and imposing man who didn't stand for any messing around when I was a youngster but I loved him all the same and always had the utmost respect for him. One of the first of many lessons he taught me was never to bully anyone and never to allow myself to be bullied. I can remember coming home one day at the age of seven and complaining that I was being picked on by two boys at school. His response was to tell me not to mention them again until I'd sorted them both out and I took his advice. He later taught me never to start a fight if I thought I could avoid doing so, but added that if I was convinced a fight was inevitable I should make sure I got in the first blow as that was half the battle. It was another valuable lesson that has served me well over the years.

He also taught me the value of money at an early age. At twelve years old I regularly worked the cash desks at his clubs on weekends and school holidays, and when I was fourteen, I started working behind the bars. On the Mondays when I went to school, I would take bags of beer towels and beer mats to school with me, the brewery would give hundreds of them to us for the club, I would sell them to the other kids for a bit of extra pocket money. My father would keep most of my wages for me and double up whatever I was saving for later in life. I never smoked, never drank alcohol and never used drugs of any sort as I was growing up. My father also did not believe in credit cards and money on the never never, as he believed you should not spend what you have not got, he used to say to me "Son if you haven't got it in your pocket then don't buy it," to this day I remind myself of those words and very rarely use credit cards unless it's essential. I've never used one while I am abroad on holidays as I would not like to return to a debt, in my opinion he taught me well. While I feared my father, I didn't touch any of those things mostly out of respect for him. Besides which, I didn't need them anyway. My vice was always football. That's where I got most of my kicks when I was a teenager.

My father was never interested in football. He was a workaholic who spent the majority of his time concentrating on his businesses, although he loved boxing and would often go to fights or watch the boxing on TV. He was keen for me to follow in his footsteps and take up the boxing game but my mother wouldn't have any of it. My father had broken his right hand during his days as a fighter and he'd had trouble with it ever since, so that put her right off the idea.

While I didn't become a boxer, a cousin of mine called Rudi Pika did. He was a top amateur and fought Frank Bruno for the ABA British Heavyweight title at the Wembley Arena in 1980. They were both eighteen at the time. Everyone I know who saw that fight swears to this day that Rudi won it, but the referee awarded it to Bruno on points. Some say that if Rudi had been a Londoner and Bruno had been a Welshman, then the ref would have scored the contest differently. Others reckon that the promoters already had some big contracts lined up for Bruno so they couldn't afford for him to get beaten. I have no idea what the truth is. All I know for sure is that my father wasn't happy with the decision and I think he lost a lot of his respect for the sport after that fight. Rudi went on to be managed by Mickey Duff and was undefeated in all thirteen of his professional contests but he was never given a proper shot at the big time. Tragically, he took his own life in 1988 after suffering from depression.

As a youngster I often used to visit my mother's parents in Lancashire on weekends and school holidays. My grandfather, Fred, was a football fanatic and it was he who introduced me to the sport. While I was staying up there he'd occasionally take me to Gigg Lane to see his beloved Bury play. They were in the old Fourth Division at the time and I reckon I must have watched them six or seven times before I got to see Cardiff City in action.

My first visit to Ninian Park was in November 1973. The Bluebirds were due to play Bolton Wanderers in a Second Division game shortly before my eighth birthday and the club had given some free tickets to my school in Marshfield. I knew my father wouldn't take me to the match but my grandparents were visiting us that weekend so Fred was happy to accompany me to Ninian. City had a pretty poor side at the time and was fighting against relegation. A few years earlier they had been pushing for promotion to the First Division and were regularly getting crowds over 20,000, but then the club sold star striker John Toshack to Liverpool and the team went downhill from there. The attendance for the Bolton game was less than 10,000 but as a young schoolboy I thought the atmosphere was amazing. I was really impressed by the noise of the crowd and loved the singing and chanting. It was all very different to Gigg Lane, where attendances rarely got above the 3,000 mark. I immediately became hooked on the Bluebirds, especially as they won that first match 1-0 with a goal by Welsh international Gil Reece.

My grandparents moved down to Cardiff to be nearer to my mother shortly after that, which worked out perfectly for me. I began to go to games regularly with my grandfather, who bought us season tickets for the Bob Bank terrace a year later. City were relegated to the Third Division at the end of that season but they bounced back straight away with promotion in 1975/76. That was a fantastic campaign for the club and there were some big crowds at Ninian Park, including one of over 35,000 against Hereford United. My heroes back then were Phil Dwyer, Tony Evans and John Buchanan, who is still my favourite Cardiff player to this day.

Although 1975/76 was a terrific season for City, I was nevertheless the only kid in my school that supported them. Most of the other boys claimed they were Leeds or Liverpool fans, which really used to piss me off. The fact that they wouldn't support their local team didn't make any sense to me and I hated some of them for it. The playground arguments I had with those kids resulted in plenty of scraps and landed me in all sorts of trouble with the teachers. Looking back now, I suppose you could say I was involved in football violence for the first time as a ten year-old!

It was during the mid-Seventies that I initially became aware of hooliganism, although I was too young to know what was actually happening at the time. Whenever my grandfather and I used to walk out of the Bob Bank and onto Sloper Road, there always seemed to be gangs of youths running all over the place. I'd be wondering what all the excitement was about and would ask Fred if we could stay and watch what was going on but he'd insist we go straight back to the car. He'd say my father would be angry if we got home late and he wouldn't talk about what was happening in the streets outside the ground if he could help it. His club, Bury, was a small family outfit compared to Cardiff, so I don't think he liked the atmosphere around Ninian Park too much.

By the early stages of the 1978/79 season I'd started going down to watch the City with my mates instead of my grandfather. I was in my element, especially when we were playing one of the bigger clubs like Tottenham, Newcastle or Chelsea, and being in the middle of a group of lads definitely made the match-day experience more enjoyable. Easter Monday, 1979, is a day I will never forget as that was when I went to my first away game. It was at West Ham of all places and a baptism of fire would probably be the best way to describe it. The events I witnessed at Upton Park back then made a deep and lasting impression on me. I've still got vivid memories of the various incidents even now, and although it was almost thirty years ago I can remember them like they happened yesterday.

The match was a three o'clock kick-off, so I told my parents I was heading into the city centre in the morning. As I didn't want them to know I was going to the football, I claimed I was planning to watch a couple of films at the Odeon with my mate Andrew Jones and said I was going back to his house afterwards. My father allowed me to go provided I promised I'd be back at nine in time for work at his club. I remember being really excited about the prospect of travelling to London to watch the Bluebirds and it never entered my head that I was going to what was regarded as one of the scariest grounds in the country for visiting fans. In all honesty, I knew very little about hooliganism at that stage. I was as green as grass and was just looking forward to watching City play against one of the top teams in the Second Division. West Ham were on the fringes of the promotion race and Cardiff were battling against relegation as usual, so it promised to be an interesting game. That's all I was thinking about when I decided to go.

I'd booked to travel on one of the Adar Glas Supporters' Club coaches which were run in those days by a couple from Cilfynydd called Roy and Mair Daniels. When I got to Ninian Park, I found that my coach was mainly full of supporters from Valleys towns like Pontypridd and Llantrisant. I guess I was probably the youngest fan on it and I was on my own as Jonesy hadn't turned up, so I headed towards the back of the bus and sat there quietly. I was a bit nervous at first but a pair of brothers named Kenny and Vincent Ham got chatting to me and soon made me feel at ease. They would have been about eighteen and nineteen and I was only thirteen, although I was fairly big for my age and I must have looked at least sixteen, so I didn't feel too out of place in the company of the older lads.

Most of the talk on the way to East London was about how West Ham's fans were a bunch of psychos and how Upton Park was a dangerous place to go. That should have rung a few alarm bells for me but I wasn't bothered at all. It merely added to the excitement as far as I was concerned. When we eventually arrived there we were met by a large number of police who escorted us straight into the ground. Nobody was allowed to go and have a drink or get anything to eat but if the truth be told I don't think many wanted to anyway. About seven or eight hundred Cardiff supporters had made the journey and it looked to me like around three quarters of those were young men who'd be able to fight if they had to, although I sensed there was a definite feeling of tension in the air. Many of our fans seemed apprehensive about the afternoon ahead and it turned out they had very good reason.

As we took our places on the terrace behind the goal I noticed straight away that the segregation between our section and the home supporters was only a small wall which was just a few feet high. I can remember that surprised me, although I probably didn't think too much of it at the time. The crowd inside the Boleyn Ground was almost 30,000, which was one of West Ham's biggest of the season. The atmosphere was hostile right from the word go as the rival sets of fans began winding each other up and it got worse after Pat Holland headed the home side into an early lead. I found it pretty intimidating, especially as this was my first away match and our supporters were so heavily outnumbered.

When the half-time whistle blew I decided to go downstairs and get myself a cup of tea. While I was being served, the lady behind the counter said "I'd take that scarf off your wrist if I was you, son." She seemed genuinely concerned for me and I couldn't understand why. I boldly told her it was fine as I was a Cardiff fan and I casually made my way back upstairs. In retrospect, it seems she had a good idea of what was coming next but I didn't have a clue.

Out on the terraces the situation was about to take a dramatic turn for the worse. The home supporters were chanting "United, United, United," while the City fans were shouting "Shit, Shit, Shit." Then, without any warning, all hell suddenly broke loose as hundreds of West Ham lads launched what must have been a premeditated attack on the Cardiff end. They invaded our enclosure from both sides like they were on a military manoeuvre. To our right, they started pouring over the small wall that separated our section from theirs. To our left, they were charging out of the terrace they called the Chicken Run, running across the corner of the pitch and jumping into our end. It was total chaos and we were quickly overwhelmed. Like most of the City fans in London that afternoon, I was in a state of panic. We had no option but to try to get towards the back of the enclosure, although it was soon obvious there was no hiding place. A few of the older Cardiff boys attempted to stand their ground but they had no chance in the face of such an onslaught. Punches and kicks were flying in at them from all angles and they took a right battering.

The old bill had been flooding onto the terrace from the moment the invasion started but it took them several minutes to restore order and I got a kicking in the meantime. To be honest there was no real damage done, just a few bumps and bruises although I was badly shaken up. I reckon any lad of my age and with my lack of experience would have felt the same under the circumstances. The police eventually managed to form a cordon between us and the West Ham mob, and much to my relief they were slowly but surely forced back towards their own enclosures. Their assault had been swift, ferocious and very effective, as demonstrated by the fact that the majority of our supporters were virtually silent for the remainder of the match. Even an excellent volleyed equaliser from striker Ray Bishop ten minutes from time wasn't greeted with much of a celebration by the demoralised Cardiff fans. Our team may have earned a valuable draw on the pitch but we'd been well and truly beaten on the terraces. You might say we'd been hammered.

The fun and games weren't over yet though. Not by a long chalk. After the final whistle, the old bill held us inside the ground for about twenty minutes. During that time, I overheard a couple of them warning a group of our lads that we'd be on our own if we started chanting when we got outside. I reckon a lot of the policemen on duty that day were as nervous as I was. As the gates opened and we began to make our way back to our coaches, which were parked about a quarter of a mile away, a roar went up all around us and West Ham fans started appearing from everywhere. Once again we came under attack and once again some of the older Cardiff lads did their best to fight back but most of us just ran to the buses as fast as we could, dodging fists and boots along the way. A few of the West Ham mob even followed us onboard and were lashing out at us in the aisle as we tried to get to our seats.

Having totally lost control of the situation from the moment we left the ground, it seemed like an age before the police were able to get back on top of things. When they finally did manage to gain some sort of control, they gave us an escort away from the immediate Upton Park area. The number of cars and wagons they used was incredible. There must have been at least two police vehicles for every one of our sixteen coaches, but unlike today when buses full of Cardiff fans are often shadowed for long distances on the way home from matches, in this case the escort disappeared after a couple of miles.

That wasn't a smart move by the old bill, as within minutes of them leaving us around forty or fifty West Ham lads came hurtling across a patch of parkland to our left and began bombarding us with bricks and bottles. The coach drivers immediately stopped their vehicles and for the first and only time that afternoon the Cardiff boys were briefly able to turn the tables on the Cockneys. Loads of lads piled off the buses, steamed straight into the West Ham fans and chased them all over the place. It was a small victory but one that seemed to cheer everyone up no end. After I'd looked up and down the convoy of coaches, I pointed out to the Ham brothers that ours appeared to be the only one that hadn't been damaged during the battle. I'd spoken too soon though, as a large stone came crashing through one of the side windows just as we were about to pull away. Thankfully nobody was injured but the journey back to South Wales was definitely a lot colder as a result.

For a thirteen year old schoolboy on his first ever away trip, the experiences during that afternoon in East London had been frightening. However, they'd also been strangely exhilarating. Adrenalin had never pumped through my veins at such a rate before and I'd never previously felt the kind of excitement that gripped me as I watched our lads chasing those Hammers supporters across that park. Although I hadn't got off the coach and joined in, I was already promising myself that next time I saw something like that happening I would attempt to get involved.

Despite the fact that it was mighty cold due to the additional ventilation, the trip back to Cardiff was a great laugh. It seemed like everyone on the bus had cuts and bruises and we all had our own stories to tell. Three decades have passed since that game was played but I can honestly say I've never seen City fans take a worse hiding than the one West Ham dished out all those years ago. Nevertheless, it didn't put me off travelling to away matches. On the contrary, I became a regular traveller from that day forward and I actually booked my seat for the next trip during the journey home.

That game was up in Sunderland a fortnight later. They were top of the table and needed maximum points from their final two matches in order to clinch promotion to the First Division. City were still in danger of relegation despite having been on a terrific run which included four wins and two draws in the previous six games. Only three coach loads of Cardiff supporters made the long trek to Wearside, but those of us who did go witnessed a superb 2-1 City victory thanks to a brilliant penalty save by Ron Healey and goals from Ronnie Moore and Ray Bishop.

The crowd at Roker Park that day was well over 36,000. As a result, it was necessary for our fans to share an enclosure with some of the home supporters but surprisingly there was no trouble at all. Very few of us were wearing colours and we kept pretty quiet throughout, although to be fair I don't think it mattered a great deal anyway. I reckon the local lads were so concerned by what was happening on the pitch they weren't really bothered about a couple of hundred Welshmen.

Sunderland beat Wrexham 2-1 at the Racecourse in their final game but that defeat by the Bluebirds cost them dear. They ended up missing out on promotion by a point. City's fine form continued until the end of the season and they eventually finished ninth in the Second Division table, which was an amazing achievement considering they'd been marooned in the relegation zone for most of the campaign. Little did we know then but as far as the next thirty years were concerned that was as good as it was going to get for Cardiff City.

The last but one game of the season was a Friday evening clash against West Ham at Ninian. After what had happened at Upton Park less than a month earlier I was expecting a bloodbath but in truth it was relatively trouble-free. At one stage during an uneventful 0-0 draw a small group of Cockneys made a half-hearted charge across the Grange End terrace and that was about the extent of it. In recent years I've read claims that West Ham's mob caused all sorts of problems on their visits to Cardiff during the late-Seventies and early-Eighties. That's certainly not my recollection and nor is it that of the other lads I've spoken to who were following City in those days. West Ham were formidable at home, nobody can dispute that, and it's common knowledge they often made their mark on the road too, but nothing much happened when they came to South Wales. In my experience it was Chelsea who had the most impressive travelling firm back then, not the Hammers.

The boys from Stamford Bridge visited Cardiff a couple of months into the 1979/80 season. They'd been relegated after finishing bottom of the First Division the previous year and had made a mediocre start to the new campaign but their fans still turned up at Ninian Park in large numbers. A crowd of around 16,000 was easily our biggest at that stage of the season and was swelled by almost 3,000 Chelsea supporters.

About an hour and a half before the game I was with Jonesy and a few other
youngsters in a café opposite Cardiff Castle when more than a hundred older City lads
came charging past us. We leapt from our seats and tagged onto the back of the mob,
which was heading towards the Royal Hotel on the junction of St Mary Street and
Wood Street. The hotel's bar is only a short walk from Cardiff Central station and on
that occasion it was full of Chelsea fans as well over a thousand had arrived by train.
About twenty or thirty of them piled out when they realised Cardiff were coming their
way and began throwing bottles and glasses at the home contingent but they were
soon on the back foot. The City boys battered most of them back through the hotel
doors in no time, while those who got caught outside were smashed all over the place
until dozens of police arrived and calmed things down. That was the first time I'd
been close to the action while Cardiff's lads were giving a rival mob a kicking but I
didn't have long to wait for the next occasion.

After the fighting outside the hotel had ceased we began to make our way towards
Ninian Park. There were lots of Chelsea fans in evidence on the mile and a half walk
and consequently there were scuffles breaking out at regular intervals. As we passed
under the Leckwith Road railway bridge and turned left onto Sloper Road, my
attention was drawn to a gang of around fifty lads who were marching almost military
style on the opposite pavement. I didn't recognise any of them and guessed they were
a group of City supporters from one of the Valleys towns or a neighbouring district
like Barry or Penarth. The determined way they were moving caught my eye and I
remember being struck by the fact that they weren't wearing any colours. They also
seemed much quieter than most of the fans heading for Ninian Park. It looked to me
like they were on a mission, although hardly anybody seemed to notice.

When we arrived at the ground we took up our usual positions in the centre of the Bob
Bank under the television gantry. That's where the majority of Cardiff's younger lads
used to congregate in those days. There must have been about ten minutes to go before
kick-off when trouble erupted in the top left-hand corner of the terrace next to the
Grange End. Everyone started to surge in that direction and it was immediately
obvious that a load of Chelsea supporters had invaded the home section, although it
was difficult at first to see how many there were. Back in the Seventies, Ninian Park's
Bob Bank had no seated areas and was simply a huge terrace that ran the length of the
pitch. It held thousands of City fans so I assumed there were hundreds of Chelsea boys
involved in the invasion but by the time I got to where it was going off they numbered
only thirty at the most.

No prizes for guessing the mystery gang I'd spotted on the way to the ground were
Chelsea fans and were right in the middle of the action. They were incredibly game
too considering the amount of Cardiff lads they were up against. A handful of police
desperately tried to keep the battling fans apart for a short while but they knew they
faced an impossible task and soon decided to get out of the firing line. From that point
onwards it was bedlam. A burger stand got trashed in the melee and a few of the
Chelsea boys took a serious hammering as the full force of City's mob came crashing

down on them. I saw one lad get thrown over the wall at the back of the terrace, while at least two more jumped in the same direction in a bid to escape further punishment. They must've hit the ground with a thump as there was a fourteen foot drop to the other side. It seemed like an age before the old bill returned with reinforcements and got the situation under control, and by then only a couple of the Chelsea invaders were left standing. The rest had either run or got battered, while a few had to be stretchered away for treatment by the St John's Ambulance.

As one Chelsea lunatic was being carried along the side of the pitch he suddenly lurched up off his stretcher, staggered through an open gate in the fencing and attempted to attack a group of City fans who'd been laughing at him as he passed. One minute he was lying there covered in blood looking very much the worse for wear, the next he was back on his feet swinging punches. It was like something out of one of those dodgy horror movies. Everybody on the Bob Bank steered well clear of that nutcase. He was eventually dragged off the terrace and wrestled back onto his stretcher by a couple of coppers. I've often wondered if he ended up in the hospital or the cells.

The contest on the field was a stereotypical game of two halves. A Ronnie Moore goal gave the Bluebirds a well-deserved lead at the interval but they were awful during the second half and Chelsea came back to win 2-1. The visitors had defender Gary Chivers sent off for throwing a punch at Moore with about twenty minutes to go, which made the atmosphere on the terraces even more fractious.

After the final whistle, hundreds of City boys mobbed up in Jubilee Park opposite Ninian Park and began pelting the Chelsea supporters with missiles of various descriptions as they spilled out of the Grange End. Their response was to rip the park's wrought iron railings out of the ground and use them as a battering ram as they charged into the home fans. A few of the Cardiff lads fought back but most of us were on our toes and that was the turning point. From then on the Chelsea mob had much the better of the exchanges during the numerous battles that developed on the streets leading back to the city centre.

All in all it had proved to be quite a day. The newspaper stories on the following Monday said one fan had suffered a broken jaw while twenty others had needed hospital treatment for minor injuries. Both the Royal Hotel and the Terminus pub on St Mary Street were reported to have been badly damaged by brawling fans and the police claimed they'd made almost a hundred arrests – so many, in fact, that a special session had to be arranged for a fortnight later at the city's magistrates court. Thirty three supporters were eventually convicted of various public order offences, fifteen of who were from South Wales while the rest were from the London area. Notorious magistrate Sir Lincoln Hallinan had a field day. He was the scourge of many football fans over the years and on this occasion he jailed one and fined the rest a total of almost £9,000.

I found out some time later that Steve 'Hickey' Hickmott was the lad who had been at the forefront of Chelsea's unsuccessful invasion of the Bob Bank. Hickey was a very well-known character in hooligan circles and became infamous on a national level in 1986 when he and three other Chelsea fans were given lengthy prison sentences for conspiracy to cause affray at football matches during a six-year period starting in 1980. The police claimed their officers had been following the boys for months in an undercover exercise they called Operation Own Goal, which was the first of its kind in Britain. They were eventually released in 1989 when their convictions were overturned on appeal after it became clear that the old bill had fabricated some of their statements. Hickey and his mates returned to Ninian Park on a couple of occasions during the Eighties in the years before they were imprisoned. I'll talk more about that later.

During my early-teens I was a dedicated follower of skinhead fashions despite never actually having a skinhead haircut myself. My father outlawed that idea in no uncertain terms. A short back and sides was as close as I ever came to having a crew cut but I did wear the entire proper skinhead clothing. My usual football match attire consisted of a Crombie-style overcoat or a flight jacket, a Fred Perry polo shirt and straight-leg Levi jeans rolled up over a pair of black twelve-hole Dr Martens. However, I must confess I didn't roll the jeans up over my boots until I was a safe distance away from the house. My father was always very smartly dressed and he wasn't impressed with my appearance at the best of times, so I never risked the consequences of him catching me with my bovver boots displayed in all their glory. I valued my health too much for that.

I was also a big fan of some of the skinhead bands from that period such as Sham 69, the Angelic Upstarts and the Cockney Rejects. In fact, the first record I ever bought was Sham's 1978 single 'If the kids are united'. The Cockney Rejects were ardent West Ham supporters but I loved them all the same, especially as several of their songs were about football violence. I had their name emblazoned across the back of my jacket and I bought everything they did, including the version of I'm Forever Blowing Bubbles they released when the Hammers reached the FA Cup final in 1980.

Talking of West Ham, we made our return to Upton Park about a month or so after the Chelsea game. That one ended up being a miserable trip. The coach company couldn't get any damage insurance after what had happened in East London on our previous visit so the drivers refused to take us all the way to the ground. The three hundred of us who travelled were dropped off at Paddington and we had to take the tube from there. Thankfully, the old bill were waiting in large numbers at Upton Park station and we were escorted in and out of the ground without too many problems, although the locals still made their presence felt in the surrounding streets. The game itself proved to be a nightmare for Cardiff. Welsh international defender Rod Thomas gave away two penalties and City ended up losing 3-0 after being totally outclassed. West Ham's side that day included the likes of Frank Lampard, Billy Bonds and Trevor Brooking, and featured ten of the players who beat Arsenal 1-0 in the Cup final at Wembley six months later, but that was no consolation to us at the time. Still, I suppose there was one positive. At least the journey home was a lot warmer than it had been the previous season.

Towards the end of 1979, my father relocated the family to the village of Wenvoe in the Vale of Glamorgan. Situated halfway between Cardiff and the seaside town of Barry, Wenvoe's a really nice place to live and it was perfect for me as several Bluebirds players also lived in the area. I managed to get friendly with a couple of them, including one of my all-time heroes, the legendary Phil Dwyer.

A born-and-bred Cardiffian from the Grangetown area of the city, Phil was a rugged defender who could also play in midfield and attack whenever required. He was a huge favourite with the supporters and made no less than 576 appearances for City in all competitions between 1972 and 1985 – a club record that will probably never be beaten. Phil was always as good as gold with me and would often sort me out with tickets for away games. We are still good mates to this day. In fact, he recently wrote the foreword to my first book.

Three more characters I met for the first time while I was living in Wenvoe were Bradley Ashford, Peter Mannings and Colin Howells, or Little Colin as he's better known. They became very good friends of mine following an extraordinary incident that occurred in the village one evening a few months after I'd moved there.

In those days, Wenvoe Village Hall used to play host to a youth disco every few weeks. They were staged mainly for the benefit of the local kids but due to the fact that Wenvoe is slap bang in the middle of Ely and Barry, gangs of lads from those two districts would often turn up and gatecrash the event. As a result, the hall would sometimes resemble a mini battlefield. You'd have the Barry boys at one end of the room and the Ely boys at the other, while the Wenvoe lads like me would be stuck in the middle doing our best to stay out of the way.

On this particular occasion the disco itself passed off without any problems, which was a rarity considering the amount of kids who used to attend these things. They were always packed and there was usually trouble of one sort or another, but this time the evening was a peaceful affair. Shortly after the disco had finished, I was standing around outside the hall with Catherine Davies, who was a friend of mine from the village, and a small group of girls from our school. One of the Barry boys came over with a couple of his mates, introduced himself as Bradley and began talking to us. I must admit I was pretty impressed with Bradley from the word go. Although he was only a little older than me, he was well over six feet tall and solidly-built with it. He had a genuine skinhead haircut and wore braces, a Fred Perry and Doc Martens, so his choice of fashion immediately met with my approval. You could tell just by looking at him that Bradley would be a right handful if he wanted but he seemed like a nice guy all the same.

After chatting to us for a little while the lads said their goodbyes and set off towards their bus stop, which was on the main road about quarter of a mile away. They hadn't been gone more than a minute when I noticed a gang of around twenty Ely boys heading off in the same direction. It was obvious trouble was brewing but I didn't really know any of those involved at that stage so I decided to stay out of it. Sure enough, it wasn't long before we heard a commotion coming from the main road. I feared the worst for the Barry lads, but much to my amazement it was the Ely boys who came sprinting around the corner with Bradley and his mate Ollie in hot pursuit. Bradley was wielding a pitchfork while Ollie was armed with a pair of garden shears.

The story goes that the Barry lads had been set upon by the Ely contingent and chased across some gardens. One of Bradley's mates was caught and given a bit of a kicking while the others escaped and took refuge in somebody's garage. While they were hiding there they gathered up a few gardening tools and then launched a spectacular counter-attack. Twenty lads being chased up the road by a manic six foot-plus skinhead brandishing a pitchfork was a sight to behold. I bet the good people of Wenvoe had never seen anything quite like it. I know I hadn't. The police arrived on the scene soon afterwards and Bradley was arrested if memory serves, although I'm pretty sure he was never actually charged with anything.

At the next City home match I was approached on the Bob Bank by several Ely boys. They wanted to know all about the big skinhead from Barry as a couple of them had been in Wenvoe on the night of the disco and had apparently seen me talking to Bradley outside the Village Hall. After I'd explained that I'd only spoken to him for the first time that evening and knew very little about him, I began chatting to two of the lads about the football. They were Mannings and Little Colin, who I'd spotted at Ninian Park on several previous occasions. I immediately got on well with both of them and we began going to games together from that point onwards. The friendships we formed that afternoon have stood the test of time and we are still good mates almost three decades later.

Overall, the 1979/80 season was a mediocre one for Cardiff. The Bluebirds maintained a steady mid-table position right the way throughout the campaign and they eventually finished fifteenth in the Second Division table. While it wasn't exactly the most exciting of years, at least the team was never in any danger of relegation, which made a pleasant change.

City's final match of the season was against Sunderland at Ninian Park. A win for the Wearsiders would have guaranteed them promotion to the top flight so they brought a huge travelling army to Cardiff. Before the game the city centre was full of visiting fans but there wasn't much trouble if the truth be told. Although there were a few minor skirmishes, the only genuine fight I witnessed happened outside the Castle opposite the Angel Hotel, where a mob of around fifty local lads waded into a similar number of Sunderland supporters. There was a big police presence in the area at the time, so the disturbance didn't last long.

At Ninian Park the visitors took over three sides of the ground. In fact, so many Sunderland fans had travelled down that the kick-off had to be delayed by fifteen minutes in order to let them all in. The crowd was just short of 20,000 and I reckon at least 11,000 were from Wearside. The only area of the ground we had to ourselves was the Bob Bank. That's where Jonesy, Little Colin, Mannings and I were situated in our customary position under the TV gantry.

As a dull and goalless first half drew to a close, Colin went missing. I assumed he'd gone to get something to eat, but shortly after the half-time whistle had blown a roar went up on the terrace and he suddenly appeared in the middle of the pitch kicking a tennis ball towards the Grange End. How he got out there I don't know. He dribbled the ball into the penalty area, slammed it into the back of the net and celebrated his 'goal' in front of the visiting supporters. Then he took off his Cardiff scarf, laid it on the ground in the goalmouth and bowed down in front of it. By this time the Sunderland fans in the Grange End were going bananas. A couple of coppers went onto the pitch and tried to grab hold of him but he dodged them easily, jogged back towards the terracing and vaulted over the fence, much to the delight of everyone on the Bob Bank. That incident was typical of Colin in those days. You never knew what he was going to do next. Not only was he fearless but he was crazy with it.

Ray Bishop put City ahead during the second half but Bryan 'Pop' Robson equalised for the visitors soon afterwards and that was the end of the scoring. A draw wasn't quite enough for Sunderland to secure promotion but they finished the job a couple of days after the FA Cup final when they beat West Ham 2-0 at Roker Park in their final match in front of a mammoth 47,000 crowd.

While the Sunderland game wasn't memorable in itself, the scenes in and around the ground that day certainly were. I've watched the Bluebirds play some big clubs in my time but I've never seen another side bring as many supporters to Ninian Park as Sunderland did back in 1980. Considering the distance their fans had to travel it was an amazing turn-out. I have to give credit where it's due even if it was embarrassing for us to be outnumbered at home. In these days of restricted ticket allocations for away supporters I don't suppose we'll ever see anything like that at Cardiff's new stadium, which is a pity as far as I am concerned.

CHAPTER TWO

MODS, SKINS, JACKS AND WURZELS

After the 1979/80 football season had ended, my mates and I turned our attention to our favourite summer pastime, although in 1980 it wasn't cricket, baseball or tennis that kept us entertained. Throughout that particular summer our sport of choice was mod bashing.

During 1978, the Jam's chart successes had sparked a mod revival which gained momentum in 1979 with the release of the film Quadrophenia. By 1980, mod bands such as Secret Affair, the Lambrettas and the Chords were having hit records, and kids wearing fishtail parkas and boating blazers were a regular sight on the streets of South Wales.

Like most of my friends I hated the mods with a passion, but to be honest I never really knew why. Maybe it was the fact that they were often surrounded by lots of pretty girls, whereas most of us football boys were hopeless in that department. We never had any groups of good-looking females following us around town. Our gangs were always made up of lads only, so I reckon we were probably a bit jealous of the mods and their modettes.

Credit to them, the kids who followed the mod fashions during the early-Eighties couldn't be accused of choosing an easy option as they had plenty of enemies to contend with. I think I'm right in saying the only serious rivals the original mods faced in the Sixties were the rockers, but by the time the mod revival came around the new generation had to battle with punks, skinheads, rockers, bikers and football trendies. I bet half of them were afraid to leave their houses!

Our numerous encounters with the mods during the summer of 1980 not only increased my fascination with gang fighting but they also helped to boost my confidence. I quickly progressed from watching while it was kicking off at the football to getting actively involved in clashes with the mods. Most of the action took place in and around Cardiff city centre on Saturday afternoons. Lots of mods would congregate at the Transport Club, which was situated on Garth Street just around the corner from the Vulcan pub. The football lads often teamed up with the skinheads and we'd either launch attacks on the mods outside their club or chase them up and down Queen Street. It must have been a nightmare for the old bill, who were attempting to control large gangs of youths running riot in a busy shopping area.

Occasionally, if nothing much was happening in Cardiff, a load of us would jump on the train and go mod hunting in Pontypridd. On Bank Holiday weekends the place to be was the Barry Island seaside resort, which is where some of the most memorable battles occurred. The 1980 August Bank Holiday Monday stands out in my mind because that's when I crossed paths with Bradley Ashford for a second time.

I travelled from Cardiff to Barry on a train with Jonesy, Mannings and a handful of other lads from the football. We arrived at the Island station at around midday and were surprised to find that the streets outside were already swarming with mods, but despite being heavily outnumbered we just piled into them anyway. In truth we had little option, as they were on top of us as soon as we walked out of the station doors. There were only eight or nine of us and although we were giving it our best shot we seemed sure to come unstuck until a dozen or so of the local skinheads came to our rescue. Led by Bradley, the Barry boys came charging across the road and steamed straight into the mods, scattering them everywhere. What had looked like a certain defeat quickly turned into an easy victory following their intervention. After the mods had been chased off I shook Bradley's hand and thanked him and his mates for helping us out. He recognised me from the Wenvoe disco incident, so we got chatting and discovered that our fathers had known each other for many years. Bradley's father, Lyndon, was a well-known and much-respected man around the Barry area. I could see that his son was going to follow in his footsteps and we became firm friends from that day onwards.

My mod bashing exploits continued for a couple of years until I moved to live in Bradford. Looking back at that period now I'll admit I feel a little guilty about some of the things we did, particularly as the mods were often accompanied by girls while we were scrapping with them. Although the modettes never got hit they did seem scared at times, especially when fights were breaking out in and around the Transport Club. I suppose most of them knew what they were letting themselves in for when they decided to go there, but nevertheless the fact that they were involved at all doesn't sit comfortably with me if I'm being honest about it.

During the 1980/81 football season my terrace education moved up a gear. By that stage I was completely obsessed with Cardiff City and very rarely missed a game home or away. Trips to places like Blackburn, Derby and Bolton brought me into regular contact with some of the older lads who were following the Bluebirds at the time and I loved being in their company. Going to matches with them was a big ego boost for a boy of my age.

The first away game I travelled to independently of the official supporters' clubs was a midweek League Cup second round tie at Chelsea in September 1980. A week earlier, City had beaten the Londoners 1-0 at Ninian Park thanks to a Ray Bishop goal, but only around four hundred of us headed to Stamford Bridge for the second leg. I went with Mannings and Little Colin on a coach that set out from the café which used to stand next to the Leckwith Road railway bridge. On board were some of Cardiff's top boys of that era such as the Baker brothers, Mad Les, Roy Riot, Boozer and Black Jammo. Mannings and Colin are both a few years older than me and they already knew a couple of those lads, so I was accepted without question. Once again I was probably the youngest on the bus.

On our arrival at Chelsea we were met by a large number of police who escorted us to the away end. We parked about a quarter of a mile from the ground and had to walk past several pubs on Britannia Road including the Princess Royal, the Lord Palmerston and the Imperial. Each one of them emptied out as we passed and some real monsters came into view, but although a few bottles and glasses were lobbed in our direction nothing serious happened. I remember I was feeling ten feet tall as I marched through the streets of London with the rest of lads from our coach. I doubt I would've felt quite so confident if we hadn't been surrounded by the old bill, but that's hardly surprising considering the bruisers who were lining the pavements.

At Stamford Bridge, the game hadn't long started when huge centre-half Mickey Droy netted to bring the tie level. It looked like it was going to be a long night, but although Chelsea were well on top for most of the contest our defence held firm. Striker Peter Kitchen, who we'd signed from Fulham for £100,000 a fortnight earlier, scored his first goal for the club with five minutes remaining to give City a 2-1 aggregate victory. To say we went mental on the away terrace would be an understatement. The way we celebrated following the final whistle you'd have thought we'd just won the Cup, not got through to the third round!

After the match we were kept inside the ground for almost half an hour while the police cleared the streets, but nobody complained. We were in no hurry as we anticipated a rough ride on the way back to our coaches. They were parked in several different locations, which meant we'd be split up once we got outside. I can remember us singing 'we'll meet again, don't know where, don't know when' while we waited to be let out. We were sure Chelsea's boys would be gunning for us, especially as we'd knocked them out of the Cup, but it turned out the old bill had done their job well. The walk back to the buses was relatively uneventful as hardly any home fans were still hanging around.

That night was a real adventure for me. Although they didn't bother to have a go at us, the Chelsea mob we passed on our way to Stamford Bridge was awesome. Easily the most fearsome I'd ever seen. Nevertheless, I hadn't been afraid. While I enjoyed travelling with the supporters' clubs, I found that going to an away match with some of Cardiff's older lads was a different experience altogether. It was a much bigger buzz and I wanted more of it. I felt like I was growing up fast.

Something that may surprise younger Bluebirds fans is the small numbers we sometimes took to away games in the early-Eighties. For instance, I recall going to a midweek Division Two match at West Ham during the first week of October 1980. The Hammers were third in the table at the time and City were twelfth but less than a hundred of us went to Upton Park. If I remember correctly there were only about twenty on our coach. Bear in mind the division we were playing in was the equivalent of today's Championship, so that was a dismal turn-out. Our home crowds that season were also very poor more often than not. In fact, the club's average attendance of just over 6,700 was the lowest in its Football League history at that stage.

Four days after the West Ham game, City were playing Sheffield Wednesday at Hillsborough, but I couldn't afford two away games in a week, so six of us decided to go and watch Newport County play Portsmouth instead. Both teams had won promotion to the Third Division at the end of the previous campaign and County had some decent players in their squad such as John Aldridge, Tommy Tynan, Steve Lowndes and Nigel Vaughan. Back then, most Cardiff fans regarded Newport as our friendly neighbours and a fair few Bluebirds would go along and support them if our side was playing away. Therefore, I decided a fifteen-mile train journey to Somerton Park was the ideal way to get my weekend football fix, but that didn't turn out to be the wisest choice I've ever made.

When we arrived at the ground we made our way onto the Cromwell Road End, which was a covered section of terracing split between the home and away supporters. We tried several different vantage points, but wherever we stood the view was diabolical. Whoever designed that terrace had ensured it was virtually impossible to see the pitch regardless of where you were standing. Considering County's miserable history, this had probably been a deliberate move by the architect. Anyway, we ended up positioning ourselves towards the front of the terrace next to the Pompey fans and I could see there were plenty of them in a crowd of just over 7,000. While the view was terrible the atmosphere was pretty good, although we were surprised to hear a few anti-Cardiff songs coming from the Newport supporters.

Central defender Keith Oakes scored twice in the space of a minute just before the interval to give County a 2-0 lead. Maybe it was the fact that we didn't celebrate the goals which gave us away, but shortly after the half-time whistle had blown we were surrounded by a group of Newport lads. They'd obviously worked out we were City fans and it kicked off almost immediately. We traded punches with them for a minute or so and considering there was only half a dozen of us we did ourselves proud until a gate flew open behind us and we were dragged out of the enclosure by a combination of police and stewards. They initially put us in the away section, but that was a stupid idea. Pompey's boys were charging in our direction within seconds, so we were hauled back out of there and slung out of the ground altogether. As we strolled to the train station we laughed and joked about what had happened and reflected on the fact that the local lads were nothing like the friendly allies we'd imagined they'd be. I can honestly say that none of us went to Somerton Park looking for trouble that afternoon, but we found it all the same. That brief scrap on the Cromwell Road End didn't seem particularly significant at the time, but it later proved to be the beginning of a bitter and violent feud involving the Cardiff and Newport youngsters which rumbled on for the best part of two decades.

Our fierce rivals Swansea visited the Welsh capital during the 1980 Christmas period for what turned out to be one of the most memorable local derbies in Ninian Park's ninety nine-year history. Clashes between Cardiff and Swansea are almost always lively but this particular game had extra spice as the Swans were challenging for promotion to the top flight under the management of Bluebirds legend John Toshack. His side was sitting second in the Division Two table, three points behind leaders West Ham. City, meanwhile, were just one point above the relegation zone, although Richie Morgan's team had been showing signs of improvement and were unbeaten in their previous six matches. The South Wales derby looked set to be a cracker and it didn't disappoint.

As Boxing Day fell on a Friday in 1980 there were two sets of Football League fixtures within the space of forty eight hours. The Swans beat Bristol Rovers 2-1 at the Vetch in the first of their holiday games, while the Bluebirds drew 0-0 with Bristol City at Ashton Gate. I travelled to that match on one of the supporters' club coaches. Our right-back, Linden Jones, and their striker, Kevin Mabbutt, were sent off for fighting just before half-time, but apart from that incident it was a dull affair both on and off the field.

On Saturday morning the city centre and the Canton area near the ground started to fill up a lot earlier than they normally did on match days. Everyone had been looking forward to the derby game for months and it seemed like nobody wanted to miss out on any of the action. The big question as far as the lads were concerned was whether or not the Swansea Jacks would be bold enough to have a go at us before kick-off. Around 5,000 of them were expected at Ninian Park, although the majority were known to be travelling on official coaches or special trains. In the event there was no sign of any gangs of Jacks on the streets or in the pubs during the hours leading up to the match, so hundreds of us headed towards Ninian Halt station at about half past one in order to wait for their two specials to arrive.

The first train pulled in shortly before two o'clock and we greeted its occupants with a hail of missiles as they were escorted off the platform and along Sloper Road by a huge number of police. With their truncheons swinging and dogs snapping, the old bill just about managed to hold our mob at bay. The Jacks never once attempted to break their escort and I couldn't blame them under the circumstances. City had played Swansea at Ninian eight months earlier but the levels of hostility on that occasion had been nowhere near as intense. This time around the air was so thick with hatred you could almost taste it. The second train arrived about twenty minutes after the first and again the Jacks were escorted to the Grange End without any major problems, so I took my place on the Bob Bank along with my usual group of mates at around half past two. The crowd of just over 21,000 was the club's biggest for almost four years and the atmosphere inside the ground was electric.

The Ninian noise levels increased further when lanky striker Gary Stevens converted a terrific forty-yard pass from John Buchanan to give City an early lead. Swansea improved steadily as the match wore on and drew level five minutes before the break. Former-Bluebird Brian Attley took advantage of a Phil Dwyer error and set up Neil Robinson, who scored from eighteen yards. The visitors went in front a couple of minutes later when Ron Healey failed to hold a powerful Robbie James drive and Alan Curtis netted the rebound. City pressed hard for an equaliser during the early stages of the second half but they looked dead and buried as Leighton James headed home a third for the Swans with a quarter of an hour remaining. Much to their credit the players kept battling away, although thousands of fans had given up hope and were drifting towards the exits when Peter Kitchen pounced on a poor Nigel Stevenson back-pass and slotted the ball home in the eighty-sixth minute. What happened next is now a part of Cardiff City folklore and is a moment that will never be forgotten by those of us who were fortunate enough to witness it.

Within a minute of the restart the Bluebirds were awarded a free-kick around forty yards from the Swansea goal following a foul on Billy Ronson by Welsh international John Mahoney. After John Lewis had made a dummy run, Wayne Hughes tapped the ball a few inches sideways to John Buchanan, who unleashed a thundering right-footed drive that was still rising as it crashed in the top right-hand corner of the Grange End net. Goalkeeper Dave Stewart got nowhere near it despite a full-length dive. His defence hadn't even bothered to put up a wall, which goes to show how far out the free-kick was. I can't recall seeing a shot hit harder than that either before or since and I don't think I've ever seen a City goal celebrated as wildly. The scenes on the Bob Bank were unbelievable.

Amazingly, both sides had decent chances to win the game during stoppage time. Ray Bishop wasted a good opportunity when Peter Kitchen was better placed to score, while Ron Healey made a terrific save from Robbie James just seconds before the final whistle.

The post-match reactions of the two managers to John Buchanan's wonder goal were funny. City boss Richie Morgan told reporters "when he shaped to shoot I turned to Dave Roberts on the bench and asked 'surely he's not daft enough to have a go from there, is he?' I'm very glad he did!"

Meanwhile, Swansea chief John Toshack said "I've never seen a goal like it. I was hoping Buchanan would shoot because you cannot score from that range. I couldn't believe it when he did."

The Scottish midfielder's stunning effort was all the more extraordinary as he had seven stitches in a right foot injury he'd sustained during the previous day's game at Ashton Gate. The papers reported it had been touch and go whether he was going to play against the Swans. Apparently, he'd only declared himself fit an hour or so before kick-off.

To tell you the truth, I can't recall anything significant happening outside Ninian Park after the game had finished. Perhaps the Jacks managed to sneak back to their trains and buses while all the Cardiff lads were still inside the ground celebrating Buchanan's goal. A South Wales Police spokesman later told the press there was no serious incidents on the day, and that's how I remember it. However, he added that fifty one arrests had been made in relation to a variety of minor public order offences. That's an indication of how much times have changed if ever there was one. Can you imagine what the reaction would be today if fifty one arrests were made at a Cardiff v Swansea match? The press would be claiming civil war had broken out!

After the euphoria of that late comeback against the Swans, we were brought back down to earth with a bump a week later when we travelled to Leicester for an FA Cup third round tie. The Foxes were second from bottom of the First Division and were on a run of three successive defeats, so an upset was on the cards, but in the end they were much too good for City.

I went to the game on a football special along with several of the other youngsters. It was the first time I'd travelled any sort of a distance to a match on the train and we had a great laugh on the way up there. Every carriage was packed and all of our top boys were on board so it looked like being an entertaining day out and so it proved. We pulled into Leicester at around the half one mark and, as expected, the police were awaiting our arrival, but surprisingly there weren't many of them. However, there were plenty of local lads waiting for us outside the station and it kicked off almost as soon as we walked through the doors. The rest of the journey to Filbert Street took nearly half an hour as there were running battles all the way to the turnstiles. The old bill tried their best to contain the trouble but they didn't have much success. The escort broke apart on countless occasions and a few of the resulting clashes were fairly nasty. I'd been used to travelling on coaches that parked up near the grounds we were visiting, so a long and chaotic walk from the train station was an entirely new experience for me and it was a very exciting one too.

Inside Filbert Street we were housed in a large pen on the Spion Kop end. The Leicester fans were on both sides of us and the atmosphere was really hostile. We had loads of missiles of various descriptions thrown at us throughout the ninety minutes, but it was good fun nonetheless. The same couldn't be said for the game though. While the honours had been fairly even outside the ground it was a different story altogether on the pitch. City started well enough and Peter Kitchen missed a glorious early chance but then Gary Lineker put Leicester ahead on the half hour and that was the end of that. We finished up being stuffed 3-0, which meant we were dumped out of the FA Cup at the third round stage for the fourth year running. The walk back to the station was a bit intimidating, especially as it had got so dark, but although there were a few skirmishes along the way the police had things under much tighter control and we made it to our train safely enough.

Another rail trip I have vivid memories of was a visit to Bristol Rovers in late-February. The match was billed as a relegation dogfight beforehand, but in reality Rovers were already doomed. Having won just twice all season they were rock-bottom of the table and eight points adrift from safety, while City were seventeenth, one point above the drop zone. Around 2,000 of us made the short journey to Eastville, with the majority travelling by train. I went on the special with about ten or twelve of my mates.

There was mayhem in Bristol from the moment we arrived at Stapleton Road. Despite the station's proximity to the ground, the escort took about twenty minutes as there was trouble all the way. Mobs of Rovers fans were waiting on every street corner and they were surprisingly game considering they were heavily outnumbered. Some of the fighting became pretty vicious at times, especially as the police had adopted a 'take no prisoners' policy. One battle under the motorway bridge involved dozens of lads from either side and was amongst the most violent I've ever witnessed at the football.

At Eastville the majority of us occupied a large open terrace on the Muller Road End, although loads of our boys also got onto Bristol's Tote End behind the opposite goal. Unsurprisingly, brawling broke out there as soon as the teams took to the pitch. For a little while it looked like there were more Welshmen than Wurzels on the home terrace, but the fighting resulted in large groups of City fans being ejected every couple of minutes during the early stages of the match. A rare goal from midfielder Steve Grapes midway through the first half was enough to secure a valuable victory for the Bluebirds from a poor quality game. The old bill completely lost control after we'd left the ground and the route back to the station was like a mini war-zone. It took the police almost an hour to round everyone up and get us all on the train, and by the time we finally pulled out of Stapleton Road our Wurzel friends had put half of our windows through. Although City are easily the bigger of the two Bristol clubs and have always been considered our fiercest rivals, for some reason trips to Rovers seemed a lot more eventful during the late-Seventies and early-Eighties.

The return match with Swansea took place on a Saturday in mid-April during the Easter holidays. Before the game, City were one point above the relegation zone and the Jacks were one point off the promotion places, so it was a vitally important fixture for both clubs. Once again I travelled on the special with the rest of the lads and it seemed like there were thousands of us on it. Every carriage was heaving. When we got to Swansea's High Street train station we were loaded onto a fleet of double-decker buses and taken straight to the Vetch. A few of the bus windows were kicked out en route and there was a bit of squabbling with the old bill outside the ground as everyone tried to squeeze through the set of three tiny turnstiles, but there was no sign of any Jacks in the vicinity and no serious trouble to speak of. Inside the Vetch around four thousand of us were housed in the West Stand behind the goal. A group of about thirty or forty City fans invaded the North Bank ten minutes before kick-off and it was chaos over there for a while until the police managed to drag the Cardiff contingent out.

The game proved to be an exciting contest. Swansea were well on top for most of the first half and it was no surprise when Leighton James put them ahead just before the interval, but he wasted a golden chance to increase their lead midway through the second half when he had a penalty brilliantly saved by Ron Healey. Striker Peter Kitchen headed home a late equaliser from a John Lewis cross and midfielder Tarki Micallef almost won it for the Bluebirds deep into injury time with a decent effort which went just inches wide. I can't remember there being any significant problems after the game, although the newspapers reported that the South Wales Police had made a total of sixty arrests on the day. Forty lads, the majority of who were City fans, were later fined a total of almost £4,000.

The point earned at Swansea was a valuable one, but the team was then beaten at home by Bristol City on Easter Monday, so the battle against relegation went right to the wire. The Bluebirds won one and drew two of their last three games, including a 0-0 draw against West Ham at Ninian Park in the final match of the season. That result was a huge relief as it was enough to keep City in the Second Division on goal difference. However, the reprieve from relegation later turned out to be a temporary one.

CHAPTER THREE

MEETING UP WITH TOM JONES

In May 1981, my mother and father took me across the Atlantic to the United States of America for what I consider was our first-ever genuine family holiday. Previously, whenever we'd travelled abroad, the trips had always revolved around work at my father's Spanish nightclubs. However, on this occasion he was prepared to put pleasure before business for an entire fortnight, which is something I don't think he'd ever done before.

Originally, we anticipated spending a week in San Francisco before flying south to Las Vegas. I was especially excited about the first leg of the holiday as I was very keen to visit Alcatraz Island in the San Francisco Bay. I've always been a big fan of prison movies and the Birdman of Alcatraz is one of my all-time favourites, so I was looking forward to seeing the famous old jail for myself. Unfortunately though, when we got to San Francisco the weather was awful. It was either foggy or teeming with rain for the entire time we were there, so all ferry trips to the island were cancelled.

After four days we were fed up of getting wet, so we flew down to Las Vegas a little earlier than planned. Naturally enough, the weather in Nevada was in marked contrast to how it had been in San Francisco. The heat was incredible and was such a shock to my system that I almost passed out as soon as I stepped off the plane. Nevertheless, I fell in love with Vegas from the moment we arrived. I'd never seen anything like the main strip with all its amazing hotels, restaurants and theatres, and everything about the place appealed to me. At the time I was virtually addicted to fruit machines, so I was immediately drawn to the numerous casinos, although fortunately I didn't manage to blow much of my holiday money. Gambling in Vegas is restricted to over-twenty ones, so I was quickly thrown out of every casino I went into.

We hadn't been in Vegas for more than a few hours when I spotted that Tom Jones was playing at Caesar's Palace. His name was displayed on billboards and posters almost everywhere we went. I was really keen to see Tom live but initially my parents weren't interested as they'd seen him many times before and all the shows were sold out. I was aware that my father had known Tom back in the days when he lived in South Wales, so I kept asking him to get in touch with his old friend. After a couple of days of my nagging, Mum managed to persuade Dad to leave a note for Tom at the Caesar's Palace reception desk. He did so reluctantly, as he wasn't the kind of man who liked to ask anyone for favours, no matter who they were. I think he was embarrassed by the whole episode and I'm sure he only left that note in an attempt to shut me up.

Early the following morning, an envelope was pushed under the door of our hotel room. It contained a note from Tom welcoming us to Las Vegas, three tickets for that evening's performance and backstage passes to meet up with him after the show. The seats he'd arranged for us were in the front row of a private box. I couldn't believe our luck.

The concert lived up to all my expectations. Tom was brilliant live and the atmosphere inside Caesar's Palace was fantastic. We had a great evening. As soon as the show was over we made our way backstage, but we were told by the security people that Tom would probably be at least an hour as he usually had a sauna following his performances. My father was almost as impatient as I am which is saying something, so he wasn't prepared to wait around for long. After quarter of an hour or so, he asked the security guys to pass on our thanks to Tom for his hospitality and we headed back to the hotel. At the time I was upset that we hadn't stayed to meet the star of the show, but it turned out to be a good move on my Dad's part.

The next morning I answered a knock on our hotel room door and was stunned to find Tom Jones standing in the hallway. He greeted my father warmly, apologised for the fact that we'd been kept waiting the night before and invited us for lunch. Needless to say I was over the moon. Tom was great company; very laid back and surprisingly down to earth for a man with his fame and fortune. It was obvious that he'd never forgotten his Welsh roots as he spoke with pride about the South Wales Valleys and his hometown of Pontypridd. He talked about the mansion in the Bel-Air district of Los Angeles that he'd bought from Dean Martin a few years earlier and then, as lunch was drawing to a close, he told me "If it hadn't been for your dad, I don't think I'd be where I am today."

Tom explained that during the early stages of his singing career, my father had helped him out with his living and travelling expenses and had set him up with a number of important show business contacts. He revealed that he'd even asked Dad to manage him at one point, but my father had instead advised him to link up with some of his contacts in London. Tom said he would never forget what Dad had done for him all those years ago and told me that if I ever needed a favour, then all I'd have to do was ask. I've always been very proud of my father and his achievements, but maybe never more so than on that particular day. To hear someone of Tom Jones' stature speaking so highly of him was wonderful. As for Tom himself, I've often considered writing to him and asking him to do me the favour of buying Cardiff City Football Club, but I don't think I'd get much joy. By all accounts he's a rugby fan.

When we got back to Britain, my father decided it would be a good experience for me to work for somebody else during the summer holidays. By that stage I already knew pretty much all there was to know about working in his nightclubs. I knew the cellars inside out, I knew how to serve every drink behind the bars and my math's was excellent as you had to add up the orders in your head back then because the old mechanical tills weren't up to much.

My father was friendly with a man named Monty Smith, who had a couple of garages in Barry and Penarth. He let me have a job as a petrol pump attendant at his Penarth garage on Windsor Road and I worked there from Monday to Friday for seven weeks. As well as physically serving the petrol, my tasks included checking the oil for the customers, putting air in their tyres and cleaning their windscreens. Although Monty only paid me something like 50p an hour, I enjoyed working for him. The garage was always busy, we had some good laughs and I found it easier working for someone other than my father. Although Monty was fairly strict with his employees, he wasn't anywhere near as demanding as Dad. Besides which, I think Monty had a bit of a soft spot for me as he was also a Cardiff City season ticket holder, so we used to have regular chats about football.

On Friday and Saturday nights I regularly worked on the cash desk at a rough little club in Barry my father had bought earlier in the year. It stood next to the Barry Island pleasure park and was known locally as the Pelican, although Dad renamed it the Feathers when he took it over. The place was a notorious trouble spot and working there proved to be a real eye-opener for me. I'd seen plenty of fighting at my father's other clubs, but the violence inside the Pelican was on a different level altogether. The problems often started almost as soon as the doors opened and they would carry on until closing time. At least two or three major rucks tended to develop every night.

In a bid to get the place under control, Dad employed several well-respected Barry-based doormen such as Jiffy Smith and Ray Diaf, and a number of the top lads from the Cardiff club circuit, including heavyweight boxer Winston Allen and well-known nightclub bouncer Marlow Offside. Winston fought the likes of Frank Bruno and Joe Bugner during his professional career, while Marlow, or Oxo as he was nicknamed, spent much of his spare time in the gym sparring with the best Welsh boxers of the day. He was the sort of man you wouldn't mess around with if you knew what was good for you. In readiness for any trouble at the Pelican, he used to keep a gum shield above the door, a baseball bat behind the cash desk and an Alsatian dog in the car outside. It took him and the rest of the boys about three months to stamp their authority on the club and some of the violence I witnessed in the meantime was really heavy. The fighting at the football was like a Sunday school picnic by comparison.

By the age of 15, I knew how to work the bars and cellars inside out and for the next two years my weekend nights were spent there; personally I felt that experience of working hands on and not being taught it in college etc. I believe gave me more of the skills and the ability to help me in later life. The club had been dying to death and by the end of the second year, the fighting had been cleared up and the club was packed with customers four nights a week, a Tuesday night being for the Butlins staff when they got their wages. So as my father had done in the past he found a buyer and we were now looking for another run down business to build up.

My football life had not been affected and I was still able to go to every home game and about 17 away games that season as long as I was back for 9.30pm to start work.

Our group at football matches was more you could say like a youth firm of lads, we all were regularly going to away matches together. Peter Manning was probably the oldest amongst us, he and Little Colin were two years older than me, between the three of us we would organise our away trips.

Rotherham (a far cry from Las Vegas) away on Saturday in September 1981 will not be forgotten in a hurry by Mannings, about 10 of our group travelled up on a supporters coach and we all sat at the back of the coach believing we were the bee's knees. When we got to Rotherham we left the rest of the supporters and took a stroll around, well away from the ground, but to be honest it was quite boring and we felt there was no opposition around. The match itself felt exactly the same, boring, with a one nil loss to add to it. The only excitement during the game, came when Mannings kept running over to a group of about 20 Rotherham fans who were giving it the big one, knowing there was no way we could get to them. Mannings kept trying to get to them and eventually resorted to sticking his fingers up at them, having had one warning, Mannings ended up being nicked and receiving a £125 fine for his troubles, the only good thing was in those days you never got a banning order to go with the fine.

Sheffield Wednesday away in October was the next game we all went away together; our numbers in our group had now swelled to about 25 of us, with the likes of Frankie D and Dexy now joining our group. The team was struggling now or you could say as usual, we were once again looking on course for relegation already this early in to the season, our previous home game we had lost one nil to Newcastle, who incidentally only brought about 200 fans(where were their so called great support in those days). About 800 Cardiff had travelled to Wednesday included in that was well over 500 lads. Nothing happened before the game, but as I entered the away end behind the goal, Wednesday fans were throwing things and spitting down at us on the left stair case which took them to their stand.

At half-time we all made our way to the food areas and once again Wednesday fans started their antics, but this time City fans stormed up the staircase, tearing open the gate and running Wednesday fans back along their gang way, that soon shut them up for a while. We lost the match 2-1, with Dave Bennett a class looking player scoring for us, having Bennett playing for us gave us some hope for the future. After the game the coaches were all outside in the main street at the back of the stand, Wednesday fans virtually came out alongside us all and running battles between us and them soon began. A lot of it was not the usual bravado like they do today bouncing around, it was straight in to each other, and if I was honest it was most of the older Cardiff fans doing most of the battling for us, with us including myself giving them back up. There were no winners as both sides received the usual cuts and black eyes, with the police eventually stepping in after say what felt like a five minute brawl.

A game that I will always remember was Charlton home on a bank holiday Monday December 28th 1981, which once again we lost one nil, but it was not what happened on the pitch that stands out in my mind, it was what happened after the game, I will remember it for. Because after one of the most miserable games of the season so far, I ran with about 100 lads including our group of about 25-30 youngsters around to the away end which in them days, the away fans were housed in the enclosure beneath our main grandstand. During the game Charlton fans had been really mouthy with a lot of big fat bear belly blokes continually calling it on. As soon as we saw the Charlton fans coming out, we steamed straight in to them without even thinking about it, they had a quite a few big lumpers at the front, I remember for the first ever time at Ninian Park smashing this fat lump to the floor, the police were now smacking everyone with their truncheons and as I ran to make my escape, I was grabbed by a copper and frog marched to a room which had a couple of cells right opposite our souvenir shop on the corner of the Grandstand. I said to them that I had lost my way and he had hit me first, the copper said it was my lucky day and said because it was Christmas time he was just going to give me a ticking off and did not want to see me by the away end again. I was chuffed and couldn't wait to get out, I wasn't really scared of the old bill, it would have been my father who I would have been scared of, if he had found out, so I was more chuffed that he would never know.

Our season finally came to life as we had drawn Man City away in the FA Cup 3rd round a daunting task having to go to Maine Road, but an exciting one nevertheless. Two football specials were put on for our fans, we all booked on including all the older lads, suddenly our group of 25-30 younger lads became 70, oh how they come out of the wood work, but never mind, I just hoped they would come again with us. Our team and our lads were going to be severely tested, but that's what makes playing teams like Man City so exciting, you never know what's ahead.

We were all on the first train and when the train pulled in, Little Colin decided to do one of his mad stunts, he jumped out of the window while it was still going, you should of seen the shock on the faces of the old bill as he landed on the beginning of the platform, a couple of them rushed over to try and nick him, but they had no chance as the train was coming to a halt, Cardiff fans just charged off the train and were rushing down the platform like a stampede of elephants, the police had to all rush to the exits to try and stop Cardiff getting out of the train station. Mannings and I picked up Little Colin; thankfully he only had minor grazes, so we joined up with the rest of Cardiff who had managed to get outside the train station.

Cardiff were trying to run here, run there and anywhere they thought would get them further from the old bill and hopefully meet some Man City. But there were no Man City to be seen, I was quite shocked by this. They tried to put us on buses but Cardiff were having none of it and so in the end they walked us through Moss Side and let me tell you that was a sight to behold, run down and looked 5 times rougher than Cardiff docks. There was a massive Asian area and a lot of abuse was directed at them by Cardiff fans, that did not interest me one bit, what I could not understand was there were no Man City still to be seen.

Finally we got to Maine Road, as we were all queuing up to go in, groups of Man City lads started to appear and coming towards us, our lot did not need to do anything as within seconds hordes of Valley lads sent them packing and these lads I can tell you are a match for anyone, they don't care about the Casual scene or things like that, they just get pissed up, support their team, but if anyone is looking for trouble from the opposition the old bill no one will stop them having their say fun for the day. The atmosphere was electric inside the ground, over 31,000 fans packed in there including over 3,500 Cardiff fans, the singing was nonstop from both sets of supporters, what made it better was that their lively fans shall we say were right next to us. The old bill did have the segregation well under control throughout the game, which we lost 3-1.

After the game Cardiff fans did their usual steaming out of the away end, but once again it was virtually Man City free. The walk back to the train station was a quiet one, maybe everyone was tired now and with Man City not turning out for us, most of the fans just wanted to get home now. On the pitch the season just went from bad to worse, we were now going to be in a relegation battle for the rest of the season.

CHAPTER FOUR

BOMB THREATS AND TEARS

Chelsea away to me was one I was looking forward to, as I had a soft spot for their team and supporters as they reminded me of us. It was in February 1982 on a Wednesday night, but I had a problem, my parents had said that was one match I was not going to as they knew the name Chelsea guaranteed trouble. Had they forgotten that I had been to West Ham already on a couple of occasions and if you've been there you can fear nowhere else. The good news was they were going away for a few days and that was at the same time we were playing Chelsea in February of that year, so I was going to be staying at my uncle Garths, I was still in school so I told him that I would be staying at my mates after school that night. I took my clothes in a bag and as soon as I was out the door, I was out of my school uniform and changed in to my football clobber.

We weren't being picked up from Ninian Park until about 1pm, so I went off to the amusement arcades, where I was hooked at the time on fruit machines. I met up with a few of the other lads who were going and so eventually we made our way down Tudor Road towards Ninian Park, having already lost half our money to the Bandits (machines).We would meet the rest of the lads at a Cafe, which in those days, was just under the Ninian Park bridge on the right hand side opposite the Ninian Park halt train station. As we were making our way down the road and being young lads and not thinking, just running across roads, I got hit by a car, which was soon to put pay to my Stamford Bridge trip. An ambulance was called, with of course the police arriving too, I was able to get back on my feet even though I felt dazed and had a painful arm and leg. I ended up arguing with the police as they said I had to go with the Ambulance, I was refusing and said I was off to see Cardiff play at Chelsea, they said if I hadn't they would lock me up, so off I went to hospital, telling my mates to go off and enjoy themselves.

My uncle picked me up, where I then had to explain to him with my arm in plaster what had really gone on that day; he just laughed and said I don't think you will be able to tell the same story to your parents. As we drove home, guess what? We were only passed by the Cardiff supporters' coaches heading to Chelsea!

Another game in which our fans turned up on mass was Hereford away in the Welsh Cup semi-final in April 1982.We all decided for this one we would go on the service train, Little Colin, Mannings and a few of the usual suspects were going up early for this one and of course myself, even though it was a night match, we actually left in the morning for less than an hour's trip. As the train made its way through all the small Welsh towns, a couple of lads got on at Pontypool, these lads were quite a few years older than us, but we soon got into a good conversation with them about their past experiences with the City, we eventually exchanged names and one of them, a lad called Alan Rawlings who was in the army and in years to come we would be side by side on many occasions, was to later become involved in a big football court case with me.

We arrived in Hereford a small market town, it looked like it was in a coma, and the main street had no life at all, so we sat around in a pedestrianised street, outside some of the pubs. Some of Rawlings' other mates, Stan and Carl, would also become good friends of ours and travel around the country with us; they were good lads to be with. As the day went on the street filled with City fans, lads from all over South Wales converged on this small market town. The nearer it got to kick-off time, the more the atmosphere seemed to change; the streets were packed with drunken Cardiff fans.

Us younger lot decided to leave the main group of Cardiff fans and make our way to the ground, on passing one pub we saw that all its windows had been put in, this pub turned out to be where Hereford's lads would drink. We decided for a laugh, to all go in the home end, in them days' pay on the day were the usual thing, so we all paid to go in and stood on their end behind the goal and the opposite end to where Cardiff fans were housed. We went and stood by their singers. I remember Little Colin dragging a Hereford fan down the terraces because he wouldn't fight him. We stood on there for most of the first half even bursting out with the odd Cardiff song, but the locals pretended not to notice we were there.

So at half-time we decided to make our way to join the rest of the Cardiff fans, as we jumped over this small wall, we noticed fighting had broken out in the Cardiff end, the Cardiff end had erupted into a near riot, the police had been chased out of there. A wall had now been dismantled and everything they could lay their hands on was being pelted at the police, Len Ashurst, one of my all-time favourite managers for Cardiff went over to the away end to try and calm the situation down, but even Ashurst came under attack, with bricks and bottles being thrown his way. By now we had got down to the away end, Cardiff fans had formed a half circle and if the police tried to arrest anyone, City fans would stick together and attack them like a pack of wolves. We jumped into the away end and merely watched from the side. The fans started to calm down as the police stayed out of the end, to this day I don't know what triggered it all off, but it was the worst fighting I had ever seen at football before that day.

The second half of the game, which just about got completed, sent Cardiff through to the Final of the Welsh Cup where we would meet Swansea. At the end of the game, as we tried to leave the stadium, the police started to try and grab people out of the blue, at this time there was no trouble going on as everyone was just trying to get out. As we were walking away from the away end, Colin was grabbed by the police and they accused him of having a knife. Now Colin is one lad, who speaks his mind, but with the police you can't have your own mind, Colin started mouthing at them and told them what to do with themselves. They searched him and found it was a comb that was sticking out of his back pocket, we went to try and help him, but with snarling dogs and police lashing at us with batons, we were unable to help him, they still arrested him and put Colin in handcuffs, which we found out later was for threatening behaviour and abusive language. The night ended with three pubs being totally ransacked by older Cardiff fans and many shops on the way back to the train station having their windows put in.

Two weeks later Colin appeared in Hereford Magistrates Court along with 57 other Cardiff fans, a few of us went up with him, but Colin being a cheeky bastard went and sat himself on the Ushers desk in the court room and refused to move, eventually after being threatened with being locked up and the crowd in the court in raptures, Colin moved. Most lads were given between £50 to £75 fines and some were laughing their heads off afterwards, as they had given false names and addresses and had got away with it, but Colin was given a £200 fine for contempt of court, but it did not bother him one bit, as that was Colin for you. Everyone then went for a drink in Hereford. We now had Swansea to look forward to in the Final.

Back to the league games, Luton Town at home was our final home game of the season, on Monday 17th May 1982,this was it, all our previous games meant nothing now, as this was a must win game, lose and we were relegated. Luton were already promoted as champions and came to us with nothing to play for, but as the best team in this division, we had also in recent weeks put a few good results together. I went to the match believing we could do it, nothing is impossible I kept saying to myself, the unthinkable won't happen to us, we just can't be relegated. Over 10,000 City fans turned up with little over 200 Luton fans there, yes it was a Monday night, but surely as champions you would have thought Luton would have brought more fans than that. The City fans got behind the team right from the start, you could feel the tension, I was singing and cheering them on every second of the game, as much as I liked the fighting side of football, I love my club more and I did not want relegation no matter what. Well my beloved club, let me and thousands of other City fans down once again, we were beaten 3-2 and of course with that came relegation.

I don't know what happened to me that night, but when the final whistle went and the ground was emptying and most of the lads had ran off to have a go at the Luton fans, which at this moment in time did not interest me one bit, I just stood there in the middle of the Bob bank terrace in disbelief, my eyes welled up with tears. All we had to do was win the game and we would have stayed up and Luton had nothing to play for, they did not even need a single point. But only Cardiff could let you down, I kept saying to myself. I eventually walked out of the ground, but my tears turned to anger, how my club could just give in and let us down. I can't exactly explain why I did the following, but I had become so wound up and hurt by what had happened, I wanted my club to feel some of my hurt, as I walked past a phone box, all the emotion I was feeling took over me and rational thinking was not at the forefront of my mind, I turned around and went back to the phone box and phoned the club up and when my call was answered I did the daftest thing ever, I said I was going to blow the club up and with them all in it and then just put the phone down, pointless really and it was probably laughed at by the person who listened to my outburst, all I can say is, at that moment in time, it made me feel better for the next five minutes and I had managed to get some of the hurt out of me. Looking back now, yes you could say I must have had a screw missing but I was 16 years old at the time and that's how I managed to deal with my club hurting me, I bet everyone has done something they regret and feel silly about it afterwards. I later found out that hundreds of Cardiff fans had tried to get at the Luton fans after the game, the Luton fans had apparently huddled in the corner of the Grange End terrified, but were saved by the police and dogs who continually charged at the Cardiff fans for up to half an hour after the game had finished.

I was still hurting for the next month, but as they say time is a healer, having Swansea away in the final of the Welsh cup second leg at the Vetch field was the perfect match to get the nightmare of the Luton game out of my mind and also take all our frustrations out on the Jacks. We had drawn the first leg 0-0 at Ninian Park, with them once again failing to turn up at our place. So only two days later we were all off to Jackland, thousands made their way for the forty odd mile trip, every train was packed. All our group of lads went on the train as well; it was now becoming a regular thing with us. When we are arrived in Swansea, hundreds of lads just marched straight through the entrance of their train station, the police just let us go (in our dreams nowadays), there was at least four hours to go before kick-off. We took over their pubs not far from Swansea seafront and in the areas around Swansea Quadrant. For the first hour we just sat there drinking and many you could see were already bored as no one could believe there was not a Jack in sight.

About twenty of us decided to go for a stroll, everywhere we walked, there were just Cardiff fans looking for pubs, we had now wandered further a field and of course the inevitable was going to happen, we bumped into about sixty Jacks. Our young firm was as game as they come, with lads like Dexy, Peg, Little Colin, Mannings, Beards, Pricey etc. We had no intention of running and we were soon taking a bit of a hammering off them and eventually we were all over the shop with most of us then being split up and in the end being run back to our pub, near the Quadrant. All the older lads saw us and within seconds had piled out of the pub with pool cues/balls/bottles, the Jacks saw this and before Cardiff could even get to them they were gone and that was the last we saw of them.

As time went on, we made our way to the match, there were scuffles going on down every side street, with police sirens coming from everywhere, to be honest it was beginning to feel like a home game, with Cardiff fans everywhere. Even during the game pockets of Cardiff fans were all around the ground and a few did take a bit of a kicking, but they were never run out of the Jacks end. For the first half an hour dozens of Cardiff fans were being taken out of their end by the police, was this going to be a repeat of the season before? I thought to myself, but no, this time the police were well prepared and soon got the fighting under control.

We lost the final 2-1, Cardiff fans were not prepared to watch the Jacks lift the trophy, so thousands descended onto the streets, with the police outside making sure no one made their way around to the Jacks ends. As we slowly made our way back to the train station, we never saw anyone and it became quite easy for the police to keep order. To this day I have always wondered where they were in those days, as I knew they had quite a few hundred lads. Maybe they knew that it was quite impossible to take on thousands of lads from all over South Wales, with hundreds of lunatics from the Valleys always making the journey to Jackland.

By the summer of '82, a lot of lads were fed up of being picked on by the old bill, most lads were skinheads or lads with Doc Martin boots and scarves around their wrists. A new look at football had hit London and the North big time, it had become known as the casual/trendy look, as some of us called it, with clothing known as Fila, Lacoste, Tacchini, Ellesse tracksuits, polo shirts, expensive designer trainers, smart trousers and jeans were now being worn at football, personally I really liked the new look. It took a while to take off in South Wales. So by the beginning of that summer of '82, I had totally changed my look and actually to the relief of my parents as they had hated the skinhead look.

CHAPTER FIVE

THE FORMING OF THE SOUL CREW

This is a true story and has never been told before and to some people who were not around in those days they will probably find it difficult to understand why all this happened. You have street/neighbourhood gangs in every town in the country, but in the Eighties a lot of lads/boys turned to football and joined their clubs gang/group. My life was work, work, and work in the early Eighties when I was 15/16 years old, I never liked drugs or drank alcohol so football was my vice, my way of letting off steam shall we say.

As you have now read, during the Seventies to about 1980, Cardiff fans had been wild and unorganised and some would say one of the Scruffiest mobs ever seen. In 1980 the Casual look arrived big time in Cardiff, we were now wearing Pringle, Slazenger and Lyle and Scott, we still had many lads who were skinheads, but by the 1982/83 season Cardiff had moved upmarket in the casual world and moved onto Lacoste, Fila, etc. Some were even wearing Armani, how times were changing fast. Cardiff were only getting average crowds of 7,000 fans at home games, yet this coming season we would take over 1,500 fans to most places and included in that would be well over five hundred Casuals. Before we go any further the Casuals, soon to be known as the Soul Crew, were actually very loyal to Cardiff and these lads had been through many years of watching utter rubbish on the pitch.

Our team had always been at the wrong end of the table but no matter how bad the team were the lads were always there and most night games the lads would outnumber the 'Shirters'. We had not been in the top division (Division One) since 1962. One thing that everyone must remember is that these lads would never look for fights with the average Joe Bloggs; they only wanted a row with like-minded lads and if nothing was happening on that front then most of the lads would watch the game and support the team. We were not the animals that we were being portrayed as in the media, everyone had jobs and football was about meeting up with mates and following the team with pride. Most clubs visiting Cardiff would be anti-welsh and would sing songs like "sheep shaggers," some would even go further with chants of "Aberfan," which was well out of order!

This would hurt the fans, especially those from the Valleys that followed Cardiff, Burnley did it once and I will never forget how the Valley lads tore down brick walls to get to them and I don't think Burnley have or will ever sing it again. Football is about your club and the lads that you go with but sometimes people take it too far.

Getting back to the 1982/83 season, Cardiff had been very active and was finally going together as a mob on the train; we were sometimes 400-500 strong. I was living in Bradford at the time and I was still only 16 but I was following City everywhere that season but the game that I will never forget was Sheffield United away. We were top of Division Three and were regularly followed by over 2,000. Cardiff's mob was never less than four hundred plus many of Cardiff's normal supporters would get stuck in if needed. That day I once again went by train and two lads from Bradford's Ointment firm, who I had got to know, came along with me. When we arrived we went to a pub on a hill not far from Sheffield train station where we met up with the rest of Cardiff, the Bradford lads were well impressed. Standing outside the pub was a lad called Parsons, who at the time must have been about 24 years old and he travelled up from London with about a dozen or so lads who followed the City.

I was 16 years old and a very impressionable kid who looked up to Parsons and his little firm as they were the lads everyone seemed to want to know and follow. Parsons was not one of those who hung around and got drunk in the pub all day, he would never stand still and was always on the lookout for the other teams firm; he always wore the best gear and made himself noticed.

That day I was standing outside the pub when Parsons asked me and a couple of others "Do you want to take a walk into their town and leave them lot here drinking?" without hesitation we were off in a shot. In less than five minutes Parsons had found a row, there were six of us and about a dozen Sheffield, to be honest we would have backed off that day but Parsons was having none of it and steamed straight into them, I thought to myself what the fuck.....if I want respect I have got to get stuck in and I did, the six of us give one hell of a battle and ended with Sheffield running back to get the rest of their firm. We returned back to the pub where the lads were and Parsons shouted for everyone to leave the pub and fuck the drink!

There I stood side by side with Parsons and 400 Cardiff casuals behind us, oh my God, I was 16 years old and the adrenalin was unbelievable, I felt like I was leading an army into battle. As we were marching along, Parsons was talking loudly to us saying "We should be organised Cardiff, not pissing it up!" he hated people getting drunk. "Keep it together, come on!" he shouted, then out of the blue he said "this mob needs a name!" and he just came out with it, with anger and frustration he chanted "Soul Crew, Soul Crew, Soul Crew" and within seconds an army of 400 Welsh lads were echoing the words of our new name "Soul Crew."

By the time we finally met Sheffield's mob, Parsons had us so pumped up we would have fought 1,000 lads, Sheffield's mob came steaming down towards us but it felt like we went straight through them and within minutes most of their mob were on the run and those that stood took a right beating that day. Sheffield came back with planks of wood or whatever else they could find, they tried to stand their ground and for a few minutes it was toe to toe, but in the end the Soul Crew numbers were too many. The Soul Crew continued right through to the shopping centre chasing, by now, a few hundred Sheffield, they tried to stand but this army was not going to stop. The old bill eventually rounded us all up and marched us to Bramall Lane. When we got there Parsons had other ideas, the old bill wanted us to stand on the terracing but I remember these double doors being opened from inside and a couple of hundred of us running up the stairs and all sitting in their seats. I later found out that Parsons and a few others had paid to get in then opened the fire exits for the rest of us. That was the beginning of Cardiff's mob sitting in seats at away games in the home end in big numbers.

During the game we sat there and watched the match and you would not have thought there had been trouble that day, the Bradford lads continually kept saying "We have never seen anything like this and the Ointment had nowhere near the numbers of Cardiff."

After the game, Sheffield wanted revenge and all the way back to the station their numbers grew bigger and bigger, both mobs were now virtually equal in numbers and the old bill were finding it hard to keep us apart. Parsons picked up a traffic cone and threw it straight over the old bill and towards Sheffield's mob; both sets of lads flew at each other and for about a minute fists were flying everywhere and neither side were giving an inch. The old bill finally took control, for now. As the Soul Crew got to the train station, Sheffield came charging down again with bottles, bricks and anything else they could get their hands on. The old bill came steaming down and went straight through us and sent Sheffield packing and at the same time the dogs seemed to have been let loose on us.

On my journey home the lads later told me (I returned to Bradford) that everyone had agreed that from now on Cardiff were to be called the "Soul Crew" and nothing else, (during this era Soul music was at a peak and that is where Parsons took the name from) and so this was the start of 'The Soul Crew Years'.

Bradford away came soon after; I was still living there and had met their firm "The Ointment," when I had gone to watch Bradford v Oxford earlier that season. Soon after I had moved to the area I had gone to see that particular fixture as the following Tuesday Bradford were playing down at Ninian Park and I wanted to book on one of their coaches. I had gone in the Oxford end and the Ointment was on their end too. I ended up talking to them which led to me going on their coach to Cardiff on that Tuesday evening. Nothing happened that night as it turned out to be a wet dreary evening and their coach didn't get to the ground until kick off. I got off their coach about a quarter of a mile from Ninian park, but I will say they treated me with the utmost respect, maybe because I was only 16 and was on my own and most of their lads were in their 20's and 30's.

Bradford away though was a totally different matter especially after what the Bradford lads had seen what Cardiff were capable of in Sheffield. Right from the build up to the match everything seemed to go wrong, first a floodlight was damaged and the game was set for a Wednesday afternoon. I knew not many of the Soul Crew would travel but most of my mates were still coming up. That morning Mannings phoned me to say that he was sat on a coach with fifty 'Soul Crew' and that Little Colin was coming up on the train with another eight lads. I knew from that minute that the nine from Cardiff would be in trouble as the Ointment would have anywhere between sixty and eighty at the train station waiting. If only there were mobile phones back then as I needed to get hold of Little Colin and warn him, even though I knew Colin would relish any trouble that would come before him, and if need be would stand by himself in front of sixty lads. But that wasn't the point, Colin and I had been friends since 12 years old. I made my mind up I was making my way to the Bradford interchange with a friend called Catherine, who was staying the week with me up from Cardiff. When I got to the station it was virtually empty, there were no direct trains to Bradford from anywhere in those days and everyone would either have to go to Leeds or Manchester and then change to Bradford.

A train pulled in and one solitary lad got off and guess who it was? . . . . . It was Parsons. I was so pleased to see him I started rambling on about what I knew, that fifty Soul Crew including Mannings, Boozer etc. had probably arrived by coach and would be in a pub near Valley Parade. I said to him that the Ointment were more than likely in a pub called the Queen's, which was just around the corner from the station. I also said that I didn't have a clue what time Little Colin was arriving. Parsons suggested we go and get Mannings and the rest of them and then come back, the only problem that this was at least a good mile walk.

We walked as fast as we could, virtually running and we soon found them, we now had fifty good lads and I was trying to tell everyone what I thought would happen but as I was only 16 I don't think many of them were interested in listening to me except for Mannings. Parsons said "We should all go now," but the majority wanted to stay and thought that if Bradford were so good they would come to us, so Parsons, Mannings, myself and a few other youngsters went outside and debated what we should do, with this a Cardiff fan from the supporters club came over and warned us to be careful as Bradford had just attacked some Cardiff in the train station.

The few of us outside the pub shouted to the others to quickly come and we made our way to the away end. When we got there we met Little Colin who was sporting two black eyes, a lad called Wurzel, who didn't look much better, and six other lads and a girl. I rushed over to Little Colin and asked him what happened?

Annis My story

The following story is written by Little Colin:

"I was 18 years old when we played Bradford away and I will never forget the Bradford fight in 1982-83 season, as being outnumbered is a big buzz to me and when the odds are stacked against you, you find out who your real mates are and you can always sit back afterwards and have a laugh about it. We boarded the train at Cardiff central, eight lads and one girl but if I am honest I knew the only one I could rely on was Wurzel. Yes we knew there would probably be some kind of reception as in those days every team in the Country made a show. The journey was a seven hour long and boring trip. I did expect more than eight lads to go but there you go I thought "this could be fun."

Eventually we arrived at Bradford interchange, we got the train but there was no reception for us, everyone you could feel started to relax a little, we went down the escalators and as we approached the end I noticed a few lads at the bottom, I'd say about six lads. I thought these were the spotters, little did we know that there were much more than six and a mob of about sixty Ointment seemed to come from literally nowhere. Most of the lads that were with me were edgy as if to say "what the fuck are we going to do?" Wurzel and I just carried on walking to the exit where they were crowded, I knew I was going to get a kicking but that's life, if you don't want to know, don't go!

I think Bradford were disappointed with our turnout and then they suddenly came into us shouting "Ointment, Ointment."Wurzel and I were suddenly fighting everyone or that's what it seemed like. I hit as many as I could but the amount of punches raining down on me sent me and few of the others flying back. I could see Wurzel was getting a worse hammering so I went back to help him as no matter what I would never leave a mate. They seemed to stop for a couple of seconds and it gave us chance to regroup by the bottom of the escalators.

They came at us again, our lot did have brollies with them and they were whacking them whilst Wurzel and I tried to punch them back, eventually we were forced back up the escalators and to the platform. I don't know why but Bradford just seemed to disappear, yes they had a result in their eyes but if they were so good why were we not battered? I actually felt exhausted and shattered rather than battered and I was glad I could recharge myself ready for whatever happened next. The old bill eventually appeared.

At the ground I met my old mates Annis and Mannings, they said they had heard there had been trouble, but everyone knows what I am like. I laughed as I told them the story, I have since met the Ointment for a drink on a few occasions, some for a drink on a non-football day and to be honest we laughed about that day and they bought me drinks and said that they will always have respect for me. We also met up about fifteen years ago at the Valley and we showed them how it should be done.

I am 48 years old now and in my opinion those were the best days. To this day Annis and Mannings remain my good friends and since that day we have been side by side on many occasions, I would trust them with my life too."

As we all went into the ground we looked over to their main stand and there were about sixty to eighty Ointment chanting "Where's your famous Soul Crew?" This made our anger worse. If I remember correctly we lost the game 4-2 and at the end of it Mannings and Little Colin were arguing with the old bill as they were demanding we walk back to the train station but the old bill were having none of it and put them in a meat wagon to take them back to the station. I said cheerio to everyone and Catherine and I walked back and as we came around a corner we walked straight into Bradford's firm! One of their main lads, who was in his late twenties, whacked me straight in the face and said " You're lucky I don't do more, now fuck off you Cardiff c...," with that about sixty of them walked passed and a couple did say that that was out of order by him.

The following day I rang Little Colin and asked how he was but as usual he thought the whole thing was a good laugh but one day he would get his revenge on them, which he did some fifteen years later when the Soul Crew returned and ran the Ointment around their town centre and after the match run them outside their own end.

My next away game was Preston and as usual I made my way by train and when I got there I went to the nearest pub by the train station, it was packed full of Soul Crew. As I made my way in Parsons approached me with his little mob from London and said "You are not welcome anymore, it was through you we got done in Bradford," I replied "What are you on about I was with you all day and it was only us who wanted to help the lads," to which he said again "You heard, you're not welcome," I thought what can I do? Parsons, as everyone knew carried a blade and wouldn't hesitate to use it, had already cut up another good lad's, Carlton, arm over something minor so I walked away but straight away I thought no-one is going to stop me following Cardiff, they are my club and always will be. I went to the game with Mannings and a few other mates of mine, Mannings said "Don't worry, he doesn't like me either," Little Colin had nearly come to blows with Parsons over the situation a few days previously.

The atmosphere was quite extraordinary that day as while we were fighting for points on the pitch, Britain was fighting with the Argentineans over the Falklands, one group of Cardiff fans were chanting "Argentina!" to the Preston fans and within minutes Cardiff were fighting Cardiff, as you had lads from the Valley's and other parts of Wales whose brothers and other family members were fighting in the Welsh guards out in the Falklands, sense prevailed and the mass numbers of Cardiff's firm outnumbered the idiots who had sung it and they silenced them. That actually made me feel sick, our boys are fighting for our Country and some idiots are singing Argentina, that is lower than low. When there is war, we are all together side by side; you don't bring war into football.

At the end of the game as the gates opened the Soul Crew came steaming out and up went the chant "Soul Crew, Soul Crew" and Preston were run straight down the middle of the main road. Preston were feeble compared to Sheffield United and Portsmouth and this time it didn't need the old bill to control Cardiff as they peacefully walked back to the train station with no more opposition along the way. I never saw Parsons after the game but Mannings and Little Colin phoned to say that Parsons had been doing a lot of shit stirring about me, they told me he had said "Annis is a foreigner as well and we don't need him," both said they had been sticking up for me but due to Parsons popularity he was number one amongst the Soul Crew because every time there was a battle he was always there and the Soul Crew had been terrorising the rest of the firms in the third division.

At 17, I moved back to Cardiff as my family had sold our business in Bradford but before I moved back some of the Ointment came to see me at the nightclub I was working in, in fairness they apologised for what had happened on the day with Bradford and also said it was out of order attacking such a small group of Cardiff, but one of them did say "Fucking hell, you had a small skinny lad who wouldn't go down and had hurt quite a few of us and in the end we left him alone," I replied "Fair enough but my mate Colin will live to fight another day."

That season Cardiff had been the most organised I had ever seen, we had battles with Oxford, Hereford, Bristol Rovers and even Newport but there were three other places that stuck out that season as well as Sheffield United away were Lincoln City, Portsmouth and Wigan away, each one of them gave the Soul Crew a run for its money. I have let a few of the other lads tell the stories of those places in another of my books "Diary 2" but I will confirm that these three firms were well up for it and did not let Cardiff have it all their own way. I was at all those places and I can tell you the Soul Crew left with nothing but respect for these three firms. The football we were watching was the best I had seen from a Cardiff side in years and this was helping swell our numbers too.

I moved back to a place called Barry, where over the years I have made many good friendships, Barry is near Cardiff and a few occasions when I went into Cardiff I did have some grief from some of the lads over what happened in Bradford, but I stuck to my guns and said that what happened at Bradford interchange was not my fault and the only thing, if any, I was guilty of was trying to impress the Ointment by taking two of their lads to Sheffield United with us and showed them how good we were, so the

Ointment knew from there that they had to put a good show on for us. The mouthy ones at the time I have since seen later on in life and they have apologised. Anyway these idiots who gave grief weren't even there in Bradford that day and during the late Eighties and early Nineties stopped following the City anyway and I was still going. All my true mates and some who were even there at the time know the truth and have always stuck by me.

As I have already said it was Parsons who came up with the idea of naming the Soul Crew and whether you liked him or not he led the Soul Crew into many battles and during this time I believe was the time that Cardiff were ever really organised. Since the Eighties Cardiff have been getting bigger crowds but I will say again they have never really been that organised as too many different areas in South Wales have always gone their own way, so you could say whenever other firms have had battles they might have been lucky or not so depending on what area they met from South Wales. Cardiff have got different mobs from Neath, Port Talbot, Barry, Bridgend, Llantrisant, Rhondda Valleys and many other valley areas, Merthyr, Ebbw Vale and then probably ten different areas of Cardiff too. In the Eighties I would have said Cardiff were a much tighter group but as the years went by, all these areas I just mentioned formed their own firms.

Parsons was Cardiff born but was originally with the Yid's (Spurs) and then came back to Cardiff. I don't really know why he left the Yid's but when he arrived on the scene at Cardiff he had many ideas but a lot of them were well out of order. After virtually organising the Soul Crew by himself as well as naming it in the 1982-83 season, by the end of it Parsons decided that the Soul Crew should only be people from the Cardiff area and he had some of the lads to tell others who were from Newport and the Valleys that they were not welcome, this caused a big rift amongst the Cardiff mob and didn't go down too well with some of the local Cardiff lads including myself. An example of Parsons attitude was on the way to Millwall, he went up to a lad on the coach who had long hair and said "You'll be getting off at Reading as you're not coming to Millwall, Reading rock festival suits people like you." On another occasion he even said to one of my mates that he was too fat to be in Cardiff's firm. He wanted us to have no blacks or Asians in our firm and this was the last straw as Cardiff always had lads from different cultures especially blacks, as the docks of Cardiff has always been the heart of the City.

During the years the docks have produced some of the Soul Crew's top lads, by this time Parsons had made many enemy's and one particular day outside the Ninian Park pub, one of the older lads named Bubble, who was as meaty as they come and someone who was not to be messed with, went up to Parsons and told him he was not welcome anymore and then knocked him out cold, leaving an imprint of his ring on the side of his face. Parsons went back to London and was not seen for a very long time. He later teamed up with Millwall's mob but this lasted less than six months as he made enemies there very quickly.

The next time I would see Parsons was at Stamford Bridge, it was Chelsea v West Ham and nine of us from Cardiff (Richard E, Chris Beer, Daryl Lewis were just some of the lads who went). We had gone there to see my old friend Chelsea Pat and this was a game not too be missed. We were meant to go into the West stand but West Ham had taken it that day so we stood on the Shed, as we stood a mob of Chelsea came up to us and who was at the front . . . . . Parsons!

I'll never forget what he said that day as he tried to belittle us, "Mr Annis and his young Cardiff Casuals, what a nice surprise, trying to take the Shed now are you?"

"I've come to see Chelsea play and see some of my mates" I replied. Parsons continued "Do you fancy your chances on here?" As he said it a roar went up from behind me, West Ham had invaded the shed, fighting erupted on all sides and we found ourselves toe to toe with West Ham and eventually helping Chelsea run West Ham off the Shed End.

After the game I told Chelsea Pat what had happened and he said he would have a word but by now Parsons had become a name with Chelsea after leading them against Portsmouth and a few other firms. The next time I saw Parsons he was standing in a shop doorway selling the Bulldog magazine (N.F magazine), I went to approach him and he seemed to just disappear fast into the crowd. A few weeks later Chelsea Pat told me that Chelsea had enough of his bully boy tactics and had also kicked him out of their firm.

A couple of years later I heard a story that he had got back in with Chelsea as one day on a match with Man Utd, ten Chelsea were getting done and Parsons had been nearby with a pit bull terrier, he ran to the front and with a growling dog by the side of him and ten Chelsea lads behind him he had Man Utd on their toes, but once again his friendship didn't last and Chelsea soon wised up to him again. Years later he was seen following Tooting and Mitcham AFC in the non-league.

I was to see him again and that was to be in the old Top Rank nightclub in Cardiff on a New Year's Eve. I was there drinking with Nils, Darryl and a few docks lads and I spotted him at the bar, I said to Nils "I can't believe it, its Parsons the racist bastard!" and with that I ran straight for him, Parsons saw us and him and his mates ran, we chased them down Queen Street where we eventually lost them. But the last ever time was at Fulham v Cardiff, it was half time and we were near the gates, Parsons and a couple of lads approached the gates and he shouted over to us that at the end of the game we had better have a good firm ready and then he disappeared. Yes, we did have a good firm, there was over one hundred of us including Dexy, Little Colin, Mannings, Dio, Darryl, Jammo and many others, we looked up and down many of the streets but we were never to see him again.

As much as I ended up hating Parsons he was the one who started the Soul Crew, make no mistake about it. Whatever has happened to him since I don't know and truthfully I don't even care but he does know that he is not welcome in Cardiff!

Something that may surprise you as you read this is that the Soul Crew was originally formed by lads from good backgrounds, the likes of Dai H, Nicky Parsons, Simon Williams, were all from areas such as Radyr, Whitchurch, Rhwbina all in Cardiff, they grew up in middle class families and since have very good jobs such as directors, manager's, they were not from the working class background as many may expect. But as I have said in this chapter the younger lads who came through and eventually took over the Soul Crew were from the working class families.

We went up that season and the real test was to come for the Soul Crew with firms like Chelsea, Boro, Man City, Leeds and Pompey (once again), all of them had top firms and would test the Soul Crew to the max.

When I got back I hung around with Little Colin and Mannings, who introduced me to their small firm, which was part of the Soul Crew, they were known as the "Ely Trendies" (some knew them as the Millbank boys) but as their ages were mainly between 15-18 years old a lot of the older Soul Crew never took them seriously until eventually they did as you will read. The younger lads eventually took over from the older ones. Mikey Dye, Siccy, Zeddy, Rayer (RIP), Jammo, Zub, Duller, Derym, Mexy and many more – these lads were a close knit group but made me feel really welcome.

A few of the original Soul Crew like Alan Rawlings, Peg (Denmark), Stan, Dai H, Simon Williams, Carlton, Beachy, Big Bubble, Carl (Hereford), Ducky (The Oppressed), Wurzel (Gloucester), Peter Mannings, Little Colin, Glen Waithe, and Chris (London) never stopped going and a good friendship with them developed.

In time a group of Barry lads, Daryl Lewis (who would stand with you no matter what the numbers were, became one of my best mates too), Kersy, Tonto, Wally, Marshy, Melvyn, Chris, Jeff Lloyd, Joseph, Coddy, Staples, G Wallpole, Terry, Jeff and Clayton Smith. There were the Llanrumney lads Steve Wilson, Shoulders, Beards and Pricey. There was Mac, Richard E, Dexy, Chris Beer, Mallo, Anthony Lewis (Bomber),Steven Kadget, Dave Roberts (Conwy), Digger, Mojo, Dixie, Matty, Simon Neads (Neath Punk), Fulman, Scouse, Guff, Hue, Taffy Anton, Gonk, Richard Sandam, James, Moorie, Harrison, Ginger Jones, Oggy, Conrad, Summerfield, Young Peg, Robert Penny, John and Aaron Weaver, John (Simmo), Joe Mullins, D Rhys, Ginger Nick, Kev Ederle, and others joined up with us in the coming years.

Nils, Jonathan Evans, Jellyhead, Rusty, Toddy, Derek Ford (RIP), Blond Simmo, Brummie, Princie, Icksy, Brownie, Greckson, Ivor, Bear, Big Foot, Maxwell, Weller,

Chop Chop, Santos, Polcock, Webber, Lancastle, Frankie D, Rotters, Winky, Quinny, Woody, Bolton, Marksy, Dowy, Chongo, Rhys and there were also two girls who regularly travelled away with us, Helen and Nadine, there were many more who I have not managed to name. There were many good lads like Steven Deacon and Anthony Rivers (Lakey) who joined up in later years.

On some games there could be as few as thirty young 'Soul Crew' and yet on another day the numbers would swell to around one hundred and fifty, we have gone to daft places like Worcester in pre-season friendlies and taken three hundred. We would go to Exeter, Hereford, Reading, Walsall and Shrewsbury and take over three hundred lads each time but let's remember these were the type of teams that we were playing against in those years. At the same time you then had different areas from the Valley's going their own way and with no-one ever willing to organise or to even try, Cardiff were never going to be as organised as Chelsea or Boro were in those days.

But at home games no firm was ever going to take the City of Cardiff as every lad from every area would turn out and if it was heard that a firm, like Chelsea, had entered the City then Cardiff would be spontaneous and 1,000 lads would converge on them, that is probably why the Soul Crew was never raided like Chelsea, West Ham, Boro, Leeds or Spurs etc.

The old bill could never go undercover and arrest anyone as there was no-one to blame for any organising. Our spotter in those days was a copper named Jeff Richards (RIP), Jeff knew everyone by first names, a lot of the lads did have respect for him but also knew why he was there and it was not to congratulate us!

Jeff knew my dad from the Sixties', so I will be honest with you, whenever he was around I would cringe as I had a lot of respect for my dad, I was actually more scared of my dad than the old bill as he was strict but fair. I was not a big drinker and never touched drugs out of respect for my dad.

The team was soon to go back down the league once again straight after our great promotion from Division Three and virtually all the old heads from the Soul Crew gave up following the team away unless it was Chelsea or Leeds away days of course. Over the next twelve years we spent nine of them in Division Four and so a lot of the bigger firms forgot that we even existed unless we drew them in the cup. So the name Soul Crew was literally only ever heard at places like Carlisle, Stockport, Wolves, Exeter, Tranmere, Plymouth and Hartlepool. I mention these names as every one of these teams had a firm and some of them even had the upper hand over the young Soul Crew. We weren't the best out there and never pretended to be but we were game and formed a good friendship between us all. I will say it again we never fought anyone who did not want to fight.

CHAPTER SIX

A NEW LIFE IN BRADFORD

When I was 15 years old I had become an addict to gambling on fruit machines, even when I had been with my parents in Las Vegas I had sneaked off on numerous occasions and gone gambling on the fruit machines, but to be caught every time by their security and told you had to be over 21 to play them, I was eventually threatened with being thrown out of the hotel. Thankfully for me I saw the truth about the machines when I moved to Bradford at 16 and half years old. Each and every day I would empty the seventeen machines we had in our club and seeing what was being taken out of each machine made me realise that there was only one winner, the house!

In September 1982,I had moved to Bradford six months before my parents did, originally I was all set to do a hotel management course at home in Cardiff. But my father had bought a club in Bradford called Tiffany's owned by Mecca, they were losing thousands on this club and Mecca were desperate to rid themselves of business's that were in dire straits. My father bought it nevertheless and renamed the club to Caesars Palace; it quickly became apparent that the then manager was skimming from my Dad's business. This manager had gone from driving a clapped out old banger to within two months of us taking over he had two brand new motors.

My father said to me "Son I need you to go to Bradford and run the club for me," I had worked in the clubs since the age of 12 and my father needed someone he could trust. I went to Bradford and the first thing to do was to put myself on the cash desk, as expected there was an immediate upturn in our nightly takings, we were now taking an extra £500 per night with myself handling the cash. The manager was obviously sacked.

Bradford was an eye opener for me, being brought up in Cardiff surrounded by my mates and living with my parents, it seemed like another world to me. I lived in a tiny little backroom in the club and I was alone up there and having to fend for myself at a young age, this was at the time of the Yorkshire Ripper, Peter Sutcliffe, being caught and prostitutes worked Lum Lane which ran parallel to where the club was situated on Manningham Lane.

There were severe problems amongst the Blacks and Asian gangs during these times and also the white gangs, mainly the Bradford Whites (Leeds fans living in Bradford) would fight with the Blacks too. Bradford was in turmoil and this resulted in the nightclub suffering, women were not going out, they were still scared of what had gone on in the previous months with the Yorkshire Ripper. To turn this club around I had to somehow get the crowds back in.

I met up with a local entertainment's agent and after much talking we decided on the best way forward for the club. Every Thursday we would have a band playing at the club, not just any band, we would have some very big names playing there or new up and coming bands which had large followings. We had Big Country, New Order, Aswad, Marillion and Marc Almond (Soft Cell) to name just a few. These acts would help turn the club around and pull the punters in. Thursday night was previously the Ballroom evening where we were only attracting 80-100 people, I knew I had to change it and modernise the club. The club was the biggest in Yorkshire at the time and it could hold up to 3,500. The club was right, the area had the potential, and I had to figure out a way to get them in.

The agent and I came to an agreement, he would bring the big name bands to the club, he would promote them and he would do all the leg work. I agreed that he could take the money at the door but I told him he would have to pay for all the staff that worked on a Thursday night and I would take the bar money. It was a fantastic bit of business for the club, not only would we sometimes have over 3,000 people spending money at the bar but the club was becoming a huge hit and was soon seen as the place to be, we could not lose.

There were some perks about having these bands, I got to meet all of them after their gigs and they would have a drink in our function room with some of the staff. There was also some funny, mad moments I experienced during these times, Marc Almond walked around the club before it opened and because he did not like the posters of himself on the walls of the club he tore every one of them down, he then later, in my opinion, became quite arrogant with the crowd whilst he was singing and was teasing them at the edge of the stage and in those days there were no barriers between the artist and the crowds and someone pulled him by the leg and he fell into the crowd and by the time the doormen got there to help him out, half his clothes were torn off him. The lead singer of Marillion climbed up on to the lighting rig and then hung from it above 3,000 people, imagine health and safety nowadays they would have shut me down there and then.

Bradford was really struggling with its gangs and their fighting and their hatred for each other. Opposite our club, nightclubs opened up solely for Blacks, there was a serious divide in the City and it was getting worse. One evening in the town centre, there was a truly awful event where a young black girl had one of her breasts cut off with a machete by members of Leeds whites. The hatred was immense and for the next few months the blacks of course wanted revenge and gangs of blacks and the

Bradford City's football lads who were from all different back grounds and were known as the Bradford Ointment were all out in full force every weekend looking for any Leeds fans who might be out drinking, this of course did not help the nightclub business at all.

I kept trying to keep the club going and become successful; I tried different themes for each night. Saturday nights were holding their own, but Fridays needed a boost, so we held the Malibu British disco dancing championships and ran this for over four months, we then followed it with a Miss Caesars competition, the crowds were coming from all over the North of England to compete and to watch. I also helped build up an under 17's disco on a Monday night, 7pm-11pm,starting with a dancing competition, Michael Jackson's Thriller album was out at that time and the kids were all copying his dancing techniques, a couple of thousand kids would regularly turn up, many coming from Leeds, Halifax and of course Bradford. I did the same on Friday nights for the under 17's between 6pm and 9pm and then about twenty kids would help us clean up the place for the over 18's that would start at 10pm, for that they would get free entry and a free slush puppy the following week.

After months of hard work and trying different themes for different nights the club was making money and I had managed to turn around a business that was heading downward. Around this time my parents had moved up from Wales and had bought a house in Guisley in Leeds, where we were overlooking the original Emmerdale farm, many times we would see them filming the show. Next door to us the first ever Harry Ramsden's was opened in the UK by none other than Margaret Thatcher. I was glad to be out of the pokey little room I had occupied for six months at the club and have a bit of comfort again, I would travel back and forth to the club on a scooter I had bought until I passed my driving test.

I would use as much of my spare time as possible to watch football and one day in particular I made my way to Bradford Interchange to get on the train to Wakefield where I would meet up with Pat from Chelsea and other Chelsea fans I knew, whenever I couldn't watch Cardiff I would watch Chelsea if they were nearby, that day Chelsea were playing Leeds.

As I got to the train station a lad I knew called Wayne, who lived in Bradford, who followed Chelsea was there waiting for me. I had met him on the train the previous game, when he saw me he said "I've just had a smack off those Leeds lads over there," I said "Which one?" he pointed over to a lad who stood with five other Leeds lads. In those days I was well up for it, especially if someone had been bullied, without hesitation I walked over casually and landed one straight on this lad's chin and the whole group backed off immediately. I fronted them up and none were prepared to step forward, I turned to walk back to Wayne when he shouted "Quick they got blades," I looked back and they were reaching into their socks, there was no hanging around we ran up the escalators and got onto the next train out to Leeds.

We arrived at Leeds station and there was a wait until our train to Wakefield arrived, I took a wander down to the ticket barrier and the same Leeds lads were there hanging around, probably now waiting for yours truly. Luckily they did not notice me, so I walked back up to the platform and waited until the train arrived for Wakefield. When I got there I met up with Pat and there were around 500 Chelsea fans congregated around two pubs. When I say 500 Chelsea fans it was probably one of the finest firms I had ever witnessed. Only once have I ever seen a firm better than this and it was when Cardiff played at Millwall many years later and we had 800 lads on two trains and the police inspector at that time said "What Cardiff have here is an international mob and only England could match this mob."

The 500 Chelsea was not the only mob they had out that day, there were in fact over 10,000 Chelsea in Leeds that day and amongst that was 4,000 lads. The group I had met up with was all the main faces and Pat knew every one of them, he introduced me to each of them and I was made to feel very welcome and they only had praise for Cardiff. I was a child compared to most of these Chelsea, as their ages were anywhere from 20-45 years old and I was only 17. West Yorkshire police mounted their biggest ever operation that day and managed to keep the two sets apart all day. Even after the game over 3,000 lads walked back the two miles to the station and we did not see one Leeds fan, apparently Leeds fans had been trying to get at Chelsea fans but the police numbers that day had been so big they had kept them well away and forced them back with dogs and horses and blocked all the roads off to where we were walking, boy that must have cost a fortune.

A month had passed and I was in the club working on a midweek night, as we had a private function on in an area of the club that held about 400 people and was separate to the main part of the club, I went down the stairs of the club and could see there was a group of dressers larking around, the bouncers were in the middle of them sorting it out. Then suddenly one of the group stepped out and said to me "I know you!" it was the Leeds fan I had hit on the station. Trouble nearly broke out, but I thought this is my place of work and I was not going to allow it to happen in my father's club. I said "If you've got a problem we can sort it out another time" I turned and walked back upstairs. I had not been upstairs for long when I got a message to say the club was going to get wrecked. I went to my office and got my Alsatian called Caesar, and steamed down the stairs, already the doormen were taking stick not only from the Leeds lot but from the other idiots who had been larking about earlier. There was a standoff and I have to admit it was the Alsatian who did the trick as if I hadn't have had the dog there would have been around thirty of them against three doormen.

I called this lad over and said to him to talk to me on his own, we went upstairs and after twenty minutes of chatting and talking mainly about the day against Chelsea and him saying how they managed to run me and my mate by pretending to have blades in their socks and how I got lucky with my punch, our talking turned to laughing. We agreed to shake hands and introduce ourselves properly, his name was Muffy.

Over the next few weeks Muffy came into the club regularly and I ended up going out with a girl who was his best mate, over time we eventually became good friends but always begged to differ on our views of Cardiff, Chelsea and especially Leeds. To this day he doesn't rate either Cardiff or Chelsea and that is the view of Leeds lads in general, they only rate themselves. Whilst I lived up in Bradford I got to hate Leeds more and more mainly because of their attitudes.

I remember one Sunday a few of us had gone ice skating in Bradford, Muffy, Manny, Paul, Ashley and myself. We met a few girls from Pudsey whilst we were skating and we got chatting and they asked us to come back to Pudsey with them, so we did. When we got to Pudsey it became apparent very quickly that we were not welcome and we were told in no uncertain terms to leave, Pudsey at that time was very much a National Front area of Leeds fans and the fact that Paul and Ashley were of Asian descent was the reason of our dislike. Muffy did not know any of these Leeds fans and let's be honest, I can't tarnish all Leeds fans with the same brush, as Muffy was Leeds and he did not share their pathetic views. Muffy was able to live in Bradford without many problems really as his cousin was one of the Bradford Ointments main lads.

I was mad in those days and did not take situations like what had happened that well, it was decided that we would go back to Pudsey and rectify the situation. There were three cars full of us friends including the original five who had been there earlier. We found the group of National Front in Pudsey and we got out of the cars and steamed into them. There was a huge brawl and during the melee there were no fewer than seven of them who needed hospital treatment.

As quickly and unannounced as we arrived we got out of the area and headed straight back to Bradford where we went to Indian restaurant off Lum Lane where you could get a curry for as little as £1, I remember distinctly that this particular Indian restaurant had no knives or forks, you ate with your fingers! Gull was the owner and over time we had used the place regularly. We were enjoying our food when in walked the police, they asked who the owner of the blue Capri was, I had only past my driving test a few weeks earlier and it was my first car, I stood up and said it was mine. The number plate had been taken by a witness from the scene and I was arrested along with Muffy, Paul and Ashley.

Thankfully each and every one of us stuck to the same story and denied what had taken place. We were all eventually released without charge. I was becoming more and more popular in Bradford and was beginning to make some very good friends but along with becoming more known and the club doing so well it also brought about other problems. There was a black man who was simply known as George.

George would walk up to the bouncers on the door of the club and was constantly looking for trouble and in particular with me. George was known as a tough man in the area that many simply wouldn't get involved with and certainly did not want to fight. Night after night he would come to the door asking for me to come outside and meet him. Eventually one night I went to the door and met with George, he said he wanted me to come outside and fight him. I told George I would but not at that time as the club was full of punters and if he still wanted to meet me then it would be at the end of the night.

Closing time came and it was time for me to go and meet George, I went out the front and told him we would go out the back and out of sight. There was a group who was watching but they were all told that this was between George and me. George was tough and very strong but I was no mug myself and was very fit at that age, don't forget I was only 17 years old but I did not care I would fight anyone and George was a challenge. I beat up George and battered him quite badly; I had to show this group watching that I would not be pushed around or have the piss taken out of me. Because I had beaten up George, word quickly spread and I now gained respect from a lot of people in Bradford.

I was invited more and more to different places to meet different people and one evening I went out for a drink with Muffy to a Leeds lad's pub in Leeds and most of their main faces were there including Griff. All I heard all evening was Leeds this, Leeds that and Leeds everything and a few of them were trying to belittle Cardiff and I was having none of it. The arguments became heated and I will admit thanks to Muffy I never got done, as I could tell what was on their minds. I eventually left but on bad terms with the Leeds lot and I have never spoken to them since.

Muffy and I remained good friends and even when I moved back to Cardiff we continued to maintain our friendship. I had not long moved back to Cardiff when Leeds came to play Cardiff at Ninian Park in a midweek night game in the old Division Two. I asked Muffy if he would be coming to the game and he said don't worry we will be there as Leeds are always everywhere. Muffy had got to know Little Colin, Mannings, Jonesy and some of the Ely lads quite well and as long as Leeds was not mentioned they got on well, even so much so that we had our own football match on the fields by Ely bridge. I went to the game and sat in the Grandstand with my usual mates and sat next to the Baker brothers from Llanrumney, who at that time were probably our main lads, they were about ten years older than me.

We had not seen any Leeds before the game and then out of nowhere about ten minutes into the game Muffy appeared behind me and as he was the one who would always go in and out of different clubs ends he had managed to get over to us. I turned around and he said to me whilst smiling "I told you we would come, where were Cardiff? Nowhere." I said "Shut up its all Cardiff here and anyway which way did you come?" he said that him and Griff had left the coach near Penarth Road and walked nearly a mile but did not see one Cardiff lad. "You stupid idiot, no one drinks that end of the City or even walks down that way" I said to him, (in the Eighties no one did, it was all Tudor Road end of Cardiff that everyone drank), "No wonder you didn't come across anyone" I kept laughing, Muffy managed to get back to the sixty Leeds lads he had been with, at the other end of the Grandstand.

At the end of the game Muffy, Griff and the sixty lads with them came steaming out and the usual Leeds chant went up "We are Leeds, We are Leeds!" but they were backed off straight down Sloper Road by around 300 Cardiff, it only lasted thirty seconds or so before the old bill took control. Muffy had fallen over onto his arse and luckily for him the lads around him were Mannings, Little Colin and a few others, Mannings told Muffy to get up off his arse and go back over to Leeds. There you go Muffy the favour was returned that night.

Even when Leeds played Cardiff in the FA Cup in 2002 and they were top of the Premiership and we were two divisions lower than them Leeds still never showed up, in all the years gone by they have never come to Cardiff in numbers so why they say they don't rate us is anyone's guess. I suppose there was one time that they could claim they turned up and that was in the Eighties when a few Leeds went to the King's Castle pub giving it large but they bumped into the wrong group which included Jimmy Tobin, who sparked four of them out by himself and that is no exaggeration.

I had spent eighteen months of my life in Bradford, of which the first six were on my own but I still tell friends to this day it was the best education I could have had, I don't wish to sound cliché but I left Cardiff a boy and returned a man from Bradford. No one can teach you about life you have to experience it and I had witnessed many things that I had never seen before socially. I became more understanding of business and how to run a successful one at that, despite working in the club's since the age of twelve, my time there had definitely been more than an eye opener.

During the time spent there, we as a family, had turned an ailing business into the most successful club in Yorkshire in a very short time, my father announced that it was time to sell whilst the club was at its peak, this is how we made money, taking them from nothing and turning them into a money making machine and then eventually selling them on for huge profits. As much as I understood my father's decision to leave Bradford, the pain was still there, I did not want to leave Bradford as

I had made many good friends and I can honestly say I feel living in Bradford, other than Cardiff, felt like it was my home.

I have lived in no fewer than 28 different homes throughout my life and this place just seemed at that time the place I wanted to stay at. But I knew that I had to return to Cardiff and continue to help the family business prosper. I got into my Capri and with a small bag of belongings and Caesar the Alsatian in the back, I drove back to Cardiff in what I can only describe as the saddest day of my life at that time. Muffy now lives in Tenerife and has finally settled down and came back to the UK a few years ago to come to my wedding, his mother and father, Pat and Stuart came too, they have become very close friends of mine and over the years I have gone to stay at their home on many occasions, where they have looked after me and any friends that have been with me and I have been treated as if I was their son. Ashley has moved to America, as to Paul, no one seems to know where he has gone, sadly Manny passed away a few years ago with bowel cancer. There are many other friends that I made during the time I lived there and all I can say is thank you for making me so welcome.

CHAPTER SEVEN

COMING HOME TO CARDIFF

Cardiff as a place had not really changed, it looked and felt as though the place had stood still for the last eighteen months, I had been back on quite a few occasions to watch Cardiff City's home games, but I had literally gone straight to the match and then straight back to Bradford.

My father had already found our next challenge, an old listed theatre in St Mary Street in the City Centre of Cardiff called the Prince of Wales, many football fans from all over the country in years to come have drunk in there during their visits to the Capital watching their team play at the Millennium stadium. We bought the building in March1984 a month after we had returned to Cardiff and the building was run down and was being used as a sleazy x rated cinema. The first thing my father did was let me get a team of lads together and including a few travellers (Gypsies), we stripped the building to its bare bones, filling thirty odd skips. The travellers were happy to take all the old seats with them, as they were heavy solid steel seats under all the materials and worth a few bob in scrap. Within weeks of us starting work on the building we had Cadw (listed buildings inspectors) on our backs wanting to dictate on how we should alter the building inside and wanting us to put every detail in writing. Being honest once the building was emptied, we closed the doors and locked them and just got on with doing the job without listening or having other people tell us how to spend our money.

By October 1984, the building was finally finished and had been transformed into one of the finest nightclubs ever seen outside London, that's what all the newspaper reporters were reporting in the weeks leading up to the opening of the club after we had shown them around the place. Some of the quotes from the Welsh and National newspapers were:

"WELCOME TO THE GLITTER PALACE"

"THE MOST EXCITING, GLAMOROUS DISCOTHEQUE THAT WALES HAS EVER SEEN OPENS IN CARDIFF TOMORROW"

"VEGAS LOOK FOR CITY'S NEW LUXURY NIGHTSPOT"

"CARDIFF HAS NEVER SEEN ANYTHING LIKE IT BEFORE"

I was very proud of the look of this place, especially as I had worked from day one on it and I had not only helped strip it, I had helped in every department in making it such a beautiful nightclub, from painting to knocking nails into plasterboards, I had done my part. The person I was most proud of was my father, he had totally designed the club himself, no expensive architects, just my father's brain and at the age of 62 which my father was then, he too was unloading vans and clearing all the rubbish up, but then that's what made me so proud of him, nothing was beneath him, at heart he was always a docks boy, who knew how to make money but never forgot where he was from. We opened the doors to the public on Friday 9th November 1984; our new club was called Caesars at the Prince of Wales, the name Caesars had caught on so well in Bradford we thought we would continue the trend.

Over 1,200 came in on the opening night and with hundreds not being able to be accommodated, the queues to get in stretched halfway down St Mary Street. I was 18 years old when this club opened and I was assistant manager under the manager who was called Eddie, who I had worked with at Caesars in Bradford, we put a good team together, we had a local DJ called Jeff Deere, a few mates of mine Christopher Beer (Lighting technician), Daryl Lewis and Richard England worked on the Bars, Richard was in charge of the cocktail bar, Malcolm McCann (Mallo), Amoir Mear (Bear), Paul Grexson and Ivor all helped out from glass collecting to helping behind the bars. Little Colin Howells worked the cellars and did all the repairs. There were 35 staff in total, the rest of the staff were mostly attractive girls on the bars and a good team of doormen. Dave Bennett, Simon Brown, Ozzy, Brian Willis, Trevor, Mark Chancellor, Lawrence (ex SAS), Eugene Tucker and Gary Pemberton (Boxer), Dave Bennett who was the same age as me, but taller and probably twice as strong (builder/carpenter during the day) eventually became our head doorman, he knew how to speak to people, but at the same time if you were out of order, he knew how to control the situation without a doubt. Years on we became best friends and Dave became well respected by both my late parents, especially my father as Dave would always pop in for a cup of coffee and a chat with my father in his later years. You meet a lot of people in the world I was in and I can honestly say you won't meet a more honest and nicer man than Dave, no jealousy there whatsoever and he has come from Ely one of the biggest council estates in Europe and has built up his own building business which he now has up to forty men working for him. I had no hesitation in asking Dave to be my best man when I got married in my later life.

At the same time as all this was going on Cardiff City were struggling in the old Division Two, after just having a great promotion season from Division Three. My old friends Little Colin and Peter Mannings were, as usual, there for me when I came back and ready and waiting to continue like the old days of following Cardiff, they were now hanging around in an area called Ely Bridge which is at the beginning of Ely, there was a new group of lads who had now started going regularly to Cardiff home games and had just started going away, they were known as the Ely Trendies, the main face was a lad called Mikey Dye, known as Dio to most, we immediately hit it off and became good friends and in the coming years we organised many exciting away trips to places like Colchester, Burnley, Bolton, Halifax, Stockport, Shrewsbury, Blackburn, Watford to name just a few, we would go to the home teams town centre's before every game and on nearly every occasion go on the home teams end. At the least unexpected places like clubs like Colchester we even took a good hiding, but that was part and parcel of being a football lad and the buzz and the excitement that came with it, it is very hard to explain to other people if they were not around in those days. To this day Mikey and I are still good friends and he too was to come to my wedding nearly twenty years later.

I had fallen out big time with Newport fans. I knew they despised Cardiff fans from when I had gone to see them play a few seasons ago against Portsmouth, but what I did not realise was they had taken it to another level, as I was about to experience. I went to Newport one afternoon with Colin to look at a Club on Stow hill; I had been invited to have a look at its lighting rig. After we had been there we were walking back to our car, when 5 Newport lads approached us and told us to give them our Fila and Lacoste jackets to them, we told them to get stuffed and do one, they did, but five minutes later they were back and now there was fifteen of them. Colin pulled out his work knife and they all backed off, as a taxi was going by, I flagged it down and jumped in it, grabbing Colin at the same time, if Colin had had his way he would have fought the lot of them. We went back to our car and drove back to Cardiff, I was not going to leave it there though and I went back the following day with Chris Beer and a few others. The personal battles between us and Newport were about to begin and actually went on for the next sixteen years. Fighting between us and them became a weekly occurrence and would happen in parks, at Barry Island, in pubs, town centre's to even roller skating rinks. What Newport did not realise was that they were not fighting the Soul Crew or Cardiff City fans; they were just fighting the lads I went about with. They even sent a girl in to Caesars when we were stripping the club and she was told to tell me if I did not come and face them in Cardiff bus station there and then twenty odd of them would come in to my place of work .Now for me this is going way too far and I was seething with anger and with Chris Beer and Colin the three of us went straight round to them without even thinking of the consequences. There they all were standing there, I said 'You've come to my place of work, if you want, no problem I will find out where everyone of you live and visit your own homes', with that I noticed them all walk slowly backwards, but they were not going back because of what I had just said, the Gypsies who were working with me had sensed that we had a problem and half a dozen of them had come around to help us with shovels in their hands. Now I personally would not have wanted to tangle with the Gypsies and it was obvious Newport felt the same way. They then shouted name the place and time; just off the cuff I said "This Saturday afternoon Cardiff Castle grounds 3pm."

We spread the word and the turnout was unbelievable by us, it was towards the end of the summer and the football season had not yet started, over 300 lads turned out from skinheads to Casuals for us and guess what it was a total no show by Newport. Everyone got bored and quite a few decided to go mod bashing down Queen Street, which ended up with a few large brawls and had the South Wales Echo writing about it on the Monday. Like I said these types of incidents became a regular occurrence over the coming years, with Newport actually coming to Cardiff unannounced and running us ragged a few times.

I actually had a lot of respect for Newport until I was attacked by them, when I was with a girl in the year 2000, which I have written about later in this book. To this day they hate Cardiff and even sing about us at every game and cheer every time they hear we are losing, Cardiff don't even talk or think about them.

Back to Caesars nightclub, the first year was an amazing success, a club called the Top Rank in Queen Street, Cardiff who were our biggest rivals at the time, tried to compete with us, for two months they were charging a penny in and with that you got a voucher for a free pint at the bar, it made no difference to us whatsoever, as the crowds just continued to come. But then the troubles happened all over the country, with riots in Brixton, Toxteth and London, places like Cardiff tried to copycat them on a much smaller scale and opposite us was a street called Caroline Street, known to many as chip alley. In those days this street was a no go area for the police in the early hours of the morning. Young Docks gangs used to meet up down there and have fights with groups of Valley lads who had come for a night out in the town centre, and then these groups of lads would hang around outside our club and attack our customers coming out at the end of the night. Our doormen were warned by the police not to go outside of the club and get involved yet the police would not get involved themselves, but in the coming months they tried to blame our club for the trouble, even though inside our club we hardly ever had trouble. Yes we all know I liked a fight, but I actually hated it on my own doorstep and at my place of work, I sometimes feel I must have been two different people, as I could totally turn off from the fighting to be 100% business minded and be respected for that by other people in the nightclub world.

My father had had enough of this and went down to the docks and visited some of these young lads' homes and spoke to their parents, but by now small riots were happening down the docks with police one night being locked in a building with cars put up against the doors of the building and then set alight. Luckily no one was killed, these type of mini riots spread to over parts of Cardiff in areas like Ely. My father said to them, by their kids coming to his business they were messing with his families' livelihood and he would not stand for it. Some of the older ones like Paul Santos and Richard Cordle had a lot of respect for my father and took care of it and over the forthcoming weeks less and less of the young docks kids came near our club.

The Success of Caesars had caught the eye of many club owners in London, in particular Peter Stringfellow, who contacted my father and asked for a meeting. Stringfellow then came down to Caesars one afternoon and met up with my father and myself. I did not realise but their paths had crossed before and Stringfellow knew all about my father and I could see how impressed he was with how my father ran his nightclubs. Many years ago my father previously had "Go-Go Girls" (topless dancing) in his cabaret clubs, but Cardiff wasn't ready for it at the time and so my father just stayed with normal cabaret. The reason why Stringfellow had called this meeting was because he wanted to ask my father if he was interested in becoming partners with him in London in the first ever lap dancing club. Stringfellow said 'It had worked elsewhere in the world and believed it certainly would in London', my father said 'You're probably right it will, but we've just come back to Cardiff after working away in Yorkshire and Spain' and he wanted to now spend a few years back in his home town running business'. Fair play to Stringfellow he went on to become very successful with his idea of table top dancing which is now virtually in every City in the UK. We continued with Caesars for another twelve months and had a few celebrities come to the club during that period, Steve Strange, Simon Bates Radio 1 DJ and groups like Shakatack, we eventually sold the club on to a Swansea based company who did the daftest thing of all and had the club security run by all Swansea doormen, the club was eventually wrecked one weekend and the doormen chased out, the club closed down and was eventually re-opened many years later by Wetherspoons who now just call it, The Prince of Wales.

As we are on the subject of trouble in nightclubs, people go on about how bad the trouble at football matches is and these fans should be birched, banned, locked up and are disgraces to society, some of these people need to take a good hard look at themselves, especially those that are in higher circles. At the same time as I was managing Caesars, we had just bought another club called the Double Diamond in Caerphilly, which my parents would concentrate on more, with a manager working with them. They had a graduation party for over 600 of the medical profession booked on a Tuesday night, so I went up there and helped out. We needed extra bar staff, so I took four up with me, as these were all now qualified doctors etc. We decided to only have a few doormen.

The night started well and in they all came dressed up to the nines, in their dinner suits and gowns, polite as anything as they arrived. We had booked an outside catering firm to prepare the food and serve it all out; I just helped with the bars. As the evening got in to full swing and they were coming to the end of their meals, the waitresses were trying to clear up but the male medical graduates started harassing the waitresses and let's put it this way in today's years they would all be up on sexual assault charges. Then came the food fighting, with them throwing their food at each other back and forth from table to table. I saw all this and went to the organisers of the catering and said forget about silver service; just get your staff to clear up everything as fast as possible.

They had their after dinner speeches, which went well, by the way these graduates were not kids, they were all 25 plus years old. The disco then started with the few doormen and myself now on tenterhooks, but the next hour or so also passed by peacefully. Out of the blue just when we had started to relax the alarm bell went on the front door, which meant there was trouble inside. I was at this stage serving a customer behind the bar and saw two of the doormen run past my bar, so I passed the customer on to one of the other staff and rushed over to see what was happening, an argument had broken out between some medical staff, who by now were well drunk. We calmed it down but asked the aggressor of the two parties to come and have some fresh air by the front door, he was having none of it and suddenly the ones who had been arguing with him, had now turned on the doormen and myself. We were well outnumbered and had to make our minds up, I took the decision to back down and let them all be, with just a polite warning. As soon as we went away they started up again and this time the same aggressor was going out, the third doorman ran in to help us, but we got attacked from everywhere, we got ourselves out and pulled back to the front door. In the meantime I told the bars to stop serving and pull the shutters down as now these medical staff were fighting a free for all and had even gone into our kitchens and were running around hitting each other with anything they could get their hands on from saucepans to plates, it was total chaos in there and these were people who were supposed to be from our upper class society, and who we are expected to look up to were now well out of control. They were now even fighting in our kitchens and the three doormen and I were helpless, I now even had the music turned off.

Two van loads of police arrived, I had not called them and I never have in my twenty odd years in the nightclub business. About a dozen of them clambered out of their vans and the Sergeant in charge was about to ask what's going on, when he saw for himself what was happening, so instead he shouted to us, "Just clear everyone out of the building and someone put the floodlights on." The night ended with sixteen medical staff locked up and guess what none of them were ever charged, yet I was asked to report to a police Inspector in Caerphilly two weeks later to explain what had happened and even he admitted, this profession can be some of the worst people to deal with, once they've had a drink. I had to tell this story, as I really get fed up of society looking at football fans as though we are scum.

After the sale of the Prince of Wales, I sold ice cream for a few months out of the doors of a shop we had kept; the shop was situated on the side of the Prince of Wales. It was actually a good laugh and very profitable, I had a proper ice cream machine and in those days, one ice cream would cost about two and half pence to produce and it would sell for about 25 pence. In the meantime my father would be looking through every business paper for any struggling business for sale.

'We want people to walk through our door and be in a fantasy world . . .'

❽ The dance floor — with the massive lighting gantry.

Welcome to the glitter palace!

WESTERN MAIL, WEDNESDAY, AUGUST 1, 1984

● Mr Annis Abraham junior and Mr Annis Abraham senior in the Prince of Wales theatre.

Vegas look for city's new luxury nightspot

By SHARON DAVEY

A LITTLE bit of Las Vegas will be coming to Cardiff when Annis Abraham opens his Prince of Wales club and restaurant on September 29, his 63rd birthday.

For so impressed was Mr Abraham by Liberace's own club in Vegas that he decided to import some of the star's ideas for his own club.

"It is the first time I have copied anyone, but Liberace is a good man to follow," said Mr Abraham, whose son Annis junior and wife Beatrice Dawn are co-directors in the scheme.

The nightclub itself will feature mirrored walls and tables, laser beams, hydraulic lighting that will go up and down with the music, and a top-class disc-jockey.

But the luxuriously-decorated club will only be part of a vast entertainments complex.

There will be five bars, including one for cocktails, late night eating facilities, and during the day Mr Abraham will run a restaurant serving breakfasts and lunches.

When these two ventures are open and making money he plans to open a classy boutique and shoe shop, utilising some of the shop space he has bought up with the Prince of Wales Theatre.

But perhaps the most adventurous scheme of all is what Mr Abraham plans to do with the Prince of Wales cellars, which he only recently discovered.

If all goes well these will be transformed into a Portobello Market-type complex, with space for 32 shop units.

The Cardiff business tycoon has already received calls from con-

tacts in London interested in renting space.

But Mr Abraham's plans to not even stop there. He has also discovered space in the vast old building for an office suite which he reckons he could rent out for £140 a week.

Things are moving fast at the Prince of Wales. Already the old cinema has been re-floored and it is looking less dilapidated every day.

There will be no membership for the nightclub. It will be open to everyone over the age of 18, but Mr Abraham may run an under-18's disco as well.

He will probably charge £1.50 entrance fee during the week and £2.50 at weekends. For this visitors will have the run of the club and all its bars.

The Prince of Wales should hold 800 people in all, and the project will mean jobs for up to 40 staff.

Caesars change hands — for a reputed £1m.

8/11/83.

BRADFORD'S biggest nightclub is changing hands in a deal believed to be worth more than £1m.

Caesar's in Manningham Lane is being taken over by the Northern-based Dollar Leisure group, which runs a number of other clubs throughout Britain. It inherits the plush nightspot, which has seen about £100,000 of improvements take place over two years.

Caesar's, formerly known as Tiffany's and The Mecca, now boasts the largest stage in any Northern nightclub. Its laser-controlled lighting and video system is believed to be the most comprehensive around.

Ready to move

Present owner, Annis Abraham, plans to return to his native Wales where he already owns two other clubs. He said: "I've enjoyed the time in Bradford and have seen Caesar's built up into what it is now.

"I've spent a lot of money doing the place up but me and my family are ready to move on again."

The new owners are expected to maintain the disco and restaurant side of Caesar's, and also the live rock groups staged regularly. New licensee at the club is Kevin Quill.

THURSDAY, MAY 10, 1984

Abraham in bid for top night spot

ANNIS ABRAHAM, whose son has bought Cardiff's Prince of Wales Theatre, has now made a bid for the Club Double Diamond, Wales's premier night spot.

"The agents said we made the highest bid," said Mr Abraham, also revealing plans for a new restaurant in Cardiff city centre.

Nightclub king sells up and moves out

ONE of the most well-known nightclub and restaurant owners in South Wales is selling all his interests in the area and moving to the North Country.

CHAPTER EIGHT

THE DUNGEON LEAGUE AND THE NORTH EAST

Cardiff City had a new manager, Alan Durban, in 1985 and we were still in the old Division Three, our away support had dwindled to sometimes less than one hundred and those that were still going away were mostly lads, many fans describe the Durban years as the worst in Cardiff City history. As I am writing about Alan Durban I will never forget Tuesday night on the 5th of November 1985 at Walsall away. Chris Beer, Daryl Lewis and I travelled up in my Ford Capri; we set off in the middle of the afternoon hoping to arrive in plenty of time to have a drink before kick-off. Less than twenty minutes from outside of Walsall and two hours before kick-off, we were well chuffed, when suddenly my clutch gave up and we had broken down on the M5. The next three hours were spent waiting for the AA and having the clutch fixed at the side of the motorway, the match was well and truly underway but I was adamant we would see as much of the game as possible. We didn't have mobiles then so we had no idea of the score, when we finally arrived at the stadium there was less than ten minutes of the game remaining.

We ran into the nearest entrance, which happened to lead us to just behind the Cardiff City dug-out in the Walsall end. I went over to the dug-out and shouted "What's the score?" we are losing 6-3 was the reply, after everything that had happened so far that evening and now this dreadful score line I was fuming. I looked over to the Cardiff end and there were less than sixty hardy souls amongst the crowd of 3,282. The full time whistle blew, Chris, Daryl and I walked out with our heads down and made our way into their social club. While Chris was playing the bandit, Daryl was at the bar getting the drinks, I said "Fuck the bandits and the drinks lets go back and tell them what we really think!"

I led the way and we went straight to the players entrance, with no security on the door but even so they would not have stopped us, we made our way through the entrance and found ourselves outside the Cardiff City dressing room, without thinking I went straight in, and first person who was stood in front of me was Alan Durban! It was a red flag to a bull, for some reason I grabbed hold of Durban and verbally launched into him, a scuffle ensued with players and staff trying to get me off the manager. Daryl shouted "We better go; the police and stewards are here!"

I let go of Durban and my parting shot was "You're not fit to be our manager," I turned on my heels and left a stunned dressing room in my wake, did I feel better for doing so, yes I did! The following day the headline of the Western Mail read *'ANGRY*

FAN ATTACKS DURBAN'. Thankfully that was the end of the matter.

I was eventually proven right; Durban was not fit to be our manager because at the end of the 85\86 season Cardiff City were relegated to the Fourth Division for the first time in the club's history. As if that wasn't bad enough, it was almost like the Football League deliberately rubbed salt into the fans' wounds when the fixture list for the 1986/87 campaign was announced. They gave us a 600-mile round trip to Hartlepool on the opening day of the season. What a way to welcome us to the dungeon!

The club was in a terrible state on and off the pitch at the time, and crowds at Ninian Park were down as low as 1,800 on occasions. Many so-called City supporters had turned their backs on the Bluebirds, although the young Soul Crew hadn't. Cardiff's away following was often tiny during the mid-Eighties, but we were among the small number of fans who stuck by the team regardless of what division they were in and what sort of results they were getting. Although the opening day of the 86/87 campaign was sure to be a very long one, we were all up for a journey to the North East.

Believe it or not, we had as much fun in those days travelling to places like Hartlepool, Scarborough and Darlington as we did when City were playing away to some of the bigger clubs. You never knew what to expect when you were turning up at a northern lower-division club for the first time and there was hardly any old bill on duty at some of the smaller grounds, so we usually had a laugh.

In the weeks before the Hartlepool game we sorted out a batch of cheap family rail cards. When we eventually caught the train there was about eighty of us, and most us were travelling on dodgy family tickets. The lads I was with included Viking, Beer, Rhys, Rusty, Rawlings, Jonathan, Derek, Dowie and Steve from Llanrumney. Some of the Ely Trendies such as Dio (Mikey Dye), Jammo, Sissy and Jerky were along for the ride, as were a number of the Barry Casuals including Darryl, Kersey, Melvin, Bowcher and Staples. You could say we were one big happy family!

The night before the trip, forty of us had been over in Barry Island for the evening and we ended up staying out until the early hours of the morning. Our train was due to depart at around 5am, so it was pointless going home. Most of the lads were so drunk by the time we left South Wales they just wanted to sleep the beer off, but amazingly a few managed to stay awake for the whole journey.

As we were leaving Cardiff Central station we were apparently spotted by the police. They phoned ahead to Bristol Parkway, where we had to change trains, and told the local old bill to expect us. When we got to Parkway, two of Bristol's finest came over and told us they thought the Cardiff coppers were winding them up when they'd said eighty of us were heading their way so early in the morning. We assured them we wouldn't cause any problems and said all we wanted to do was sleep. Surprisingly, they let us board our train with no objections. I think they just wanted to go back to sleep themselves.

We arrived at Darlington station at about 10am. As we were waiting for our connection to Hartlepool, we noticed a load of local lads further down the platform. They were setting off to watch their team play a Third Division game in York, so Rawlings wandered over and began chatting to a group of them. They numbered around fifty in all, and they looked a decent little firm. Most of them were a good few years older than us and they were dressed in all the right gear. Jonathan, Viking, Darryl and I strolled over to where Rawlings was standing and listened to what was being said. Rawlings told us they were asking who we were and he said they were talking about how much they hated Hartlepool, but I sensed they were just weighing us up. Then this fat Darlo lad looked down his nose at us and sneered "You Welsh wankers won't be able to do anything in Hartlepool anyway. You're just a bunch of kids."

Having some chubby northerner taking the piss out of us was all the encouragement our boys needed. A roar went up and everyone was straight into them. Without going into too much detail, it's fair to say that the Darlington lads came badly unstuck. There were bodies flying everywhere for a couple of minutes until the old bill flooded onto the platform and split us up. After things had calmed down we couldn't help laughing at the local boys. They had tried to belittle us but it backfired on them big time.

The transport police ushered us onto the next train, and about nine or ten officers followed us on board. It was their intention to escort us straight to Hartlepool, but we had other ideas. This particular train was one of the local services that stopped at every station between Darlington and Hartlepool, so when it pulled into Stockton-On-Tees we jumped off and legged it out onto the streets. The coppers tried their best to stop us but as soon as we made it off the platforms they were powerless to do anything as we were out of their jurisdiction.

We managed to find ourselves a nice little pub within a few minutes' walk of the station. I promised the landlord we'd fill up his tills and said we'd be the best-behaved football fans he'd ever encountered provided he didn't telephone the old bill and let them know where we were. He had no problem agreeing to such a deal and was as good as gold with us all lunchtime. We kept the doors firmly closed and made sure everyone stayed inside the pub in an effort to avoid detection. Either the police couldn't find us or they couldn't be bothered to look, as we managed to stay there for almost two hours without any interference from the local constabulary. When we were ready to move on, I asked the landlord to show us the best way to Hartlepool. He said a bus pulled up outside the pub every half hour and it went straight to the town centre, so that was that. Pretty soon, eighty pissed-up Soul Crew youngsters were on a double-decker bus heading for Hartlepool, and it was rocking. Literally rocking at times!

As the bus arrived in the middle of the town, one of the lads at the front of the top deck shouted that he could see a load of mods a bit further up the road. That was like a red rag to a bull for us. Back then, mods had become an unhealthy obsession for our firm of young casuals. If we weren't fighting with other football fans we were fighting with mods, so the bus started emptying and half of our drunken loonies were staggering down the street chasing after them. To be honest, we must have looked a right bunch of clowns. We made so much racket that the mods were on their toes long before we got anywhere near them, but although we didn't manage to give them any grief, what we did do was alert the old bill to our arrival. The next thing I knew there were coppers everywhere and we were all running off in different directions. It didn't seem too bad at the time as we'd agreed beforehand that if we got spilt up we'd meet up later in Hartlepool's seats. Things didn't work out quite that way though.

Plenty went wrong before we got to the ground. Jammo's small group walked into the middle of a shopping square and stumbled upon fifty Hartlepool lads. By that stage he was pissed out of his brains, so with only a handful of boys behind him he just went for it and steamed straight into them. When we caught up with him later it was obvious he'd had a right kicking, and apparently he didn't get much in the way of back-up from those who were with him. The local lads had even nicked his shoes, which was out of order, although to be fair Jammo wasn't using them anyway as he could hardly stand up!

I was in a group of about twenty and we were involved in a few scuffles with the Hartlepool fans on the way to the Victoria Ground. I remember they were pretty game and never once took a backward step. The old bill had to get between us on several occasions before we got to the ground. When we eventually did arrive we went straight into the main grandstand as arranged, but we were disappointed to find the others hadn't managed to join us.

Nothing much happened for the first half an hour or so. Then we noticed the enclosure below the stand was suddenly starting to fill up, but the lads who were arriving weren't Hartlepool or Cardiff supporters. They were in fact Middlesbrough fans. The situation was that Middlesbrough Football Club had gone into liquidation over debts of £2 million a few weeks earlier. As a result, the bailiffs had locked Ayresome Park and Boro were left with nowhere to play. A group of local businessmen were supposed to be putting a rescue package together, so the Football League allowed Boro to play their opening Third Division game against Port Vale at Hartlepool's Victoria Ground. Bizarrely, instead of their match being played the following day, it was scheduled to kick off in the evening just a couple of hours after our match had finished.

As we approached half time there must have been a hundred and fifty Middlesbrough lads in the enclosure below the stand and they were making sure we knew they'd seen us. I felt like we were sitting ducks. During the interval some of them began making their way up the steps towards us, so a few of our lot ripped out a load of plastic seats and began hurling them at the advancing Boro contingent. From that moment onwards it was chaos. At first the Boro lads backed off and a few of them even spilled onto the pitch, but then they got themselves together and began charging up the stand towards us. More seats were thrown at them but they were returned with interest. For a couple of minutes the air was thick with missiles going in both directions. Meanwhile, a large percentage of the six hundred Cardiff fans in the away end were attempting to invade the pitch and come to our rescue. The old bill really had their hands full trying to keep the City mob under control. A few lads did make it onto the pitch and Dowie was one of them, but he was immediately bitten by a police dog, so he got himself back into the away end a bit sharpish.

It didn't take the Boro boys long to get decent numbers up into the stand and we had no chance against them. When they reached us we attempted to stand our ground for about thirty seconds but it was a pointless exercise, so we began to retreat. That gave Boro further encouragement, and they not only kicked us down the stairs but they battered us through the turnstiles as we were trying to get out. I took a fair few slaps, as did Beer and Dio. Viking and Derek did their best to fight back, I could hear Viking shouting to Derek by the turnstiles to hit them as hard as he could and smash them like me, but they didn't last long before they had to clamber over the turnstiles and join the rest of us outside the ground. Luckily, nobody sustained anything more than minor cuts and bruises, which was amazing considering the punishment we took while we were trying to escape.

Beer was seriously pissed off with what had happened and demanded that we try to do something to get our own back, so we ran around to the stand's main entrance and tried to make our way down the players' tunnel. However, the old bill saw us and managed to stop us before we got very far. We told them we were only trying to find the away end and surprisingly they believed us, so they led us to the Cardiff section and let us join up with the rest of the lads. As soon as we got into the away end we began swapping tops with the boys who were already in there, just in case the coppers decided to come looking for those of us who had been involved in the battle with Boro in the grandstand.

The match ended in a 1-1 draw with striker Rob Turner scoring City's goal. Afterwards, the old bill had a nightmare job as they tried to escort hundreds of us back to the train. There were lots of Hartlepool lads about and there were plenty more Middlesbrough fans arriving for their game, so by the time we reached the station it had kicked off numerous times. No side could claim any sort of victory though, as the police were generally on top of things. Nevertheless, I should mention how impressive Boro's firm looked. Despite the fact that their club was at death's door and they weren't playing in their home town, they still had a large number of lads out. The transport police arranged a special train to take us back to Cardiff and at least a dozen officers joined us for the journey. Nobody was really bothered as most of us were knackered and just wanted to sleep after such a hectic day out, and that's hardly surprising under the circumstances.

When we got back home our phones were red hot. Bear in mind these were the days before mobiles and the internet, so information didn't travel anywhere near as fast. Those who hadn't been with us up in Hartlepool wanted to know what had happened as the trouble had made the national news on TV and radio. There was also plenty of press coverage over the following few days. The media seemed amazed that the first outbreak of violence of the new season had occurred at a Fourth Division match. The fact that the start of the second half had been delayed for fifteen minutes while the police tried to calm things down was the major talking point.

Cardiff City were destined to spend ten of the next fifteen years in the league's bottom division, but although the football was often rubbish, most of us stuck together and kept supporting the team all the same. The Eighties and Nineties are now considered by many fans to be the worst period in the City's history, and that's fair enough really. The club was often in turmoil back then, but the Soul Crew lads still managed to have plenty of good times. Having said that, the day we spent up in Hartlepool in August 1986 was definitely a one-off. After all, I can't remember any other occasion when we had to take on three rival mobs in one day.

CHAPTER NINE

MAD DAY AT WOLVES AND A RUDE AWAKENING BY NEWPORT

It was Saturday September 6th 1986 and we were away to Wolves, we always knew this would be a good trip, Wolves have a big support and their firm has got huge numbers who were known then as the Subway Army. I knew of three hundred lads, who were going by train, but the ones I was hanging around with at that time sometimes liked to do their own thing, either they would go by our own coach or transit. On this occasion it was a transit.

So in this transit were sixteen of the best lads you would wish to be with, Richard E, Chris Beer, Daryl Lewis, Mallo, Dexy, and Docks lads Wella, Maxwell, Woody, Bigfoot, Grexson and Ivor were part of the group. Beer was the driver and we were on our way and we were not on the road for too long before we were in Wolverhampton town centre by midday. The decision was made to park the van near to the main train station so it would be a good walk back after the game with the train mob. With no mobile phones in those days we did not know where the train mob had set up, so we wandered into the town centre.

On our way in we bumped into a group of thirty City lads which included Rawlins, Stan, Karl, Wurzel and Mikey Dye. We made our way together into the town and we were walking past a shopping centre when one of the lads at the front called back saying that it looked like it was Wolves pub, it was at the bottom of the road next to the department store Beeters.

I cannot remember why but Richard E, Daryl, myself and a few others made our way around the back of the pub, as the rest of our lads walked down from the top of the road to where there was around seventy Wolves lads congregated outside their pub. We ran into the pub from the back and what a surprise we gave them, with Richard knocking out two of their lads. We had taken them totally by surprise and not even given them the time to think about standing, as the main bulk of our lads just ran straight in to the disarrayed Wolves lads; they were on the run with us giving them chase through the shopping centre. I'll never forget how Rawlins and a couple of others came from the side of the pub and put a shopping trolley through the pub window, Wolves were being attacked from all sides.

They tried to stand on a couple of occasions in the shopping centre but we had the momentum and we were now well on top of them and it wasn't until the old bill showed up that we stopped giving them the run around. The lads could not believe we had run Wolves so easily out their own pub and right through their shopping centre. Yes we had caught them by surprise but it was still a good result.

With now a massive police presence all around, we split up and made our way to the ground, but before we did, we agreed that we would still go in Wolves seats if we didn't manage to meet up before the game. Most of us managed to find a pub where the main lot of Cardiff's crew were drinking, plus a good set of lads from the Valleys. Our tale was spreading around the pub and we were aware that Wolves would want their revenge before or after the game. Cardiff were put in a police escort to the ground but our lads from the transit had gone out in two's and three's and went straight to the ground and met up with each other in the Wolves seats as we had all agreed on.

Only a few minutes before kick-off and I heard shouts of "Fuck off out of here, you sheep shagging bastards!", we stood up and faced the Wolves lot coming down the stand toward us, we were ready for an off with them until Jeff Richards, our spotter, along with Wolverhampton police started to shout out our names, "Dexy, Annis, Mallo, Richard, Mikey" he virtually named every one of us before he said "I want you all out of here before you're all nicked." As we were escorted out of their end, Wolves shouted abuse but we strolled slowly out with the police shoving us in the backs to hurry us along. It felt like we were being treated as naughty school children.

The match was a good one with about 1,500 City fans making a lot of noise; we went on to win the game 1-0 thanks to a Paul Wimbleton goal and our players all coming over to us to acknowledge our great support, taking 1,500 fans to an away game, when our home attendances were some times less than 4,000, in my opinion was great support.

After the game the old bill tried to escort about four hundred of us back to the train station, but they were finding it difficult to do so as each and every one of us was a lad only interested in getting to Wolves who had about the same numbers congregated on the other side of the dual carriageway. It was about half a mile walk back, but during this time Cardiff were jogging and trying to cross the dual carriageway and Wolves were doing exactly the same, as we got to the station the mobs managed to meet head on and for a few seconds punches were landed and both sides wanted it, but the old bill again got between and let the police dogs do their work for them.

Once everyone was in the train station, the sixteen of us who had travelled in the transit knew it was going to be fun for us trying to get back to our van. To my surprise we got to the van unnoticed as the police had formed a line to stop Wolves going into the station. We drove out but within minutes we were caught up in traffic and sat there for a few minutes before Beer said "They're here, they're here," he had seen about forty Wolves running up the road toward the van, we all got out of the van as we would have been sitting ducks in the traffic jam. Fair play each and every one of the lads ran straight up the road and into the Wolves lot which ensured a proper toe to toe. It was going off for at least five minutes until the noise of sirens ensured the Wolves lot got away and then the old bill were on the scene and they made sure that they made a point of taking it out on us.

We were thrown against their vans and told that we were all arrested, then given the third degree and searched, we kept saying what were we supposed to do, sit there and take a hammering? They eventually got us back in our van and escorted us out of town, telling us not to come back again.

In the Eighties Wolves were always well up for it, they always had big numbers and game lads but by 1988 the old bill had had enough of them and Gilly (One of their main faces) along with sixty seven others were dawn raided in an operation the police called Operation Growth (Get Rid Of Wolverhampton Troublesome Hooligans), most got fines and bans but eleven of them got prison sentences including Gilly.

On our journey home we all chatted amongst ourselves about the mad day we had in Wolves. We arrived back home around 7pm and dropped half the lads off on Newport Road, we then took the van to Cardiff Central train station, where four of the lads wanted to get dropped off. At this point there were only eight of us left and as we pulled up outside the station the area was packed with people. It looked like a rugby match had been going on. I was sat in the front of the van with Darryl and when he got out to open the back door of the van I noticed a group of fifty or so lads hanging around just inside the station doors, a couple of them came out and noticed the van and then me. They came closer towards the van and one of them shouted "It's Cardiff," Maxwell got out the van and when I say he is 18st and 6'2" I mean he is every inch of it, the rest of us got out to back him up, Maxwell knocked the first one out with his first punch and we legged the other few back into the station.

A shout went up from inside the doors and out poured the lot of them, with the fifty of them and the eight of us we were soon back footing it and heading back to the van, Beer got the van started and shouted for us to get in, when we were all in, Richard E said "Fuck it, they're only Newport," so back out we all got, one with a car jack in his hand and with a mad charge, we had them going back again but this lasted just a few seconds as we were soon being punched and kicked into the van and totally overrun, with a few of us literally hanging out of the van still fighting, Beer put his foot down and got us all out of there in a flash.

We had been done, we couldn't believe it, and after going to Wolves and doing them and returning home to be done in our own backyard by Newport was unbelievable.

Afterwards we found out that Newport Old Boys were playing in a South Wales Cup Final in the Old Arms Park and all their football lads had come down to see the match.

CHAPTER TEN

A DAY I'LL NEVER FORGET

Saturday January 10th 1987, we had been drawn away to Millwall in the FA Cup 3rd round, the season up to this point had been diabolical and the crowds at Ninian Park were barely 2,000. Off the pitch though, the lads had had their fun at the likes of Stockport, Shrewsbury, Northampton and many other clubs that season. But Millwall away was the big one to the young Soul Crew.

I had been to Millwall before and had seen firsthand how good their firm was and how they terrified many other teams mobs going to the Den. For weeks leading up to the game the lads had been building themselves up, but as the time got nearer the numbers gradually dropped that were travelling by train. A lot had decided to either go by coach or on the special (a special train that run straight to London).

All the lads I knew very well were still going though, Toddy, Little Colin, Mannings, Mikey Dye, Jammo, Rawlins and many more. We were a bit apprehensive if I am honest as going to Millwall could not be compared to going to places like Shrewsbury or Stockport; these lot were a different kettle of fish all together, but for me this was the real buzz of following football at that time.

We had arranged to meet at 8am at Cardiff Central, around 120 lads turned up and the ages ranged from 16 to 25. None of us knew what the plan was, as there wasn't one, we would set off for London and take it from there. When we arrived at Paddington we were surprised that there were no police present. It was 10.30am and some of the lads suggested we go over to Soho for a laugh, the lads were absolutely buzzing with Rawlins and Little Colin in particular psyching everyone up.

For the next few hours we stayed in Soho and out of sight of the police, the lads drank and chatted about what they thought lay ahead, that soon changed though when Rawlins got up on a table and started a chant "WE WANT MILLWALL, WE WANT MILLWALL", Little Colin jumped up on the table, whilst the whole pub were chanting and he shouted "Fuck all the talk let's just fucking do it!."

Little Colin led us out of the bar that we were in and out onto the street with the chants ringing out "WE HATE ENGLAND" and "MILLWALL, HERE WE COME, MILLWALL-MILLWALL, HERE WE COME."

When I think back now we were pretty daft in doing that as we were bringing all the attention onto ourselves, how we never got picked up by the police and escorted was surprising, but the people of London were staring and even taking photos of us. We jumped onto a tube over to King's Cross, but with some of the lads not paying eventually the police were called and caught up with us. A young lad of 16, called Benson, was apprehended, I hadn't noticed until Dixie shouted "Annis, over here" I went over and there were two police officers, one holding Benson and the other stood in front of the pair of them. I asked "What you holding him for?" and one replied "We are going to have a quiet word with your mate about not paying his fare" and before another word was spoken the second officer, who was a lot younger, whilst pulling out his truncheon said "He's nicked; now fuck off out of our way."

By this point there were twenty or so Cardiff lads who had come over to us, there was a surge forward and I remember two lads from Llantrisant and a couple from Barry went straight into the police and knocked them down, I never touched them once, but I recall the police taking a few kicks. I don't know if they had called for backup before the situation escalated but another two turned up on the scene but this mob were not going to be stopped, the four police backed off to behind a set of black gates and pulled them shut. Mike Dye, Toddy, Jerky, I and a few others left there, but quite a few stayed to keep battling the police through the gates. I was game as anyone when it comes to fighting another mob of lads, but had no interest at all in fighting the police.

Eight of us caught the next train down to Millwall and now we were shitting it as the numbers were so low. Eight of us going to Millwall, we were asking for a beating I thought. But when we arrived it was quite the opposite, there was no welcoming committee, just around twenty police standing around and they never even looked at us. We walked into the Old Den with huge smiles on our faces. Little Colin and I took it another step further and went and sat in their seats on the right-hand side to the away end, perhaps we were feeling that we were the governors for the day.

The two of us went in, got a cup of coffee and sat down, it was a little early yet and hardly any Millwall were in their seats, but the nearer it approached kick off the more came in, but so were Cardiff too. Millwall's attention was taken by looking at Cardiff goading them in the away end. I was surprised at Millwall's turnout if I am honest, maybe they thought Cardiff wouldn't come but I had certainly seen better from them in the past.

A boring first half 0-0, Little Colin and I made a stupid mistake of going to get another cuppa at half time, at the kiosk we were swamped by Millwall giving it the big one. I stood there thinking 'fucking hell' yet Little Colin the lunatic shouted "Come on try and fuck me up," but lady luck was on our side as not only had the police spotted it, but Cardiff's very own spotter Jeff Richards came to our rescue and with about eight other police took us out, Millwall jeered at us and I kept thinking for once the police turned up at the right moment and put us on the Cardiff end.

The game finished 0-0 and there would be a replay to come at ours, they tried to keep Cardiff in at the end but Cardiff were having none of it, drain pipes, toilets and anything else was smashed up and thrown at the police. The police had one charge at Cardiff and then the gates were shut on us to keep everyone in. We were held in for over half an hour and when we were eventually let out, it had given them enough time to clear the streets of any Millwall.

The train back was packed with lads from the earlier special; they had decided to go back with us. When the train stopped at London Bridge there were at least 250 of us and we were all stopped and then let past in two's. As I walked up the stairs I saw two of the police from earlier in the day, one had a shiner and the other with his arm in a sling and cuts and bruises to his face, one of them shouted "That's him!" and two plain clothed officers grabbed me and put me straight in handcuffs and dragged me into a room and told me to stand in the corner with my back to them like a naughty schoolboy. Within a minute the door opened and two other lads were brought in, one was Rawlins and as he said "Alright Annis" he was instantly told to shut it.

We were then taken away into vans, but as we all knew the police liked their fun and our heads were banged into the back of the vans before we were actually put in the back of them. Unbelievably we were first taken to Holborn police station, and then we were taken to two other police stations before then settling for the night in a police station in Baker Street. That night no-one questioned us or even spoke to us and on the Sunday I was asked if I would make a statement and I said "No, I just want to see a solicitor," "No-one is available" was the answer. I shouted to Rawlins, whilst the door was open, to not say anything. The third lad did make a statement and said something about us both, he said that we were there but he didn't know if we had done anything, but the truth is we hadn't done anything so that's why he couldn't say if we had.

They kept coming in to my cell and asking me when I was willing to be interviewed, I just kept replying, "When you finally get me a solicitor." When they called back in again, I said "You let me ring home first, and then I will make a statement." Late that afternoon they allowed me a phone call on condition I made a statement, I rang home and speaking to my Mum my heart sank as she kept ensuring me and telling me, "not to worry, we'll get you a solicitor and get you out." My mother kept saying to me, "If you make a statement, say you will answer everything once your solicitor arrives." I went and made a statement and I still have the tape today, from beginning to end I kept saying the same thing "I can't believe what you're saying" and "I am innocent." I was accused along with Rawlins of battering the police and they said I was the leader, they said they had three witnesses to which I kept saying "Show me their statements then." They also said "You travel the length and breadth of the country following

Cardiff City and hundreds follow you," I laughed at them and said, "Yes I do, because I love my club and yes hundreds of others love and follow Cardiff City and we have no leader." I said "You're missing the point, I am innocent of what you are saying and therefore because you won't let me see a solicitor and are making up stories, I am not prepared to say anymore, than that I am innocent and no comment from now on." Their reply was "We have witnesses who all put you there at the scene and involved in the attack on our officers." They kept repeating this and other accusations for about half an hour. They were getting wound up, because I would not reply anymore and if I ever did it was just simple, "No comment."

At the end of the interview they said I was being charged with Affray and assault on the police , I couldn't believe it, yes I had been there but they were lying, as all I had done was speak to the police and stick up for a fellow Cardiff fan, not batter them.

The Monday came and Rawlins and I were driven to the Magistrates and put once again in a cell, separate from each other. The cells were full, but not for football, as everyone was shouting to each other, "What you in here for?" when I told them, there was a big cheer, but I wasn't smiling. The other Cardiff fan must have been let go for now, as he was not here with us. My solicitor came down to my cell and said he would do everything he could to try and get me bail, but the police were strongly asking for me personally to be remanded. Eventually they put us both before the court. The prosecution claimed that a blind man and a mother with a child had been knocked over and as well as the two police officers statements, they had two further police officer statements to come, also they apparently had three independent witness statements. My solicitor said that we both totally deny the claims. They wanted me remanded but my solicitor said that my parents were in the court and had travelled all the way up from South Wales this morning. I looked around and a tear rolled down my cheek as I realised how much my parents cared for me. My solicitor then told the court my parents were prepared to post bail for me and that I would agree to sign twice a week at the nearest police station. My parents had to sign a £1,000 security for me and with that the Magistrates then granted both Rawlins and I bail, much to the annoyance of the prosecution.

My parents, Rawlins and I drove home, we told them the truth, my father always knew if I was lying but he knew I was telling the truth otherwise my head would have been knocked off my shoulders.

About eight months passed before the trial and we had four visits to London Magistrates to keep answering the charges, the charges never changed, even though the police had put boards up around Kings Cross Station, asking did anyone see this attack on police officers by football fans and the date it happened. I was still able to go to football but I was going more and more in the car, the only problem was I wanted to be with the lads but I knew I had to hold back.

The Magistrates put the case to go to Knightsbridge Crown court, the trial was set as a two week trial, they hadn't got anyone else as Rawlins and I had stuck to our guns and not named another soul. I took seven witnesses, Helen and Nadia (the two girl casuals), Toddy, Jerky, Tim, Daryl and Little Colin. At the same time as our trial in Knightsbridge Crown Court, the Chelsea head-hunters and West Ham's ICF trials were on, they had been raided a year previously. It seemed trials against football fans were the in thing at that time and the Government and police were determined at no matter what cost to stamp out fighting at football and in my particular case, even if they had to lie to get a conviction. Of course I was a lad and enjoyed fighting, but I had never attacked police in my life and never intended to do so. As far as I am concerned I am totally innocent of these charges.

During the trial the jury was of mixed nationality and I could tell right from the beginning they were not police believers, this jury would make up their own minds. The prosecution had made Benson, the 16 year old boy who had not had a ticket, their witness, but that was about to back fire on them. They had no video footage of the actual fight, but only of when we got arrested at London Bridge, the Judge saw that we all had Aquascutum, Burberry, scarves etc. and made a comment, that we looked like an organised military outfit, so he was not on our side from the outset.

The youngest police officer was adamant that it was Rawlins and I, by the way, the third lad was charged and in court with us, so little did the help that he gave them, help him. My brief kept repeating to this officer "There were twenty lads kicking and hitting out at you, you were on the floor, and these two were the ones, you are saying, without a doubt, whilst kicking you and shouting 'kill him', not only can you only remember these two, but they stood out as twenty others were doing the same." The officer wouldn't change his mind no matter what, he even went on say that I had shouted over him, "Kick him in the head," the lying bastard! If it was not for him in the first place, the trouble would not have erupted.

The other police officer was honest, he was the officer who was originally just going to tell Benson off, said that we were there, but with everyone laying in to them, we were part of the large group, but he was not sure what we had done. The other two police couldn't identify me as I had already gone by the time they arrived at the scene. Next up was their star witness, Benson, or so they thought. Benson told the truth and no matter how they tried to get him to say that Rawlins and I were the leaders he would not agree with them. He then told the court that he was told by the police that he had to be a witness or he would be charged and taken to court himself. He also told the court that I had not done anything.

Now where were these other three witnesses they claimed they had, the blind man and the mother with the child? Simply they were never real, that was only said at the beginning of the case to try and get us remanded. They then put my witnesses on and each one that took the stand the judge said to them all that we looked military and organised, Helen took the stand wearing her famous Burberry skirt. Toddy and Tim had Hugo Boss blazers on and the Judge remarked on this too. To be fair every one of them they spoke well and did not get caught out as they were telling the truth. I would also like to thank you all once again for turning up for me.

At the end of the two week trial there was a good chance that we could be found guilty as the young police officer was still adamant it was us and the judge was totally biased. When the Jury retired we honestly felt we would be found guilty and sent down due to the Judge's summing up, so much so that my barrister was ready to appeal on the words the Judge had used in his closing statement to the jury. The Judge thought of remanding us, while the Jury was out, but my Barrister stood up and said "For two weeks now, the defendants have travelled back and forth from Cardiff and have not failed once to turn up and not even been late." So we were granted bail, whilst they were out. The Barrister told me that if I was to be found guilty with this Judge I would be looking at four years at least. My parents and I went to a cafe nearby and I actually said to them, I wanted to run away, my mother said "And yes you would be on the run for the rest of your life, so you would never be free, we will be here for you no matter what."

Three hours passed before the jury returned, but they wanted to go over Benson's statement again and in particular what he had said about me. The Judge you could see was not happy about reading Bensons statement out again and even my Barrister felt he rushed it through. At this point I handed all my personal belongings to my parents and had said my goodbyes, I was going down, I was convinced. The jury came back after half an hour and were ready with their verdict.

Rawlins was first, not guilty to affray (which was a riot in those days), he clenched my hand as the jury returned its verdict on me, again not guilty. We hugged and kissed and screamed for joy, we never even heard the third lad get not guilty. The Judge demanded silence in the court, we turned and thanked the jury, and the Judge let them go without even a thank you. We ran over to our parents, it was one of the happiest days of my life. I then said a personal thanks to my Barrister, whose name was Graham Ford, he replied "I always believed in you, but it was the Judge that worried me, you owe a lot to your parents for the work they did behind the scenes," I said "I know, thank you." I believe I got not guilty in this case was because for months before it, my mother studied every word of the prosecution's case against me and worked endlessly with Graham Ford, my mother actually put most of my defence together for me, Thank you Mum and Dad.

The media didn't even write about it back home, well they don't when you're innocent, do they? Yes we were lads but we weren't into attacking police.

CHAPTER ELEVEN

BROWNHILLS

Brownhills was an old ex-merchant Navy pub/hotel virtually run down to the ground. As you came out of Cardiff Central train station the pub was tucked away on the right hand side. In the late Eighties my father and I gutted the ground level of the pub and put two bars in there. One bar was used as a starting point for people before they headed off into town and the other was used by the regulars, who were made up of retired Navy and Sea men. The first and second floors were rented out to the Social Security and kept totally separate to the pub. The pub was popular with ex-sailors who would come in and share their tales with the regulars and many a tale I would get to hear.

At first just a few of the football lads I knew would pop in on their way into the City centre but as the weeks went by more and more would come in as it had become known as the place to chat and meet anyone to do with football, the lads all started using Brownhills on a regular basis.

We opened up the one part of the building and had designed and decorated it more like a wine bar, it was officially opened on the 19th February 1988 and was called Vineyards, but somehow everyone still called it Brownhills including all the football lads. On weeknights alone there was guaranteed to be between thirty and forty lads in the Vineyards part of Brownhills and on the weekend we had in, anything up to four hundred lads, depending on whether City were playing home. At this time everyone was wearing Tacchini, Lacoste, Fila, etc. The pub was probably one of the cheapest decorated pubs in the town centre, but with the most expensively dressed clientele.

These were the days when Cardiff's young up and coming firm emerged and for about six years they were Cardiff's finest. Brownhills will bring back memories for the lads who hung around there or even the ones who would just pop in occasionally. Brownhills helped merge the Docks lads with those from Ely, Splott, Canton, Barry, Fairwater and the Valleys, even lads from as far as Neath and Abergavenny were brought together at Brownhills. This had never happened before as Cardiff were well known for in-fighting which went back many years.

Some of the lads from Neath and Port Talbot, Simon, Fullman, Scouse and Guff (Anthony Ridgeway) would travel up regularly just to come and chat to the other lads about our next game, over the months it was great to see the Docks boys and Ely boys now getting on and drinking together in the pub, they had a history between them and the fighting used to get well out of hand. The Ely boys were known as the Millbank boys, because of the area they hung around and they protected it against other areas of Cardiff. They were very good friends of mine especially Little Colin, Mannings, Dio, Jammo, Seddie (Billy the badge), Cissy and the Dock's boys were also good friends of mine, Nils, Jonathan Evans, Wella, Darren Rees, Big foot, Rusty, Grexson, Maxwell and Ivor. Away from football they had had many fights in our town centre and even gone to each other's areas and fought each other. But now Cardiff City through Brownhills had united all together. I met many a good friend through Brownhills, Joff (Jeff Lee), James, Dexy, Peg, Conrad, Brummie (Stephen Byrne), Mark Todd, Ginger Jones, Matty and many more.

For away games in the Eighties Brownhills proved to be a good pick up point for the lads and on match days at home there would be as many as four hundred lads in there and never ever a need for bouncers. On an egg chasing day (Rugby) I would have to have as many as eight bouncers working, and at the end of those days there would be windows, chairs and even drainpipes smashed or broken, but because it was rugby you were supposed to laugh it off and say it was all done in jest. If that had been football other Landlords would have had the police come and have many of them arrested and claim there had been a riot.

During the years Brownhills was open City were getting low crowds again and were in the lower leagues so most away teams would not bring any lads/fans on the trains except for our rivals Bristol City, Bristol Rovers, Newport and the Jacks and the only mob to ever attack Brownhills was Newport and that wasn't even on a football day. It was a Saturday night and Brownhills was packed out and there must have been at least fifty lads in there having a drink before they either moved on or made their way home. Someone came in to the pub and said Newport were drinking in the Owain Glyndwr and there was about forty to sixty of them, with that every lad except for Little Colin, Chris Beer and a couple of others stayed by the front doors in case it was untrue and they were closer to Brownhills than what we had been told.

By the time the lads had reached the Owain Glyndwr other lads had joined up with them and the numbers were around eighty lads by now. Newport had left the Owain and they seemed to have vanished. Everyone made their way from the Owain and walked back in different directions and not as one group, as the group I was with got closer to Brownhills we could hear shouting and we ran toward the pub, there Newport were, fighting in the doorway of the pub. Little Colin had been glassed in the face, but still never moved from the front door, he would probably die before they got past him, Chris Beer was throwing pool balls at them and then whacking them back with a pool cue. The Cardiff lads who were coming back just steamed into them, led by Nils and Jonathan, Cardiff went ballistic and Newport were just annihilated, they got ran back and hammered all the way to the train station and continued to take a hiding on the platform. I was left with a pub with three windows smashed and a front door hanging off, but thankfully no damage inside, thanks to Little Colin and the others who were with him. Colin for his bravery ended up down the hospital with 8 stitches in his forehead but somehow kept smiling, that was Colin for you.

During those days there is a bit of a funny story to tell, the casuals of Cardiff at the time would have quite a few battles with the mods during the summer when there was no football. There were many battles ranging from the transport café, the Model Inn, Ely Bridge, Barry Island and even in the City Centre of Cardiff, 90% of the time the casuals had the upper hand as they fought like football lads and always stood together but there were occasions when they would come unstuck particularly when they attacked the mods who were on scooters, as there was a scooter club called the cougars, which were led by Mac, Shep and a lad called Letterman. For years we kept hearing this name Mac and that we'd all been lucky in the past as he hadn't been there. On one of the Sunday's he was there, a few lads took a bit of a pasting on Ely Bridge. Over a year passed after this incident and I still hadn't met Mac or even seen him but his name was always coming up.

On one particular game I was stood on the Bob Bank chatting to a lad about the game and I ended up chatting with him for twenty minutes or so and when the game finally finished I said "By the way I'm Annis" and he introduced himself as Mac, we both paused and looked at each other and burst out laughing. Over the years we have since gone together on many an away trip to follow the City. We have remained friends ever since and Mac along with Jonathan, Nils and Little Colin are the most reliable lads you would ever want by your side.

So Brownhills over the years became a place where it didn't matter what part of South Wales you belonged too, as long as you were Cardiff you knew you would meet some of the lads any night of the week and could catch up with what had been happening.

Brownhills was eventually sold at the end of January 1989 to a group of Asians from London; it ended up being ruined by a fire and totally destroyed. Now it is a car park for British rail.

CHAPTER TWELVE

THE ZULUS

As the season went on we now had a regular one hundred and fifty young Soul Crew going to the away games no matter how poor the team were playing. We had Birmingham away on a Tuesday night in October 1989 in the old Division Three.

I had never forgot the Zulus (Birmingham's Firm) coming to Cardiff in December 1984, I had just turned 19, we had a good young group of lads who now knew each other very well and had become a very good firm in the lower leagues. We were about to play Birmingham home and what a day I knew we would be in for. It was going to be fun and games all day long. Before the game we didn't see much of the Zulus other than going toe to toe with them for a few minutes near Ninian Park, I've got to say they were a well-dressed mob kitted out in Burberry and Aquascutum, a few of our lot took a few whacks from their Burberry umbrellas, which were smashed to pieces in the coming together, we had the upper hand with the initial mob but they were joined by another seventy or so more and had us on the back foot for a spell but with lads such as Dexy, Little Colin and Richard E, we were never going to be run. The old bill eventually sent both firms packing into the ground.

Birmingham won the game 2-1 and after the match the battles continued. Ten of us were walking down St Mary Street around forty minutes or so after the game had ended, Peter Mannings said he was sure they had some lads in town, we got chatting to some of our lads who said that there were around sixty Zulu's making their way towards us from the Castle. One of our lot went to the Philharmonic Pub, to get the older lads of Cardiff's firm to come and join us.

We headed directly towards where Birmingham were coming from and it was not long before we bumped into them, at this point there was only ten of us and we gave it a good go but we were overrun by the Zulus, not only because of their numbers but by a show of more Burberry umbrellas, which they were using more than their fists. We tried to stand on the corner of Wood Street by the Prince of Wales, waiting for the other lot from the Philharmonic but they never showed.

What happened next was quite funny, Chris Beer and a couple of other lads had gone into a place called Asteys, a big café near the bus station, some Brummies had followed them in there, Beer threw bottles of tomato sauce and mustard at them to try and fend them off, the Zulus were covered by the condiments and their Burberry umbrellas were too. Eventually around ninety Cardiff arrived on the corner of St Mary Street, it was about to be game on again but for the old bill, who turned up again and took control of the situation, escorting the Zulus back to their transport by the castle.

To be fair to them they had a bit of a result because other than us young Cardiff, the rest of Cardiff were too disorganised and took too long to get it together and also by coming back into our City Centre such a long time after the game had finished they had certainly caught us well and truly out that day.

Also a month before we were due to play Birmingham in October 1989, ten of us went to St Andrews, where Birmingham were playing West Ham in the Littlewoods Cup (League Cup) on the 19th September. We had a transit and Chris Beer, Jonathan Evans, Jellyhead (Chrissy Williams), Derek Ford (RIP) and a few others travelled up in it. What were we doing? I don't really know as it was about to turn in to a nightmare. On the motorway we even stopped for a hitchhiker, who wanted to go to the Midlands, but somehow ended up with us outside Birmingham's ground. We arrived at the ground with about half hour to spare before the kick-off, but we were going around in circles not knowing where to park. As we were going past the side of the ground a mob of about sixty lads were all standing there, a couple shouted at us, "Pull over you Cockney c....!" Jonathan was by the window, I was in the middle of him and Chris Beer who was driving. Jonathan Shouted "We're not Cockneys we're Cardiff, come on." Now I know Jonathan is mad but this went even further, to me this was suicide, "Stop the van, everyone out," Jonathan said to us all. With that Beer slammed the brakes on and the three of us in the front jumped out and ran around to the back of the van, the Zulus, couldn't believe their luck and came storming towards us. Jonathan's still calling them on with Beer and myself by his side, I tried to open the back doors of the transit to get everyone out, but they would not open, shit I thought we were done for.

I shouted to Jonathan, we have had it, forget being mad get back in the van, with that I grabbed Jonathan's arm and the three of us jumped back in, but by this time, the van was surrounded. Through Jonathan's window one Zulu tore Jonathan's jacket with a knife, Beer tried to get the van to go but I had ended up sitting on the gear stick. The transit was getting smashed all over and we really thought we were dead. The Zulus were shaking it and trying to get all the doors open. Eventually Beer got the van to go and sped off up a hill, we were then stopped by the old bill. We all got out, typical all the doors opened now, but the sides of the van looked like they had been hit by a dozen hammers. We all pleaded our innocence to the police and said we had been attacked, their reply to that was, "You shouldn't jump out and offer people out in the first place," they had watched the whole attack.

They allowed us to leave our van by the West Ham coaches, Jonathan and I asked who was coming in the West Ham end, most of the lads said they would prefer to stay where they were and not bother with the game. So Jonathan, Beer, Derek and Jellyhead came to the game with us. As it was the early stages of the Littlewoods Cup, West Ham only had about 400 fans in the away end. Within minutes of us going in, some Cockneys asked who we were; we told them and also what had happened outside. They turned out ok and invited us up to their place if ever we wanted to go up.

Luckily after the game our smashed up transit had a police escort out of Birmingham, but what a lucky escape. Oh by the way, the Hitchhiker had never been to a football game before and he muttered a thank you to us, for the lift, as by now he was shaking all over and was about to have a nervous breakdown. We promised him that this does not happen every week, but I don't for one minute think he believed us.

So back to the Tuesday night game away to Birmingham in 1989, the lads who were aged between the ages of 18-25 were well up for it. The Docks lads, Ely Trendies, Canton, Barry and all other areas of Cardiff were now united as one at football, but outside of football it was completely different. During a football match between the Docks and Ely lads it had descended into a riot and the night life wasn't much better between them either, but Nils, Grexson and Ivor, who were all from the Docks, were always trying to keep the peace amongst them all.

For this fixture we had two coaches leaving Empire Pool in Cardiff at 5pm. Every one of the lads turned up, including Lakey (Anthony Rivers), who was 15 and was attending his first Cardiff away match, there were no problems on my coach but on the other coach run by Mo Jo (Paul Mohamed), he was having issues with lads who would not pay, I had to jump on his coach and help him get the money in, as neither of the drivers were willing to leave until they had all the money.

We finally left forty five minutes late, so there was no stopping off on the way, it had to be straight there and we also knew we would be pushing it to make the Kick-off in time. Luckily enough we had a lad on our coach who was originally from Birmingham, who we nicknamed Brummie (Stephen Burn), he got the coaches to drop us off at Digbeth bus station. It was 7.30pm and Brummie said "Don't worry I know a shortcut," we got to the ground at 8pm and the game was already underway, we couldn't believe it, there was no old bill. We decided that this was it, one hundred of the Soul Crew onto the Birmingham end.

About ten of us had just got to their turnstiles and were ready to pay to get in when we heard singing from behind us, when we turned around it was our lot singing and throwing stones over to the Birmingham lot who were looking over from their end. With that hundreds of Birmingham fans steamed down to the turnstiles, there was no way we were going on their end now. The old bill had arrived by now and were chasing our lot back with their dogs, we felt let down by our lot who had sung and got us noticed. A lot of insults were traded between our ten and the Brummies as the old bill escorted everyone away. Cardiff were all taken and put on to the away end. Arguments went on throughout the game over the singing that got us spotted.

At the end of a 1-1 draw in front of a paltry 7,000 crowd about a dozen Cardiff had managed to get away from the escort, the old bill had no idea of where the coaches were that we had travelled up on. As Jellyhead, Jammo, Little Colin, myself and the other eight Cardiff made our way around to their end, Brummie (Stephen) was sent back to try and get some more lads. As the dozen of us made our way, we were spotted by a group of at least one hundred and fifty Birmingham.

Birmingham steamed towards us and a few bricks were thrown as they made their way towards the dozen lads. Jammo and Jellyhead were caught by the bricks and sent to the floor, Little Colin just ran straight into them followed by the next lad who took a right hiding and if it wasn't for the old bill turning up and wading in with their batons there would have been serious injuries, I got smacked all over the place just trying to rescue Colin.

The rest of Cardiff got as near as they could, because they told the old bill that our coaches were where the fighting was happening, but the old bill kept them back and stopped them getting involved. Little Colin had two massive cuts on his head and he was dripping in blood. When we finally got to Digbeth bus station, Little Colin and a few others received medical treatment from staff at the bus station.

The old bill weren't amused by all this and started to pull the lads and asking for their names and questioning them, thankfully no one was arrested. After twenty minutes the two coaches were escorted to the motorway and out of Birmingham.

A few years passed and we were to play Birmingham again but this time on a Saturday afternoon at their place again. By this time I had become good friends with some Sunderland lads who had been to a few of our home games, Mac, myself, Little Colin, Lakey, Dibble (Sean) and a few others had been to a few of their games too and we were made to feel very welcome up in Sunderland. They had arranged to meet us outside New Street station at 12.30pm, two car loads had come down including Brooksie and Daz and others, all good lads. We had travelled there in two cars ourselves, Glenn Villis, Huw, Little Colin, Chris Beer, Scouse and a few more and there was also around two hundred Cardiff lads coming up on the train.

As we arrived at New Street Station, the Sunderland lads were already waiting outside for us, we all went inside to wait for the train lot, and we were told that the train had been delayed, due to Cardiff fans playing up on the way up, at Cheltenham train station. One of the lads said, "Have you noticed we are being watched?" we looked around and there was a black lad who had clocked us and his mate who had been with him had darted off. We made our way over to the doors of the station and at the end of the walkway were about seventy Zulus. I noticed a lad at the front was someone I knew called Big Al. I told everyone to wait there and I will go and speak to Big Al, Little Colin came with me. I went over to Big Al and he shook my hand and the seventy odd Zulus were just staring at me and a few shouted out "Where are your lads?"

I told Big Al that there were only sixteen of us and the rest of the lads were still on the train that was delayed. Big Al told the Zulus to back off and go back to the pub; I said cheers to Al and turned around to walk back to our group. As we were walking back to our lads a roar went up behind us and suddenly there was seventy Zulus running past us and steaming straight into our lads, Little Colin and I ran in to help, but the group had been scattered. Everyone had got away apart from Little Colin and me, but luckily for us Big Al had run over to us and was having a go at the Zulus and saying they were out of order. I was having a go at Big Al telling him that it was well out of order what just happened.

The old bill arrived and grabbed us lot and asked who we were. Big Al had got away but not before apologising. Within minutes the train pulled in and the two hundred Cardiff got off and went straight through the ten old bill, who were taken by surprise. Cardiff marched straight down the road and turned left; we joined with them and by this time the rest of our group were back amongst us. We walked straight past a pub and standing on the door was Big Al, I stopped and spoke to him and remember him saying "Fucking hell maybe it's a good thing they didn't wait around for the rest of your firm to arrive" but he did say again that they were out of order and that he had tried to stop it, in fairness to him he had tried and he even came over to help Little Colin and I and pulled his lot away.

The old bill were doing their best to keep up with Cardiff, but Cardiff went straight towards the shops where vehicles were unable to go at that time. For the next five minutes Cardiff were wandering around like lost sheep and it was inevitable that they would be rounded up and they were, and escorted straight to the ground. Twenty of us broke off and went back to the pub where Big Al was, and he told us that Birmingham had been rounded too and he said that they were not as big in numbers as they had not expected as many Cardiff to turn up but said it would be different after the game.

The atmosphere at the game was superb and went by peacefully, after the game Cardiff tried to get out of the car parks and Birmingham had around four hundred trying to get at them but the old bill had everything under control as Cardiff were like headless chickens trying to get out. Eventually the old bill got everything under control and escorted Cardiff back to the station; the Sunderland lads were surprised and impressed by the turnout of Cardiff. We heard later on, that a coach full of Valley lads had it off with Birmingham outside a pub, where the Brummies had thrown bottles and bricks at the coach whilst it had broken down and then everyone on the coach got off and it was like a free for all, both sides giving as good as they got.

On the four occasions Birmingham have been in Cardiff, three of the occasions they have turned up and taken it to Cardiff and we have always had respect for them.

CHAPTER THIRTEEN

THE HOUSE OF COMMONS TO LOCKED UP IN STANDARD LIEGE

For a while my family came out of the entertainment business and opened up a chain of shops called Beauty Care Shops in Cardiff, Pontypridd and Neath, more or less on the same lines as The Body Shop, the main difference was that for products that they were selling for say £6.99 we would sell them for £1.99. My mother bought over 100 products of theirs and sent them to a chemist in Scotland who copied the ingredients; the cost to us was 50p per bottle. At this time they had no rights to nearly any of their products, even their famous White Musk perfume was not registered as their own, so we were able to copy it. They never had and still have no rights to the names Strawberry, Orange, Banana etc. as they are all natural names, the colour scheme in all their shops was green, they also had no rights to that either. But I think we went a bit too far, as I will now tell you. My father had decided the entertainment business was more now for the big public companies that were spending millions of pounds on renovating their clubs at least every two years, some even every year and were now even dictating the price of how much a pint was, a bit like Asda and Tesco today. I personally think we got out at just the right time.

So my father visited about half a dozen Body Shops and my father even had the cheek to go inside them and say he was from Egypt and could he take photos of their shops inside, the shelving, the products, their set up and he even got their staff to pose for him in their Body Shop uniforms, they could not do enough for him. We then copied the whole layout of their shops, if you walked in to ours, you would have thought you would have been in a Body Shop. We opened our shops up in 1990, with all these products, plus my uncle Garth and myself went to Cheetham Hill, next to Strangeways prison in Manchester to buy loads of cheap beauty products to add to all the Body Shop stuff, I was stunned at how cheap everything was and as long as you were paying in cash and buying in bulk the owners of the shops who were mostly Asian, would work on pennies just to get your business. Our Beauty Care shops immediately took off and word soon spread how cheap we were compared to Body Shop.

Within weeks Anita Roddick the owner of the Body Shop chain, who had hundreds of these shops worldwide was told about our three shops, they even had someone come down from their head office and photographed ours and wrote up a twenty page file on our shops. We were then warned if we did not close the shops down immediately we would be taken to court; we ignored them for over a year and were eventually taken to the High Courts in London. They filed a case against us, that we were passing off as a Body Shop and making people believe they were actually in a Body Shop, of course we were and we knew we were, but they could not stop us selling the products, they had to find other grounds to shut us down, it took them long enough.

Eventually I had to go to London with my solicitor John Dole who is now a days Judge in the civil courts, we had to meet a Barrister in London who specialised in these cases and prepare a case for our defence, what a day this turned out to be. On the train up to London we bumped in to John Smith a Labour MP, who John Dole knew very well and even though I am not a Labour supporter, after having quite a debate with him, I have to say I was well impressed with him and I told him so, but at the same time, I told him he would still never change my views on the Labour party, he laughed. He invited us to come in and look around the House of Parliament as his guest after we had seen our Barrister. I only had to be asked the once, as a child in school I had always had a big interest in politics, besides football of course.

Back to our visit to our Barristers, John Dole and I were both told there was only one winner, The Body Shop and if we tried to fight it, our costs could run into one hundred thousand pounds, but they had said to him, if we go quietly and not make a fuss about it and bring no publicity then they will let the matter go. I later went home and told my parents the bad news, but my father's brain was ticking over and he came up with an idea. We agreed with what the Body Shop had asked us to do, as long as we could have a month to sell our stock off. We would then change a lot of the colourings etc. they agreed. At this time we were also in a battle with Cardiff Council over our signs and the shops frontage, they had said we had not had planning permission for them and they had said the front of the shop was too bright for St Mary street and especially by the traffic lights, so we went to the newspapers and said we were going to shut down due to the council and their demands and that a closing down sale would start on the following Monday. A bit of luck had come our way and we used all this to our advantage, it became the biggest closing down sale in history, our business trebled, with everyone wanting a bargain, I kept going to Manchester and buying more and more cheap stuff, from perfumes, to teddy bears to children's videos and at the same time, we still sold the Beauty products but under a different label, which Body Shop could do nothing about.

While I am on the subject of where we got all our stock from to sell in the shops, I will never forget one of the journeys I had to Manchester, with my uncle Garth and Derek (Derek Ford RIP).We did the usual thing and hired a transit and drove up to Cheetham Hill, went and bought all the flannels, videos, baskets etc. and then called into a shop which sold beauty products and perfumes. Peter the owner was going through a bad time and wanted to do a deal on all his perfumes, we struck up a deal, which we felt was a price that could not be beaten back home, the problem was, we had to get all the stuff in the van. Well somehow we did and the van looked like it was weighed down by a ton of bricks, so off we went and made our way slowly back to Cardiff. We were all chuffed with ourselves as this journey really felt it had been worthwhile as the van was jammed full to the rafters, we even had stuff under our seats, by the handbrake and right up to the back of our heads.

As were driving down the M6 between Stoke and Stafford, Garth said "The police are behind us and they are flashing their lights to pull us in." So we pulled over and the police told us to follow them to a ministry of transport weighbridge, where they made us get out and they weighed the van. The truth is, you could tell just by looking at the van, it was too heavy; you didn't even need to have it weighed. They then told us we would have to empty half of the stuff out and leave it there; otherwise we could not complete our journey. So we did so, but we were not at all amused and our minds went in to overdrive thinking what we could do. Half the goods were now under a trailer by this weighbridge, we asked Derek to stay by the stuff, whilst we came up with a plan. The police told us that he could not stay there as it was private property and that he would have to go with us, "You're having a laugh" I said, "Ok give us a receipt" they wouldn't as they said they could not be held responsible for the stuff and that they were not confiscating it, and just that we were not allowed it on the van, yea I thought to myself and this will all be here tomorrow, do they think I am thick? We told Derek to sit on the side of the hill, a public area and just watch over our stuff and we would be back.

So off Garth and I went, we drove to the nearest services, where we unloaded the other half of the van and I sat in the services with it all, what a site it looked like with me sat by the side of it all. Garth then drove back to get Derek and the rest of the goods, but at the same time hoping that the police had gone on their way. They had, but Derek said they had offered him a lift to the nearest services when it started to rain, but of course he turned it down, even though he had got soaked and much of our stuff was too, but at least it was all there. Garth and Derek then drove back down to me and we filled the van back up to bursting point again, happy days or so we thought, as about an hour later just past Birmingham, Garth who was driving had to suddenly brake and due to us not packing the van like we had originally, bottles and box's flew forward, smashing and breaking all over the place, including all over us. What a site we must have all looked, covered in nail varnish, lipsticks and women's perfumes. We eventually made it back to Cardiff, but with half the goods soaked through and smashed and two weeks later Garth received a three hundred pounds fine, it turned out to be a total whitewash, in the end being too greedy had been our downfall.

The sale of all these products lasted for over fifteen months and just before the Council were about to put an injunction on us regarding our signs, on the 1st September 1992, we shut all three shops down, selling them off at the same time as people could see that these shops had plenty of trade.

As to the House of Commons, we met John Smith who, true to his word invited us in as his guests, where I met MP's like Michael Heseltine and John Prescott. Boy what a life they have, in those days they had bars galore, where away from the camera's half of them from all different parties would sit and drink cheap drinks together, seeing what I saw, you would not think they were at each other's throats every day, you would actually think they were best of friends. I appreciated what John Smith did for us and I have actually chatted to him on quite a few occasions over the years since.

For the next few months I helped my Uncle Garth sell cars at a garage called J&B Motors on Penarth Road Cardiff, but I don't think I was ever cut out for this job as I am an outspoken person and I definitely feel you have to be a bit of a conman or an Arthur Dailey and I am certainly not either of those.

On the football side of my life, in my opinion, the 1992/93 season under a manager called Eddie May had been one of the best seasons I had ever had, watching Cardiff City, we had won promotion back to the old Second Division in style, with thousands of City fans going to places like Shrewsbury, Scunthorpe and Wrexham, we had also won the Welsh Cup and had qualified for Europe, so we really had enjoyed our football and finally had something to look forward too.

In July 1993, I was back to doing what I knew best, making failed businesses into successful ones, I just loved the challenge and thrived on it, I always wanted to prove to my father that I could do it for him, on the rare occasion my father ever said well-done Son, that to me, meant more than anything. Going out drinking with mates, meant nothing to me, I was used to working on the nights my mates went out and I had more of a buzz telling my parents that we had beaten last week's takings. As you all know by now my downfall in life was my addiction for football and enjoying fighting in my younger days. An agent for Mecca who had previously sold us Caesars in Bradford contacted us and said they were selling of all their hotels and they had one for sale on our doorstep in Cardiff, were we interested ?

The hotel was called the Celtic Bay hotel, the building was over 115 years old and was an ex-railway warehouse, just on the outskirts of Cardiff Bay, which at that time the bay, had not been redeveloped yet. The hotel was losing £10,000 a week and had sixty full time staff. My father offered them a very low price, but at the same time offered to complete the deal within a month, not really expecting them to accept. In the meantime I was still travelling the country looking at clubs for sale in Mansfield, Blackpool and as far as Newcastle. They contacted my father back and said the offer had gone to their board of directors and that we would know within the next ten days their answer, my father told the agent to tell them he had no intentions of increasing the offer, due to the high losses and them stating we had to take all their staff on. Ten days later they accepted our offer, as long as we completed as we had said within a month, which we did.

On the day we completed all the staff were asked to come and see my mother and myself one by one. A few didn't even turn up, also quite a lot of staff had been on the so called sick for months and many that did turn up, accepted our offer of redundancy pay. Within 48 hours we had managed to reduce our staff from 60 to 29, with me bringing myself in to work seven days a week and you guessed it Little Colin as a help behind the scenes. I also contacted three experienced bar staff from my previous businesses, which jumped at the chance to work in our new venture. We also had bought thousands of pounds worth of drink, cleaning materials and stationery etc. off Mecca, but within a week I started to notice stuff going missing. I set traps and also I started going back to the hotel in the early hours of the morning. I caught one of the duty managers loading his car up with our wine and cutlery and I made him take me to his home there and then, where I found much more of our stock, the night porter Howard was renting some of our bedrooms out at night to prostitutes, but the silly bugger forgot to tidy them up after they had been used, that's how I initially caught him out. I then caught two of the cleaners leaving after work with bags full of our cleaning materials; these were just a couple of the many things I caught the previous staff up to. One of the main reasons the hotel was also losing money was that many companies were not paying their bills, those that were bad payers, were now told to pay up within 28 days or all credit was immediately stopped. Some never came back, others paid up. Also from pictures on walls, to flowers and plants, which were costing hundreds of pounds a week to the televisions in the bedrooms, everything was rented, they were all immediately told to come and collect them, we then bought our own televisions. The hotel started to work better with half the staff and seemed to be running much more efficiently now.

Our main function room was redesigned by my parents into a wedding room, stunning is how I would describe it, when it was finished. We advertised our new function room and soon we had booked over 50 weddings for the following year. I decided to shut our main restaurant and an adjoining bar, as they were losing a fortune and I then turned them in to more of a nightclub, with a small stage, now this was all my idea and I then advertised for local bands. The response was better than I could have imagined, so Friday and Sunday nights became known as the band nights and on Saturdays I organised an over thirties Soul/60's night. These bands brought their own followings as well and played more for the fun of it, than the money. Then twice a month I would have more well-known local bands, which were of course more expensive, but guaranteed you a full house. A band called ACAB, who had a lead singer called Smithy were a massive hit and sometimes I would have them on three times in a month as they became that popular. At first we were getting crowds of a couple of hundred but word was spreading and I would send Little Colin to other pubs and venues around Cardiff where he would leaflet every car and even have the cheek and go inside the places and hand everyone a ticket or leaflet to come to our club which now had a 2am license and we had also managed to get the capacity up to 500. Three months later Friday, Saturday and Sunday nights were full houses and by 10.30pm we were refusing people.

We called this part of the hotel CB's and it had its own entrance, eventually CB's was making more money the three nights it was open, than the hotel was in seven nights.

During the two years that I worked there, it was agreed I would not have any holidays and that the only days I would have off were to watch Cardiff City. But Cardiff City were in Europe in the European Cup Winners Cup and to me this was a dream come true, we had drawn Standard Liege in Belgium away on the 15th September 1993. I had to go; and my parents could see how much it meant to me. I know I was the only one who did the day to day running of the hotel, but both my parents went down to the hotel for the next two days and worked with the staff for me. I was able to get a flight direct from Cardiff, one of those 30 odd seated planes, Colin and I managed to book on one cheap. Now this really did excite me, most of my mates were going to meet us over there as I had to work times around our business. We got on the plane in Cardiff and to our surprise the whole team was on there, there were some spare seats by Nathan Blake, so we sat next to him and to this day I have kept in touch with him and even now I meet up for an occasional breakfast or lunch with Blakey.

When we arrived in Brussels the first thing Colin and I had to do was find digs for the night as the game was not until the following evening in Liege. We walked for what seemed like an hour as most were full, after eventually booking in a bed and breakfast; we went for a drink down by the red light area as we knew that's where most Cardiff would head. There had already been trouble down there with prostitutes trying to rip some Cardiff fans off and in return the Cardiff fans smashing their premises up. For a while we just kept ourselves with a few others in a quiet pub and then made our way to the Kebab/food area with about twenty other City fans. Most City fans were now drunk and an argument broke out with some local Turks, who pulled out knives on us, which in turn we threw whatever we could get our hands on at them. More and more Turks came and more and more were armed with weapons, we were soon running for our lives. We ended up outside this bar, where we decided to all make a stand against them, with chairs and tables as our weapons. The noise of sirens was soon ringing out and I shouted "Just get out of here and get back to your hotels." At this point I had lost Colin, a few lads went with me, we tried to find him and as the police arrived we just stood aside and they thankfully just ran on past us.

I got back to the hotel to find Colin asleep but his face was battered and bruised. The following morning, I asked him what had happened, but he said he could not remember. We had breakfast and then we both made our way to Brussels main train station to go to Liege. As we were walking through the station, I felt a hand on my shoulder, as I looked around these two men were standing there, with one of them saying "Passports, passports, police, police" and holding his hand out at the same time. We handed them to him and then the same police officer kept pointing at Colin's face, a few police in uniforms joined us saying "Come this way." We were both taken away and locked up in police cells in the train station. They were not like British ones these were like holding cells with just long bars and we both could speak and see each other which, at least, was something. The two of us both said if one was released without the other, the first thing to do is go to the British Embassy. The only thing I could think of was why were we locked up, was it because of the fight with the Turks the night before?

Every ten minutes different police officers or different Belgian men would come back and forth and look at us; it felt like we were animals in a cage. We would ask them "What is happening, why are we here?" but we got no response. Four hours had gone by and I was beginning to think we were in some serious trouble, but I kept thinking to myself, but we never hurt anyone, it was them who had the knives. As I was just sitting there deep in thought, both our cells were then opened and this Belgium police officer said to us both, in broken English "You're both free to go, enjoy your match." When he was handing our stuff back to us, I asked him "Why were we locked up?" he pointed to Colin's face and then replied with "No one identified you both, so you can go." He did not need to say anymore, we were gone. Because of what we had both been through, when we arrived in Liege we both stayed low-key, everywhere we went there were City fans drinking. Over 1,200 Cardiff fans had made the trip and amongst the fans were hundreds of lads who by now were well pissed up.

Liege fans were well up for trouble and even came around to the train station area where Cardiff fans were drinking and soon began taunting them, with that Liege fans were attacked and chased off, but then the police came in so heavy handed, fighting broke out all over the place. It ended up with Cardiff fans fighting the police for the next half an hour, police cars had their windscreens put through, pubs started getting wrecked and the Belgium police just continued wielding and smacking any Cardiff fan they could get near with their batons. The worse part about it was that, yes many Cardiff fans were causing trouble now, but the police left that area and went to another area where 200 Cardiff fans were drinking in total peace, rounded them all up, put them in cages, before they deported every one of them, yet every one of these fans were the innocent ones.

We went to the game, where we had netting twenty feet high in front of us, but it did not stop us creating a brilliant atmosphere and seeing our side go 2-0 up with local Cardiff lad Anthony Bird scoring the two goals. We thought we were going to celebrate a famous victory, when Liege stormed back into the game with 5 goals and left us all dumbfounded and leaving the stadium in total silence and disbelief.
The police put as many Cardiff fans as they could on the trains out of Liege and on trains bound straight for Ostend. Colin and I managed to avoid this by going back to our mate Simon Williams' hotel and staying there until it had all quieted down. We then caught the train back to Brussels and in the early hours of the morning caught the plane back to Cardiff. Well, all I can say is, that was one hell of a European trip and one I will never forget.

So it was back to work at the Celtic Bay hotel, The club was now a success, the function room was sold out with weddings and private parties, the hotel side was plodding along, so something had to be done regarding the hotel side of the business. Cardiff was now staging big boxing fights and many big concerts, so I got hold of the agents and offered them blocks of bedrooms with private conference facilities and areas of the hotel where their stars could be in private at reduces rates to get our hotel on the map. We ended up having Barry McGuigan's boxing camp taking half our hotel over on a few occasions and the pre-fight boxing weigh-ins were also staged at our hotel. I have to admit we hardly made anything on these types of bookings, but it certainly got us well known and more bookings from the public started coming in, if truth be known the hotel business side was not for us.

In August 1994 we sold the hotel to a London based company, my father made a statement to the local media, "We were offered a good profit if we sold the Celtic Bay to them by the beginning of August and it was an offer not to snub your nose at and to be honest, I'll never look at another hotel again." My father was right hotels were not for us, but on the bright side thanks to the weddings and the club part of the business, we were able to turn the business around from losing £10,000 a week to when we left earning £4,000 a week. But I think I aged during the time I worked there.

Green shop shuts in colourful clash

April '91

GREEN FOR STOP: *A splash of colour which caused councillors to see red has led to Annis Abraham Jnr putting closing down sale signs in the windows at the Beauty Care Shop, St Mary Street, Cardiff.*

CLOSING DOWN signs have gone up at one of Cardiff's most prominent sites . . .because green paint has made planners see red.

The owner of the Beauty Care Shop — opened less than six months ago — is calling it a day because; "I can't take any more hassle from the planners."

CLEARANCE

Mr Annis Abraham said he will board up the building on the corner of St Mary Street and Wood Street because of a row over its appearance.

Cardiff City Council are ready to take enforcement action because the shop

BY GEOFF WRIGHT
Business Editor

front's illuminated signs, plywood panels, doorways — and green colour — do not match the approved plans.

They said no application was made for neon signs and the design was inappropriate and harms the character and appearance of the St Mary Street conservation area.

It "detracts from the setting of the listed Prince of Wales theatre." It is claimed.

The shop is run by the developer's son Mr Annis Abraham Jnr, who said it will be shut and boarded up after a clearance sale.

"My father is 70

years old and he does not need the hassle. He is not desperate for the money and, anyway, the site will increase in value."

HOLIDAY

He claimed the corner looked much better now than it did before Beauty Care was created out of the former Red Onion takeaway, the Bear tobacconists and adjoining newsagent.

The council's criticism had come out of the blue while his father was away on holiday, he said.

"Since it appeared in the Echo we have had a lot of people coming in and asking if we wanted to start a petition.

"But that's it now, we are going to board it up."

CHAPTER FOURTEEN

TROUBLE IN ALL WALKS OF LIFE

As time went on and the more responsibility I was given by my father, in fact my father had virtually handed the reigns over to me and rarely visited our businesses now, once they were up and running, he was only interested in looking at the figures. I was the hands on manager controlling everything, so I now saw the lads less and less. I was still going to every match but I was a manager of a nightclub and the strictness of my father and the respect I had for him meant there was no way I was going to let him down. The new nightclub was in a small town called Bridgwater in Somerset, which we bought in May 1995, after I had visited the club for several weeks beforehand and had seen why it was losing money. I would work the club until 4am then drive straight back to Cardiff, so I could see all the home games and for the away games I would leave Somerset in the early hours after we had cleaned the club up and it was all ready to be opened for the next session. I would leave the away games before they had finished so I could get back to work, well in time before the club would re-open as I was the only one with the keys. Also I knew my father would ring the club one hour before it was due to open, to make sure that I was there, I can tell you now there were some close shaves. So I was never going to have a chance of a social life or even a quick drink with the lads.

In the years I have worked in clubs, I have seen men refused entry, go home only to return later with an axe or a hammer and knives to try and attack the doormen. I have seen many people have their noses broken or their faces glassed, I have witnessed doormen saving people's lives because they have been so drunk or acting the idiot they have fallen over balconys or they have been hit over the head in a fight. I can tell you now the ones who mouth at you at the door usually end up doing nothing, it's the ones who quietly go away are the ones to be most wary of and the axe man I have just mentioned was exactly that type of person. In June 2008, hundreds of people ran riot on the London underground as a result of binge drinking causing thousands of pounds worth of damage and hurting many people along the way, yet those who are charged are likely to be slapped on the wrist, yet if it was football related it would have meant a custodial sentence.

Whilst I was working in Somerset the local police had been tipped off by their Cardiff counterparts to watch me because of my association with football. At first the licensing Sergeant didn't give me the time of day. The club and the town had mini riots every weekend, but we were aware that this was a problem club before we bought it; the police probably thought it would either get worse or they could blame some of the incidents on me. Another problem we faced at the club was anyone who thought they were someone never ever paid to get in. During my many visits to Toffs nightclub before we had bought the club, I would watch up to a hundred potential paying customers be either let in for free or given free drinks from the bar, it was madness and the management seemed to have no care about it.

Well that was about to change, within the first four weeks I received every threat under the sun, including "You Welsh c..., we'll be waiting for you," "Fuck off back over the bridge" and many more. I stood firm and even though I could tell the doormen were very nervous everyone was made to pay and the local idiots were banned.

One night in October 1995, four local so called body builders who thought they were untouchable and had previously said to me "We're never going to pay to come in" came in, threw their money on the counter and went straight in without saying a word. They then waited in the club until the final twenty minutes of the night before the club closed its doors and watched as most of the doormen went into the club leaving just one on the door, as I approached the front door I felt a tap on my shoulder and as I turned around I was punched and pulled to the floor, I tried to get up but I was repeatedly kicked in the head, mouth and back by the four men. The doorman, who was left at the front door and was new to the club that night, ran out the doors and was never seen again. Eventually the other doormen came but it was too late the cowards were off and gone.

I lost three teeth and spent a week in hospital and the following five weeks were spent having a collar on. I never went to the police, in fact it was quite the opposite, and all I'll say is that they had a return visit and two of them spent two days sat in a police station while the other two ran away up north. The C.I.D visited my father and had the cheek to ask my father, who was 72 years old at the time, if he had any guns in the house as they had two men shitting themselves in their station at Bridgewater fearing for their lives. My father said "Feel free to search, but once you are done go and see my son and tell me how you would feel if it was your son." They did and off the record one of them said "If it was my son I would want to see them sorted."

Anyway the idiots and so called body builders made a full confession and asked to be put on remand, I didn't even need to go to court. The amount of apologies they kept sending my parents was unreal. I returned to work and at the same the time employed a few new doormen, I continued to work and manage Toffs for the next three years and kept the local idiots on the other side of the door without ever having to call the police to the club. In those three years I was able to build up Thursday nights from having seventy people to regularly getting crowds of over six hundred. I made all drinks £1 and charged £3 entry and during the weekdays I would visit every major supermarket and cash and carry to buy everything on offer, I got banned from

Sainsbury's as customers were only allowed five cases of Beck's when they were on offer and they reckon that they had monitored Little Colin and myself over two days buying fifty cases. I would never pay more than 20p a shot for spirits or more than 25p a bottle for lager, if I could not get certain drinks that week or month then we would not sell them on a Thursday night. The bar money would pay all our overheads for the night and the door money would be our profit. Friday's became the over Thirty's night and we were strict with that and that became a success and Saturdays were the usual Saturday nights where you never needed to look for customers, you were usually turning them away. Everybody paid, there was no such thing as a free night and I would do stock takes on my alcohol every month.

Even after what had happened to me, I loved working Toffs nightclub and the only time I would worry, was if my father walked in, as I would want everything to be spot on. The club would open at 9pm and my father taught me that even if there was only one customer in the club, the DJ would play as if it was a full house and the rest of the staff would be on their bars cleaning them down and ready to serve.

The reason why I have told this story about what happened to me in Toffs nightclub was because at the end of the day the point is I suffered more injuries in a nightclub than I ever did at football and over the years I saw a lot less violence in football than I ever did whilst working in clubs. The fights at football were never much more than a boxing fight and people were never attacked for any reason, it was like minded lads who wanted the same thing. The government has spent millions of pounds eradicating violence at football yet when you consider the state of the country they forgot what was happening in society, pick up your daily paper today and you will read of family's living in fear of knife crime, child abduction and at least twenty more serious crimes than what happens at football.

A funny thing happened when I left the club after working there for three years, the licensing Sergeant said to my mother and I that he was sorry that I was going as during these years there had been very little trouble and the police were rarely called out to the club and that the trouble at that end of town had been next to nothing.

CHAPTER FIFTEEN

LOVE IS BLIND

Many Cardiff City fans, including myself were totally fed up of previous chairmen who had promised the City fans a future, a new five year plan, no more players to be sold, a new stadium and once again stick with us because this club is now moving forward. Excuse my language but they were all talking 'utter bollocks' and I, like many other loyal Cardiff City fans, were taken in by all this, time and time again. We, as fans, as usual always stuck by them, listened, were patient, paid our money and followed our team from one end of the country to the other because we all had one thing in common; we love Cardiff City and love is blind or so they say.

The three seasons before Sam Hammam arrived, the fans had started to finally stand up and be counted. They believed and I believed that the club wasn't in very good hands. There was no money and our club was now, for the second time in four years, in its lowest ever position in the football league. On Saturday May 2nd 1998, Cardiff City ended up fourth from the bottom of the football league and to make matters worse only one proper director out of seven could be bothered to turn up and that was Mr Steve Borley, the only director who cared but didn't have enough power to change the way things were. But, while Steve Borley was on the board, the rest of them thought the fans would just keep quiet. They thought wrong, as hundreds of Cardiff fans invaded the pitch after the last game of the season against Darlington. At the end of the game, the fans raced towards the players' tunnel, some trying to burst through the stewards, others demanding the head of the chairman, Samesh Kumar, and in the main part of the grandstand, hundreds chanted "Kumar out." This went on for over half an hour. The fans frustration was totally understandable. They had paid good money to watch rubbish for much of the campaign. Their loyalty to the club remaining fierce, their eyes almost disbelieving at events which had unfolded over the last nine months and all that our so called chairman could say in his programme notes, was that our position was due to bad luck. What planet was he on?

The problem was that this current board had totally failed but they seemed quite happy to remain at the club. At the same time, the media kept talking about David Sullivan, the Birmingham City multi-millionaire director who was born in Penarth and had always said that one day he would like to end up taking control of his boyhood team, Cardiff City. This was making us the fans even more frustrated. On the 8th May 1998, the board agreed to meet a group of City fans. Seventeen fans including myself went down to Ninian Park and into the boardroom. Once again, Samesh Kumar couldn't make it so Paul Guy, the vice chairman, met us but as he had only been on the board for a year, Guy was unable to answer most questions. He managed to calm down the situation by telling us that the fans were going to be given an opportunity to become financially involved and that the shares at £1 each would be made available and all the money would be given to the manager, Frank Burrows, for team strengthening. We asked how many shares and Guy said half a million. We also established that there was no need for a hasty move to a new ground at the bay because the club still had a 44 year lease on Ninian Park at a nominal rental. The board promised to compensate existing shareholders and, for the dire season the fans had just endured, there would be concessionary prices for the next season and that they would consider reintroducing a sliding scale for entrance charges depending on our league positions. This had been operated very successfully by one of our previous chairman, Rick Wright. Yes, once again we went away believing things might get better, but knowing deep down in our hearts that many of our questions were still unanswered.

I went home and told my parents about the chance to buy shares. My father and I had a successful company and, at the time, were looking to invest in a new business. My heart was ruling my head and I started to talk my father into investing. We talked and talked and both came up with an offer that we thought was totally fair. We agreed that we would offer exactly the same as Celtic Leisure whose directors were Paul Guy - the Cardiff City vice chairman, David Temme - a director of Cardiff City and Bob Phillips. They had all paid fifty pence each for their existing shares. We found out that 580,000 unissued shares were available so my father and I faxed the current Cardiff City financial controller, Sean Murphy. I was doing it more for the love of my club but my father was doing it for business reasons only.

A week went by and our company's offer was turned down. Around about the same time, director Steve Borley stated that the City board had no intentions of selling the Bluebirds to multi-millionaire David Sullivan or anyone else interested in a takeover. So the current board was going to do it alone.

Cardiff City supporters now had a summer of wondering whether we would even have a football club next season. The Cardiff fans I know, live, sleep, work and breathe Cardiff City. All their money, holidays, free time whatever you want to call it goes into following our club but, unless you are a devoted football fan, you probably won't understand what it means to us when our club loses week after week and when people in charge of your club constantly give you false hope and then sell your best home-grown players such as the likes of Toshack, the Bennett Brothers, Blake, Delaney, Howarth and another fifty I could mention through the years. It hurts you so much. Some fans show it in different ways; some demonstrate; some drown their sorrows in the pub and others just go home and moan to the wife, kick the dog or the mother in law until the next game.

Over the years, my family and our company have helped Cardiff City through sponsorship for players and some of the managers. We usually aimed at the local Welsh players who I always felt were the future of the club because they generally cared more for the club and, as fans and kids, had stood on those terraces. So therefore, they had been through some of the up and down experiences like us. Scott

Young, Lee Phillips, Christian Roberts, Lee Jarmen, Andy Legg and Dai Thomas were just a few of the names we sponsored. We even sponsored matches, the match ball and Scott Young's car for a season. Cardiff was finding it hard through the 1990's to get businesses to back them. Sometimes they struggled so badly that some players didn't even have sponsorship at all and the team shirt also struggled to get sponsors. In the summer of 1998, Joan Hill who was the chief executive at the time rang me and asked if we would be interested in sponsoring the shirts for the season 1998-99, I asked how much and she said £25,000.

I said I would speak to my family and then get back to her. Joan had said they were struggling to get a sponsor and the season was virtually upon us so she needed one urgently. I can tell you how times have changed. The sponsors in 2008 now pay approximately £250,000, ten times the amount then. I went and told my parents and they thought about it for 48 hours after which I rang Joan and told her the good news that we would. She asked me to fax it to her so she could show the board. A few days went by and I never heard from her again so I rang her and she said they had had another offer. I said OK but you know we were going to pay the money up front and not in instalments like some of the past sponsors. Joan's reply to that was it had been taken out of her hands. I thought about this conversation and thought that we had been used and taken for fools. I did some digging and was told from a reliable source that Sports Café had been given the sponsorship and for only £15,000 and in three instalments. I was gob smacked.

Now I knew Paul Guy and Bob Phillips had something to do with the Sports Café and were also directors of the club at the same time so I thought, "There you go, that explains itself." Later on towards the end of the season, I was told that the final instalment was never paid. Whether that was true or not I will probably never ever know. The Sports Café never did well and it soon closed down. Once again, I felt the current board was determined to never let me come on board but I can always say that I tried to help when the club was going through its most difficult years.

Well, the next season came around fast and the Sunday Express newspaper had even tipped City to plunge into non-league soccer. The good news was that Frank Burrows the manager supposedly told Chairman Samesh Kumar to stay out of team matters. Burrows had heard rumours that under the last manager's reign Kumar had too much say in the team's selection. Burrows and Bill Ayres, City's assistant manager, stated "There would be no excuses this season." The fans began to feel that at last we had a manager that didn't bullshit and would take no nonsense so maybe we could get out of the dungeons (Fourth Division) that season. We then signed Caerphilly-born Dai Thomas from Watford for £50,000. The previous season we couldn't afford to buy Barry Town goalkeeper Mark Ovendale, for a nominal fee so maybe things were starting to look a little brighter. We went to Shrewsbury Town on Friday night, the 21st of August 1998 and came away with a magnificent win 3-0 and Dai Thomas scored on his debut. Even the newspapers were praising the fans on how much they were backing the club. Dai celebrated that win by taking his top off and running over to the ecstatic City fans. This just showed how much hunger the Cardiff City fans had to see City do well. If a win on a Friday night at Shrewsbury Town sent them ecstatic then what would happen if we were playing and beating Premiership clubs every week?

By October 10th 1998, we were top of the league and Frank Burrows then asked the club for money to go into the transfer market and strengthen his squad. It never happened and players like Matt Brazier were sent back to Fulham which then caused shareholders and directors to start arguing in public with some saying that money was available and others saying that it wasn't. Samesh Kumar then turned down an offer from David Sullivan to take control of the club and we, the fans, could not understand this as the current board could not afford to take the club forward or buy quality players. Then the newspapers were saying that the other directors were having secret talks with David Sullivan behind Samesh Kumar's back. It had already been reported that Sullivan had had a one and a half million pound takeover bid for the club turned down; it was an offer that thousands of us fans believed that the club could have accepted and should not have turned down.

We, the fans, were getting so frustrated. To say we were pissed off would be an understatement but we just kept cheering our team on. We even went to Carlisle on a Saturday only to find the match being called off half an hour before kick-off due to the heavy rain and then returned there on a Wednesday night in December but the journey was well worth it when Cardiff won 1-0 and we went to the top spot again. The Echo the following day said on a cold wet night at Brunton Park, Cardiff City went top of the table for the second time this season to the booming sound of 100 Welsh voices singing "Frankie Burrows Barmy Army." We sang it time and time again, like a stuck record. At the end of the scrappy game, the players strode across the pitch to thank their loyal fans. This was a night for celebration.

The fans started to see a bit of success and suddenly we were taking nearly five thousand fans to Brentford on a Monday. Surely someone like David Sullivan should finally be allowed to take control of the club. But, once again, it all went quiet on the proposed takeover deal. At that moment in time, the current board wasn't getting any flack and was being left alone. As we were top of the 'dungeon league' and just that little bit of success was keeping the City faithful happy. Then suddenly out of the blue in March 1999, Mark Delaney another Welsh born talented player was sold to Aston Villa for £500,000. How could they do this to us? The crowds at home games were up from 4,000 to 11,000. We then heard that the board had turned down David Sullivan's money.

The next home game saw thirty loyal but angry supporters storm the boardroom and demanded answers. When it calmed down a little, it was agreed that, if we delegated six fans as spokespersons, the board and Samesh Kumar would meet us around the table. The date was set for Wednesday March 18th 1999. Here we go again I thought, as myself, Kevin Murphy known as Big Sam from the Valleys Independent Supporters

Club, Alistair a supporter from Barry, Simon Williams an Ex-Director and season ticket holder for more than 30 years, John Simmons known as Simmo and Will Dixon another ex-boardroom member and passionate Cardiff City fan, met up on the night at the Ninian Park pub and decided who and what questions would be asked. We went to the boardroom at Ninian Park where we were met by Paul Guy, Steve Borley, Kim Walker, Mike Price and Phillip Jardine. As I looked around the room, I thought to myself 'Yet again, no sign of Samesh Kumar and they probably won't be able to answer everything we were about to ask'. But low and behold, in walked Samesh Kumar who apologised for being late as he had been in a meeting with Frank Burrows. We wanted to be assured about the future and that the directors would pledge that there would be money available for Burrows to strengthen his squad should he need to and before the transfer deadline and that there would be more cash next season to give fresh impetus to the new campaign.

Paul Guy said "We will back Frank Burrows in every way we can and he makes all the decisions on the football front - we have never said no to any player he's requested, the board has never said no, not once." Then they outlined the background to the signing of Andy Legg. Steve Borley then pointed out that Burrows had been at a board meeting and then asked if he could introduce someone and in walked Andy Legg. "That shows" said Borley, "that we are willing to back Frank Burrows."

They then said to us that there were nine directors at the club and that they all agreed they wanted to take the club forward and had big plans for the Bluebirds in the future and that over the next few years things, including major ground improvements, a new training ground with three pitches, offices and changing facilities and of course the centenary season celebrations, were all in the pipeline. Now let me remind you all who are reading this book that this was said on March 18th 1999. They then said to us, "Look, we are joint top of the Division. Let's all work together for the rest of the season so we can get promoted." We all agreed on that but I don't think many of us supporters believed anything else. In the end and in a nutshell, yes, we did get promotion. However, a few weeks later Samesh Kumar resigned as chairman but remained as a director with the biggest share holdings of 37%. So yet again the fans would have to wait and see if yet another chairman could keep his promises.

So on the 11th May 1999 we had another new chairman, namely Steve Borley. This time it felt a bit different as we all knew Steve was as passionate as us about the club. He had been a Bluebird since he was a kid. Yes, we would all be behind him but the big question at the back of my mind which I made public to him and the newspapers when asked what I thought of him was "Yes I'm glad to see Steve Borley as chairman because he loves the club and Kumar never really had an affinity with Cardiff City but the reality is that Borley doesn't have the money that we need. Frank Burrows may not have spent much this season but he is going to need a lot more in the Second Division. It's a catch-22 situation. We want local people involved but we also need someone with more money."

Deep down many of the supporters felt Borley was a smoke screen because the rest of the board knew we the fans had a lot of time and respect for him so it meant that if things went wrong or tits up then we would probably not make our voices heard so much. I did say to Steve Borley that I felt as long as the rest of the usual suspects were on the board then I couldn't see us doing well and things not being any different. Fair play to the man, he was willing to give it a go and had put some of his own money into the club. Steve Borley was being described as a fans chairman in the local newspapers. Borley was quoted on the 7th August 1999 as saying, "All I'm trying to do is move the club forward and bring in more investors to make the club stronger. If I do nothing more than rekindle interest in Cardiff City, I'll be pleased and, if someone else comes along and is able to improve on what I have been trying to achieve, then fine, I'll be the first to say good luck, carry on and see what happens and I'll continue to be a loyal supporter in every way that I can."

The season started quite well and we played some good football with Andy Legg, Jason Bowen, Scott Young, Jeff Eckhardt and Kevin Nugent, etc. all playing well. But as the season went on, the team started to struggle and could not score goals.

The crowds went from 10,000 to 5,000 and the board once again had or wouldn't spend any money on the team. This time, there were no demonstrations or angry scenes. The fans were all very patient and behind Steve Borley who and I will say again, was I believe used as a smoke screen by the rest of the board - that's why he was made chairman. I started to think about all of the promises that they had made and they were even daft enough to say that by Christmas 1999 they would guarantee that we would be in at least 8th position in the Second Division. Even then I said you could not guarantee such a thing but they repeated their ludicrous guarantee. Were we as daft to believe them? The simple answer was no. We carried on wanting and hoping it would come true.

The club continued to slide down the table and Steve Borley was now the one who had to answer all the questions raised by the fans and even he had given promises that were now hard to keep. Borley was not the majority shareholder. Some fans started to see that it was Samesh Kumar pulling all the strings behind the scenes. Steve Borley they said was no more than a puppet. He even started to take stick from me but to his credit, he took it on the chin and kept on fighting in his own way to try and keep the club going. All I and other loyal fans were trying to do was to show Steve Borley that we thought that some on the board were using him; maybe I and others went about it the wrong way. I've had quite a few one-to-one chats with Steve over the years and the one thing I will always say about him is that he has Cardiff City at heart. Maybe he was just a little bit naive. He was always good for a bit of banter and always gave as good as he received. I really believe that if Steve had not been on the board during those tough years, then half the support we had left would have finally just given up watching City and the other half would have all have probably been banned for what the authorities would have called over the top demonstrations.

Steve Borley tried his best, dug deep into his pockets and made money available for Frank Burrows. One of Burrows signings was a player called Schwinkendorf. To this day, there are a lot of questions not answered concerning this signing. There were big rumours that the signing of Schwinkendorf aroused a rift between Steve Borley and Frank Burrows. Many things have been said including that Frank took a backhander but nothing was ever proved and so it remains a rumour. I believe that after this signing the relationship between Borley and Burrows went steadily downhill. Schwinkendorf on the other hand did prove to be one of Cardiff City's worst ever signings. So make of that what you will?

Steve Borley did try later on to get David Sullivan on board after he had previously said he did not want him at the club. Now things were getting desperate. Steve turned to David Sullivan's brother Clive. This seemed more realistic as David Sullivan could not have taken control of Cardiff City unless he had relinquished most of his shares in Birmingham City. Christmas 1999, Steve Borley even went as far as parading Clive Sullivan around the pitch as the new saviour. Within weeks, the whole episode turned around and suddenly the whole thing was off with no real explanation to the fans. We believe that the others members of the board had blocked it and so yet again another false dawn for the Cardiff City fans.

The results were getting worse and in Frank Burrows last 46 league matches, there were only 9 wins with just 4 coming at Ninian Park in the last 12 months. Yes you guessed it, Burrows was on his way out of Ninian Park and it was said it was by mutual consent. The majority of the fans felt he was sacked and yes, by the results, most managers should have been but it was only eight months ago that Steve Borley had gone public and said "My first job as chairman is to extend Frank Burrows contract as he is the most important man at this club." My questions were, was Frank Burrows to blame or did he not get the support from the board? Maybe he left of his own accord and maybe he felt that the board wasn't backing him. My opinion is the latter and maybe because I was a big Frank Burrows fan that I totally had no confidence in the current board.

I bumped into Borley on quite a few occasions and we were able to have some long decent chats about the current state of the club and hopefully the future of the club. I mentioned that my family's company would be interested in investing, Steve said, "Put it in writing and I will give it to the board to consider."

The offer was made on the 9th March 2000 and these were the conditions:

1:- The shares to be bought at 50p each.
2:- The money had to all go on players.
3:- Eventually a say on the board.
4:- Myself not to be liable for anything that may have occurred before my company's money was invested.

I had a response sent on the 14th March 2000 telling me that nearly everything in my offer was unacceptable and that they were having another meeting on the same day that I had received this letter. The whole thing did not make any sense. They also wanted a response by the 14th March. What? I sent another letter stating I would be sticking to my offer and what happened to our meeting but that was the end of the matter. I wonder if I will ever know if Steve Borley was blocking me all the time. He was also on the board in 1998 when the same thing had happened to me. Did the board have something to hide as no one else seemed to be able to join and people with a lot more money than me were being turned away? What did shock me though was they were not even willing to even meet me to discuss the matter and it was just turned down flat. I believe we should have met as you can always negotiate things. Realistically, I believe I had been a thorn in the board's side all along and too much of an outspoken critic and that was because I cared and was passionate and maybe because my face didn't fit. Then again, did Clive Sullivan's face fit? I also think that the final decision was not down to Steve Borley. So on went the miserable season and yet again City was staring relegation in the face.

They did eventually buy a player called Kurt Nogan who I had previously said I was interested in helping to buy. Any player that the manager felt would help us to stay up; I would have tried to help sign. The signing of Nogan showed that pressure from the fans and I, maybe forced them into the transfer market; we will never know. By now, I believe the rot had set in far too deep into Ninian Park and things on and off the pitch were going downhill so fast that even David Sullivan could not have saved the season.

We were virtually condemned to relegation at Stoke away on Saturday 28th April, I had gone up by car with four other cars full with City fans, this game was later to be known as the battle of Britain for what happened off the pitch which resulted in over a 140 arrests with their faces all over the national tabloids and dawn raids to coincide with them. Most of the actual fighting was not between rival fans, but more the police versus the fans, some to this day believe it was a set up by the authorities. What I saw that day was baton wielding Staffordshire police attack any Cardiff fan who dare walk too fast or say anything that they disagreed with. Yes there were few scuffles before the game and our little group was part of some of it.

We had drunk in Newcastle-under-Lyme about three miles before Stoke and then parked up about quarter of a mile from the Britannia Stadium, but after going around and around in search for car park spaces, we had lost three car loads. Eventually we parked up and the two cars that were left got out, as we were crossing the main road, a similar number of Stoke lads appeared in front of us and started bouncing around calling us on, "Come on Cardiff" came the call, the ten of us stood there for a second and shouted, "We're here if you want it," that soon slowed them down as they came to a standstill realising we were not running anywhere. We took advantage of this and just ran straight into them, but little did we know they had forty more lads coming to back them up. Listen, of course I had moved on from those kind of days, but when you're confronted you've got no other choice but to stand your ground and have a go back as if you don't they are going to attack you anyway.

Now with me were some good mates amongst the ten lads, Alan Swain, Emlyn and Patrick from Bridgwater, Michael Harvey, Topman, Johnny Bywater and Mike Pedlar who now lives in Darlington, after sending their first group of lads running back to get the others, we then just all stood in the middle of the road, we were on a hiding to nothing, I got smacked all over the place, with Emlyn smashed to the floor and the bastards ripping his stone island badge off his jacket and tearing his jacket to pieces, a couple of our lads did run and they know who they are. During all this happening a copper was sat in his van, he eventually got out of the van with his dog and set his dog on the fifty Stoke lads, but it was too late for us, we had been annihilated. With that about half a dozen police arrived and escorted us to the ground battered and bruised.

As we were walking to the ground, Stoke kept walking up to the side of us, saying "We've done you Cardiff" and laughing at us, I replied "Yes well done fifty onto ten and we never run, what do you want a medal? You'll soon have your comeuppance; I can assure you of that." Well the rest of the story that day has been told many times about what happened in the ground and after the match, with Cardiff fans and the police. A book I've written called The Diary of the Real Soul Crew tells the story in full. We of course lost this game, sending us even nearer to relegation. Our next game was Gillingham away.

So on Tuesday night May 2nd 2000, nearly 600 diehard City fans including me travelled the long journey to Kent. We knew that if we lost tonight, we were relegated. We all went there believing that maybe we could pull off something. Yes, I probably went over the top as I took a banner saying 'Borley Out' - not because I disliked him but because I believed, and still to this day believe, that there were other members of the board that put Borley on top of the throne knowing we would back off while our beloved club was being drained, ruined or whatever .The point was we had seen our beloved club sink deeper into trouble and to me and many others we had to blame someone and Steve Borley had taken the reins, so in the end the person at the top takes the blame and we wanted him to see we thought he was being used. The match began. Minutes after kick-off Cardiff took the lead with a fine strike from Jason Bowen. The Cardiff supporters leapt around in ecstasy as the goal offered a glimmer of a lifeline to the Bluebird's troubled season. It was soon 1-1. Then Andy Legg was sent off and from that minute it was all downhill. By their third goal, we were all talking about Halifax here we come and then Gillingham's forth goal just compounded the Cardiff fans misery. But despite taunts from the Gillingham fans, Cardiff fans kept their humour (I don't know how we did though) and we chanted back, "You might as well go home as we are going to win 5-4." With only minutes of the game remaining, we shocked the Gillingham fans with a chant, "We're going down in a minute" and yes, within minutes, the final nail was in our coffin. We were down and totally buried.

We all headed back to the nearest pub to the ground and gathered there were some reporters. They were asking what we thought and how we felt. Also in some of the local papers the headlines were, "City are back on the road to nowhere."

On Saturday May 16th after watching City's last home league game with Bristol Rovers, I went to the player of the year event at the Sports Café at Cardiff Bay. There was a very poor turnout from the City fans that night, probably no more than 30 City fans attended, a far cry from today where over 600 regularly attend, oh how times have changed, but then who could blame them?

Later on that evening, I sat and chatted with Steve Borley for about two hours. We got on well and agreed on many things. I could see he was passionate about our club but I still had this belief that he wasn't in control down there as many of our shared views never materialised. What a Centenary Season that was; one we will never forget but for all the wrong reasons. Well, the 2000-2001 season would be around within a couple of months. Just maybe, a saviour could be found and if so, we had to hope the board would let him or her take total control. But one thing was sure, we couldn't continue as we were. The club felt dead. It was the beginning of June 2000 and due to our club having another poor season and the fans having lost trust in the owners of the club, the fans had started to stand up for themselves. You already had Cardiff City Supporters Club whose numbers were well over 1,000 strong lead by Tony Jeffries and Vince Alm and other members. You had the Valley Independent Supporters lead by Kevin Murphy (Big Sam) and now we had Bluebirds 2000 who were growing stronger day by day.

Bluebirds 2000 was formed towards the end of February 2000 by Julian Jenkins and Steve Day. Julian Jenkins himself was an ex-professional footballer who started with Cardiff City and then went onto our local rivals Swansea. He finished his career at Bradford City with an injury but he had always remained a big City fan. Steve Day, a wealthy businessman who sold pine furniture, had over the years helped out the club with sponsorship and advertising. Their plan was to try and raise money along with other City fans and then try and buy some shares. They believed they had to try and buy enough shares to dilute Samesh Kumar's shares from 33% to 28%. This would then reduce his power and hopefully enable someone new to come on board that over the last couple of seasons had been blocked. Bluebirds 2000 had also contributed to the signing of Kurt Nogan.

From March 2000 to June 2000, Bluebirds 2000 had raised over £120,000 and were able to buy shares. Steve Borley had helped them along. What I couldn't understand was why Samesh Kumar wasn't trying to stop it. Maybe he had finally given up. The rumour was that the board was now totally divided and Steve Borley had had enough. Steve even gave his blessing to the formation of Bluebirds 2000. Borley and Steve Day were friends and this probably also helped spur on Bluebirds 2000.

Then I was totally confused and shocked when David Temme announced the new ticket prices for the 2000- 2001 season. I had a good chat with Borley at the 'Player of the Year' supporters' night. As I understood it, the board was supposedly going to work alongside the supporters on future things so the announcement of the new prices caused uproar and all the supporters' clubs joined forces on this one. Cardiff City supporters told the media that the board was out of touch with the common fan. That's not how Borley had portrayed himself to me. He seemed to only want to work with the fans. Maybe he was totally outvoted on this, only the board could answer that.

Tony Jeffries of the Cardiff City Supporter's Club spoke out and said that, "For pity's sake, we've just been relegated. It's a bit thin when you have to pay £12 for a junior considering all the talk of being a family club." The 1,000 plus members of CCSC held their Annual Meeting on June 12th and Tony Jeffries urged all members to attend so that they could help give guidance to the committee on how to tackle this atrocious hike in prices. Bluebirds 2000 and the Independent Valley Supporters were also behind Tony Jeffries and Vince Alm of the CCSC. I also stated to the local media, that 'City had failed to show faith with their loyal fans. Steve Borley promised at the 'Player of the Year' evening that he would look after the present season ticket holders but he had unsurprisingly given us nothing back. I was hurt by that, he had given us nothing'.

So fans agreed we had done enough talking and now it was time to put our words into action. We had heard that there was a new person interested in taking over the club and for a while now his name had been mentioned but not really as a serious contender. The fans were hearing again on the grapevine that certain directors were trying once again to block anything to do with this person. So as the weeks went by, all of the heads of the Supporters Clubs rallied behind Steve Day and Julian Jenkins of Bluebirds 2000 and agreed to march from the Lansdowne Pub to Ninian Park. Roger who was the landlord of the Lansdowne Pub was a Cardiff City fan. His pub was covered in Cardiff City memorabilia and I always enjoyed a good chat with Roger. Usually it was only about the dark side of our club because it was all we knew.

Roger agreed on his pub being the meeting point. Steve Day and Julian Jenkins managed to get Sky TV and the Welsh media to turn up. The fans were totally united that this board had to go. We all turned up and, whilst I was standing next to Steve Day, his mobile rang. It was Sam Hammam ringing from New York. He asked Steve to call the demonstration off for Sam himself was saying that if the club was willing to negotiate then let's try it that way. So the fans had started to fight back and were finally making this board of directors see sense. I don't think there was a Cardiff City fan alive who now believed there was a future for Cardiff City under the current board.

City fans demand meeting with Kumar

CARDIFF City fans, unhappy at the way the club is being run by the eight-man board of directors, are insisting that Chairman Samesh Kumar meets a six-man delegation at Ninian Park this evening.

The Bluebirds stand joint top of the Third Division, but many supporters are fearful they will miss out on promotion or they will crash straight back down from Division Two.

"We want Samesh Kumar to come and talk to us," said Annis Abraham Junior, who will be among the six fans at the ground tonight.

"It will be a peaceful meeting. All we want are truthful answers to our questions.

"We want to know what money will be made available to Frank Burrows to strengthen the squad for next season."

Tonight's meeting was arranged when a 20-strong group of fans burst up the stairs at Ninian Park and confronted vice-chairman Paul Guy outside the boardroom.

They were unhappy over the sale of Mark Delaney to Premiership Aston Villa for half a million pounds and bitterly disappointed over a third successive home draw against Torquay.

Last night's 1-0 defeat against Rotherham left City fans even more fearful over their teams chances of earning promotion.

All the main directors will attend today's board meeting and at least three of them will stay on to meet the fans.

"We want to be as truthful as we possibly can," said Guy. "There is nothing to hide."

Cardiff City have been drawn against Wrexham in the semi-finals of the FAW Premier Cup, while Barry Town will face fellow League of Wales club Inter CableTel.

The winners of the trophy will earn £100,000, while the runners-up collect £40,000.

South Wales Echo **Friday, March 17th, 2000**

Abraham offer is snubbed by City

By Mark Bloom

CARDIFF City fan Annis Abraham's offer of a £300,000 investment into the Bluebirds has been snubbed by the cash-strapped Second Division strugglers.

Abraham, a Ninian Park season ticket-holder for the past 26 seasons, offered to buy Preston striker Kurt Nogan for £100,000 and pay for the player's wages to the end of the season in a move to help the club.

But Abraham has received a thanks, but no thanks, letter from the club's chairman, Steve Borley indicating that the board could not agree to Abraham's request.

Property developer Abraham made four key demands – that the £300,00 investment would involve 600,000 shares (at 50p a share); he would get a place on the board; he would not be responsible for liabilities occurred before his investment, but acceptable after; and that the money was spent on new players.

Abraham told the Echo today: "The letter stated that the points were not acceptable to the board, but this is a time of need and City could not guarantee the money being spent on new players.

"Everybody at the club has known for sometime that we needed a striker to stay in Division Two.

"But when all is said and done I and other supporters will be there next season watching City in the Third Division and I'm not looking forward to it.

"I feel sorry for the players and the backroom staff because they have worked hard and deserve more than this."

It is understood that City made a bid of £70,000 for Nogan earlier this week and it was turned down by Preston who have said they do not want to weaken their squad.

121

CHAPTER SIXTEEN

A RELAXING DAY AT LORDS!

When a friend of mine Mojo (Paul Mohammed) offered me a chance to go to the NatWest Cup Final of cricket at Lords involving Glamorgan v Gloucestershire, I thought why not, it will make a change from the terraces of following Cardiff City and the heartache that goes with it. So I said yes, Mojo arranged it all for another mate of mine Simon Williams and I and of course himself, booked the train tickets and got the match tickets, it made a change from me always rushing around for football tickets.

I had never watched a cricket match in my life, not even on TV, it looked boring from the outskirts, so I had never even given it a thought, so for this match, you could call me a glory hunter. I knew that Cardiff City fans had followed Glamorgan all over the country in the past and I had heard plenty of tales from people. Many had said it was just a big day out on the piss, with no hassle, others had said they had had fights in places like Brighton, but had then gone home with no problems from the local police. Like I just said cricket had never appealed to me, but the footie season was over, everything was being laid on, so why not finally give it a try.

The three of us travelled up early morning, Mojo had said how really strict they were up in Lords, no singing, no standing in your seats and not even allowed to use a mobile phone during the match in the area we were going to sit. I was gob smacked to hear all these rules, but fair enough I thought, that's their rules if I don't like it, I don't have to go again.

As we walked to the ground, we bumped in to Simmo and a coach full of Cardiff lads in a nearby pub; they said tickets were hard to come by as the match was sold out, so they had given up trying for them. We had a couple of drinks with them and then made our way to the ground. I couldn't believe who I bumped in to next, our old police spotter Jeff Richards (RIP) who was now retired and had been put in charge of the security outside Lords cricket ground. It was now starting to feel a bit like I was going to a football match, as to the left of us was a couple of police vans parked up. We went in to the ground and I could not believe it, everyone was able to drink beer and wine in their seats whilst watching the game and the food was even steak sandwiches. There were no police in the ground, but the stewards were well busy telling everyone to sit down and non-stop telling people to put their mobiles away.

We sat down in our seats with our drink and food, I thought to myself, if only it was like this at Ninian Park, the sun was out, what more could you want? But me being one for atmosphere, I did at first think it was missing big time. It did not take long to start, thanks to hundreds of Cardiff City fans from the South Wales Valleys who all started arriving, putting their flags up where ever they could and then standing on their seats, singing Wales, Wales. I looked around and there were faces I knew everywhere, I knew then that these stewards were going to have their work cut out.

The more Cardiff fans that arrived, the more songs that were being sung, then the anti-English songs started towards the Gloucestershire fans, there must have been well over 10,000 fans from South Wales and the majority seemed to be Cardiff City fans. Nobody seemed to be sitting down now; the stewards were trying their best but were getting nowhere, just given abuse and told to get on their way. Within an hour all the bars were closed, but by then the atmosphere had turned into a football atmosphere with both sets of fans taunting and bating each other. But still no police had yet entered the ground, I was actually starting to cheer on Glamorgan, even though I never understood the rules, I never imagined I would be at a cricket match, never mind cheering them on. Well Glamorgan lost and the match was followed by a full scale pitch invasion by the Gloucester Fans to celebrate winning the cup.

The three of us made our way down on to the pitch and walked around on it, the scenes of jubilation were soon changing to Gloucester fans taunting the Glamorgan fans, you idiots I thought to myself and they were, as hundreds of Welsh then poured on to the pitch. A few scuffles soon broke out, but the taunting continued from the Gloucester fans. As we were watching the trophy being presented to the Gloucester cricket players, Soul Crew Soul Crew suddenly rang out and two hundred Valley lads stormed towards the hundreds of Gloucester fans, the Gloucester fans were trying to fight back, but even the bravest of the Gloucester fans had to just turn and run in the end. It was unbelievable as all you could see were hundreds of Gloucester fans running away in to the stands, whilst their team was lifting up the cup. As we made our way out of Lords the police were now going in to the ground, whilst at the same time scuffles were now breaking out all over the place and with so many fans drunk they were fighting over the smallest of incidents.

We just carried on making our way back to the train station, on the way we bumped in to a few Cardiff lads and asked them why there were sirens going off all over the place away from Lords cricket ground. Apparently about forty Cardiff fans had had some run-ins with the locals and it had escalated onto the streets and the police had blamed the Cardiff fans for it.

On the journey home to Cardiff, I said to Mojo and Simon, "I never knew Cricket was like this," they both just laughed, Mojo replied by saying "I have never heard of this happening at Lords before and there will probably be a full stewards enquiry," we all gave a grin. That was the first and last time I have ever been to Cricket, an eventful day but I will still stick to my football and boxing.

CHAPTER SEVENTEEN

MY BRUSSELS HELL

Cardiff City yet again had just had a terrible season. They had just been relegated to Division Two, which I still call the Fourth Division otherwise known as the 'Dungeon league'. So all we had to look forward to next season was Darlington, Halifax, Hartlepool, Macclesfield, etc. I'm sure the floating City fans wouldn't be paying to see that opposition and even less chance of them going down to Ninian Park now that David Temme has put the prices up.

I was just driving the long journey home from Gillingham after seeing the club relegated once more and I started thinking what there was to do this summer. I needed something to cheer me up. I started ringing some of my mates. The first mate I rang was Dai Thomas. Dai was actually a Cardiff City player at the time but currently wasn't in the 1st Team. I said "Dai, do you fancy coming to the European championships this summer and getting away from this miserable season we have had." Dai said, "Yes, I haven't got anything better on" and so, one by one, I rang my mates. Next was Paul Mohammed, known as Mojo to most people and he had done very well for himself. He was then a criminal solicitor and is now both a solicitor and a Fifa football agent. Mojo said, "Definitely count me in." I then rang Michael Harvey and Mike Flynn known as Flynny who had his own tiling business and had done a few jobs for me. They were both up for going as well. Flynny actually said, "It can't get any worse than what we've seen this season."

I bought the tickets from the Welsh FA and then booked a hotel for two nights in Brussels. We managed to get some cheap flights direct from Cardiff. After speaking to some other Cardiff fans, there was apparently anything up to fifty Cardiff fans that were going over at different stages of the Championships. When we arrived we bumped into quite a few Cardiff fans from the Valleys.

So, on Friday 16th June 2000, we all met up at Cardiff airport. We sat in the bar for a drink and it was mentioned by one of the lads, wonder what the English fans think about us being from Cardiff and especially with Cardiff's reputation. I said it should be fine as I had previously seen England, Scotland and Republic Ireland play abroad and I had been cheeky enough every time to put up my Welsh flag with Cardiff City on it. Yes, there had been sarcastic comments from some English fans. I had even had some banter with some Hibernian Fans during the Scotland v Morocco match in the

World Cup 1998 in France but, overall, most fans say good on you for coming and it's a pity Wales never qualify. As we sat there drinking, a bloke who must of known me asked if Mac was with us and enquired if any other City fans were making the trip? Why? I asked. "Just be careful as the police are on the lookout for known City hooligans."

After another drink at the bar our flight was called. The five of us made our way to passport control. As each one of us showed our passports, we were all asked individually by plain-clothes police officers why we were going to Brussels and where we were staying. We all answered them except Michael Harvey who jokingly said, "I'm just following them." I did wonder what was with all the questions but everyone was in such a good mood and excited that I just nodded, took back my passport and went on my way.

We arrived in Brussels just after 10:00am and there were hundreds of football fans coming off flights from all over the place. What surprised me though was that there was hardly any police or security at arrivals or on the other side of passport control. We made our way straight to the hotel and checked in. Dai, Michael and I went straight across the road from the hotel and sat outside a small bar while Mojo and Flynny were still probably fluffing their hair or whatever. The sun was fully out and it looked like it was going to be a scorcher of a day. They came and joined us and we then drank up and all said we were starving. As we walked through the streets we were shocked to see them so empty especially as this was one of the host nations for the European Championships. Maybe everyone had gone straight to Charleroi where some of the games were being played.

As we passed some bars, there was a sign hanging up outside which read 'Lasagne and salad'. I'm sure I heard Dai say I fancy that so I stopped and turned to go in. Then I noticed about forty Man United fans sitting and standing around drinking. They clocked us straight away and we could see from the looks and the stares that we weren't going to made very welcome so, without saying anything to each other, we all carried on walking past. We finally arrived at a place that looked like the main square. It was called 'The Grand Place'. We looked around it and it seemed really quiet; maybe because it was still early. We sat ourselves down in a bar called 'Bar Manuel'. Then, as usual, I had to do what I always do when I am abroad and that was to put up my Welsh flag with Cardiff City on it. I am proud of where I was born and Cardiff City is the only team that has ever meant anything to me and the days have long gone when Cardiff City used to be in Europe every year. So at least now they were being represented over here even if they weren't playing and, by the look of it, we were the only football fans drinking in Manuel's. That surprised me.

I'm not usually a big drinker and people who know me know I never used to drink at all; maybe because I'd worked in pubs and clubs all my life and seen pissheads and binge drinking and that had put me off the booze. Also, my father was teetotal. Here I was, abroad with a group of my mates in the boiling hot sun and I felt comfortable drinking so by lunchtime, we had had quite a few. Quite a few England fans had now started to drift in and have a drink at Bar Manuel. Fans from Swindon, Plymouth, Bolton, and Burnley, Colchester and Southampton and most came over and sat and spoke to us. They chatted about Cardiff City and the atmosphere was nice and friendly. They all had no problem with us being there and it actually felt like we were the centre of attention as everyone wanted to ask about Cardiff City and their fans.

Then suddenly, at about 4:30pm, a group of about twenty Blackburn Rovers fans came over. At first, they had been speaking to Mojo who was just inside the front of the bar. Mojo then pointed over towards me. I was sitting down not really taking a lot of notice and by now had had quite a bit to drink. Three of the Blackburn lads came walking over to me and said, "Are you Cardiff?" I said "Yes." At first they seemed ok but more came over and the tone of their voices changed so I stood up from my seat. One of them asked "Do you know Derek Ford from Cardiff? He's from the docks." I said I did know Derek. He then raised his voice and started to get a bit loud. "He fucking ripped me off when he lived in Blackburn." I told them he'd never done anything wrong to me. I started to realise they wanted trouble whether it was because of Derek or whether it was really because we were Cardiff City. The same Blackburn knob then ranted on about some shit or other then said, "You're a Welsh twat." I said, "Say it again" and just as he was about to repeat it, I saw all his mates coming towards me so I threw a punch at him and with that chairs, tables, bottles and glasses were thrown at me. I lost it for a few moments. "Come on you bastards," I shouted at them.

I had to stand my ground and show them that I was not scared as I could see all that they wanted was trouble. There was a bit of a standoff then suddenly we were surrounded with only Dai standing by my side. One of them tried to grab me around the throat. I backed off. A lad came and stood next to me and said, "I'm with you." It turned out his name was Tony and was a Bolton fan. Michael then hurried over and said, "Annis, the police are coming" and, with that, two Belgium police called me over and asked "What was going on?" I explained that it was a private argument and it was all finished with now. They then asked my name, wrote it down and suggested that I leave the Grand Place. So we left but minus Mojo and Flynny who had totally disappeared from the area. Little did I know at the time that within minutes of us leaving these Blackburn fans ended up fighting with some boys from Burnley which are their fierce rivals. Again more plastic tables, chairs and everything were thrown at each other, which ended up with about five fans being arrested.

A few months later I found out that the TV programme Panorama was out there setting up their cameras and had seen this incident at the Grand Place and had asked around as to who I was? Apparently the Belgium police didn't have a clue who'd been involved but unbeknown to me watching these events unfold was a British policeman who was the Plymouth football club hooligan spotter. He'd been in the area at the time and had recognised me as being a Cardiff City Fan, high profile or what? He also added that I was a wealthy businessman from South Wales. Police checks were made and, yes, I did have a criminal record. When I was 19 years old, I had my hand gashed by a broken glass by someone. I in return broke his nose. Little did I know that he had a brother who was a policeman. I was given a £250 fine. So all this kafuffle in Brussels made Panorama interested in me and from that moment on they apparently followed me for the rest of the day and night and made me their No1 target for a Panorama special.

After leaving the Grand Place and unaware that I was being followed by the BBC, myself and a few others then walked through some side streets which eventually took us to a bar called O'Reilly's; it was an Irish bar. Funny when you go abroad you always look for a British or Paddy pub. On my arrival at O'Reilly's, football fans from Wolves, Wigan and Preston were all coming over to me and shaking my hand and were all saying "Well done Taffy, for standing up to those Blackburn bastards." Nearly every man and his dog were offering me drinks. I had never seen these lads before in my life but it had seemed word had circulated that I'd stood up for myself as apparently these Blackburn lads had been picking on smaller groups of other fans most of that day. To be honest, until that day I had never even heard of Blackburn having a mob or a firm or even having any troublemakers and I had never actually heard or seen a Blackburn mob before come to Ninian Park or any scarfers come to that. When we played them at home, their fans didn't travel and up at Ewood Park their ground is virtually always empty so that whole confrontation or scuffle, whatever you want to call it, was a total shock to me. As I was standing outside O'Reilly's, I noticed across the road scaffolding had been erected and on it were men with TV cameras and equipment and it looked like the world's media had taken up residence. I'm now thinking to myself something is going on here so I decided to stop drinking. As the day went on, hundreds and hundreds of fans converged on O'Reilly's and the atmosphere was changing fast. Dai had wandered off and Michael had gone off too. I still didn't know where Flynny was. During this time, I spent most of it talking to my new mate, Tony from Bolton. We chatted about football and players and life in the lower leagues.

Then, out of the blue a German fan called Ronald came over to me and reminded me of how I had met him many years ago at Standard Liege when Cardiff City played in the European Cup Winners Cup. We shook hands and had a good chat about our time in Liege. Ronald was quite famous in the world of football as he liked to go to the big matches all over Europe. Some said he was a police informer and not to trust him. He watched a lot of English games and always seemed to pick the games where there was going to be trouble. As we were standing there chatting, a load of Turkish blokes who were standing across the road from O'Reilly's started shouting abuse and the English fans quite happily abused them back. Within seconds, the Turkish blokes were calling over the English Fans for a confrontation and by now the English fans did not need much encouragement to start fighting. Many were now totally drunk and others fancied a fight anyway. But what did seem a bit strange was why only a dozen blokes would want to take on hundreds of English fans? Were they stark raving mad? As I stood there, I noticed that all the roads leading away from the area where we were standing were being blocked off by at least a couple of hundred Belgium police

officers in full riot gear. Then the police moved down towards O'Reilly's. I looked
straight at the crowd in the middle of the road and I saw Dai at the front of the mob. I
twice went over to the crowd and, from behind, I tried to grab Dai's shoulder. I
shouted to him to come back to the bar but, by now, Dai had had too much to drink
and the noise was deafening. I also recognised a group of lads from Aberdare who
were also Cardiff fans; one of them I knew as Kenny.

These so called Turks turned out to be plain clothed Belgium police who were now
whacking the English fans with their truncheons and making sporadic arrests. To me,
it felt like the whole thing was a set up. I thought to myself that it was time to get out
of here and I tried calling Tony, Dai and a few others to a street behind me which the
police hadn't yet blocked off. As we were going past the side of O'Reilly's, the side
door burst open and England fans spilled out fighting with each other. To this day I
don't know what the fight was all about. I stood there for a few minutes watching and
then I shouted to the other Cardiff lads, "Let's get out of here." I could now see the
Belgium police had decided that they were going to arrest everyone who was in the
area whether innocent or not of any violent or threatening behaviour. It was now total
bedlam and everywhere you looked there were running battles between the Belgium
police and the England fans. I assumed that Michael and Dai had managed to get
away. I was just getting away a bit rapid when an ambulance pulled up with its light
flashing and laying there was Kenny from Aberdare who looked like he was having
some kind of fit. At the time all that the Belgium police were doing was hitting him
and anyone who tried to help him.

This angered the fans who then started attacking the police. I went over by the
ambulance and, by now, the police realised that he was injured and in a bad way. It
turned out later that he had a broken arm. I went over to see if he was OK. He was
calming down and being put in the ambulance. I asked him if he was OK and he
nodded yes. I later found out that Kenny suffers from epileptic fits.

I moved away with Tony from the bar and bumped into Dai again. We headed up
some side street that was out of the way and into a quieter area. We then came across
three of the Blackburn lads again who had started all the trouble in the Grand Place
earlier. I will admit I did go rushing over to them as I was fuming that they had caused
all that trouble earlier with me. They saw Dai, Tony and me coming towards them and
were soon on their toes and gone. We made our way up an alleyway and came to a bar
called La Fiacre. It seemed like it was a good place to get away from it all. There were
probably over 100 football fans packed in here with the majority totally unaware at
what had been going on in the streets nearby. Just as we were finally able to relax,
some fans who were at the front of the bar shouted to us at the back of the bar that the
police were at the front door with their guns out - they were actually guns which shot
gas canisters. Suddenly, with no prior warning, two canisters were fired straight
through the front door and right into the middle of the jam-packed bar. There was an
almighty panic. People everywhere were screaming and having breathing difficulties.
I went to the back of the bar but there did not seem to be an exit. Soon I was crawling

The man I owe everything too, my father. My father and myself

These lads would stand with you no matter what. Summer 1985 Blackpool, some of the lads, myself, Beer, Grexson, Eddie, Daryl. Some of the best lads i'll ever know.

Tom Jones and myself in Caesars Palace Las Vegas May 1981.

Muffy (Leeds), Toddy (CCFC) and myself by Brownhills pub (Cardiff) in 1988.

The 80's, myself, Darryl, James, Jock (Tim) and Barry lads.

Myself in 1984 painting in the Prince of Wales (Caesars)

1982, Dave Bennet and myself at Ninian Park in the managers office.

12th August 86. Pre season friendly, Gloucester City v Cardiff City, myself, Mikey Dye, Mallo and Frank Burrow the Cardiff manager.

Darryl Lewis (one of my best mates) and myself in the 80's

This was our police spotters card in the 80's our main spotter PC Jeff Richards gave it to me just before he died in 2009.

▶ **READY TO OPEN** *Bar Burges director Annis Abraham inside the new bar, left and right. And, inset, the exterior.*

The Abraham Family

▶ **EIGHTIES GLITZ** *Caesar's Prince of Wales Discotheque, ready for opening in 1984.*

Paul Grexson, Chris Beer and myself in Majorca 1980's

At Ashtongate 26th January 2010 after Cardiff City won 6 nil v Bristol City. The very first few fans to show their discontent towards Pete Ridsdale.
Thomas Fish, Geraint Handley (Cheggers), myself, Paul O Connel and Dafydd.

The March against Peter Ridsdale, 5th March 2010

The March against Peter Ridsdale, 5th March 2010

The March against Peter Ridsdale, 5th March 2010

The March against Peter Ridsdale, 5th March 2010

Newcastle away 6th Feb 2010, on a friday night just before we lost 5-1

16th March 2010, Coventry 1 Cardiff City 2 celebrating in one of Coventry's pubs after the game.

July 2008 celebrating after we had just beaten Celtic 1 nil in Portugal

RIP Ninian Park, you will never be forgotten.

Some of the lads from the 80's and 90's that I use to follow Cardiff with. Jelly head, Big Sam, Matt, Nills, myself, Frankie, Mikey Dye, Marshy, Simon Neads, Chunky, Taffy Anton, Jonathan, Wilburs.

Dibs tours Norwich away March 2009

14th October 2008, the lads and myself on Con Tours in Germany to watch Wales

My loving family, my wife Joanne and my three daughters
Alexandra, Annaise and baby Tilly.

My daughter Alexandra with the Grandstand seats and crash barrier from Ninian Park 1st July 09

25th April 09
Laura, Annaise, Alexandra and Connor
True Bluebirds !

30th Jan 2010, a very proud moment for me, my daughters Annaise and Alexandra Cardiff City mascots v Doncaster Rovers at out new stadium.

Warren Feeney with my daughters Annaise and Alexandra in the Cardiff City dressing rooms home.

Joanne and myself in Portugal

My three princesses, Alexandra, Annaise and Tilly-Annis

Jason Perry (Cardiff City legend) and myself, my Niece Isabella and my daughters Annaise and Alexandra at my book launch. The last ever event at Ninian Park 6th June 2009.

My daughter Annaise at Highbury Jan 2006, Arsenal 2 Cardiff 1

Joanne, Annaise, and myself
in the player's tunnel entrance at Ninian Park
22nd May 09

Cardiff City trophy cabinet at Ninian Park. Gone now but never forgotten

Owen Powell (Catatonia), Jonathan Owen (Actor) my daughter Annaise and myself in Ninian Park pub with the FA cup.

Forum trip to Leeds October 2010

Forum members at Play Off Final 2010

Danny Gabbidon, myself and Robert Earnshaw at Ninian Park.

Jason Perry and myself, one of our longest ever serving player. A legend in my eyes.

Cass Pennant, Dave Sugerman and myself at my launch of 'Diary of the Soul Crew 2' at Sams Bar 31st January 2009.

Diary of the soul crew 2 at Plymouth. 17th Feb '09
Plymouth fans

Launch of Diary of the Soul Crew 2, 31st Jan 2009 Simon Insole our police spotter, myself and Cass Pennant.

In Majorca, Simon Williams ex Cardiff City director and original member of the Soul Crew and now a pirate haha and myself.

July 2008 in the Algarve just before we won the Algarve cup,
Cardiff City 1 Celtic 0

Having a good time, the good old days. chairman Steve Borley, media manager
Julian Jenkins, assistant football manager Ian Butterworth and Dayo, Jonny,
Michael and myself. The club and fans were close then.

Sunday 18th June 2000. Coming home after watching England in Brussels at the airport. European Championships. Michael Flynn, myself, Dai Thomas (ex Cardiff City player), Michael Harvey, minus Mojo.

Warren Feeney (Cardiff and Northern Ireland) a legend in my eyes, called in to see some of the Cardiff fans after Sheffield United home, 24th Feb 2010.

Peter Ridsdale at my launch of Cardiff City fans through the years. The last function to be ever held at Ninian Park before the stadium was pulled down. 6th June 2009.

Peter Ridsdale and myself at my home after having dinner with my wife Joanne and myself.

A fans meeting I organised up at the Brunswick pub in Merthyr for the valley fans to meet and question our chairman Peter Ridsdale, over 250 Cardiff fans turned up. 7th Sept 2009.

San Hammam at my home also Vince Alm, Gwyn Davies, Carl Curtis and myself 11th Nov 2010.

One of the happiest days of my life, my wedding day July 29th 2006, Sam Hammam, myself, Joanne and my daughter Alexandra.

Sam Hammam (The last supper), The Holland House Hotel, Nov 2008.

1910 - 4th July 2009
Ninian Park: The end of an era

Jono (Zulu), myself, Cass (ICF), Jason (Zulu), Fat Pat (Headhunter), at my launch of "Diary of the Soul Crew 2" in Cardiff 31st January 2009.

on my hands and knees, not being able to breath and I couldn't see where I was going. I did not really know what I was doing. The CS gas had taken hold of me and I was disorientated. Eventually, I scrambled through the front door and out on my hands and knees.

I tried to wipe my eyes and my vision started to come back. As I looked in front of me, all I could see was hundreds of fans all sitting there with plastic handcuffs on and there were flashes of light that were coming from cameras. I tried to cover my face and then realised that, if I stayed where I was, I would be arrested like everyone else. There was a fan on the floor next to me and a big gap in front of me. I tried to tell the fan to distract the police but he wasn't listening. I thought "Fuck it anyway" and decided to get up and make a run for it. A shield was whacked against me as I hit a brick wall. The next thing I knew I was flat out on the floor and for a second I didn't know where I was. As I was starting to come around, this Belgium police officer was saying, "Are you ok?" He then brought water over followed by oxygen. I thought if I open my eyes and reply I will be arrested so I just lay there with my eyes shut. I eventually opened them and made out I was having some kind of fit. With that I was put on a stretcher and into the back of an ambulance. During all this, I put my hand on my back pocket to make sure I had my mobile phone with me. I opened my eyes and saw a lad in the back of the ambulance with his head all cut open. He saw me and for a minute he thought I was dead. He was just about to shout for help when I said; "I'm ok mate" and I put my thumb up to him.

The ambulance eventually took us to the hospital. I was in a ward that was absolutely full of fans. I looked around the ward and everywhere there were fans with every sort of injury. It seemed like the Belgium police had declared war on the English fans. In the next bed to me was a Stockport fan. We had a chat about what had happened to each other. The next minute a lad came running in shouting there's no police outside or anywhere and that we should all get out of here. With that I jumped out of bed and went outside where there must have been a dozen taxis lined up. I climbed in a taxi with the Stockport lad and told the driver to just drive. I then pulled a card out of my pocket with the name of the hotel on it and told the driver to go there. On the way, the Stockport lad jumped out and I have never seen him since. As the taxi was heading towards my hotel, my phone rang. It was Michael. I asked him where he was. He said, "I've just left the hospital." I said, "You're not going to believe it but so have I," and, with that, I told him we would meet at the hotel.

When I arrived at the hotel, there was Michael standing outside with his jeans cut right up to the top of his leg. I asked him what had happened and he said that the police had beaten his legs and, when he screamed out that it was broken, that's when they stopped and they then panicked and put him in an ambulance as well. A nurse had cut his jeans right up to the top. We both burst out laughing. We wondered what had happened to the others. I said that I thought that Dai had been locked up and the last time I saw him was in the bar called La Fiacre.

We both went up to the hotel room where we found Flynny fast asleep on the bed. We woke him up and told him what had happened. I think he thought we were having him on. We asked where he had gone. He explained that he had become so drunk that he had fallen asleep in the Grand Place and had woken up later to find himself on his own, so he had made his way back to the hotel. I then rang Dai and Mojo's mobiles but their phones were still off. I turned on the television and all over the Belgium news was pictures of the night's events in Brussels and then I saw myself. I felt sick. It was about midnight now so I rang home and my mother answered. She was half asleep. I said, "Don't worry if you see me on the news, Mum. It's all ok now" and I said goodnight without giving her the chance to answer. We all talked for an hour or so and eventually I never appeared on the television again, to my relief.

The following morning at about 8:00am, my phone rang and it was my mother saying, "What were you on about last night?" She said she had been half asleep so did not really catch what had I said. I said that it was nothing really and changed the subject. I told her that we were off soon and going to make our way to Charleroi. I then woke up the other two. Dai and Mojo still had not come back and their phones were still off. We went down for breakfast and the three of us discussed the whole situation. We decided to keep a low presence during the day ahead as it was clear that the Brussels police had been indiscriminate as to whom to arrest or not to arrest. We used a taxi for the forty minute journey to Charleroi and, during the whole journey, I just kept trying both Dai and Mojo's phones but it was still the same, both phones were off.

When we arrived in Charleroi, the sun was out again but this time it felt we were in a different country. The Belgium police were all in short sleeve shirts and their attitude and look on their faces towards the English fans was different. They had smiles on their faces and were going out of their way to be helpful or even to just say hello to you as you passed by. We all said to each other, "Are we sure we are still in Belgium?" We kept out of the main square and even drank in a bar and restaurant full of Germans. We did hear later that there had been trouble in the square but apparently nothing on the scale of the night before.

As the evening approached we made our way to the stadium. There was trouble by some of the turnstiles with hundreds of English fans trying to get in without tickets but they were soon dispersed. We entered the stadium and were looking for our seats. I then saw Mario, a police spotter from Cardiff. I said to him, "Is this a setup?" He replied, "No, I've come over for the tournament with my mates." I said, "Then how come our seats are right next to yours?" He said that we probably bought them from the same place, the Welsh FA. I believed him as I knew he was a keen football fan and had for years followed Leeds United. He had previously told me that the Leeds fans had threatened him and his family and eventually he had to put in for a transfer and that's how he ended up in Cardiff as a policeman I had seen Mario at hundreds of Cardiff games over the years and he had always treated me and other people fairly.

A year later, Mario was in trouble with his superiors for being over friendly. In 2001, the night before a match up in Hartlepool, he and a couple of other football spotters were staying in the same hotel as me and about another seventy Cardiff fans. Mario had drunk with us and even played the piano and sang in the bar with us. The following season, he was taken off being a football spotter and virtually demoted to making cups of tea for officers on match days. I didn't see what he had done wrong as it actually brought a bit of bonding between the fans and the police.

Years have passed and Mario is back on football duty now but this time his job is to gather evidence at football matches. He carries a camcorder everywhere now. A lot of City fans now feel he has actually gone totally the other way and goes too far and that a case involving Chelsea/Cardiff fans in 2011, many felt a lot of them were totally stitched up by him.

Back to the match in Charleroi, as I sat next to Mario awaiting the match to start, I told him that the previous night in Brussels was a nightmare and that I believed the Belgium police had set up the English fans. We watched the match and England beat one of their biggest rivals, Germany. Michael, Flynny and I decided to make our way to the nearest train station. As we were walking back, thousands of England fans were celebrating. You would have thought they had just won the Cup, not just the match

The trains were totally packed. They jammed us in like sardines. On arrival in Brussels the fans were again met with a hostile reception from the Brussels police. When we exited the train station, the police would not let us go straight on or turn right. Instead they sent us left and stood there banging their riot shields with their battens. They were directing everyone down towards the Turkish area. After walking for about five minutes, we managed to slip away and make our way back to the hotel. We heard the following day that there had been battles between the Turks and the English fans. During the last two nights up to 700 English fans had been arrested and over 400 had been deported just from Brussels. Yes, there had been troublemakers over there but from what I saw and experienced, I believe the Brussels police caused more than half of it themselves with their attitude and I would even go as far as saying a lot of the trouble and arrests were virtually set up by the Belgium or Brussels Authorities. That's how it really felt.

We had a bit of a lay-in the next day and I was awoken by my phone. It was Dai ringing to say he was on the way back to the hotel. I rushed down to Flynny's room to tell him the good news. Then the three of us made our way down to reception as fast as we could as we were all eager to find out what had happened to Dai. As we stepped down to the front doors of the hotel, Dai pulled up in a taxi. He looked tired but relieved to see us all. We then went for a walk and sat down outside a quiet bar. Dai said he had only been released after he had faked an asthma attack. He then went into detail about what had happened. We all sat there quiet, totally concentrating on what Dai was telling us.

Dai had spent two nights in a cell that had held about 30 fans at a time. He said he was starving because they had only fed them wafer biscuits and had thrown packets of water to them every six hours. On the first night, two Watford fans had recognised him from when he used to play for them and they went and told everybody. Everyone was saying we can't believe it; we've got a football star locked up with us. Banged up in there was a lad from Wolverhampton called Gilly - some people knowing him as Lenny. He started talking to Dai and said that he was going to fake an illness to get out and if he didn't come back after an hour, then Dai should do the same. So that's what happened. Dai called for a guard and was taken down a stairs to a makeshift hospital room where there was only one doctor. Dai really then play acted about this asthma attack. Well, the doctor didn't have much equipment, Dai told us. He asked where his inhaler was and Dai explained that it was back at his hotel room. The doctor told the police to release him at once. Dai then said that as soon as the gates opened he just ran and ran. He couldn't believe he was out of there.

He was even more determined to get away because he had told the police that his name was 'Lee Richards' but the whole of the holding cell knew that he was in fact Dai Thomas. Dai then flagged down a taxi and even borrowed the driver's phone so he could ring me. We all then told our own stories to Dai as he gulped down his food. I said that I wondered what had happened to Mojo. Michael smiled and said, "Well, he is a solicitor. He is probably representing everyone." I tried his phone again but it was still switched off. I thought to myself 'Mojo's a sensible lad. You have to be to be a solicitor. He surely couldn't be locked up, but where was he?'

I said that we had better get our bags from the hotel and make our way back to the airport. When we arrived at the airport of all the people we could of bumped into, it had to be the 'Blackburn lads'; they were there checking in. There were only five of them now. The lad who had caused all the trouble came over and apologised and then said that the rest of his mates had been deported and that they had all been out of order and blamed it on drink. We then just went our separate ways and boarded our plane.

On the journey home, we were surprised to see a couple of Cardiff City Supporters Committee members, Sue Goodfield and another woman who I knew but did not know her name. Sue Goodfield was later able to verify the fact that Dai had come back on the plane and was not deported like the papers eventually reported. We also later found out that Mojo had been arrested and deported. In fact, 965 fans had been arrested and deported including people who had just been standing there and weren't even football fans!

We arrived back in Cardiff and, in Dai's mind and mine; we thought that was the end of the whole event. Then suddenly on Tuesday night, 20th June 2000, a Panorama Special called 'England Shame' was shown on TV. I was sitting there at home watching and there I was on the TV. I couldn't believe it. It was like I was having a bad dream but worse. It was like all your worst nightmares coming at once.

I felt I'd brought immediate shame to my parents. They didn't deserve this. My mother was calm about it but my father who was 78 years old at the time went mad. It was a good job he wasn't a lot younger as he would have knocked me to the floor. All I could keep saying to them was that I was so sorry.

The following day my phone wouldn't stop ringing with reporters; some even came to my house, the Daily Mirror and the Sunday People wouldn't leave me alone. I really felt for my parents. My mother said to me that we would get through this together. She even said there were much more serious and worse things happening in this world than just a fight at a football match. The next day Dai came down to my house and for the next few days we kept ourselves well away from everyone and out of the public eye as we were both being hounded by the media.

I did say at the time that I wasn't involved in any violence whatsoever. Yes, I blatantly lied; one because the fight I had was a private one and totally not started by me and two, I wasn't involved in any running riots and leading mobs through the streets like Panorama had said on their programme. They had also made out that my punch was virtually what started the riots. My punch was actually at 4:30pm and the so-called riots started over 4 hours later in another part of the city and which were incited by the Belgium police.

They also said that I was calling everyone on. I was actually calling on my mates to get out of the area because where I was standing was the only place that wasn't blocked off by the fighting. Maybe I should have put up my hand and said "Yes, I did throw that punch," but the BBC never came to me and asked me my side of the story and have never done even to this day. The media were pressing my club, Cardiff City, to ban me. I wrote to Steve Borley who was still chairman at the time and apologised for any embarrassment that I had caused to the club and I did at the time state that I had not done anything that I considered wrong. David Temme wrote back sarcastically and said that this time we will not ban you but instead read me the riot act. I felt he tried to belittle me at the same time but I didn't care at that moment. All I wanted was still to be able to go and watch my club.

I said to my mother that I wanted to sue the BBC because I felt they had totally portrayed me wrongfully and made me out as a ringleader and a racist. Before Brussels 2000, I hadn't even seen 99% of these fans before in my life and I am actually half Egyptian and very proud of it so I'm definitely not a racist. Look I've enjoyed many a fight in my life growing up, but this programme had gone too far, in parts of it they were even trying to connect me to people on drugs, which is one thing I've never done or even gone near and every lad who knows me, knows that I can't stand anything like that. Personally it was more that I had brought shame to the family that was hurting me and that my parent's reputations would now be hurt.

My mother said that it's best to leave it alone - for all it was worth, the papers would be tomorrow's fish and chip wrapping, as usual my mother was totally backing me all the way.

I then read an article in the Wales On Sunday (25th June 2000) that interviewed BBC news correspondent Gavin Hewitt who was asked about the football related trouble and me and about some of the racist chanting. He actually states, "*I'm not referring to Annis Abraham in this regard*" and later says again "*I'm not talking here about one individual or Annis Abraham but certainly some of the people outside O'Reilly's were chanting in an aggressive, racist and intimidating manner.*" But that's not how I was portrayed on the programme. On the night, you would have thought that I had been one of these people.

I showed the article to my mother but she still said to leave it. Even if I won and did prove my innocence, the press would try and turn it around against me. The Times were the only ones who wrote a fair and neutral article on me. A week later, I had a phone call from a firm of solicitors called David Price & Co of Great James Street in London who said they had been following and reading the media reports about me and thought I had a case against the BBC and Panorama. So, against my mother's advice, I went to London to see them. To this day, I wish I had told the truth that I had thrown that punch. I now believe it would have helped me more. After a few meetings with Price & Co, I decided that I was going to fight the BBC.

On 17th July 2000, I put a claim into the High Court. This went on for months with solicitor's papers back and forth and, let me tell you, when you're fighting the BBC, they don't care how much it costs to them, they will just keep the case going. Later on that year, sadly my mother passed away at the age of 55. She died on 29th October 2000 of a heart attack. My mother was my rock. She was always there for me no matter what. About the same time, my father had two strokes, one after another. My father lived with me and needed me more than ever now. I decided in 2001, after my daughter Annaise was born in February, that all this was irrelevant to life and it should be put to rest and I should concentrate on looking after my father and my daughter Annaise, so I withdrew the case.

You were right Mum, God bless you. I should have listened to you.

Going back to just after Panorama programme, I was getting snubbed in business. I was the manager and licensee of a pub called Burgess House in Park Place in the centre of Cardiff and I was in the middle of selling it to a London based company. They were suddenly asking what type of person they were dealing with after they too had seen the programme. Everywhere I went; people were looking at me with disgust. I remember walking to the ground at an away game at Cheltenham and two young children with their parents pointed over at me saying, "Look, it's that hooligan off the television." I later said to my mother that I felt the whole world was against me. She would reply, "Hold your head up high and ignore them."

The media had been demanding that I be banned from the club and were putting immense pressure on Steve Borley, the chairman, to ban me. Thankfully, Borley resisted and took my word for it that my incident was a private one unlike how Panorama had made it out to be. Thanks Steve.

A few weeks after that programme, I went to Ireland with some of my mates, Johnny, Chris and Frankie who were all staunch Cardiff City fans. Cardiff City was playing there and whilst I was there, a few Cardiff City fans who I had known for years only just to nod to, but nonetheless Bluebird fans, started shouting abuse about me supporting England. My reply to that was that Cardiff City are my team and always will be and that when Wales play England I always will without doubt support Wales but as Wales never qualify for any tournaments and because I love football I will always go and watch a British nation be it England, Scotland or Northern Ireland or even the Republic of Ireland abroad. To this day Brussels is still brought up and many fans/people ask me about it.

Then suddenly everything changed for me in football. Tony Jeffries, head of the Supporter's Club rang me and invited me to a private meeting at The Friendly hotel with a man called Sam Hammam. Only a dozen fans were asked and Tony said to me, "I've asked you because I know you are loyal to Cardiff City and with what you have been through lately you deserve a break."

ABRAHAM . . . Sam adviser

'Hooligan'

From Back Page

named in a Panorama investigation in June 2000 as "one of Britain's most choice hooligans" — even though he has no football-related convictions.

He was filmed ringed by screaming fans, who were taunting Belgian police. And a reporter alleged Abraham helped plot the mob's movements when they were in danger of being trapped by lawmen.

Abraham threatened to sue the Beeb. But, though he issued a writ, the action never went to court.

He has organised fans' forums for Hammam and insists the TV allegations should not embarrass the Bluebirds. Abraham said: "I didn't even have my name taken in Belgium."

Hammam's minder Neil MacNamara was revealed as a convicted football hooligan earlier this week.

Meanwhile, the FA of Wales have banned Hammam from walking round the pitch during matches.

FAN IN THICK OF FIGHTING

DAILY MIRROR, Friday, May 10, 2002

FLARE-UP: Cardiff fan Annis Abraham in the crowd at Euro 2000

PUNCH: Abraham raises his clenched fist as trouble breaks out

FLOORED: Riot police move in and Abraham is on the ground

MEETING: Sam Hammam, left and Abraham are seen talking

CARDIFF fan Annis Abraham, a wealthy businessman, also features prominently in the video.

Abraham was captured on TV footage mingling with troublemakers during riots at Euro 2000.

He always denied any involvement but the new BBC footage clearly shows him throwing a punch as Cardiff fans gathered outside a Brussels pub. He is also seen being slammed to the floor by riot police.

At another point in the programme, Abraham is shown drinking with Hammam, and the pair allegedly discuss going on to a nightclub together.

Abraham has since said he and Sam were friends and he would never let him down by being involved in hooliganism.

Abraham said: "One of my proudest moments was that the owner, someone as great as Sam Hammam, got to know me.

"Do you really think I would betray his trust? I wouldn't."

Sam in 'hooligan' link No2

EXCLUSIVE

By DAVID FACEY

A SECOND member of soccer boss Sam Hammam's inner circle has been accused of being a football hooligan by the BBC.

Annis Abraham — one of the Cardiff chairman's closest advisers — was alleged to have helped organise violence during Euro 2000 in Belgium.

Wealthy businessman Abraham, 36, was Turn to Page 67

ABRAHAM . . . Sam adviser

'Hooligan'

From Back Page

named in a Panorama investigation in June 2000 as "one of Britain's most choice hooligans" — even though he has no football-related convictions.

He was filmed ringed by screaming fans, who were taunting Belgian police. And a reporter alleged Abraham helped plot the mob's movements when they were in danger of being trapped by lawmen.

Abraham threatened to sue the Beeb. But, though he issued a writ, the action never went to court.

He has organised fans' forums for Hammam and insists the TV allegations should not embarrass the Bluebirds. Abraham said: "I didn't even have my

New bar opens on historic site

September 8th, 1999

End of three-year fight in sight

ONE of Cardiff's most historic buildings, which has lain empty for 10 years, is to re-open as a wine bar next week.

The project to open Burges Bar has been in the making for three years, but has faced continual delays over planning and conservation issues.

The façade of the neo-gothic style listed building in Park Place conceals an intriguing history.

Designed by renowned Victorian architect William Burges in 1871, it was originally home to John McConnochie, chief engineer of Bute Docks and Mayor of Cardiff.

Its architectural style was highly influential on other buildings in Cardiff and it is a significant historical landmark on open bus tours in the city today.

Over the last 12 years the building has passed through the hands of five different owners, including international air operators TBI and was also inhabited by squatters for two years.

Manager Annis Abraham

By Suzanne Stevenson

Junior has more than 14 years' experience managing bars and nightclubs in South Wales.

He bought the building in 1996 but faced a long wait for his project to materialise because of differing opinions over refurbishment plans between conservation and planning officials and fire officers.

"I am pleased everything has finally come together," said Mr Abraham.

"It has been quite stressful over the last few years trying to listen to all the different bodies involved. I did feel like giving up at times.

"However, I love this business. It is such an achievement to build something up from scratch and then see the place when it is full of people."

The three-floor bar features a grand teak staircase with turret-style banisters and includes a sports bar and downstairs restaurant which will open in November.

The bar will employ 18 people and open on September 17.

▶ **READY TO OPEN** *Bar Burges director Annis Abraham inside the new bar, left and right. And, inset, the exterior.*

Businessnews   South Wales Echo **Thursday, July 8th, 2000**

Businessdaily

Edited by Geoff Wright
call 029 2058 3629
geoff.wright@wme.co.uk

Club in a million for the professionals

By Geoff Wright
Business Editor

geoff.wright@wme.co.uk

ONE of Cardiff's most historic and best-known buildings is to become a private club for professionals in a deal that could be worth more than £1m to the company of local entrepreneur Annis Abraham Jnr.

The lease of Burges House in Park Place has been bought by Exclusive Events of London and a group of Welsh investors.

A spokesman for the event management specialist said the members-only club would be designed for people "in corporate, professional, managerial, media, education and the arts, as well as private individuals from Cardiff and the surrounding areas".

He added: "One thing it will not be is a gentleman's club."

South Wales-born Mark Wallace-Jones, managing director of Exclusive Events, which has similar projects in London and Birmingham, said the venture was a "very exciting opportunity."

"I am looking forward to working with local businesses and creating a successful venture," he added today.

The building, described as "the finest house in Cardiff" when it was completed by world famous architect William Burges in 1874, will reopen early next year.

"It will be a place to meet, to eat and be entertained," said Mr Wallace-Jones.

Mr Abraham Jnr described it as a "great deal" for his family's company.

"It is a package and, if all the options are taken up, it should be worth more than £1m after three years."

Mr Abraham Jnr – son of one of the country's early major club owners – was recently in the news for another reason.

He finalised the deal at the same time as preparing legal action against the BBC programme Panorama, which filmed him with other football fans at Euro 2000.

The case is in the hands of his lawyer.

▶ **CLUB ENTERPRISE** *Annis Abraham Jnr at Burges House, which is set to open as The Town House early next year.*

CHAPTER EIGHTEEN

A DREAM COME TRUE FOR OUR CLUB

Sam had already been down to the City of Cardiff and its new bay area. He had had a good look around it and apparently had been very impressed with what he had seen. He had been in meetings with ex-chairman Tony Clemo (from the Eighties) who had been acting as a bit of a go-between for Sam and the current board. A South Wales Echo reporter, Mark Bloom, managed to be the first reporter to get in on the action when Sam had been visiting. Sam had done his homework on Cardiff City Football Club and had already come to the conclusion that it was a football City crying out for some success. There was an estimated 1.5 million people living in South Wales and the nearest Premiership Club was well over 100 miles away so Sam knew that the people were already here and that Cardiff was really a big football City. It was just a myth that we were more of a rugby City. Sam later told me that Cardiff was one of eleven clubs that had approached him and had asked him to become chairman but it was Bobby Gould who he knew from his days at Wimbledon that had talked him into coming to Wales.

On Saturday July 1st 2000, I went along with two good football mates, Lee Beames and Johnny Bywater, to the Friendly Hotel on the outskirts of Cardiff. My mind was ticking over fast. One minute I was on a high with the excitement of meeting Sam Hammam; the next minute I was thinking what if he has heard about all the bad publicity that I have had of late and think I might be an embarrassment to be with. I decided I would go into the meeting and just keep myself to myself and just listen to everyone else. We all sat in the reception of the hotel, Tony Jeffries, Vince Alm, Big Sam, Lee Beames, Johnny Bywater, Brian Clark (ex-Cardiff City player from the Seventies), and the late Ronnie Bird (ex-City star of the Seventies and one of the nicest people you could ever meet), Paul and Brian Morgan and a couple of other City fans.

I will never forget Tony Jeffries for inviting me to that first ever meeting with Sam. I know he took a lot of stick off certain fans for inviting me. Maybe Tony had never forgotten our trips to the Hartlepool's and Darlington's when all these other fans weren't there or maybe he felt like giving me a break when no one else would. Tony had been speaking to Sam a lot on the phone before this meeting and you could say Tony had a helping hand in bringing Sam onboard. Well, we were all here, us lucky chosen few.

You could feel that every one of us sitting there was nervous but excited at the same time. Here was a man who had taken Wimbledon, the smallest football club in the Football League from the Fourth Division to the old First Division and could still only ever attract crowds of a little over 6,000 at best. Sam had not only taken them into the best league in Europe and kept them there but also they were never relegated under Sam. Wimbledon even beat the mighty Liverpool against all the odds and shocked the football world. They won the FA Cup at the old Wembley. We had been told that Sam had bought Wimbledon for as little as £15,000 and 20 years later sold it for £29 million. Sam was one of the highest profile chairmen in the football world. So was this the man that could, hopefully, make all our football dreams come true. We had had many false promises and so many big names mentioned in the past that would come in and takeover Cardiff but it had never materialised. Now, finally, a big name in the world of football had come down to Cardiff to actually meet us, the fans, and talk to us about taking over our club. He was going to hopefully tell us what we had only ever dreamed of and that was to take over our dying club and in years to come take us to the Promised Land, the Premiership.

No press was allowed at the meeting. Sam had spoken to Mark Bloom of the South Wales Echo to find out who was head of the Supporters Club and then he specifically stated he wanted only the fans at this first meeting. Mark Bloom was told by Sam that he would ring him after the meeting to say how he felt it had gone.

As we sat there eagerly awaiting the arrival of Mr Hammam, the doors opened and in he walked with a big smile on his face. Immediately you could feel the warmth and passion in the air that he generated within seconds of him speaking. Behind him walked our ex-chairman Tony Clemo. We all stood up to greet Sam and straight away Sam told us all, "Please, please, sit down." One by one he asked us our names and when my turn came, I said, "Annis" and he looked at me again and said, "Where does your name come from, is it an Arabic name?" I said my father was Egyptian and from that second onwards he seemed to want to talk to me more and more.

Sam asked us many questions about our club and he repeated on several occasions the same question, "Why had the club failed?" Most of us answered him with the fact that most owners or chairmen had always bullshitted us with lies and false promises. We all told him our love for the club. I personally kept saying that all my life I had believed and still believed we could be as big as Liverpool or Manchester United. Big Sam (Kevin Murphy) said our ground wasn't big enough and was totally run down and that we had to put up with over thirty years of shit from previous owners. We all kept telling him that we were bigger than rugby and that the media had always been totally biased against football. I've always said rugby in Wales has been a national day out whereas football is an every week sport, watched and participated by more people and that local park football in Cardiff is actually in the top five in England and Wales for the highest amount of players registered.

Sam then said he could and would only purchase the club if he could purchase 83% of the shares as he needed to be in total control of the club. Sam talked to us for over three hours. He said he had £3.5 million to invest and that he would not put a penny more in as the real success would take between ten to twenty years to achieve. He talked about changing our colour from Blue to Green as he felt green was more of a Celtic thing and he believed that this would reach out to the whole of Wales and not just to the Cardiff people. This didn't really go down too well with us and I do believe Sam noticed that.

A few of us noticed that when Sam was introduced to Brian Clarke as being the player who scored the winning goal v Real Madrid in the quarter final of the European Cup Winners cup in 1971, he didn't seem to be that interested and didn't really take a lot of notice or give any praise or even comment on the fact. But later on in that year we were to realise why. Sam was actually more interested in seeing our response to him saying that, "I hear you lot all like a good fight?" which did get everyone laughing. "You're always guaranteed a fight if you're looking for one in these parts," we told him. Sam said he liked our passion. He went on to state that he wasn't a flash person and always paid his way. He then thanked each one of us individually for coming to meet him. Before he went, he asked for my telephone number, which I gladly gave to him. Sam then left with Tony Clemo.

He left us all feeling on top of the world and believing we may have finally found our saviour. We later heard that he had gone to meet Borley our current chairman who at this current time was trying to keep the club afloat and was now personally paying the player's wages out of his own pocket. In all my years of supporting Cardiff City, I would say that only two chairmen stood out to me as really caring for Cardiff City and that would be Bob Grogan and Steve Borley. Sam that night, as promised, rang Mark Bloom and told him that the meeting with the fans had been a total success and that we had given him a warm welcome. We were passionate supporters and that he had a good feeling about everything. Mark Bloom later told me that Sam had been like a bottle of pop ready to explode.

The next few days were agonising as we were hearing all sorts of different rumours. One minute we would hear that the deal was on and then the next it was off. The biggest rumour that was coming out of Ninian Park and from a very good and reliable source was that certain members of the board were trying to block Hammam's takeover. We all knew that Samesh Kumar was one but we were suddenly hearing that Michael Isaac was also trying to block the takeover and that the board was all divided once again.

The fans were starting to talk about how mad Sam had been at Wimbledon and out of the closet came all the stories about the crazy gang. Some of these stories about Sam sounded beyond belief. One such tale was that he was supposed to have set fire to John Hartson's clothes. If it were true and judging by what I saw of Sam in the years to come, nothing would surprise me with him, then, as John Hartson was and still is a

Jack (the name of our rivals Swansea though he has never played for them), this episode, true or false, would have brought a lot of smiles and laughter to the faces of Cardiff fans. I know for a fact Sam was great at getting his own players gee-d up before a game and he also knew well and truly how to wind up the opposition the wrong way.

I also found out that Sam had visited Ninian Park the week before he met us and that Mark Bloom had been tipped off that Sam was going to be there through board member David Temme although he strenuously denied this accusation when asked. Bloom decided to stick with his tip-off and went down to Ninian Park. He just sat in his car by the main entrance. His tip-off was proved right as a Mercedes turned up with Tony Clemo driving and Sam in the passenger seat. Bloom rushed over to introduce himself as Sam walked into the reception entrance. With that, Sam turned around and asked the receptionist "Was this man a convicted rapist?" She just sat there with her mouth wide open and unable to reply. Sam just continued to walk through the reception and, at the same time, asked Mark Bloom if he would like to join them. They went to the away dressing room where Sam called Bloom and Clemo inside it. He then drew on the wall of the dressing room a tree. On this tree, he showed the future plans of the club and how the club's future would grow and branch out. Rolf Harris, eat your heart out!

We the fans didn't care how mad Sam was. We felt you had to be a madman to buy our club in its current state. At the same time all this was going on, the media still wouldn't leave me alone and the Daily Mirror had printed on their front page how Euro 2000 row fan had quizzed Sam at the specially arranged meeting and had been allowed to renew his season ticket. I was wondering if they would ever leave me alone and just let me get on with my life.

About two weeks had gone by since I had met Sam at the Friendly hotel. Rumours, stories, newspaper reports were all changing daily. I had a strong feeling after meeting Sam that day that this man wanted to be in charge and be top dog at Cardiff City. When he wanted something, he normally got it and nothing would get in his way until he had it. Then, early one evening, I had a phone call from Sam.
"What are you doing?" he asked "When?" I replied "Right now," said Sam. "I'm about to have my tea, Sam." "Come and meet me for a drink," he said.

I didn't need much persuasion. I slipped on my shoes and coat and I was at the Marriot hotel where he was staying within twenty minutes. As I walked into reception, Sam came out of the lift and greeted me with a handshake and a hug. We sat down and talked and Sam mainly asked the questions. "Do you speak Egyptian or Arabic?" I said "No, I wish I did though." He asked me all about my family and by this I could tell he was the type of person that a family meant everything to him. In future conversations, I found out that Sam's children worked in New York and Sam had grandchildren. Sam would visit them many times in the years, he was very proud of his children. They in turn would visit him. He even brought them down to Ninian Park and I had the pleasure of them all visiting my house.

Sam brought up the subject of Brussels and, at first, I cringed thinking of what he was going to say. Sam said he had seen the Panorama programme and then said, "Never let anyone knock you down in this world and feel proud of yourself. What have you done? Had a fight? In Lebanon, we shoot each other," and then he joked, "I even have guns in the boot of my car." This was just Sam's sense of humour.

He then asked me what I thought of our club badge. I said that I loved it. Sam said that he thought it was weak. Bluebirds in Lebanon are a sign of weakness and we must never show that we are weak. We shoot Bluebirds in Lebanon like any other bird. We chatted for hours and he made me feel like the last couple of months had never happened and that not only was this a new beginning for him and for Cardiff City but for me as well. Before I left, I told him I was off to Dublin to watch Cardiff City on their pre-season tour. He said that he wasn't able to go as there was so much to be done if he was to own Cardiff City but don't worry, I will be given the total run down on the current squad. I thought to myself, I wonder who will be keeping Sam updated. I said my goodbyes and Sam said that we would speak again very soon. I drove home and I was feeling on top of the world. Not only was Cardiff City getting one of the greatest chairmen in football but he also wanted to know me personally when so many others had turned their backs or were slating me behind my back.

So off I went to Dublin to see the City play but now with a smile on my face and a little bit of hope in my heart. The local police were at Cardiff airport but even they couldn't upset me when they went out of their way to call me over, taking me into a side room and questioning me on where I was going and what for. This was all just minutes before the plane was due to leave. I just said you know why I am going to Dublin and you shouldn't believe all that you read in the newspapers. They did say sarcastically they could make sure that I missed my flight. So I replied "I'm going to see Cardiff City play" and their pathetic reply was, "That's all we wanted to know. Have a good time." Maybe a few more terrorists and the like could be caught if the police paid less attention to football fans. Then again, I suppose Panorama had made me high profile and it was to be expected. Some of my other mates, Frankie, Johnny and Chris, went on the trip out to Dublin with me. They were ardent fans that rarely missed a match. While we were over there, we went to see Shamrock Rovers v Rosenburg in the European Cup. We ended up having a great night and the atmosphere was electric. The Irish certainly know how to enjoy themselves and made us feel right at home. A group of Irish fans sat next to me and asked me if I was the Cardiff fan off the television. I said I was. I'm thinking this is all I need but they were great and made a joke about it.

The following night we went to see the City play against St Patrick's Athletic and again another great night with everyone relaxed and having a bit of a laugh. It was also nice not to see a policeman in sight. I thought, 'It's a pity it's not like this at home'. As we were watching the game, my mate Johnny said to me, "I'm sure that's Bobby Gould over there." Johnny must have had good eyesight because, if it was Gould, he was right on the other side of the pitch standing there on his own. We all said let's go over and ask him if Sam had sent him over to watch the team for him and was Bobby going to be the next Cardiff City manager? It was fairly obvious that Sam had sent him as Sam had previously said that Bobby Gould had spoken highly of Wales and Cardiff City and had recommended to Sam that Cardiff could really appeal to him. As for him being the new City manager, that was the real question to be answered. We strolled over and engaged Bobby in a bit of a chit-chat on football but Gould just smiled at the new manager question. Before we left him, we had our photos taken and wished him good luck. The rest of our time in Dublin was spent mainly talking about the club, Sam and Bobby Gould.

After I returned to Cardiff, I continued to watch some of the other pre-season friendlies. I took in games at Swindon and Brentford home, Bath and Llanelli away followed by Newport County away on the 8th August that was on a Monday night. I had a strong feeling there could be trouble at this match; one because Newport had a strong hatred towards Cardiff and two, because Newport's firm and I go back a long way - it all started far back when I was a fourteen year old kid. For this particular game, I had heard that Cardiff's lads were all going together but, after all the unwanted publicity and trouble I had recently, I didn't need any more so I went without the lads and the only other person with me was a girl.

I drove to the match and parked my car in the stadium's car park. It was nearly kick-off time. We were walking through the car park towards the turnstiles when about fifteen Newport lads came running over towards me. Just then, three Cardiff fans pulled up in a car. The Newport boys started calling us on for a fight. "Come on you Cardiff scum," one of them shouted. I don't know why but one thing I've never done when it comes to Newport is show them any fear and so I said to the lads who were now with me, if we just go towards them they will probably back off and that's what we did.

Two coppers, who had come from nowhere, were now standing next to us and could see what was going on, and told the locals to get on their way. With that, they went off a bit sharpish towards the turnstiles. As I pulled my money from my pocket to pay to get in and go through the turnstile, the side gates swung open and about thirty Newport lads came pouring out. The other three Cardiff fans that I'd been talking to suddenly vanished. I just stood there on my own with a girl with me. I told her to quickly just go and get the car. Apparently these Newport lads had been attacking any Cardiff fan in a shirt inside the ground and had even hit a father and his young son. The thing was that my arm was bandaged up from where I had burnt it cleaning out some drains. Acid had exploded and burnt the whole of my arm and on the side of my stomach. None of this mattered to the Newport lads, but I suppose they had waited a long time to finally get one up on me, they started shouting, "You and your boys thought you were all it in the Eighties. What's it like standing here now on your own?" Deep down I was shitting myself but I could not let Newport know this as I had to show face no matter what. One of their lads just kept walking in a circle around me and just kept giving it the big one. I just replied, "Well, you lot are all so hard, thirty onto me," and with that all I can remember was being jumped from behind and then being kicked in the head, time and time again. Finally the police came over, sprayed some CS gas and whacked a few of them, which restored some order. What helped break it up most though was that a shout had gone up that there were about fifty Cardiff lads walking down the road towards the ground!

One of the police, who had finally stopped the attack, said to me, "If you had not taken such a beating I was just about to arrest you" I could not be bothered to even reply. An ambulance was called for me but I said I didn't need it. Apparently my head looked like the elephant man from the film. The police asked me if I wanted to press charges and I said, "No." One officer said, "We've caught three of them anyway for public disorders," to which I replied, "You can do what you want with them but I'm not pressing charges."

I found out later that the fighting between Cardiff and Newport went on for a full half hour in the streets while the match was on, one of Newport's main pubs was smashed up, but Newport gave as good as they got and many Cardiff lads have said they were well game and in some of the fights some lunatic girl had been leading them and had steamed into Cardiff on two occasions.

The next night the incident was all over the Welsh news and on the front and the back page of the Argus paper. Luckily at the time the media didn't know it was me. I rang Sam and he said "Come right over now." I told him what had happened at Newport but he said that he already knew and that none of this would hurt our friendship. We talked about Cardiff City and the hooligan problem that was associated with the club. I told him that during the Seventies, Eighties and Nineties that the majority of Cardiff's away support were lads who would fight if they had to and that City's support was different than most of the other clubs in the league. We had a much larger pool of lads who were very volatile but at the same time probably the most loyal type of football fans you could ever get. Yes, at times, it had given Cardiff City football club a bad name and I was not singing the hooligan elements praise. But at the same time it had also helped City become a fortress for the big games. Over the years at Ninian Park, the likes of Tottenham, Chelsea, Manchester City, Real Madrid, Middlesbrough and even Arsenal (twice) could not beat us at home. Nearly every club has said that the intimidating atmosphere had helped us beat them. At one point during the Eighties, during away games, it seemed it was only the lads who were following City. I will probably be slated for saying this but it is true. Sam replied to what I had said with yes he loved all that type of atmosphere but, if Cardiff City wanted to get into the Premiership with the big boys, one day that image would have to totally change. I agreed. We also both agreed that we would still like to keep an intimidating atmosphere but without any fear of crowd trouble.

Over the next year Sam would virtually ring me seven days a week and I would usually meet up with him at least five times a week. He was so passionate about football and the future of Cardiff City that it wouldn't matter what hour of the day you rang him or if anyone else connected with football had a question or a query, he would always answer the phone to them. If you left him late at night he would then read books about Barcelona or Real Madrid and then the following day he would say to me, "We will be bigger than both of them." He would say that the Welsh had been too negative and that they didn't believe in themselves. "I will make them believe they are great because they are." He asked me what I thought about the current team and commented that he wanted to have three players for every position so that our squad would be strong when injuries and suspensions arose. The thing was, up to this point, Sam had not yet been officially unveiled as the new chairman but that didn't stop him from turning up at the club every day. You couldn't take the fact away that Sam wasn't afraid of hard work. He was a real grafter and his enthusiasm was infectious. It was a good two or three months before Sam took over the running of the club and when he did, good or bad, it was like a breath of fresh air.

Sam would get me to show him all around South Wales. As he was driving through these places, I would say, "Sam you've just gone through a speed camera at 50mph in a 30mph zone." He would laugh. I once asked why he laughed about it. He explained that because he was Lebanese and that his car or driving license was not registered here in Britain then the police or the authorities could do nothing about it. A couple of years later that came back to haunt him. Sam had bought four Audi cars through the club and they were all registered to the club except for Sam's car. That had been registered in his name. Sam was booked for speeding. At first, he never turned up in Court. A summons was sent out and Sam was given a six-month ban. During those six months, Sam hated having to rely on people to drive him everywhere.

When Sam first arrived he had a number plate on his car, W1 DON, which stood for Wimbledon and he used to say that they, Wimbledon, were his baby and always would be as they had been his first club. Then something happened one day when Sam saw a member of the ground staff wearing a Manchester United top. He went mad and threatened to sack him if he wore it again to work. But the bloke turned around and said, "You can't talk to me like that. You've got Wimbledon on your car." Within two weeks Sam turned up with a new number plate, C4 RDF. So now Cardiff City was his new baby and we the fans were to be soon called his babies as well.

I was in the car one day when Sam said that he needed to ring Ninian Park to speak to someone regarding the website. There was no answer from the club and I could see from Sam's face that he was angry. He asked what time it was. It was 5:28pm and he said angrily that no one was supposed to leave until 5:30pm. I said that the staff were probably used to going home early as it is usually like a ghost town around the ground at that time of day. Sam was going potty and was ranting that someone would pay for this. The next day Sam was down at the ground by 7:00am even before the cleaning lady arrived and yes, Sam did get rid of someone. It had played on his mind all night. I heard a few days later from someone within the club that the wrong person had mistakenly been sacked.

Sam asked me where the best areas in Cardiff were to live and asked me to make some appointments with estate agents so that he and his wife Nida could view some properties. I felt great doing all these things and helping Sam. I was a bit shocked that Sam was a bit of a one man band. He had no advisors, no accountants or anybody else come to that working for him. When he arrived in Cardiff, he just took over the place and its staff and never put any of his own personal staff into the club. I contacted the best Estate Agents in Cardiff, Kelvin Francis and James, Jones and Hentons and received some particulars from them - I even made viewing appointments for Sam. When I drove him and Nida to see some of the new apartments they had just built on Marine Parade in Penarth, Sam asked me how much they were. I said they were from £350,000 for an apartment. Sam was a bit let down with me as he said he was looking more on the lines of £750,000.

In the year 2000, I don't think there were any apartments for sale at that price anywhere in the whole of Cardiff. Sam also said that he wanted good security and plenty of privacy. A few weeks later Sam said that Nida's mother was ill and Nida preferred that they kept their existing London home so Sam never ended up living in Cardiff. He spent the next six years living out of suitcases on an average of at least five nights a week. During those years, Sam stayed in the Marriott hotel, St. David's hotel, the Holland House hotel and the Vale of Glamorgan hotel. I personally think Sam was a lonely man and that's why he liked plenty of people around him. He would usually ring me and sometimes say to come on over and bring a few of the lads with you. But of course they had to be interested in football. Nearly every time I was out and about with Sam, someone who we both never knew would say hello to Sam and he would always say hello back and on many occasions would stop and talk to them for five or ten minutes.

One day Sam came out with a saying that he really believed in and that went, "When my family are in the right, they are in the right and when people say they are in the wrong, they are still in the right." By his family, I mean Cardiff City fans and he was the father figure. Sam had another one of his ditties printed and this was handed out to every fan at the turnstiles.

"I am very, very lucky to have joined this great family. I feel proud, honoured and privileged to be part of you all. I pledge to do my best for my new family or die trying."

Sam said that every Cardiff City fan were now his family including the hooligans and that we, the family, if possible, would deal with any members of our family misbehaving or doing something wrong.
After knowing Sam for about four months, he one day pulled his car over to the side of the road, turned off the engine, looked at me and asked me a question, "Do you think the fans will ever turn on me?" I replied, "Not as long as you are always honest

to them, Sam. That's all they ask." Sam looked at me and I was stunned by his reaction. His voice suddenly went loud and the tone of it became angry. He went into a rage and said, "If ever they turn on me, I will fuck them, I mean it, fuck them and I will close down the club." With that, his feet were kicking the inside of the car. I went quiet as I had never seen that side of Sam before but, within seconds, he just started the car up like nothing had happened and drove on and just went back to his normal chatty self as if nothing out of the ordinary had just gone on. Those words and his actions have always stayed with me to this day.

Sam loved walking around the City with shouts from everywhere, "Hello Sam" or "Sam, do the Ayatollah." The Ayatollah thing was written by the media after the Cup game against Leeds when Sam had supposedly invented this and spouted something to the press about the fans being his followers. As usual they had their facts totally wrong. The Ayatollah came about under the Tony Clemo days over twenty odd years ago. Some Cardiff City fans had been to the Middle East and the Ayatollah had died. All these people were banging their heads in mourning. They were doing this because they felt so much hurt. Now these City fans who I think came from Cwmbran, learned the reason for this and did the same because they felt so much hurt and misery from following the City and so they banged their heads in rage. "Everyone do the Ayatollah" is still sung to this day at every game.

In the evenings Sam would love to eat out at the restaurants in the City. On many occasions we ate in the Brassiere or Champers. Quite a few times, when there was just Sam and I, we would go to a small Lebanese restaurant in Mill Lane (I'm not sure if it is still there nowadays). I would demand that Sam let me pay the bill as I always wanted to show him that I could pay my own way with him. After a bit of a friendly argument, he would give in. Talking about being in the City, one day we walked into a Thai restaurant in Wood Street; me, Sam, Nida, Alan Cork, the then team manager who was a player under Sam at Wimbledon, and a few others. When I walked in, there was Willie Bolland and a few of the other City players standing having a drink while they were waiting for a table. Willie saw me and said, "Hello." I told him Sam was behind me and he nearly choked on his beer. I've never seen so many players try and down their drinks so fast. I asked if there was a table for eight. They said that there would be at least a half an hour wait as the town was packed because the 'egg chasers' (Welsh Rugby) had been playing that day. Sam had no patience at all which is very similar to me on that score; it must be our Arab blood. He didn't make any comment, just turned around and walked out. Sam asked me if I knew of any other restaurants where we wouldn't have to wait. I said that everywhere would be packed but I knew of a Chinese restaurant called The Bozan in Albany Road. I rang them. Emma the owner answered and she was very helpful and said she would fit us all in somehow.

We caught two taxis over there but, when we arrived, they only had two tables available to seat four people on each. The other problem was that they were nowhere near each other. That didn't bother Sam. He made Corky and I carry them over the tops of the other diners while they carried on eating. We then put them together down the middle of the room that was actually the only walkway to get to the buffet. Emma was just about to go and say something to Sam when I nudged her and said that it wasn't worth it and not to bother and I quickly added an apology. That was Sam for you. Wherever you went, he always took control of the situation, immediately.

I will never forget one night down the Bay when Vince Alm, Jamie Sullivan, and Joanne my wife, myself and a few others, about twelve of us in all, were with Sam. We were in the Pearl of the Orient restaurant. Rhys Weston (one of the City players) was there. I knew him well and had always had a lot of time for him because when he took stick from the fans whilst on the pitch, I knew he was always giving 100% even if he wasn't the most talented player out there. Rhys had been ill for the past few days and was unable to even train. He had a stomach bug or something. I was sitting at one end of the table and Sam was at the other. Rhys came out of the toilets behind Sam and he saw me and came over to say hello. I tried to tell him not to but it was too late. As he stood there, he saw Sam at the other end. My god, the look on his face as it went white. Sam I could tell was angry but at that moment just played it down and asked, "How are you Rhys?" Rhys quickly replied that he was feeling a lot better and with that Rhys said his goodbyes to the table and quickly sloped off. No one mentioned anything at the table in front of Sam and the conversation was totally changed.

As time went on, Sam asked me to invite more and more City fans out for meals. I would try and invite fans from all areas. On many occasions, Sam would give you less than an hour's notice so Johnny Bywater and my brother in law Jamie Sullivan, who were both season ticket holders for many years before Sam came, would come out with us. Sam would also ring about a dozen people himself who were all loyal City fans, Vince Alm, Big Sam, Tony Jeffries, Steve Day, Ketty, Peter Morgan (Mogs), Gwyn Davies, Paul Corkrey (Corky), Steve Davies, Lee Beames, Julian Jenkins, Alun Griffiths (Jaffa), Paul Mohamed (Mojo) and, on many occasions, Terry Phillips from the South Wales Echo would join us. Many times I sat by Sam and many times I would see the cost of the bill that Sam would sign for - it could often range from £400 to £1000 a night. We were out one night and I remember Big Sam and myself saying that we felt the crowds at Ninian Park had looked much bigger than were announced. Sam looked at us and went quiet. We repeated it again but he never answered and would carry on talking about other things. A few weeks later, I found out from Alan Kersleg, the safety officer at Ninian Park, that Sam had asked him to take photos of sections of the crowd and then asked him to count the fans individually, one by one in those areas and report back to him with his findings. Sometimes when you would think Sam wasn't really listening to you, he was and he would go away and analyse what had been said and, if he thought it was worth his while, he would do something about it.

One thing Sam hated the most was the local football fans wearing other team's shirts especially those from the Premiership. He believed that they should wear Cardiff City shirts and I personally agreed with him. We were walking down the bay one day when some young lads saw Sam and they shouted, "Hello Sam." At that, he shouted back to them to get their Man United shirts off. "What are you doing wearing that? Are you not Welsh?" He persuaded one lad to take it off and throw it in the choppy waters; then Sam gave the lad £20 for his trouble. That night Sam declared a war on all English football shirts in Wales. He said that we should get everyone in South Wales to hand in their football shirts at the club in exchange for the club allowing them to buy a new Cardiff City at half price. He said that we would have a massive bonfire and burn the lot. Sam managed to persuade hundreds of football fans to bring their tops to the club and Terry Phillips did a big article about it in the South Wales Echo. The bonfire never happened as the authorities said it was racist against the English and it could possibly stir up a lot of trouble so that was the end of that but he made a nice few quid on the sale of shirts.

In the early days of Sam's reign, Sam believed in the players and club staff having a get together and bonding before the season started. He would arrange for them all to come together on their day off. A barbecue was arranged pre-2001/2002 season at the Vale of the Glamorgan Hotel. I felt really privileged when he invited Joanne and me as I was just a fan and was worried if the players or staff would be unhappy at us being there. It was quite the opposite as Julian Jenkins (media manager) and his wife Denise greeted us both as we arrived. We all ended up eating together. I mixed quite happily with all the players and, as I already knew Rhys Weston and Alan Cork well, I never once felt out of place. Sam even arranged for an artist to draw caricatures of us all. Joanne burst out laughing at the one of me. I personally would say that the event went well and everybody was relaxed and enjoyed themselves.

One thing I will always stick up for Sam was that not only was he a football fan but he was one of the most passionate chairmen you could ever wish to have as an owner of your club. He would watch the under 9's, under 11's or whatever age of the team that Cardiff City might have playing on the park, be it on a Saturday morning or on a Wednesday afternoon. Sam even travelled the country to watch the youth team play. He really believed in the kids at Cardiff City. Sam would say to me he had more pleasure out of watching them than the first team. Sam would say to me that three of the most important things for this club to progress were an academy for the future of the club, a new stadium as without that he felt the club would die and for the fans to stick with the club no matter what. He said that the next ten to twenty years were going to become a rollercoaster ride and wasn't he right on that?

On a few occasions Sam would ask me what I thought of the current staff. I said that the day to day staff members were very loyal to the club - they had to be as the club had gone through some very bad times and on many occasions the club had looked like it was going to go bust and out of existence. Sometimes the staff didn't know if they were going to get paid. Sam asked me about David Temme, the chief executive. I said that we the fans had had our grievances with him in the past. He asked why and what those grievances were. First, I pointed out that David's background was Rugby and Ice hockey and that some of us had felt he knew nothing about football; secondly, when he left the Ice hockey scene, the reports that came from their fans weren't good and more importantly that Ice hockey was now financially in trouble; thirdly, he called Cardiff City fans 'cherry pickers' and that statement had caused outrage amongst the fans and fourthly, his ticket pricing for season tickets and games in general was well over the top. I then asked should I continue as I could write a book about him. Sam said, "No, I always believe that the more someone downs someone in life the more that person must be doing something right." I then said, "You asked me, so don't ever say I never told you." Guess what? Some six years later, Sam said in my house one day, "Why didn't you tell me about Temme?" I reminded him of our conversation; he said that I should have gone on about him more. Sam then went all quiet with me, almost sulking and then he changed the subject.

On another occasion I sat down and told Sam how my family twice tried to buy shares into the club (1998 and March 2000) but the Board had made it quite impossible for me, even though they were desperate for money. I also said that the same had happened to David Sullivan and his brother, Clive Sullivan. Sam then told me it had nearly happened to him and, if it hadn't been for Steve Borley selling Sam some of his own personal shares at a loss, he wouldn't have been able to get outright control of the club and Sam would never have gone ahead with the takeover. The other Board members knew that and had tried their best to block him. I told him that through the years, Borley and I had had our differences but that I had a lot of respect for the man. He had always put his money where his mouth was and his intentions for the club were good. I told Sam that I still felt strongly and was quite adamant that other people had used Borley's good name to distract the fans from knowing how badly the club had really been run. I felt that the rest of the previous Board members were only using the club for their own gains.

I also believed that if they had let me on the Board, I might have opened a can of worms and maybe we would all have known the truth of what had really been going on. Sam replied, "Borley is a good man."

Sam would always ask how my family was and he showed genuine concern about my father's health. Sam knew that my father had had two strokes in the last year. Sam would pop into my house to see my father and asked me time and time again to bring my father down to Ninian Park as Sam's guest. I used to say that he was too ill to watch and that my father wasn't a great lover of football anyway. Sam was very much a family man when it was to do with your own personal family. I don't mean his Cardiff City family - I have a totally different view of Sam on that issue. He would also always ask about my daughter, Annaise, who he knew I worshipped.

Sam used to ask me my thoughts on the Egyptians and if I had any relatives over in Egypt. I said yes but I had never met them. He asked me if I was Muslim - I said that I was born in Cardiff and I just believed in God, just like most Welsh people but I was very proud of my grandfather who was from Alexandria in Egypt. We would sometimes talk for hours about politics and Blair and Bush and the Middle East. Many times, when I had been in Sam's car, Sam would regularly speak to Dennis Wise,

Dave Bassett, and Ron Noades (to whose children Sam is Godfather) and Welsh international John Hartson. I would hear everything as he would put his mobile on hands-free and their voices would blare out on the speakers. I have sat in his car when the phone has rung and Dave Bassett has said thanks but no thanks to being the next Cardiff City manager. Then there are the times when Sam has rung up Dennis Wise and joked to Wisey about being the next Cardiff manager. I had the feeling that Sam wasn't really joking; he was just sounding him out. Wise never showed any interest in taking on the job and ended up being the manager of Millwall before moving onto Leeds and then Newcastle. One thing for sure, the fans at Cardiff would have loved his tenacious, pit-bull approach to football. He wears his heart on his sleeve - that's for sure.

One day Sam phoned up John Hartson and said, "I want you to sign for Cardiff City." Hartson joked and laughed back and then he said that would never happen. Sam, as usual, likes to have the last word and replied, "It will happen." When he came off the phone, I said to Sam that it never would. Not only did I know that for a fact but it is widely known that Hartson loves our old enemy 'The Jacks' and, in Hartson's biography, he states the only thing Sam ever did wrong in his eyes was take over the enemy Cardiff.

I have met Hartson on a number of occasions, one being on one of my visits to Dublin with Cardiff. Cardiff weren't playing on the Sunday that I was there so Steve Day, Dave Allen (Topman) and a few other mates of mine decided to go and watch Bray Wanderers play Coventry City in a pre-season friendly. During the first half, we stood just behind the Coventry dugout and I couldn't help it but I decided to give Hartson who was then a Coventry player, a bit of stick. I shouted to him, "You're only worth a quid just like the Jacks," who at the time were for sale for just £1. To my surprise, during the second half of the game, he came and stood next to me and said to me "You're Annis, Dai Thomas's mate," and with that we had a good old chat and at the same time it had made me feel a bit embarrassed at what I had just shouted at him. I had a lot of respect for him after that especially as I had been standing there with a number of Cardiff City fans; it takes a lot of bottle to do that. While we are on the subject of Dublin, a large group of us went to a lap-dancing club called Angels. Simon Williams, Steve Day, Mojo, Derek, Top Man, Ian Charles, myself and a few others jumped into a mini bus and the driver said, "Where to?" We said anywhere that there is plenty of life. He drove up and down about ten main streets and side streets and seemed to be going for miles but we were all too busy laughing and looking and weighing up the nightlife before we stopped and handed over a few Euros each. We had pulled up outside this club called Angles and went in and had a couple of drinks. I think it was either Mojo or Simon said that Richard Shaw who played for Coventry City was coming out of one of the cubicles. He saw us all looking over and realised that we had recognised him so he quickly darted out of the club. I don't know why because lap dancing clubs are quite harmless and it's really just a good laugh amongst the lads. We later left the club and when we walked around the corner, we were only two minutes from our hotel. The taxi driver, the conning bastard, had done us all like a kipper. I suppose that's life when you go to other countries as tourists.

A year later, I was down Cardiff Bay in Bar Salt after a Wales game and Hartson saw me and came straight over. I introduced him to Joanne and then, with a cheeky smile, I asked him, "Well, do you reckon you will ever play for Cardiff?" I reminded him of the day that I'd been in the car when he had spoken to Sam and that Sam had said, "You will sign one day." He laughed and said, "Sam's mad as you are probably aware. My whole family would have to move out of West Wales and I'd never be able to show my face in Swansea again but, besides all that, I couldn't ever see myself playing for Cardiff." He then offered for me to go and see him play at his latest club Celtic and gave me his number. I thanked him but said jokingly, "Wrong team, sorry John," and he laughed.

I was now starting to feel as though not only was I helping Sam but also I was helping my club Cardiff City at the same time. I drove with Sam all around the areas surrounding Cardiff to see if there were any sites big enough and available for a new stadium. We went to Bridgend, Caerphilly and to all the neighbouring outskirts of Cardiff but, after weeks of looking, Sam said we need look no more as the land is there on our doorstep. I said, "Where?" He said, "I can do a deal with the local Council on the land adjacent to Ninian Park." "Fantastic," I said. Now, I'm sure that Sam said it was around a half a million pounds for the sixty-two acre site that to me was the bargain of the century. By now, Sam had become very friendly with Russell Goodway, the leader of Cardiff Council and for the first time in the last forty years it looked like the Council was helping Cardiff City for a change. Sam said it wasn't going to be easy but at least we'd found somewhere for our new stadium. He used to say to me practically every time we met, "Annis, no stadium, no future," and, as everyone knows over the coming years, Sam then set his heart on that new stadium. Every time I now left Sam's company, I really believed that Sam was the man who could do what I always thought was only a dream and that was to make us a Liverpool or Manchester United.

One night while we were driving down Newport Road outside Allied Carpets, the traffic lights changed to red. We stopped and a car pulled up by the side of us. It was Neil McNamara. We were only able to have a quick two minute chat through the window but, as Mac drove away, I said to Sam now that's someone who would be good for security and he has about fifty doorman working for him. Sam asked me for his telephone number, which I gave him. Sam said that he believed in good security, something that Cardiff City needed. Some days later Sam contacted Mac and from then on Mac and some of his security staff worked on match days at Ninian Park. Mac eventually became famous after the Leeds game when he shielded Sam from the missiles thrown by Leeds fans as he and Sam walked past the Leeds end during our great FA Cup victory. The media labelled Mac as 'Sam's bodyguard' and decided to try and find out and dig up every bit of dirt there was on Mac. Yet if you knew him well like I do, he's one of the nicest blokes you could ever wish to meet. Mac would go out of his way to help anyone and, add to that, he's a staunch diehard City fan.

So I was now enjoying my football again and I was now beginning to believe that Brussels and Panorama were now only a distant memory. The only words that were ever now mentioned to me by people were "It's great to see Cardiff City doing well now that Sam Hammam has bought them."

ATTACKED: Abraham

5 YOBS COURT BY LAW

By MORRIS HARDY

FIVE soccer thugs who took part in running battles between rival fans were sentenced yesterday.

Violence erupted when well-known Cardiff fan Annis Abraham — featured in TV documentary about soccer hooligans at Euro 2000 — tried to get into "friendly" with Newport.

Bank worker Simon Farley, 34, attacked Mr Abraham during the first half, kicking him like a "football".

Cardiff Crown Court heard police released CS gas to protect Mr Abraham.

Prosecutor Martyn Kelly told the court: "It was supposed to be a friendly but revived old memories about what used to happen when Newport was in the League."

Information technology worker Farley, of Malpas, Newport, was found guilty of affray.

He was given 100 hours community service and two years probation.

Two others were convicted of public order offences and two admitted similar crimes.

Tuesday, August 8, 2000

RUNNING BATTLES: A police officer rushes to help a defenceless fan as he is kicked by rivals at the Newport v Cardiff football match

Attacked on my own whilst with a girl by 40 Newport fans before Newport v Cardiff game

CHAPTER NINETEEN

TIME TO MOVE ON AND LOOK TO THE FUTURE

The new season started on Saturday 12th August 2000 and City fans were the most excited I had ever known them to be about a forthcoming season. Now Sam wasn't actually the official owner yet but, behind the scenes, it was now Sam pulling all the strings. Steve Borley's name was still known as the chairman whilst Sam, for the time being, wanted to be called 'Governor'. Billy Ayre was still our team manager for now but we all knew Bobby Gould would soon be taking his place. So things were starting to take shape behind the scenes. There were no big signings yet but we all now believed we were finally going forward.

So off I went to Exeter for the first match of the season. We had sold near on two thousand tickets they had given us. If they had given us twice the amount, we would have sold them - that's how much Sam's arrival to the club had inspired the fans. We were all feeling positive and looking ahead instead of how we felt in previous years. As I walked to St James Park there was a real buzz in the air. The City Fans were chanting Sam Hammam's Barmy Army and nearly everyone was smiling and we hadn't even played a league game yet. The BBC was out in force with their cameras. They usually only bring them out only for the rugby. As I passed one film crew, I recognised, from my school days, Nick Pallet who worked for them. He said hello to me and smiled. As soon as my back was turned, he told the camera crew to put the cameras on me, which I later saw on a future Panorama programme about Sam Hammam and Cardiff City. There you go; people like Pallett say 'Hello' and smile to your face but as soon as your back is turned I believe they stab you. That's how I feel the BBC have only ever treated me.

Anyway, the BBC or Pallet weren't going to ruin my day. I went into the main stand and all I could see and hear was Cardiff City Fans jumping up and down and singing "Sam, do the Ayatollah" as he walked along the side of the pitch. As he was looking up, I waved to him and he immediately came up into the stand and hugged me. "Good Luck, Sam," I said. That opening game we won 2-1 and as we left the ground we all felt like we were walking on water and finally the dream had begun.

The first home league game of the season was against Blackpool, once a big club but had gone into decline. Years ago they were winning FA Cups and boasted the likes of the great Sir Stanley Matthews in their side. They could have done with him now.

Before the game, Sam was getting the media hyped up. He was still up to his old tricks as he had done in his Wimbledon or Crazy Gang days. The City players used to train at Cardiff University playing fields in Llanrumney, which is owned by Cardiff Council. One day, while the players were all training, Sam decided to have a bit of fun. He saw a woman called June who was in the middle of putting water and oil in the engine of her car. Sam approached her and said, "Have you got any kids?" June was taken aback by that and so would anybody be if a total stranger asked you that. I wonder what some people might have said or done. She replied, "Why do you want to know?" Sam said, "I will pay them £2 for every tyre that they deflate on all my players' cars." June realised Sam was serious and was as equally game for a laugh. She said, "Never mind my son Liam doing it, I'll do it," and with that she did. It made all the newspapers and left the current squad wondering what type of new owner they had. By the way, Sam never did pay her.

Sam was back again a few days later. This time he wanted to play a trick on Andy Legg and his new car but Leggy and the rest of the team had other ideas and with the help of June's son Liam they managed to have the last laugh. Leggy had parked his car under the changing room windows. As Sam was poking his head around by Leggy's car, they opened the window on the first floor of the building and poured a full bucket of cold water over Sam's head. "One, One," Leggy shouted. I actually believe these types of jokes by Sam built up a good team spirit.

Sam continued his madness into the game against Blackpool by having our newly acquired mascot 'Mini the Sheep' in his office. It wasn't a plastic blow up sheep but a real one. Sam didn't do things by half. He then proceeded to parade it around the whole of the ground and, in return, the City fans sang "Sheep, sheep, sheep shaggers" and "Mini, do the Ayatollah." The atmosphere was a carnival one and the City team played well with a Kevin Nugent goal that nearly gave us a well-deserved victory until Blackpool equalised to spoil the party.

On the Wednesday night, we travelled to Crystal Palace in the 1st Round, 1st leg of the Worthington Cup and the City fans turned out again in large numbers. Selhurst Park was one of Sam's old grounds that Wimbledon used to share after they sold their Plough Lane stadium. Sam brought a smile to the City fans faces even though the team ended up losing 2-1. He said he was taken aback by our away support and it was a bigger attendance than Wimbledon had for a home game.

It was now September and Sam had officially taken control of the club.

The second leg of the game against Crystal Palace was a night that I will never forget as my good mate Dai Thomas had been called in by Bobby Gould and told that he was going to be given a chance. He named Dai as a substitute for the game. The game itself was dragging along at 0-0 and on aggregate we were losing 2-1. Dai was brought on and when they announced his name, I would say sixty percent of the crowd booed and barracked him whilst pockets of us City fans tried our best to cheer and clap him on and give him a bit of confidence. As one City fan said to me, he's a City player after all and when any player wears the Cardiff shirt, I will never turn on them. The game finished a disappointing 0-0 and out we went of the Worthington Cup.

I spoke to Dai later that night and he said to me how hurt he felt by the crowd's reaction and that he could see there was no way back for him with his hometown club. I tried to console him but I could see that he had made his mind up or shall we say the crowd had. Dai still continued training and I spoke to Sam about Dai. Sam said that Dai would still be given a chance and that he would always give every player a chance. I told Dai this and told him to lift up his head and stick with it but Dai told me that Sam would totally ignore him when they passed each other down at the ground. Dai at one stage had been made to train with the Youth team and was totally excluded from the rest of the First team. Dai knew he had done wrong in Brussels but just wanted a chance to prove himself on the pitch. I personally believed that, unless Dai had scored a couple of goals in his brief appearance against Crystal Palace, Sam had already made up his mind. The crowd didn't like him. It did make me wonder who was picking the team, Sam or Bobby Gould?

Dai continued to train with the Youth team and some days they would have Dai running for miles with the sixteen year olds. Dai would ring me and say, "I've had enough. I never even get to kick a ball with any of the senior players." I would still continue to tell Dai to stick with it. Then one day Dai rang me and said that the club had called him into the office. "Who called you in?" I said. "Sam," he said, "No, I don't even think Sam knows I exist." David Temme had spoken to him and Dai said to me they had offered him a payoff. "What did you say?" I said. "I took it, I've finally had enough." "But Dai," I said "you have over a year and a half left on your contract - that must be well over £100,000." "I know but I just couldn't take it anymore." So I asked Dai straight. "How much did you accept?" "£30,000," Dai replied and with that he said. "Don't say I'm mad."

Dai had also confided in me that his agent had said he shouldn't take it and that quite a few other clubs were looking at him and he should have waited.

Over the next couple of weeks, Chesterfield and Rochdale offered Dai a contract but Dai didn't seem to care anymore. Dai was hurting. He had always dreamed of playing for his hometown club and he knew now that his dream had gone forever. Dai continued to shock me as we went for a meal up at the Cwrt Rawlin Pub in Caerphilly that is near to Dai's house. Dai then informed me that he had signed for Merthyr. Well, I was gob smacked but if that's what Dai wanted then it was totally up to him. Dai would be earning £700 a week at his new club and be close to his house. It was his choice. When City weren't playing, I would go and watch him at Merthyr and I once went to Worcester away in a night game. Over one hundred and fifty Merthyr fans had travelled up and when Dai was on the pitch they were chanting "Dai, Dai the legend." A few weeks later and I don't know why but Dai decided to quit and practically gave up on football at the age of twenty-five. Personally, I think Dai should have gone away and played for someone like Chesterfield. What a waste of talent and I am not just saying it because he is my friend and a good friend at that but how could the loyal City fans forget the nights at places like Shrewsbury and Halifax away when Dai scored. He took his shirt off and ran the length of the pitch to celebrate with the fans. They were great nights. But then some football fans are so fickle and have short memories.

The results on the pitch weren't going that well and I could see why Sam wasn't a happy person. Five draws in the last five games wasn't good enough. On the bright side, the Welsh lads, Danny Gabbidon, Gethin Jones, Scott Young and Andy Legg were all playing well. Sam said to me one evening that he liked big tough mean strikers and I'm getting one. He was true to his word as along came Leo Fortune-West; not everyone's cup of tea including mine but overall I think he achieved what Sam wanted of him. On the pitch, Leo was what Sam wanted, off the pitch Leo was quite the opposite, a real gentlemen and a very shy person.

One night when I was having a meal with Sam, I asked him why he had stopped the club mascots. He said that he wanted the players to concentrate on what they do best and play football. I explained that the mascot came on the pitch before the game had even started and warmed up the crowds. Sam was adamant that he didn't want mascots. On this occasion, Sam and I had totally different opinions on the whole matter but he was the boss and had the final decision and so that was the end of the mascots.

We went for walks up the valleys and to the reservoirs where we would meet up with Big Sam, Gwyn Davies, Paul Corkrey, Ketty, Peter Morgan and many other lads from the Valleys. I did once get a right telling-off from Sam and rightly so. I dropped a chocolate bar wrapper in the countryside and Sam went mad with me and said you should never help to ruin nature. Sam could walk for miles and was a very fit man. He told me that he had regular health checks with his doctor and the hospital that always kept him totally aware of his own health. He said that everyone should do it. He said that walking helped him think and relax.

Sam produced a booklet called 'Follow the Dream, 2000' and in that booklet, Sam outlined his plans for the future of the club, our failings, his love for Cardiff City, his dream of a Welsh army of fans and that £3,139,558.64p would be injected into the club as new capital and that would be it. Cardiff City Football Club should not only be for Cardiff and the surrounding areas but for the whole of Wales. He wanted a change of name, logo, colours and nickname and a new state of the art stadium, a new game plan, directors and a new philosophy on hooligans. A lot of this didn't go down too well with the fans. He wanted to get out there and tell it in person, to those that would listen. So Sam and I drove all over Wales on a tour to deliver his message. Even if you weren't interested, he'd still tell you. I can tell you now, I was totally against any name change, and logo, nickname or shirt colour change and I told Sam so. He would listen to me and then say he would give it more thought.

One afternoon Sam phoned and asked if I would like to come out that evening. Sam then said "I have someone important you would probably like to meet, don't ask, and wait until you get here." Sam really had me thinking now but I didn't have a clue to who it might be. I arranged to meet Sam in the Brassiere restaurant in St Mary Street that was one of Sam's favourites. When I arrived there, Sam was sitting with Alan Cork, one of his ex-Wimbledon players who played in the team that beat Liverpool in the FA Cup Final and who was now Assistant Manager to Micky Adams at Brighton. As I approached them both, Sam went to introduce me. I said, "There's no need. I know who you are and it's a pleasure to meet you."

Straight away I got on with Corky; he was a nice guy and always had a smile on his face. He asked me loads about Cardiff City, the fans and Cardiff as a place. Towards the end of the evening, Sam said, "Well, do you think Corky will make a good assistant to Bobby?" I nodded and with that Corky said that he would have to go back and break the news to Micky in the morning. A few minutes later we were all saying our goodbyes and I headed off home. I was driving along thinking how I couldn't believe that I was lucky enough to meet Corky, the new assistant manager before anyone else. I laughed to myself. I even knew Corky was coming before the press. Yes, Corky took the job. That must have been a hard decision for him as Micky Adams was not only his boss but also his best friend. This meant Billy Ayre being demoted again and his new job title was now Deputy Assistant head coach or something like it? Quite a few fans thought this was actually starting to belittle Billy - one minute he was manager and now he was third in the pecking order. City had now had a couple of wins under their belt. Leo had scored on his debut coming on as sub against Halifax Town in a 4-2 win for us. We were third after eight games yet the crowds were still low. In fact, attendances had dropped on every home game. That worried me but Sam never mentioned it. I think he was so busy looking for new players and sorting out all the staff at Ninian Park that he hadn't really noticed.

Suddenly City had a couple of slip-ups and the crowd was soon on Bobby Gould's back. In fact, they had never really taken to him because of his failure with the Welsh National Football team. Personally I don't think the Cardiff fans were ever going to forgive him for that. So on Saturday 14th October 2000, well over fifteen hundred City fans and I travelled to Leyton Orient where we lost 2-1. It wasn't just about the result. It was the whole performance of the City team. They didn't even look like they were trying and that's the one thing that really gets to us as all we ever ask is for the players to give 100%. Then, even if we've lost, the fans will still applaud you for trying. So at the end of the game, the crowd became quite vicious and vocal. I would say virtually every single one of us chanted continuously "Gould out, Gould out." It was said by some fans that they had heard that Gould had ran down the tunnel shouting to Sam, "The crowd has turned on me Sam, help me," and that Sam had walked on ignoring him. I will say that this was only a rumour among fans. What is a fact is that when Gould was boarding the team coach, he was abused by some of the City fans as I was a witness to this.

The following day my phone rang. It was Sam and I could tell he wasn't a happy man. Straight away he asked me of my opinion of Bobby Gould. I said, "Sam he never really had a chance with the fans from day one as they had never forgiven him from his disastrous spell with Wales." But my overall opinion was that I didn't feel he was the right manager tactically and I felt he never really had the team behind him. Sam said, "Ok, thank you, boss. We will speak later." Sam then immediately rang another three or four fans that in return rang me. Julian Jenkins and Steve Day were two of them and both were of the same opinion as me. Later that evening, Sam rang me back and said that tomorrow morning (Monday); he was going to change things around in the Management. Monday came and Gould was moved upstairs and Corky was given the honour of totally being in charge of the team affairs and his official title was now Head Coach. Whether it was Corky's tactics, inspiration or a bit of luck mixed in with it but, from that day, the team went on a superb run and never lost a league game from the 17th October 2000 until Boxing Day at Plymouth away. During this time, City gave some teams some right hammerings; York 4-0 and Torquay 4-1 away was just a couple of the teams that we swept aside.

On October 28th 2000, I arrived back in Cardiff from our 2-2 draw at Chesterfield. I went straight home and, at about 9:00pm, I took the dogs for a walk with my mother. We had our usual chat and laugh as we walked along and it just seemed like any other night. Then in the early hours of the morning of 29th October 2000, my mother had a heart attack and died she was only 55 years old. We were a very close family and it left my father and I totally lost. My mother was the one I would always go to for advice and turn to when in trouble, she was my rock and my guidance, I still visit the grave every week and sit there speaking to her and I know she is watching over me and guiding me. For the next few days I would just drive and drive and sometimes I would just drive around in circles and actually not get anywhere. But I knew I had to be strong as my father had had strokes and was weak, he was now 79 years old and I had to be there for him. Our family doctor had said to me your father probably won't live long now due to your mother passing away, I said "He will, I will make him want to live."

As soon as Sam heard, he was on the phone to me straight away and asked if he could do anything to help. That week Sam kept saying, come to the next home game with me and sit with me. I said no; I just wanted to stay at home. He continued to ring every day. Then on the Saturday morning, he said he was coming to pick me up. "No, you don't need to do that, I will drive but I won't be there until about 2:50pm." Sam said that there would be a car parking space left for me inside the main gates. I went along and Sam was by my side throughout the whole day. I sat next to him through the first half and then at half time Sam said, "Quickly, follow me" and we went down to the changing rooms where Corky was giving his half-time speech. I felt embarrassed being there but within two minutes Sam was off again. "Follow me," he said again, "Shall we go to the centre of the pitch and wave to all the fans." "It's ok Sam; I'll stay in the player's tunnel." So off he went and as usual the home fans gave him a roaring round of applause and, at the same time, they asked him to 'Do the Ayatollah' and he gladly obliged. We then went back up to our seats for the second half and we went on to win the game, 4-0. I said to Sam that I thought it was time for me to go home. He said, "No nonsense, come down to Corky's office." So I did. I congratulated Corky on a great win even though really my mind hadn't been on the game. I think that Corky is quite a shy guy deep down but I did notice that there was a drinks fridge in his office. He pulled out and downed two bottles of Bud, one after the other and with that he wiped his mouth, straightened his tie and said "Right, I'll go and see the press now." I think the booze probably gave him a bit of Dutch courage as even though we had emphatically won. I believe the beer helped to take away some of Corky's shyness. I said to Sam, "I definitely must go now and be with my Dad." I thanked him for a fantastic day and then I made my way home.

Over the next few weeks, my father and I went everywhere together; I even learnt to cook as due to my father's strokes, he was unable to use his left arm anymore. For a while I managed to keep my father strong, but he then had another stroke and had to go into hospital for a few weeks. Going home at night became pretty lonely and thankfully Sam kept my spirits up by inviting me out for meals with him and his wife and on many occasions meeting new players that Sam had just signed.

Sam soon had another surprise for me one night when he rang and said, "I have someone else for you to meet." That person turned out to be Rhys Weston who had been an apprentice at Arsenal Football Club and had gone through the Arsenal academy. Rhys was really excited about joining the club and Sam said he would like me to show Rhys around the areas of Cardiff and help him find accommodation. I came to know Rhys quite well and I actually felt for him when certain sections of the fans were on his back during games. Every time I saw him, I used to say, "Keep your chin up, Rhys," and he would say that he was and was giving it his all.

My life was changing all the time and losing my mother, left a big hole inside me which needing filling. If I was honest I never thought I would ever settle down, as most of my life I had spent working in pubs/nightclubs and hotels all over Wales and England and I had had quite a few relationships and as I used to work away Thursday/Friday/Saturdays and the odd weeknight and then come home to stay at my parents and any spare time I had, I would put football first. In February 2001 my daughter Annaise was born and even though I was not with the mother at the time, I rushed back from Blackpool where Cardiff City was playing on a Tuesday night to see Annaise the following morning. I can honestly say Annaise being born changed my life and in my opinion for the better. As you will have read I was very close to my parents and after losing my mother I still felt lost and lonely, I know I had my father and he was now with me every day as I had stopped working in the nightclub industry after my mother had died and was now concentrating on the property world full time, but I knew he was not going to live forever as the strokes were happening too often. I would see Annaise for a couple of hours a day, six or seven days a week and to me Annaise was now my future.

Around about the time Annaise was born I went to see a property for sale and to be honest I am quite demanding and the agents who were selling the property had a French salesman dealing with it and I could hardly understand what he was saying and being an inpatient person as I am, I asked to be put through to someone I could understand better and that person ended up being my future wife Joanne. We hit it off from the beginning and I felt Joanne was good for me as she had her own independence, a good job, her own home and she stood up to me. Within weeks Joanne moved in with me and was an unbelievable help with my father and I could not have asked for any more, Joanne was amazing with my baby daughter Annaise and to this day, they are so close and love each other as if they are mother and daughter. If only my mother had met Joanne and Annaise and could have seen the change in me and for the better as far as I am concerned, I could have finally made my mother proud of me.

Sam still called on me to come out with him when anything new was happening at Cardiff City.

I went for a meal with Sam and Ian Butterworth, the new Assistant Manager. Now Butts had just come down from Darlington and he had to leave his family up there until his house was sold. Butts and I became good friends and soon he was popping into my house after training for a cup of tea or we would go for a meal down the bay and talk about the days when he played for Norwich City in the old First Division and about when he went to America and coached. Sometimes Sam would send him on scouting missions to watch other players and certain teams and Butts would ring me and see if I wanted to go. I went to Bristol Rovers once with him and was shocked by how well known and liked he was by other footballers or scouts. He was always happy in his job but it was also very lonely for him down here. The only time he would see his wife and children was when he would drive straight home after a Saturday game all the way back to Darlington and then have to be back at Ninian Park first thing Monday morning.

About a year later, he managed to sell his house in Darlington and with that he bought a house for him and his family near Radyr. Whenever I used to ring him or vice versa he always used to call me Mr Cardiff. I went out with Butts on the staff Christmas Party and George Wood (Goalkeeping coach), Corky and I were standing there having a drink in a club called Life when Billy Ayre walked in and looked very upset. He walked straight over to Corky and a few words were exchanged. I don't know what was said but it left Corky totally red faced. In my view, Billy Ayre (who has since passed away) had been given the short straw by Sam. One minute he was manager, then assistant manager, then virtually third or fourth in charge behind Gould, Corky and Butts and then no longer with the club. It looked to me as though he was blaming Corky but that's only my view. When we all went over to Corky after Billy had left, Corky just shrugged his shoulders and said he didn't know what he had done wrong. Like I said before, Corky got on with everyone and, in all the time I knew him, I'd never seen him upset anyone. I never knew Billy Ayre but I do know the players that played under him and other members of the staff had a lot of respect and time for him, so did Corky. Corky went over to the bar and bought us all a round of drinks. It was getting late now and I never used to like to leave my father too long so I thanked everyone for inviting me and went home. The incident with Billy was never mentioned again.

Another person I came to know well was the secretary Jason Turner. I have nothing but praise for Jason and there is nothing he wouldn't do to help you. Sam worked him hard and I think Sam relied on Jason a lot. I used to ring Jason for any information about things like next season's friendly's which may have been abroad and I needed to organise well in advance. He was always obliging. Every season he would go out of his way to get my autograph book and football signed by the whole squad to keep my football collection up to date. I'll say this to you Jason - I think you deserve a medal for the six years that you worked under Sam. Even though Sam was good to have as a friend, I had heard that he had made a lot of enemies within the staff throughout the years and I haven't met many staff yet who have said it was easy to work for Sam. I'm glad I just stayed his friend.

Even through all the bad press and publicity I'd had, it wasn't going to put me off following my club to away games. I'd been going to away matches throughout the late Seventies and during the Eighties and Nineties. I certainly wasn't going to stop because of the BBC or the comments of any glory hunters that had just started going because Sam had arrived. Some tried slagging me down behind my back. So I have to say a special thanks to Terry Phillips, the chief sports writer for the South Wales Echo who drove me to 90% of the matches that season. I went with Terry because he was not only a good friend but also because when I went to the first couple of away games after Brussels, I had been hounded by the police and the media. Sam had offered me on many occasions to go with him but that would have just brought more attention to me. Going with Terry meant I could just get on with supporting my club. On some of the trips Lee Beames and Craig McGowan accompanied us. We had some good outings that season, so once again, many thanks Terry.

The season became better and better and by Saturday 21st April 2001, all we needed to get promotion was a draw away at York City. The home crowds had now gone as high as nearly 14,000 and things were looking good. Sam was already planning for the next season and deciding which players he would be clearing out. I went up to York City on a Friday night with Michael Harvey, Mojo, Dave Chappell (Crystal Palace fan) and a couple of other mates. Within 30 minutes of arriving, Sam had phoned up and asked where I was. I told him I was in a hotel. He told me to go over to his hotel and bring my mates with me. We went to the York Minster hotel where Sam and some of the other directors were staying. As usual, when we arrived Sam gave us a warm welcome and made us all feel at home. Steve Borley, Kim Walker and Jason Turner were all there. After a few hours, Sam said goodnight to us all and went to his room.

By this time, everyone had had a lot to drink (excluding myself) and we were all having football debates with each other. I noticed Borley and Mojo were starting to have a heated argument and I could see Mojo was really winding up Borley. I tried to get them both to calm down a bit but Mojo would not stop and he then said to Borley that he (Borley) wanted us to get relegated. Borley said, "Say that again," and Mojo did. With that Borley smacked Mojo in the face and Mojo hit the deck. Mojo managed to stand up after Temme and myself pulled Borley off him but, by this time, Mojo was off on his toes with Borley shouting, "You're running like you always run." Borley was chasing him up the stairs and across the landings. Eventually, Borley came back down and apologised. I could see that Borley was hurt by those comments and who wouldn't be after all the hard work that Borley had put into the club and not forgetting using his own money to fund certain things. I have to say if you cut Steve Borley open, his blood would run blue. I asked where Mojo was and he said that he had run off. My mobile started ringing. It was Mojo. "Where are you?" I asked. "Outside" he said, so I said goodnight to Borley and everyone else and promised I wouldn't mention the incident to Sam which I never did. I found Mojo on the other side of the hotel outside a fire exit. We caught a taxi back to our hotel. Personally I think drink got the better of them both and maybe Mojo went a bit too far. Years have gone by now and the two of them now get on very well. I don't think there is a person alive who hasn't had an argument when they have had too much to drink.

The day after was the big one and over 2,000 Cardiff fans had made the trip. The day went well. Leo scored a hat trick in a 3-3 draw and, at the end of the match, 2,000 City fans ran across the pitch in wild celebrations. The club had been promoted in Sam's first season and I had seen it not just from the outside as a supporter, but from the inside as well and it had really opened my eyes as to what really goes on, but I felt privileged to have been able to have been part of all this.

"GREYHOUND WELFARE"

Greyhound Welfare was founded, as a not for profit organisation, by Dawn Abraham in 1998 as a result of her love of greyhounds, becoming a registered charity in September 1999.

Since Dawn's untimely passing, in October 2000, the Trustees have carried on with her message ... and her son Annis Jnr. in memory of his mother and respect for his late father's support for her work ... is our PATRON

Dawn Abraham and her dogs, Miss Beautiful (right) and Mr Pharaoh (left) taken in early spring 2000.

Sadly, Miss Beautiful passed away in April and Dawn herself only a few months later. Mr Pharaoh, however, lived a long and happy life until his 17th year.

Our connection with the Abrahams is maintained by Dawn's beloved son Annis Jnr ... a well-known Cardiff businessman and successful author who brings his wife and daughters to our events whenever he has the chance and the time ... away from a busy professional/family life. Throughout the years he has always been there for us although his active support for Greyhound Welfare and other local charities is usually overshadowed by his devotion to football.

Amongst the busy, busy pictures on his website (now on 20,000 hits per week) it's rather difficult to find the devoted father and thinking man within ... but he is there.

Paula Ambrose

Greyhound Welfare

CARDIFF CITY AFC
·BLUEBIRDS·

Follow The Dream

AN OVERVIEW 2000

To my friend Annis. Here is to
the long sweet memories. May the
DREAM continue. love

by SAM HAMMAM

28/10/06.

CHAPTER TWENTY

CHAMPAGNE ARMY

In my time of following Cardiff City in the late Seventies, Eighties and early Nineties, I personally believe that the majority of Cardiff City's fan base were lads/casuals whatever you want to call us and I believe we were loyal to our club, let's put it this way, hardly anyone else was supporting Cardiff City during those dark days of spending nearly nine years in the dungeon league (Division Four) and about fifteen years in Division Three so what Sam did in the following story I believe was right and acknowledged our support of Cardiff City and Sam in my opinion even tried to solve Cardiff City's hooligan problems.

Right from the beginning, Sam knew that Cardiff City had a hooligan problem. He could have totally ignored it but he didn't. He decided that he would do something about it and he was going to deal with it in his own way. Most chairman or owners of football clubs say what the press want them to say, "We will ban for life anyone caught causing trouble at this club," which then usually keeps everyone happy. No, Sam wanted to meet the hooligans; every single one of them if he could. He believed that if you treated people like animals they would rebel but if you tried to understand them and get inside their minds, you might be able to know why they do it. Sam also believed that if they were treated with respect then there was a better chance that they might give back respect. The media were slating Sam when he said some of these comments. My answer to them is everybody has tried to resolve Cardiff's so called hooligan problem and failed. The press should have realised that he was dealing with things in his own unique way and should have given Sam a chance. But no they didn't. Sam wouldn't listen and went about it, in his way. What I can say is that the authorities in the past had been heavy handed at Ninian Park and I believe that process had failed. Yet since 2001, when a new team from the police football intelligent unit was assigned and PCs Simon Insole and Wayne Palmer were introduced, totally different tactics were brought in and all fans attending games at Ninian Park were treated with respect. The heavy-handed approach in and around the stadium was out and probably now; it was one of the safest grounds for away fans to come to. The police numbers were reduced by about 90% and arrests were at an all-time low. Sloper Road outside Ninian Park was, at one time, a hotbed for violence but, with no trouble at all at some games, now flowed along peacefully.

As we're on the subject of PC Simon Insole, known to some as 'Potato Head' (sorry Simon), I actually first met Simon on a Tuesday night 25th September 2001 to be precise and I will never forget our eventful first meeting and neither will he probably.

It all started when I had gone to London to stay the night with my partner Joanne and planned to see City play QPR. As usual, we had the good support that we always do when we visit London. We lost the game 2-1. We were leaving the ground and were heading down the steps of the top tier of the away end when I saw two police officers on the other side of the road to us. One of them which I eventually found out was Simon, was pointing over in my direction.

I thought to myself I've had enough of the police harassment I've suffered since the Panorama programme and, without saying anything to Joanne, I let go of her hand and charged over to Simon like a bull to a red rag. I shouted something like, "What do you think you're doing? Can't I just be out at a football match with my girlfriend?" Before I could finish what I was saying, I had fallen over and landed right underneath Simon. With that, he said, "Get up Mr Abraham; go on your way and have a good night." I felt so embarrassed. I just stood up and stormed off. Later on Joanne had said she had found it so hard not to laugh her head off at me and that she felt Simon had felt the same way.

I never spoke to Simon again until Sam thought it was a good idea to invite some of the police spotters to the 'Supporters Player of the Year' event down at the Coal Exchange pub in Cardiff Bay. Sam once again wanted everyone to get on and socialise and this he thought would be a good opportunity. At first, I didn't think it was but I was proved to be wrong. As I went to get a drink by the bar, there was Simon Insole and Richie Webber, another police spotter. I will admit I intended to just ignore them but Simon, being the friendly person that he is, said, "Hello Annis." I don't remember what was said next but for the next three hours I chatted to him and of course the incident at QPR came up and Joanne was finally able to have her laugh out loud.

Now you could say Sam had played a little helping hand in that by inviting them. Police had never been invited before to a football supporters do. It was totally unheard of until Sam came to the club. I have to say this whether people like it or not, I don't trust many police and have little respect for most, but since that day Simon and I chatted, I have to say in the next 10 years Simon turned out to be a fair and genuine a policeman.

One day Sam rang me up and said, "I want to run something past you; can we meet tonight?" As usual, I went to meet him. He said that he would like to meet the Soul Crew. I want you to organise about fifty of their toughest to go on a coach to Mansfield with me. I explained to Sam that there is no such thing as the Soul Crew; that was in the Eighties; the name Soul Crew is what the media still print and what some fans do just to wind up the opposition. Sam said OK and then for me to ask fifty of the toughest fans we had. That was easy to do as City had hundreds of lads. The following night, Sam phoned me again to ask how it was going. I explained that there was too many to choose from. "No problem," he said, "we will put two coaches on."

I had a ring around and asked lads from different areas if they wanted to go on a coach with Sam to Mansfield on Tuesday night. The response was overwhelming. We could have taken ten coaches. Sam and I had agreed that everyone would originally think that they were paying. Anyway, Simon from Neath chose a couple of lads from his area, Big Sam picked out his mates, Joe Mullins, Ted, another lad called The Neck (as he looks like a white Mike Tyson), Desy, Joey and a few others, Lakey selected his mates, Deacon, Simmo and Mac did the same. I invited Dai Thomas - I was curious whether Sam would speak to him as Dai was no longer with the club. I rang Sam and said that I had spoken to Big Sam, Mac and a few others and we thought it best to limit it to about seventy. Sam said, "Whatever you want, we shall do."

So on that Tuesday off we all went. Sam agreed that he would go on one coach going there and another on the way back. The Valley Boys gave Sam a Valley Commando badge and the Cardiff lads gave him a Battle Bus badge which he put either side of his jacket. Within minutes of leaving Cardiff, Sam had arranged for some of the club staff to have food on board for the lads which they all ate. All the way up, Dai had been sitting in a seat just in front of Sam. Sam never spoke once to him but I truly believe he really never recognised him. Then Sam really surprised everyone on board both coaches. We pulled into The Swallow Hotel about six miles before Mansfield's Football Ground and Sam said, "Wait here." He jumped off the coach and went inside. I think the lads probably thought the players were in there. Sam came back and told us all to follow him. He had hired a function room in the hotel and a buffet had been prepared consisting of Prawn sandwiches, Salmon, Beef and a variety of other foods. In the centre of the room was seventy two bottles of Moet & Chandon Vintage Champagne, one bottle for every lad and to go with that were fresh cream cakes.

Yes you could say Sam was barking mad. The lads would have gone on the trip anyway without one thing being given to them and they would have paid their way as well. A lot of the lads were just happy to have met Sam. I didn't think there was any need for this but that's what makes Sam probably a bit mad. I've always said you had to be mad at the time to have bought our football club in the current state that it was in. Every lad in that hotel that day was well behaved and I don't even remember any mess being left behind. We all finished our food and drink and on we went to Mansfield. As we arrived at the ground, the match had already started. Sam jumped off the coach first as he wanted to go and sit in the dugout. The coaches then pulled up near the turnstiles. As we were rushing to get off, Mansfield had a small welcoming committee of about 30 lads waiting. I will be honest. The second that the doors opened on both coaches, Mansfield saw what was coming off and they were on their toes within seconds. The police thought they were going to have trouble and went to move in but the lads all laughed and quickly made their way in through the turnstiles. City played awful that night. Maybe it was because we already knew we were promoted but they didn't seem up for it. The game finished 2-1 to Mansfield. Some Mansfield fans had attacked a few of the lads that had left the ground early and, yes, the lads did make an attempt to go down there after them but the police had formed two lines and the only place the lads were going was back on the coaches. You could see deep down, everyone had had a great day, thanks to Sam and no one really wanted to let him down.

We all sat on the coaches waiting for Sam, so that we could set off home. He eventually arrived and said he had booked us all a restaurant to go to in Mansfield. The local police had other ideas and said no; we all had to leave the area. Sam wouldn't give up though and twenty minutes later Sam had brought fish and chips and cans of coke onto the coaches for us all. He never gives up Sam. Like I've said before, he will always have the final say. The journey home went quickly and we all arrived back in Cardiff three hours later.

As we jumped off the coaches, an argument broke out between either some of the lads and Tony Jeffries (Supporters Club) or Sam and Tony Jeffries. All I knew was that Tony had been on his Supporters coaches and wasn't happy about all the freebies on our two coaches which you can totally understand. After this argument and for a while later, Sam and Tony never spoke.

If you asked me, was the trip a success? I'd say yes it was. Sam didn't need to give anything away to the lads. They did appreciate it but the problem for Sam was that the Cardiff hooligan problem was on a much wider scale than he had ever thought. It wasn't organised hooliganism. It was sporadic. Overall, I believe the only way it was ever going to be eroded was by other police following in the footsteps of Simon Insole and Wayne Palmer and probably us getting to the Premier League and a new stadium. All Sam seemed to be doing was winding up the media and the higher authorities. I believe he meant well but saying things like, "Bring me the biggest nutter and I will tame him," only played into their hands.

The Stoke ordeal was another time that Sam brought unwanted press to the club and himself. The Stoke police asked Sam to put about fifty photos of Cardiff fans wanted in connection with trouble at Stoke in the match day programme. I didn't believe that we should have done it. These people weren't convicted hooligans yet after all, photos of paedophiles aren't put in the papers without convictions. By the way it was sent out; it looked like they were all guilty. Instead of Sam just saying yes or no, he then made a speech saying he would provide legal assistance and legal representation to every fan that was arrested at Stoke. This again brought bad publicity to the club and the funny thing is the club never did all this anyway. Sam certainly knew how to wind up the press. He also made enemies within certain authorities at the same time. The hooligan problem wasn't going to go away overnight and Sam started to realise this. Sometimes, when I think back, Sam had begun to know a lot of the lads really well and, out of respect for Sam, they met him and liked him. Under Sam on the field of play, the club was moving in the right direction and he also calmed down a lot of our hooligan problems.

CHAPTER TWENTY ONE

LOSING MY FATHER

I was buzzing now and I was really starting to enjoy following my club again, everyday there just seemed to be good news coming from our club. Sam had brought our club to life and had made us fans believe we now had a club that was going places.

The Blue Army was on the march. "The dream goes on," said Sam. "It is almost a year now since I became involved with the mighty Bluebirds and I still cannot believe it! I am still in a daze and cannot get out of this trance! Why is this happening? It is one word LOVE!"

Sam explained that he and the club were now moving at a dangerous speed and that this was dangerous because if a big enough mistake was made, we could crash. We had just won promotion in Sam's first season. What more could the fans have wanted. Sam wasn't going to let anyone even question what would happen next. Sam had spent millions that summer and with the forthcoming weeks of the new season came new signings, Neil Alexander, Spencer Prior, Des Hamilton, Layton Maxwell, Mike Simkins, Leon Jeanne, Graham Kavanagh and Peter Thorne. We now had what Sam had always said he wanted - a big squad. We actually had thirty four first team players. God knows what the wage bill was, did Sam?

Once again, I and a few others were lucky enough to go out and meet some of the new signings; some before the night they'd signed and others to celebrate their signings. Des Hamilton was a night to remember. To us fans, he was a big name. He had played for Newcastle United in the Nou Camp stadium (Barcelona) and he was still in his prime. The reports on him were excellent. The night we all went out with him, Sam pushed the boat out even further than usual. He said, "This is a real celebration; let's have the best wine and do a toast to Des Hamilton." You could tell Hamilton was well impressed with his welcome by Sam and us, the fans. He was a 'down to earth' person and seemed really excited about signing for Cardiff City. Apparently Newcastle had offered him another year on his contract but he wasn't being guaranteed a First team place. Playing regular First Team football meant more to him which is also what we wanted to hear. Alan Cork had settled in well now and Butts his assistant felt at home now that his family had all moved down. They were both excited about the forthcoming season.

Sam then said it loud and clear, "WE WILL NOT FAIL, WE CANNOT."

The season started well and Sam certainly had woken up Wales. On the 11th August 2001, nearly 17,500 fans packed into Ninian Park against Wycombe Wanderers and they weren't let down as City won 1-0. Cardiff City also now had Scott Young, Danny Gabbidon, Rhys Weston and Robert Earnshaw in the Welsh squad which, a year ago, would have been unheard of. By mid-October, the team had started to struggle a bit and was now 17th in the League and already the crowds were down by six thousand compared to the beginning of the season. I would say to Sam that the crowds disappointed me as I felt that from day one, I had always said we were a sleeping giant. Sam would say, "Don't worry; the crowds will come when we give them a new stadium."

The websites were already filled with comments about Sam's overspending and that Corky wasn't the right manager for the team. Sam wasn't happy with some of these comments but mostly with the people who wouldn't put their names to these comments - they had recorded them under Mickey Mouse names. On this point I totally agreed with Sam. I personally think it's a coward's way of going about it. If you have something to say then say it. It's a free world but don't hide behind another name.

The team steadily started to improve and we were sixth in the League by Boxing Day 2001. Sam wanted to be top by now. I could feel it every time I met him. The hunger that drove him to get to the Premier League was unbelievable. He was a man on a mission and at the rate he was buying players, you could sense nothing was going to stop him. He would still remind you that the stadium was his number one target. I felt that he was doing alright at this stage on that. Sam would invite people like Rhodri Morgan, the First Minister for Wales to see the team play. Sam would introduce me to people like Rhodri and Neil Kinnock. I wasn't too fussed on Rhodri Morgan; firstly, I wasn't a fan of his anyway and secondly, when Sam introduced me to him and I tried to talk to him about football, I felt he didn't know anything about the game and that rugby was really his only sport. With Neil Kinnock, I felt that he had a passion for the Club and really did know what was going on at Ninian Park. Sam was getting on very well with Russell Goodway, the leader of Cardiff City Council and I think that he believed that would be the way towards the new stadium.

In all my years of supporting the club, the Leeds game will go down as one of the greatest days ever at Ninian Park. We were tenth in the Second Division (which I still call the Third Division). They were top of the Premier League, two points ahead of Manchester United so what chance did the rest of Britain give to the Welsh Club, Cardiff City - no chance. Over 20,000 fans packed into Ninian Park. If the stadium had been bigger, we would have packed in another 20,000. Everyone wanted to be at Ninian Park that day. A piece of paper was put in every programme and also handed out as you went into the ground with the words to the song 'Men of Harlech' which we all sang loud and clear and to this day, we sing it at every home game. I really believe that this gets the fans excited and emotional. The packed ground was intimidating for the Leeds team that day. I don't think anyone in Wales will apologise for it. Even when we went 1-0 down, the Cardiff fans still roared their team on and when Kavanagh equalised, the ground erupted and when our local boy from the Valleys, Scott Young scored, we were in heaven and the dream was really alive. Cardiff City had done the impossible and we had beaten the best team in Britain at the time. Sam, as promised, had made one of our dreams come true.

But when you're a Cardiff fan, you're not allowed to feel on top of the world for the next week or so; in fact, the next day the media were more interested in the thousands of fans who had invaded the pitch to celebrate and, yes, a few were out of order and ran towards the Leeds fans but 99% just wanted to celebrate the moment and let the world know that Cardiff City were now a force to be reckoned with. At about the same time as our fans were celebrating, David O'Leary was saying to the media that Ninian Park was a disgrace and that it was worse than the Turkish team Galatasaray. He also went on to say that Sam Hammam was walking around the pitch geeing up the crowd. Saying all this after the game, when you have lost only sounds to me like sour grapes, or a bad loser. What he should have said was, "Well done, you deserved that Cardiff City, you and your fans." The word at the time was that there was a bit of an altercation in the directors' car park after the game between O'Leary and Sam. Sam was speaking his usual words and apparently O'Leary lost it but Peter Ridsdale (who was with Leeds at the time) managed to get between them. The media roasted our fans and once again all the papers were full of Cardiff and its hooligans instead of the main story that happened on the pitch. The funny side of it was that before this game, David O'Leary had stated he wanted to start their FA Cup campaign in Cardiff and finish it in Cardiff (at the Millennium stadium). Well done, Mr O'Leary you did! In the dressing room after our great victory, when the players were celebrating with their Champagne, they sprayed it over Sam and unfortunately for him his black dyed eyebrows turned grey! You had to be there to see the funny side of it but I don't think he ever lived it down.

Sam later called about fifty City fans including myself, to come to Ninian Park; fans who he thought could help him. We had this meeting with him and David Temme. Sam said, "They're after us; they are trying to ruin us; they said our fans are fighting; what fighting? A fan threw a cigarette lighter and then another fan threw his fucking..........shoe!" and with that, everyone burst out laughing. Sam continued, "We have to be whiter than white." What Sam or us never realised was that someone undercover was filming all of this for another BBC programme on hooligans. Sam made Simmo stand up and said, "Simmo should sing Christmas carols" and a lot of this meeting then turned out to be a big laugh. If I actually rightly remember, Sam never once encouraged any hooliganism at this meeting; he tried to play it down or make a joke out of it.

On Saturday January 12th 2002, I appeared on the back page of the Sun as one of Sam's inner circle and as one of Britain's most infamous hooligans of 2000. That day, Sam rang me and when we spoke, Sam said, "You sound down." I said, "Of course I do, I'm on the back page of the Sun for all the wrong reasons." At that, Sam replied, "You should be proud." I couldn't believe what I was hearing. I said, "You what." He repeated it and with that I told him I had to go as I was busy working. I didn't need that type of advice; my father was still very ill but he was still able to read the newspapers. I thought, here we go again, nearly two years later and the media have started it all up again. I didn't speak to Sam much for a few weeks. I wanted this to calm down a bit. I also felt Sam loved it as he had also said, "Any publicity is good publicity." Yes, I agree if you are making money out of it. I just wanted to get on with my life and look after my family, not go through what I went through in June 2000. We were soon speaking again; I just knew that was how Sam saw most things in life and I or anyone else wasn't going to change him.

Lennie Lawrence was director of football at Cardiff City by now. I hadn't really begun to know Lennie well. I felt he was a person who kept himself to himself and that's fine - probably more people in football should do the same. For the last few months, we had been hovering around mid-table in the league. Sometimes we managed to get into the top ten but this was no way good enough for our fans and definitely not Sam. The game at Wigan Athletic will always stick in my mind. It was Saturday 16th February 2002. That day we were awful; no fight, no direction. We just couldn't believe what we were watching on the pitch. There were a lot of chants for 'Corky out' but still nowhere near like it had been for Bobby Gould. All the same, there was still a lot of unrest with the fans, especially after this shocking performance. Sam used to say that Corky was one of his family and his babes and that he was like a son (he had been one of his Wimbledon players). This family thing and babes were two of the things which played on my nerves with Sam. I know that Sam cared very deeply about his maternal family but I felt that, if we, Corky or anyone else who he called family really meant anything to him, Corky would not have been treated in the way that he was when everything wasn't going according to the gospel of Sam. After the Wigan game when I was driving my mate Tony back to Bolton my phone rang. It was Sam. He had not been able to attend the match so he rang me to ask me what I had thought of the game. He had regularly done this in the past especially if he had been in America with his family. I said the performance was a disgrace and we had been done time and time again on set pieces. We talked for a good ten minutes. In the car at the time was Joanne, Jamie, Tony and myself and the phone was on 'hands free' whilst I drove; they could all hear this conversation through the speaker in the car. After I had told Sam my feelings, Sam said, "Tonight, Corky will do the honourable thing and resign," and then said goodbye. I couldn't believe what he was saying as he was telling me before he had even spoken to Corky. After Sam had hung up, we all chatted about it. Tony said he would love to speak to Sam. I rang Sam and Tony had a good chat with him and Sam asked him how bad the game had been. Tony described it about five times worse than I did. We then dropped off Tony and I said I would keep him updated on this whole affair.

As we were now driving back to Cardiff, I decided to ring Ian Butts, the Assistant Manager, as I knew he was on the team coach. I asked how everything was. He said that of course they felt down but we would bounce back; we always do, you know that Annis. I then asked how Corky was; he said that he was down too. He also said, "What's with all the questions?" I said, "Nothing, it's OK," but Butts could tell something was up as I kept repeating myself about the display. "Corky's on the coach and you're sure he's OK," I asked. Butts repeated that he knew something was up but I just said, it's nothing and to have a safe journey home. We all said in the car that it was out of order that Sam had told me that Corky will do the honourable thing and resign but hadn't even told Corky himself, his 'footballing son'.

Then on Monday 18th February 2002, the club gave the following press release:

'Following discussions between the club and Alan Cork yesterday, the club announces that Alan will be stepping down as manager with immediate effect'.

Well there you go; another of Sam's babes bites the dust. What's worse is that the four of us knew before Sam had even told Corky. That's the type of thing that makes me lose some of the respect that I had for Sam.

Lennie Lawrence took charge of the team affairs from that Monday and we went on to win 11 and draw 3 out of our next 14 League games including the first leg of the playoffs at Stoke City. Sam's dream was continuing and then suddenly disaster struck. Against all the odds, we lost the return leg at home and the dream was put on hold for the time being. What a ride that season had turned out to be. I for one couldn't moan as we had done our best.

The season wasn't over as far as the BBC was concerned. I received a phone call from Sam. He asked me to pop down the club because it was quite urgent. I went down there and when I arrived, Sam had a videotape in his hand of a BBC programme on Sam, the Club, other fans and I. I said, "Am I allowed to reply to any of this," but no, the BBC once again never let me. Sam didn't seem to be too down about it. In fact, quite the opposite. I don't think he was that bothered at all. But I was. Sam said there was nothing we could do about it although he would love to find out who had been filming undercover at the meeting.

Worse was to come. The FAW fined us £20,000 for the Leeds game which, in my opinion, if the trouble was as bad as the press had said, the fine could have been a lot worse. Russell Goodway called a crisis meeting to discuss the problems which had recently happened. All the different authorities were called to the meeting. As a result of this meeting, the use of the lower grandstand closest to the away fans was to be strictly controlled on who went in. In future games, there was to be a bigger gap between the home and the away fans in the Grange End. Sam also agreed to install extra CCTV at a cost of £500,000. Every season ticket holder and member had to have their photo taken and it was then given to us as an identity card. This fan problem did now start to worry Sam. He didn't want anything to get in the way of the new stadium project.

The media were now really on my back again. The Daily Mirror was again writing stories about Euro 2000 and about my friendship with Sam. They couldn't have had anything more interesting to write about. To me, the world must have stopped functioning. I was old news as far as I was concerned. I had started to think to myself that maybe I should distance myself more from Sam. As for Sam, one minute he seemed to be enjoying all this media attention (and for all the wrong reasons) and then the next, he would show concern. I couldn't understand him on this.

A few months earlier that year I had had a phone call from Jaffa (Alun Griffith) who asked if I could get Sam to donate a football or a shirt signed by the club as they were holding a charity fundraising event in Maesteg Social Club. Jaffa had told me that a City fan called David Roberts had had to sell his season ticket as his child was seriously ill in Great Ormond St Hospital in London and that the family was struggling financially - they had to continuously commute back and forth to London. I said that I could not see a problem and asked when it was. Jaffa said next week. I knew it was short notice. We haven't even told the family what we are going to do. Funnily enough, a few minutes later, Sam phoned me and asked me what I was doing next Friday. I told him that I was going to Maesteg Social Club and the reasons behind it. Sam suddenly said he was too busy and if the football club donated anything then they would be making a precedent; he also said that if they wanted a top, they could come and buy it from the souvenir shop. I was shocked with what he had said. I didn't want to let the family down so I made a few phone calls and the response was fantastic. Ian Butts gave me his Norwich top that he wore when they beat Bayern Munich; Julian Jenkins (without Sam knowing) gave me a ball signed by the team; Steve Day persuaded Mark Bonner to donate something; I gave two of my shirts from my personnel collection which were Scott Young's and Christian Roberts' and to top it all, my friend Tony Reece from the News of the World told Swansea City what was happening and they donated a Swansea shirt signed by the whole team. What an embarrassment that would have been to Sam if we had let this out to the Press. I went to the night with Joanne, Jaffa and Tony Reece and £5,000 was raised that night for the family. Tony Reece bid on the Norwich shirt and paid quite a lot of money for it and then gave it to me as a present. What a kind gesture - thanks Tony. Jaffa told me that he had spoken to Sam two weeks later but he said Sam didn't think it was wrong at all by what he had done. Now that's what I can't figure out about Sam; sometimes he can be quite the opposite and really go out of his way for people and then he does something like this or shall I say did nothing at all.

Yes, that last year I had done some mad and funny things with Sam. I remember Graham Lloyd, a reporter, had written a story about Sam. Sam had said let's teach him a lesson. So he persuaded the youth players to throw an ice-cold bucket of water over him. Graham Lloyd was fuming. He requested his solicitors send Sam letters and threatened to sue him. So Sam got Steve Day and myself to do it to Terry Phillips and show that it could happen to anyone and that it was all a bit of harmless fun. Terry had also had a bet with Sam that we wouldn't win more than ten games that season. If we did, Terry would let himself be thrown in the River Taff. That season, we did win more than ten games but Terry was let off being thrown in the murky waters; instead, he took it on the chin when a bucket of iced water was tipped over his head.

Sam also asked me to post a message on the internet to Celtic football club. He said that they had shown an interest in our player Robert Earnshaw.

'Hello to our Celtic brothers'

'I have just spoken to Sam Hammam and he sends all you Celtic brothers the warmest of greetings and told me that Cardiff is now the biggest Celtic club and while we love Glasgow Celtic, you have to accept you play in a Mickey Mouse League and that if Cardiff were in the English Premiership, we would be much stronger than you financially. If we were in the Premier League, our TV income alone would be bigger than your club. The conclusion is that Robert Earnshaw is worth more than your total club put together and that includes stacking all your players on top of one another and then putting your whole board on top of them. Spoken from Sam'

I have to admit that's when Sam was mad but a good laugh at the same time. Then he would go serious again like when he decided to ban Mark Bloom, the South Wales Echo reporter, from the ground for three months because, once again, Sam disagreed with what he had said. He arranged a meeting of a group of us around the table one night and asked, "What shall we do with him," and that's what Sam came up with. Remember it was Sam's way or no way.

As time went on, I decided to spend more and more time with my family and just stick more to watching the football than being in this so called inner circle as the media called it. I did go out once every few weeks with Sam. Nine times out of ten when he rang me, I would say I was with my family and to be honest I was.

The next season came along and this time Sam would not have taken anything but promotion. He said that he wanted to offload quite a few players who had failed. The problem was everyone was on high wages and a lot of other clubs could not afford them.

One of the games that I was really looking forward to was Nottingham Forest away and I didn't have long to wait, August 23rd 2003. My mate Michael Harvey drove Roy and his son Lewis Jones, Joanne and myself up to Nottingham, I had watched a few games at Forest over the years but I had never seen my team, Cardiff play there, and due to the success Brian Clough had brought them over the years, it felt like we were going to a Premiership club. We stopped off for a drink in a pub called the Robin Hood a couple of miles just before Nottingham, it was full of Cardiff lads, Nils, Jonathan (Docks lads) etc. I didn't see any trouble before the game, but I had heard that there had been plenty in the town centre, not long before kick-off and that about a dozen Docks lads had been fighting with over sixty Forest lads and apparently the

Docks lads had not backed down and quite a few Forest lads had been hurt, even the Forest sports paper that evening showed Forest lad's covered in blood. Even our spotter Simon Insole had had to battle alongside the Cardiff lads and said to me that "Nils and Jonathan had saved his bacon, as he had been attacked as well, but the Cardiff lads had fought one hell of a battle."

The atmosphere in the ground was superb right from the start, Cardiff fans were out in their thousands and Forest certainly knew how to make some good banter. Cardiff from the start were playing some good football and you would have thought we were Premiership the way we attacked Forest. We won the game 2-1 and I and probably all the City fans that were there, thought after this game, this could be our season, so I left the ground feeling great. The police stopped and surrounded all the Cardiff lads as they tried to make their own way back to their vehicles; I was able to walk off with Joanne, Roy, Lewis and Michael. As soon as we turned the corner, I could feel Forest fans were all looking at me, I had had problems at places like Hull and Darlington, with everyone recognising me, thanks to the Panorama programme. I could just feel there was trouble ahead, so I told Joanne, Roy and his son Lewis to walk on the other side of the pavement, they said no at first but I insisted, but Michael walked with me. As we walked up the street, the abuse began, 'Annis your dead', 'Annis you Welsh C...' Michael said to me "We're in trouble," "Without a doubt" I said to Michael, "but just keep walking," we will be attacked, I thought to myself. The abuse just got worse, but we just both kept walking, I could see at the end of the road there was a welcoming committee of about 50 lads just waiting for us. There was no turning back now, within seconds Forest lads just came in to the both of us, but at that very moment a cry of 'Soul Crew, Soul Crew' went up and Forest lads were being attacked from behind by about fifteen Cardiff, led by Taffy Anton and Stan from Abergavenny (lads from the Eighties), they were going hell for leather and Forest lads didn't know what had hit them. Michael and I quickly got in with the Cardiff lot, but I was immediately grabbed by the police saying they had been watching me, I said "Well if you have been watching me then you know I haven't done anything." Their sarcastic answer was, "If you're not looking for trouble go and stand over there with the Forest fans, otherwise you will be arrested," with that Michael arrived in his car, I jumped in along with Joanne, Roy and his son Lewis and we were gone before the police could say another word.

As we were driving out of Nottingham, Roy told me how one of the Forest lads had grabbed Joanne by the throat and called her a 'Welsh c...' I was fuming but there was nothing I could do now. To me that is lower than low. My phone rang when we were driving down the M1, it was Jamie, Joanne's brother, he was saying that it was mental at this very moment and that Nils had formed a line of Cardiff lads in a multi-storey car park on Maid Marion Way and had told everyone of them not to back off, never mind run, I said "Are you ok Jamie?" "Yes" he said, "as they have to get past Nils and Jonathan first before they can get to me." Jamie rang me later to tell us how Forest had damaged four of their vehicles whilst the game was on and had laid in waiting for them all when they got back, but they would not go in to them, due to Nils and Jonathan, they had not forgotten how both of them had knocked a few of their lads out before the game and none of them had any bottle to try again. Eventually the police had arrived and taken control of everything. I've just a few words to say, Forest wrote about me in their book and said how my brand new car had been smashed up and I wasn't too pleased, well I never took my car to Nottingham and the car we came up with went home in the same condition as when we arrived in it, secondly your right I did go home not happy, in fact, I was fuming due to my wife Joanne being attacked by one of your supporters, as I have said earlier that is lower than low.

So back to the football, we had had a cracking start and won three out of our four opening games.

Come December we were top of the league and all was going well for City and Sam. I hadn't seen much of Sam recently as my father's health had been getting worse. Sam still kept up his daily phone calls to me.

On November 30th 2003, Joanne and I went to visit my father in hospital as usual, it was probably my third visit that day, on this occasion my father did not seem to be himself at all, more confused than ever. My father started bringing up a lot of things from the past and telling me who to be wary of and who not to trust, he started to shake as he was warning me about certain people in life and then he calmed down. I was telling him that everything would be ok and that the only people I had and only really ever trusted in life was my late mother and him. My father looked weak, but at the same time was stronger than ever with his words of warning and advice. As he was now looking tired and falling asleep, we both gave him a hug and a goodnight kiss and I said I would see him in the morning and that he would soon be back home.

At about 4am on December 1st 2003, my phone rang with a nurse telling me that she was sorry to say but my father had passed away, I could not think straight and all I remember next was Joanne and I, by my fathers bedside, just writing this now brings tears to my eyes as my father was my life, I don't know how long I stood there just talking to my father, even though he was no longer with us. Joanne had phoned her brother Jamie, who by the time I got home in the early hours of the morning was waiting at our door step, Jamie had got to know my father well in the last 2 years and I could see he was hurting too; Jamie had come to try and console us, thanks Jamie. For the next few days I must have been a nightmare for Joanne as I would walk up and down the landing back and forth, thinking and talking to myself over and over again about my father. Joanne took that week off work, to be with me and help me with all the funeral arrangements. I could not have got through that week without Joanne's help.

As soon as Sam heard that my Father had died, he rang me straight away. Sam attended my father's funeral on Monday December 8th and so did Tony Clemo (ex-City Chairman) who knew my father well. The older Docks people that were still alive all attended, plus many people from all walks of life, including some of the heads of the travelling communities in South Wales. My father had never forgotten his roots and was a very proud man who looked down on no man and gave the same respect to a beggar as he would to a millionaire. I also had great support from the Docks lads my age and City lads who attended in great numbers. I had asked for 'In the Ghetto' by Elvis to be played at the funeral, as to me, this reminded me of my father coming from a rough, poverty stricken, and one of the toughest areas of South Wales and making good of himself, and when the song came on as I walked out the church behind my father's coffin, I could have collapsed, overcome with emotion.

As I walked out of the church, there was just a flash of camera lights from photographers taking photos, I just walked to the car and as I went to get in the car an elderly man with a cap on approached me with a piece of paper in his hand and handed it to me and then said "I am the young boy that your father jumped into the canal many years ago and saved from drowning," he then smiled and said "I am not that young now, but thanks to your father I am here today, I would just like to pay my respects" and then he took of his cap and shook my hand, with tears in my eyes I thanked him for being here. As I got into the car, I noticed the reporters go over to this old gentleman and start writing notes while they were chatting to him, I thought to myself that will be a nice story to be told. I was so wrong, as the following day, there was no mention of this story, a headline of 'Friends and family pay last respects to clubs boss Annis, while his distraught son Annis Jnr looks on' and a picture of me in tears. I should have known; can you ever trust the media to put a good story out? No, they only look for the bad things in life. At home I have the certificate dated 9th April 1935, by the Humane Society, apparently my father could not even swim himself and was 14 years old when he saved him. The piece of paper that he handed me that day told the whole story and he signed it off by saying he would not be here today without my father saving his life, Robert Johnson.

Did I become stronger over the weeks? They say you do, but not a day goes by when I don't think of my parents and I love it when I get stopped all over South Wales by people who have a tale or two to tell me about my parents, whether it's from going to their nightclubs years ago, to my father having helped someone out or to talk to me about a dog they may have had from my mother, I just feel proud listening to their stories, so yes, you do get stronger, but you never forget. One of the hardest things I had to do was to explain to my daughter Annaise that her granddad had gone to heaven and that she would not see him again, Annaise had been coming to the hospital regularly with me and what had pleased me was she had got to know him, as Annaise was not born when my mother was alive, I still talk to Annaise about my father and take her to the cemetery so she never forgets her grandfather.

There wasn't a League game for a couple of weeks and I was glad because all I wanted to do was be with Joanne and my daughter Annaise.

I did travel to every home and away game for the rest of the season. I rarely went out with Sam. On the odd occasion I did go out with him for a meal in the Brassiere, Andy

Legg came with us. At that time Leggy was taking his coaching badges and Sam said that Leggy would have a future with us as a coach when he retired from playing. Like a lot of things, this never happened.

Towards the end of the season we started to falter and only made the play-offs. This turned out to be another great occasion for following Cardiff; we beat Bristol City 1-0 at home. The second leg was at Ashton Gate and the authorities had made it a bubble trip (coaches only). We were only given about 1,500 tickets. Jason Perry contacted me and asked if he could go with the fans. Now Jason was one of my heroes. He was Cardiff through and through. He never made much money out of playing football as he was a one-man club. He gave us ten years great service. He captained us and made over 400 appearances. His nickname was Physco to the City fans because he was never afraid of anyone on the pitch and always gave 110% every time. I remember once standing with him at the Vetch watching Cardiff play - that's what he was like. If he wasn't playing for the City, he would be there supporting them with the fans.

So I booked Jason on our coach to Bristol City away and what a night it was. We drew 0-0 and out sung the Wurzels from the beginning to the end of the game. At the end, the players danced and sang with us on the pitch for well over 30 minutes after the game was over. We were going to the Millennium Stadium in the play-off final. As we walked out of Ashton Gate, we sang, "Cardiff, here we come, Cardiff, Cardiff, here we come." Sam had made our dream come closer again; the Premier League seemed to be not a million miles away anymore.

The final was great in one way because we had 40,000 fans there but, in another way, I preferred the night at Ashton Gate with the loyal fans that I had known for years. Sam wanted to ride an elephant or, if not, have an elephant lead us from Ninian Park to the Millennium with thousands behind the elephant. Health and Safety put paid to that idea!

The final was a tense affair and it looked like it was going into penalties when Lennie Lawrence, the Manager, took a massive gamble. He took off our top scorer Earnie to which the unhappy crowd booed. He replaced him with Andy Campbell who had practically failed since we signed him from Middlesbrough. Within a minute, Campbell had scored the winner and the whole of Cardiff erupted. That night was a night to remember. The whole of the City celebrated. We were promoted. Sam had achieved two promotions in three years. We were now certainly living the dream.

We were now in the Championship and just one Division away from the Promised Land, the Premiership. The stadium project seemed to have slowed down; the Welsh Assembly had threatened to call it all off or so the rumour went. The day he sold Robert Earnshaw, I had a massive row with Sam. He had always said that we would never sell our prized assets because without them, we would never make it to the top flight. He had said too many times that we would never be a selling club. Clubs like West Bromwich Albion, who he had sold Earnie too in 2004, would always be a feeder club. Then Sam really wound me up when he said that the money from Earnie would be put to good use and would buy four to five new players. That turned out to be a lie and I was now fed up with all the bullshit. I had always believed in what he had said. If Sam had just told me the truth that he had overspent and that the plans for the stadium were draining his resources then I would have understood the reason for selling quality players.

During the time that I never saw him, he went around with Gwyn, Big Sam, Vince, Corky and many others. I still remained loyal to my club and that's who you support no matter who comes or who goes. Thousands of other fans deserted the team and the crowds went down to below 10,000 at some games. Yet only three years ago, 17,000 were down at Ninian Park. Where had the 7,000 gone? We were still in the Championship.

Ian Butts (Assistant Manager) had been a friend of mine and to this day I can say he is an honourable person in the football world. Before I wrote this piece, I rang him to check that it was alright. Even though he was then the Assistant Manager at Hartlepool, his family still live in Cardiff (his one son is now a City fan) and he was driving to Cardiff at the time. Butts still has a soft spot for City and looks out for our results every week. One day, out of the blue, Lennie Lawrence called Butts into his office and said that he had the unpleasant job of telling him that he was being released. Sam, where were you? To this day, I don't know why Butts was sacked and I'm not saying it because he is my friend but he was a good reserve team manager and the results showed that. After Butts heard the news of his dismissal, he went and picked up all his personal stuff and drove away from Ninian Park. He drove past the Ninian Park pub and stopped at the traffic lights and on the billboard was his name and that he had been released. He couldn't believe it as he had only just been told less than five minutes ago and yet the Echo already knew that morning. This type of action hurt Butts. To me, surely Butts should have been the first to know and, in my opinion, that's when Sam never showed respect to people he didn't want to know anymore.

The fans were now turning on Sam but deep down I still liked him a lot. He had been there for me when my parents passed away and he had stuck with me after Brussels 2000. I had been living the dream with him from the start. I actually thought about ringing him but I never did. Maybe I should have. I had changed my number since the sale of Earnie as I was that hurt by Sam. Over the next year, I thought about it hard and long but was still too hurt because of all his lies to me.

One day my phone rang. Sam said, "Where are you?" I replied that I was in my house and Sam said, "I'm outside. Can I come in? I need your help." Sam came in and we gave each other a big hug and Sam said, "Hey baby, I've missed you." Joanne went and poured Sam and I a drink and then brought our new baby daughter, Alexandra, to meet Sam. A year had gone by since I had last seen Sam and the stories that had been coming out of the club were horrendous. We had also become a selling club again but not just a selling club - we seemed to be willing to sell anyone that other clubs were willing to buy.

I had heard that Kavanagh was told if he didn't go to Wigan that day, the club would go under. A helicopter was sent for him and he was sent packing with tears in his eyes. Wages weren't being paid and, in the papers, the club kept stating it was just a computer problem yet staff members were telling everyone a different story. I had also been told that any staff members who were moaning about not getting their wages, Sam had called traitors. I heard this from some of the staff and other persons close to Sam. The debts that I had been told about were that the club owed over thirty million pounds which turned out to be true. It was bad enough having these debts but, at the same time, the crowds had gone lower and lower. Everyone was saying we would be relegated. I will always remember that Sam had once stated to me and others on a different occasion, "I don't do relegation," and that's true. Sam has never had a team relegated whilst he had been the owner. It had gone that bad at Ninian Park that a section of the crowd had actually abused him after a home game outside the main gates of the club. The dream had been fading fast, virtually as fast as Sam had initially got it going.

I asked Sam how he had got my new phone number and he replied from the ticket office. Of course, every time I renewed my season ticket, I always write my telephone number down. I asked Sam how things were and he said the fans were deserting him and he wanted to know why? With Sam, you don't know whether he is really asking you that and does he want the truth or does he just want you to be all over him like a lot of fans had been and had become his 'yes' men. Before I answered him, I thought to myself he wants the truth as he knew I'd never been a 'yes' man to him.

So I told Sam straight. "You lied to them and me. You should have said the club was in trouble financially and not said you were selling players to buy more players. You should never have tried to change our name, our badge which you did and even though it pleased some, it annoyed a lot more. You banned mascots. You said we had no history before you took over. You're outspoken, but so am I, but the problem with that is you made enemies in the Council and while, you are the owner, I can never see them allowing us the new stadium. Your hatred for rugby upset many in the Council as well but I joked that I agreed with him on that one. "Sam," I said "you sold the players we all loved and broke the heart of the team and when I was by your side at the meetings, you swore to the fans we would never be a selling club again." Sam had let me speak for over an hour and then said, "We will start up the mascots again and your daughter Annaise can be the first one." "No chance," I said. "Sam, there are hundreds of young children who have been waiting these past years, just go out there and publicly apologise." With that, Sam stood up and began stomping up and down my lounge saying that I was a fucking loser and that he would do it without me. Sam was incensed and his face was twisted with rage. He suddenly turned towards me and said it again that I was a 'fucking loser'. He was venting all his anger at me. Why me, I thought? I had only ever been Sam's friend since the first moment he arrived in

Cardiff. I wasn't to blame for Sam's feelings. I said nothing, as Sam didn't give me a chance. No matter what I could have said at that moment, it would have been wrong in Sam's eyes. He then stormed out of my house without another word being said, leaving Joanne and I standing there with our mouths open.

Going back to what I said about Sam upsetting people, there was a very strong rumour doing the rounds that Sam had upset the new leader of Cardiff Council, Rodney Berman who had replaced Russell Goodway. At a meeting, Sam's usual swear words had come out but apparently he had gone too far and mentioned a sexual aid. This was Sam's problem and during these years he had upset too many people. That day in my house, Joanne and I had been left so stunned by how Sam had turned on me that we didn't speak about it for ten minutes after Sam had left. About one hour later my phone rung and guess what, it was Sam. "Hey baby, I think we should meet up tonight and discuss the whole situation again and have a meal together." I just said that I was going out but he was persistent as usual and, in the end, I said I would go for a meal in the Holland House hotel in a few days time with Joanne and him and that I wouldn't be spoken to like that again. We did go for a meal with Sam and this time Sam was totally calm and to me he seemed to want to undo a lot of the things that he had done wrong.

On the field, the club was not doing so well and the fans had started once again to turn on the manager. This time, it was Lennie Lawrence who was getting it in the neck. Like I said earlier, Lennie had kept himself to himself and just got on with the job. Many thought he was too much of a gentleman when things started to go wrong on the pitch. I don't think Sam had been concentrating as much about what was happening on the pitch anymore. He was now too involved in trying to keep the club afloat. Sam realised that he needed help fast and to the amazement of the fans and me; Sam brought in Peter Ridsdale, the ex-Leeds United chairman who, to a lot of Leeds fans, had become their number one enemy. Did we have two similar chairmen I thought and probably thousands of other City fans thought the same. Only time would tell on that question. It did cross my mind that maybe Peter Ridsdale has already been through what Sam was going through now. Maybe he was the best man to help him out of the situation.

I remember going to a game at Reading away with Jamie, and Joanne and Jamie spotted Peter Ridsdale parking up. We went over to his car. I had a cap on and decided to stay in the background while Jamie couldn't wait to ask Ridsdale some questions. I remember Jamie saying sarcastically, "Are you Sam's new partner?" Ridsdale calmly replied, "I'm not Sam Hammam's partner. I only work for him. I'm only here to do a job. I could tell you a few things and maybe one day, you'll find out," and with that he moved away from his car and said, "I've must go now chaps." That was our first meeting with Peter Ridsdale and at least he spoke to us. At the same time, he put us straight and showed he had his own identity.

As the weeks went, by I started to speak to Sam more and more. I was actually starting to feel sorry for him. Sam was coming under increasing pressure not only from the fans but also the Inland Revenue - they were owed 1.7 million pounds. We were only days away from being closed down. Sam and Ridsdale went to the Inland Revenue and Sam kept saying you can't shut us down, just speak to my consultant Peter Ridsdale but they wouldn't speak to Ridsdale because he wasn't a director. Within days, Sam made Ridsdale a director. Sam told Ridsdale he had to sort out this debt first. Ridsdale then met Terry Brown from West Ham and a deal on Gabbidon and Collins was done which was reported to be worth over £3 million. This now gave Sam and the club a breathing space once again. The fans weren't happy, myself included. We never knew the real reasons for the sale of our two most prized assets at the time. I just kept getting these sob stories from Sam that this was needed if we were to stay on course for the new stadium.

It was never really the same between Sam and me now for quite a long time. I never knew anymore if he was telling me the truth or only half a story. All I wanted from Sam was the truth even if it was bad news, I would still though stand by him or stand up to anyone who dared slate or be critical of him, as I would remind myself where were we before Sam came on board and who else wanted to know Cardiff City ? No one and as far as I was concerned Sam was my friend and was there for me, when most people had turned their backs on me. If I wanted to fall out with him, well that was just between him and me, but I would still be there for him if he ever needed me.

I did hear that while Lennie Lawrence was on a coaching course abroad, Sam and Ridsdale went to the Landmark Hotel in London and had a meeting with Dave Jones, the former Stockport and Everton manager. Within days, it was goodbye Lennie. We'll never know who was really in charge when Lennie was there; some say Sam had been the boss all along but I say, thank you Lennie, you did your best and, to work under Sam, I can only say I feel you did pretty well. The arrival of Dave Jones and the signings of Darren Purse, Glenn Loovens and the year long loan of Jason Koumas did have the fans thinking that maybe it is going to start getting better again. It also calmed down a lot of the talk of us going out of business. But overall the fans had lost their belief in Sam and the dream had virtually ended.

My Mother & Father

Thursday December 4 2003

Nightclub king Annis dies, aged 82
'He loved cabaret, his work and life'

Sian Harris
sian.harris@wme.co.uk

ONE of Tiger Bay's biggest characters, credited as the man who brought the first legal nightclub to Cardiff, has died.

Flamboyant entrepreneur Annis Abraham Snr, who owned 48 nightclubs and hotels in his lifetime, passed away on Monday, aged 82.

His son Annis Abraham Jnr, with whom he ran many of his businesses, said: "My father is what I lived for. If it was not for him today I would be nobody. I am the proudest person of my father and what he did."

Tiger Bay-born Mr Abraham worked his way up from a docklands errand boy to nightclub king, employing numerous stars including Tom Jones, Engelbert Humperdinck and Shirley Bassey.

In 1958 he opened El Cuba – Cardiff's first coffee bar – and a year later held the city's first nightclub licence. He was also the first to hold a casino licence.

Among his many businesses, which were based in Cardiff, the Valleys, the north of England and Majorca, he always said his favourite was Tito's, in Greyfriars Road.

His colourful story started when,

■ **COLOURFUL CHARACTER** Annis Abraham in one of his clubs.

aged 13, he received a Royal Humane Society award for rescuing a drowning child from the Glamorganshire canal. In 1951 after witnessing a docklands shooting he seized the gun and held the suspect until the police arrived.

He was fiercely proud of his Egyptian heritage – his father was Egyptian – and it often influenced the nightclubs he designed. As a young man he also worked as a candyfloss seller, a taxi driver and car salesman, as well as serving in the RAF.

Bert Pooley, a friend of nearly 60

years, said: "He was a self-made man who never forgot his humble beginnings. He loved cabaret, his work and life. He always made his clubs so the working man could go in."

Mr Abraham was devoted to his wife Dawn and after her death in November 2000 his health deteriorated and he suffered several strokes. His funeral is at St Mary the Virgin Church, Bute Street, Cardiff, at 11.30am on Monday. He leaves a two-year-old granddaughter Annaise.

■ **FINAL FAREWELL** Annis Abraham's coffin is carried out of the church, while his distraught son, Annis Junior, looks on.
PICTURE: Richard Swingler

Tuesday December 9 2003

Friends and family pay last respects to clubs boss Annis

IN bitter cold, friends and family of nightclub baron Annis Abraham gathered to pay their respects at St Mary the Virgin Church, in Bute Street, Cardiff.

The well-known businessman made his final journey in a silver hearse followed by two limousines which pulled into the courtyard behind the church at 11.30am yesterday.

Flowers surrounded his coffin, with two white carnation wreaths reading simply "Dad". Among the mourners

was Cardiff City chairman Sam Hammam.

Docks-born Mr Abraham, 82, pictured right, had worked his way up from errand boy to nightclub king, owning 48 nightclubs and hotels in the UK and abroad during his career.

As four pallbearers walked into the large church the first bars of Silent Night played out, marking the start of the service.

Mr Abraham was proud of his Egyptian heritage, and passed on his busi-

ness acumen to son Annis Junior.

"I loved you so much and was, and still am, so proud of you," read a card placed on one wreath.

"To grandad – me and Melissa will always love you. Thank-you for everything, love Melissa and Loretta xxx," said another.

Mr Abraham was devoted to his wife Dawn, and after her death in November 2000 his health deteriorated and he suffered several strokes.

218

CHAPTER TWENTY TWO

THE LOVES OF MY LIFE AND LOSING A FRIEND

I now had another battle on my hands, the mother of my daughter Annaise was determined to try and stop me seeing Annaise and I had to file a case in the County Courts in Cardiff, it seemed to take forever to get to court, all I wanted was equal time with Annaise, but in this world a father has to prove himself to be a worthy father and that's just to see their daughter, while a mother it seems can play all the dirtiest tricks under the sun and just sit back while a father is deprived of his rights to be with his daughter. I had heard and read so many stories about fathers always coming off the worst, it was going that way for me at one stage and my mind could not concentrate on anything but the court cases, I would dream of them and sometimes I would be hurting so much, poor Joanne could not even get a proper conversation out of me, just thinking that I might not see Annaise was killing me inside. I am not going to go through the whole ordeal in this book as it's a book on its own, I will just touch on a few things that I had to go through, I had to fight in court just to have my daughter overnight, just to take her to school, just to go on holiday with her, just to see her without the mother being present, it is endless what I had to fight for. Over forty times I went to court and every time orders were granted to me, but within weeks I was having to go back again as the mother had come up with more lies against me and then even Joanne. My problem was that because I had never lived with the mother and I never had parental responsibility, I had to start from the beginning, thankfully my name was on the birth certificate, I proved Annaise had stayed anything up to four nights a week in the past with us and I had kept every receipt of all the things I had bought Annaise for the last few years. I was paying for every court case whilst the mother had legal aid and it felt like her solicitors were loving it, as letters were coming to me non-stop and sometimes I thought there was no reason behind them, all I cared about was the welfare of my daughter and being able to be with her. These cases went on for at least three years, I can understand why many fathers give up, but I was never going to, as to me Annaise, other than Joanne was all I had after losing my parents. Joanne supported me all the way and studied every case with me, this in my opinion was making Annaise's mother even more determined to try and stop me seeing my daughter.

I got my solicitor to ask for a welfare officer to be assigned to my case, this took months and at first it was nerve racking as she was so cold to me and knew my whole past, not being married and not having my parents alive did not help my cause, I reminded the Welfare officer that I had met the mother and had been seeing her during my troubles in Brussels in the year 2000.Once she saw Annaise with me and Joanne and then got to know us all, a file was written up and sent to the court. She rang me to tell me the report was concluded and asked would I rather wait to see what was written and read it with my solicitor or would I like to know now what she had written in it. I said I would like to know now and with that she said "I have supported your application for Shared Residence," on hearing those words, my eyes filled up with tears and I could hardly get a word out of my mouth, I just kept saying "Thank you, thank you," she said she would next see me in court and that day turned out to be one of the happiest days I have ever had or experienced in my life after more than three years of battling for my daughter. I was drained through these court cases and I had neglected my businesses, but to me it had certainly all been worth it. I had sunk so low, that I had even gone to see a fortune teller by the name of Sheila. Sheila worked from her home and had moved down here from Staffordshire with her husband who loved football and supported Rotherham Utd, Jonathan a good friend of mine, his mother gave me Sheila's number, but for months I didn't ring it. Well when I did, I even gave a false name. I arranged to see Sheila and I was stunned by some of the things she came out with and only I would have known these things. But all I really wanted to know was about Annaise, which she finally hit on, by saying court case papers, not a criminal case, heartache etc.

I started going more and more to see her, by the way I apologised to Sheila for giving a false name to her, and she just laughed at me and said rub your father's ring you're wearing, whenever you need help. I probably sound potty saying that I went to see a fortune teller and I must be mad. Well I don't regret it one bit, she would tell me it straight whether I liked it or not and she gave me belief before every court case when I had been battling for my daughter. Sheila would say how the case would go and how the forthcoming months would be leading up to the cases. After the second visit Sheila refused any money, point black, so I used to leave flowers at her door after every reading. We have become very good friends and in fact, I started to feel embarrassed, as after I took my children to visit her, every time we popped in for a coffee, Sheila had presents for them. We have now been good friends for over seven years and I had no hesitation in inviting Sheila and Brian to my wedding. Sheila never advertises and stars from all over Britain come down to see her, people can believe what they want but Sheila turned out to be not just a good friend but a big help to me when I was so down in life.

Times have dramatically changed regarding Annaise as she is now old enough to speak up for herself and we are closer than ever. The mother and I are now on speaking terms and work together for what's best for Annaise.

Joanne and I had now had a baby girl together called Alexandra. who was born on the 11th September 2005 and Annaise had even been with us both right up to the giving birth of Alexandra and a nurse had allowed Annaise to come in to see her sister

Alexandra and Joanne within minutes of Alexandra being born at just past midnight. The following day I told Annaise that I wanted to marry Joanne and she smiled and said "Can I be bridesmaid," so the two of us went to the hospital and in front of Annaise and our new born baby Alexandra, I asked Joanne to marry me and when she said yes it was like Annaise was more excited than myself as she would not stop hugging and kissing Joanne, to me this is surely what every man in this world would ever want.

As to Cardiff City, the season ahead looked like it was going to be a case of surviving both on and off the pitch, the club were now skint and on the pitch we were struggling in the first few months, we had our usual win against the once mighty Leeds Utd, but overall the season never really took off and the crowds dipped many times below 10,000. After the New Year we had a decent run and at one stage looked like we would make the play-offs, but then that was followed by one win in our last nine league games. What did shock me was finishing the season in the top half of the league and managing not to go bust off the pitch. Taking over 6,000 fans to Highbury was probably my highlight of the season, we became the last ever team to score and play there in the FA Cup before Arsenal moved to their new stadium The Emirates, I went with my wife Joanne and my brother in law Jamie and of course Annaise, we lost the game 2-1 but it had been a good day out with a superb atmosphere created by Cardiff fans.

The pre-season tours in Scotland, Sweden and Denmark over the last few years had been more enjoyable than the actual seasons themselves. No police in your face and going to watch Cardiff abroad for me are some of the best times I've had watching City, the trips are just so relaxing and are about just having a laugh and a good time. In the old days going to places like Standard Liege and Admira Wacker in the Cup Winners Cup will always be up there as some of the best times I've ever had following Cardiff.

I was getting married on July 29th 2006 and I had invited Sam, Nida (Sam's wife) and Jason the club secretary to the wedding. When Sam received the invitation, he rang me and said, "We may have a problem boss but I will sort it." Over the next month, Sam was first of all telling me that he was going to come to the church, then dash off and see City play our only pre-season home friendly game on the Saturday and then come back for the night reception, then next he said that we won't play on the Saturday, I will make sure no matter what that Saturday 29th July will be kept football free and Sam kept his word. Months went by and Sam refused bigger clubs than Udinese (Italian side) who eventually played City on a Friday night as the bigger clubs would only play City on that Saturday. We got married in my local church in Marshfield, where I had lived when I was 7years old and opposite was the school which I had attended when I saw my first Cardiff game and had now moved back there after moving around all over the UK and abroad and had lived in 28 houses and gone to 14 different schools growing up with my parents, it certainly had been an experience, I can tell you that, but that was how my parents and I had made our money doing up run down houses and nightclubs and selling them on, whilst looking for the next place and it did not matter where it was, as long as there was money to be made we would go there.

Of all the hotels we could have chosen to have our wedding at, we chose the Holland House hotel where Sam Hammam had spent his last years having his chats and planning Cardiff City's future with us.

The wedding day went well and was one of the happiest days of my life. Friends of mine who all follow the club, Bradley, Vince, Matthew, Joff, Jaffa, Beer, Nils, Rusty, Dio, Bear, Big Sam, Top man, Lakey, Frankie, Tony Reece, Daryl, Lee Beames, Simon, Ben and Mojo all came and mixed well with all the other lads who I had met over the years following football such as Fat Pat from Chelsea, Dave from Crystal Palace, Muffy from Leeds, Paul from Millwall and Steven, known as Brummy, from Birmingham. I thought the day went superbly as the lads mixed and laughed with other friends of mine who came from all walks of life, accountants, solicitors, newspaper reporters and even a QC. Ninety percent of the conversations that day were about City. Even in all the speeches, the word 'Bluebirds' kept cropping up. Sam was given a lot of attention by the lads from the other clubs because, like the Jacks had said before, their chairman didn't even know they existed. That was exactly the same for these lads, and yes, like Sam or hate him, in the football world, he was a showman and was still a big name.

One of the most dreaded parts of the wedding I was not looking forward to was the first dance in the evening, as I can't dance, so I had a word with the DJ, without Joanne knowing and said when you call the Bride and Bridegroom up for the first dance, make sure within a minute of the record playing, you call the guests on to the dance floor, which he did and also my daughter Annaise was a great help as she joined in the dance within thirty seconds, thanks, you were both life savers. We also had an Elvis impersonator to sing later on and I had him sing "In the Ghetto " as a remembrance to my father and of where he had started from and to let my parents know I was thinking about them on one of the happiest days of my life.

We took the children to Majorca for two weeks after the Wedding and then Joanne and I went to Mexico for a week, which turned out to be one of the best holidays I've ever had, I would recommend Mexico to anyone, beautiful place, perfect weather, lovely people and to top it all, you certainly get your money's worth.

When I arrived back from my honeymoon the new season had already started and you could feel that Sam wasn't totally running the show anymore. We were still selling our star players; even our top striker Cameron Jerome was sold. Jason Koumas didn't sign even though Sam had been promising us that he would. I had the feeling that Sam couldn't write the cheques anymore and that Peter Ridsdale was running the show. Ridsdale had been brought in to stop the crisis; you could say even stop the club from folding. He had done that so far and we were still in the Championship. The new stadium project also seemed to be on stop. The Council was fed up with Sam not giving them all the details of a £24 million pound loan that Sam had taken out. The stories became bigger and bigger about these millions of pounds worth of loan notes but no one could and still never have found out where they had come from. Sam said Langston, an overseas company, lent them to Cardiff City and that without this money, the club would not have continued.

Anyway all this didn't seem to matter to a lot of City fans as long as the team was winning. 2006-2007 season got off to a winning start with a 2-1 away win at Barnsley and this sent the near 1,700 fans home happy, not only with the result but also with the way our football was being played. By August 26th 2006, we were top of the Championship and packing out Ninian Park. A pity that we hadn't done this more in Sam's earlier years. Alexander, McNaughton, Purse, Loovens, Chopra, Thompson, McPhail, Parry, Johnson, Ledley and Scimeca were all on fire and with Dave Jones managing; maybe Sam's dream had come alive again. The fans were singing right through September, "That's why we're top of the League" as we started thrashing Luton, Southend and Wolves. I was, for the first time in all my years of following the club, beginning to believe that nothing was going to stop us. We were going to the Promised Land, 'The Premiership'. I know the season was only two months old but when you're a fan and you feel your team is playing like Brazil, you'll believe anything. I was just totally following the City and I didn't want to listen to anymore of the politics. If you want the truth, the politics of football had actually taken the buzz out of watching my team. Knowing what I've seen behind the scenes these last thirteen years has taken some of the enjoyment out of following my beloved team. I actually enjoyed it more in the late Seventies and during the Eighties - all I knew was what I saw in front of me, whether it was good or bad or indifferent, I just enjoyed it.

Whilst we were enjoying our football, little did we know that Sam was being forced out and one of the main reasons was no stadium, no future; yes, it was one of Sam's sayings. The Council would never allow the stadium to have the final go ahead as long as Sam was the owner of the club. So all the other directors knew that Sam had to go, if the club were to have any future. Personally I believe Sam was being stabbed in the back by people around him who worked in the club, but that's just my belief.

On October 21st 2006, I spoke to Sam and he said he was stepping down for the good and future of the club. At that point, he slagged down nobody. Later that day, we were playing away to Norwich and lost 1-0. We had just won our previous five League games and were six points clear at the top of the Championship. The fans didn't want to hear all the boardroom squabbles once again, not when we were in the best dream of our lives. After and including this match, we only went on to win two out of the next eighteen matches. Had the passion gone? Had Sam's influence gone? Was it just a coincidence that the day Sam announced he was stepping down, the team crumbled from world-beaters to total no hopers. Sam didn't officially resign until January 2007 and, instead of leaving the club still as a hero in the minds of many, somehow it was destroyed and any love they had for him had vanished with it.

One of the new directors of the consortium who took over the control of Cardiff City was Mike Hall (ex-rugby) and after the deal was completed, Mike Hall publicly stated how hard it had been to negotiate with Sam and that they had to pay Sam's company Rudgwick Holdings £500,000 and £90,000 to Sam's brother. Hall said, "That was money which would have been spent on players but instead it has gone into Sam's pocket. It was the only way the deal was going to be done. I know people say he is a complex character but, at the end, it was total greed and self-interest. It was amazing but football is a murky world."

When Sam attended his final home game at Ninian Park (28th October 2006 Derby County),which eventually turned out to be his last ever visit to Ninian Park, Sam popped in with his wife and daughter to my house before the game. We chatted for ten minutes and it was quite emotional. I was very sad to see this happening and I could see in Sam's eyes and his manner that day that this was hurting him very much. After he had left, I read the message he had written on the booklet that he had made shortly after taking over the Club called 'Follow the dream, an overview 2000' by Sam Hammam.

'To my friend Annis, here is to the long sweet memories, may the dream continue'
Love
Sam Hammam 28/10/06.

You see, when a man like Sam writes that to you, how can you dislike the man? Sam had never really done anything personally bad to me, Sam had actually always been there for me, if I had ever needed anything or was ever feeling down. Yes, he lied but maybe he thought the problem would go away if he did get the stadium. I also believe that nearly seven years of battling to get the stadium and the promotions at the same time had aged Sam and I didn't think he was the same man compared to when he had arrived. I felt like I had lost a very close friend as Sam seemed a broken man with his heart torn out, but I would always be there for him, like he was for me if he ever he needed support against those that betrayed him.

In a couple of press conferences, Sam actually forgot the name of Riccy Scimeca and the press had to remind him of who the latest signing was. When he went to introduce Neil Cox, Sam said, "Where are you?" Neil Cox replied, "Sam, I'm here." I feel Sam had become tired and his sharpness had gone. Seven years ago Sam was one of the fastest people ever on the names of footballers.

Sam had started to lose his temper more if things weren't going his way and if you disagreed with him, he just lost it. We had a meeting on one occasion up in the Canton stand and he requested some of his old football family to attend and about forty of us did. Now this word 'family' that Sam had virtually used every day to the fans, in my opinion came back to haunt him. If ever a fan disagreed with him during a meeting, he would try and shout them down, belittle them or just tell them to fuck off. I witnessed this on many occasions and one in particular stands out. This was when Peter Morgan from the valleys who owns his own pub, once asked Sam at this meeting, "Sam, why are you selling all our players and not replacing them?" Instead of Sam just talking back to Peter Morgan in a civil tone or maybe telling us the truth, Sam said, "What do you know about running a football club? All you know about is running a pub so stick to your pub." Now Peter Morgan is one of the hard-core loyal fans and a very emotional person but he had dared to ask Sam a question that Sam didn't like and Sam had turned on him. That, in my opinion, is when Sam used to let himself down and this started to make the fans lose respect for him. I personally wouldn't treat my so-called 'family' like that.

Sam had upset so many people in his seven years at Cardiff including players from the past who were legends to the City fans. Phil Dwyer and Don Murray are just two names to mention. They weren't made to feel welcome at the club anymore. To Sam, they were part of Cardiff City history, not his history. Phil Dwyer holds the record for number of appearances for the club. I have known him since I was fourteen years old when we both used to live in the same village of Wenvoe. I will never forget him. When I used to travel to the away games as a kid, he would always have a ticket for me and in those days they weren't left in envelopes. He would have to come out of the entrance of the away ground and I'd be there. Sometimes at places like Charlton on a Tuesday night, he would give me three or four tickets for my mates. Phil and Jason Perry were two players who really were Cardiff City through and through and had genuine love for the club and the fans. They are our history and they are proud to be part of it and we as fans are proud of the contribution they have made to the history of the club. So Sam you were totally wrong on this. A BBC reporter was allegedly marched out of Ninian Park and his tape taken out of his recorder before he left. That type of incident is never forgotten with reporters and one day, that incident will come back and haunt you.

As the months went by after Sam's departure, City slid down the table fast and even after we had a mini revival with a couple of wins in January and February, the passion to succeed and the dream that Sam had given us had finally gone. The team finished the season with just one win in their last eleven League games. I will say it again. Was it a coincidence that, when Sam stepped down, it all went wrong? Remember the day Sam was forced to announce he was leaving, we were runaway leaders of the Championship and the passion was still there with the fans at that point and the team. Should Peter Ridsdale and the new board of directors have strengthened the team when all the injuries occurred and the players seemed to have lost their confidence? That is the question that I have asked myself, time and time again. I really felt that we were giving up that season especially as I have never felt so on top of the world as I did during those first few months. I had seen many promotions over the years and near misses but I had never seen us on top of this Division before. What really went wrong?

Sam phoned me out of the blue during the bad months after he had left and, during our conversation, he said to me, "I wish I had signed Jason Koumas for £2 million and put us in more debt but I would have got us to the Premier League." In all fairness, I believe a player like Koumas was the type of player that was missing but we couldn't have taken on any more debt and the banks were closing in on us. You can look at the other side of it. If we had reached the Promised Land, over £50 million would have been given to us.

Sam also made me aware that he had heard that I had stuck up for Peter Ridsdale and he sort of insinuated that I had downed him to which I explained that I had been asked by Terry Phillips what I thought of Ridsdale after Ridsdale had rung me and we had spoken for over 50 minutes. I said that I had been wrong and Ridsdale seemed very passionate about the club. "As to me downing you," I said, "Sam, if you've read it, I never downed you once and I have told Ridsdale that I will never side with him over you, never!"

When Sam had stepped down, it was announced that all the debts would be cleared because firstly, the Council would now give the go-ahead for the new stadium and secondly, the £24 million of loan notes taken out by Sam (when he was the owner) to secure the club's future did now not have to be paid back to Langston, the company who loaned them, until 2016. To this day, no one and I mean no one other than Sam seems to know who they are. I have asked Sam straight on a number of occasions, "Are you Langston?" and he says, "100%, no." So the fans were told the future would now be great.

It seemed to start to get better and better off the field. On the 4th May 2007, the Council agreed and signed the go ahead for the new stadium, totally unconditional. Peter Ridsdale had been negotiating with the Council and it seemed that the future was once again looking bright. The papers were all writing about the club going forward and Ridsdale had been the one to take us forward. I have a strong opinion on this issue. Yes, Ridsdale did fit the final piece in the jigsaw for the new stadium and I know for a fact that he has worked tirelessly on the project but I, for one, no matter how I feel that Sam has let us down, I believe that Sam Hammam is the man who deserves some recognition for this new stadium. He started the project and put seven years of his life into it and this stadium was part of his dream for Cardiff City's future. Over the next few weeks, I popped down to the new site in Leckwith opposite Ninian Park to see the bulldozers had moved in and the work had finally started.

But trouble was once again looming over the club; has it ever not been? Langston says they want their money back now and, within months, the club was involved in a court case. We were told we might go into administration and, by the way, all this suddenly happened just after the sale of Chopra for £5million. Does it sound like a coincidence?

This is the way that I saw it, at the time and this is only my opinion on this threat of administration. If we go into administration, Langston would get nothing and Cardiff

City Football Club would lose ten points; however, the directors and chairman would owe nothing anymore and the slate would be wiped clean. So I can't understand why the newspapers and everyone were saying Langston was going to bankrupt us or put us into administration. To me, that was never going to happen. They stood to lose everything. I could only ever see the club putting itself into administration. That's my opinion. I also believe a lot of this is just scaremongering. I have spoken to Sam and Peter Ridsdale on this situation many times and I still haven't really reached the bottom of it.

Sam over the next four months had rung me only about five times. One of them was on the weekend of December 15th 2007. Sam didn't sound his usual self to me and seemed very down and withdrawn as though he had given up. He kept repeating to me that he was only trying to help Cardiff City Football Club. I was worried about Sam, if I am honest, as he really sounded a beaten and broken man. But I need not have worried as within weeks, he sounds like his old self once again. Sam's first words were, "Annis Abraham, you have bought shares in Cardiff City?" "Yes I have Sam, and if rugby people are going to make money out of my club then so am I." Sam then said, "If you were owed money, wouldn't you want it back?" "Of course," I said. "Well, why do you Cardiff fans just sit there and just talk to each other and do nothing about it?" I really couldn't work out why or what he meant by this. We fans aren't owed anything. It's Langston that's owed money and Sam says that he is not Langston so why is he going on about it so much?

On Friday 4th January 2008, Sam phoned again and wished my family and myself a happy New Year. Sam said he was glad to see Cardiff City doing so well to which I replied, "Yes, it's great." Then his voice and conversation changed when he said, "These people want to take as much out of the club as they can. The club will be put into administration." He then called Terry Phillips, a sports writer of the South Wales Echo, a 'brownie'. I asked Sam if he was losing interest in Cardiff City with which he said, "Me losing interest? You see Langston is going to win, that is a fact, in my opinion. I can't say how the club will do. The only thing on earth that the directors of the club want to do is to take the club into administration. They want to sell as many players and get as much money as they can and then get their money. That is their plan and that is why they are selling to be ready to take the club into administration. You see, I feel the danger is Langston do not really want to run football."

After Sam had finally stopped for some air, I asked him that if the club went into administration then Langston wouldn't get anything, would they? With that Sam said, "It isn't like that. That's what Peter Ridsdale is saying it is like but it is not like that at all. I don't think it's like that, Annis. The important thing for me at the moment is that I would be able to protect the football side. If I lose because Langston doesn't want to do football, as long as they or whoever is owed money get what they want, nobody wants to be running the football side of things. That's it, say fuck it, and I don't want to do anymore. It will be very bad for the club. That's what I have been sticking around for."

I wasn't really sure what Sam was going on about but it seemed to me that he still wanted to be involved with Cardiff City yet only a few weeks before he said goodbye forever to the club. Sam still continued, with me just sitting back and listening.

"I know, Annis, I think I have been let down by the fans to be fair. I am not angry with anyone or anybody." Sam went on to say how much love he still had for football and I believe that. He said Jimmy Floyd Hasselbaink and Robbie Fowler had proved to be no good and he reminded me that he had told me this when they were first signed. He had a small go at the fans again by saying the fans had proved to be ineffective. "What are they doing just sitting there?"

Sam finished off the conversation with, "The club is going into administration, every action they are doing is pointing this way." With that, Sam said he had to go. It was 4th January 2008 and for quite a while I didn't hear another word from him. I did want more questions answered and I will never believe the dream that Sam had taken us on was purely money driven. I honestly believe deep down Sam was in love with Cardiff City, but he had felt he had been stabbed in the back and had the club taken away from him and he had not been able to do a single thing about it and that this had hurt him and he was angry, would you not be if you had been in his position?

CHAPTER TWENTY THREE

PETER RIDSDALE

The name Peter Ridsdale, ex-Leeds United Chairman, did make nearly all Cardiff City fans very sceptical when we heard he had come to Cardiff City to help out Sam Hammam with our debts and the new stadium project. As I've said earlier in the book, having someone who's already been through this type of mess could be a benefit to the club. Remember, Ridsdale hadn't made our mess, Sam had. To this day, I don't think Sam himself knew how much debt or mess we were in at the time. I just think he knew we were in trouble and he needed help and, for the first time in six years, he finally decided he should get some. Nearly everyone was now snubbing the club and it owed money including £1.7million to the Inland Revenue and £2million in architect's fees on the new stadium. We were over £24million in debt with only a £9million turnover. Ridsdale was given the job to reduce the debt immediately and get the stadium back on track. Sam originally only brought in Ridsdale on a three day week but soon it became apparent that he was needed seven days a week. Peter Ridsdale was then employed permanently. He later joined the board of directors and started to have a much bigger say in the running of the club.

To the fans, Peter Ridsdale seemed no better than Sam Hammam.

The fans did not know that Ridsdale was unable to attract investors as long as Sam was still owner of the club, that's what Ridsdale led us to believe. To do that, Ridsdale said he had to persuade Sam to reduce his shares from 82% to 4%. That to me must have been one of the hardest tasks any person could ever do. That's one job I could never have done because Sam was a controller. Sam had put seven years of his life into Cardiff City and considered that this was his club. Ridsdale made Sam realise how bad the situation really was and that everything could be lost including the £24million loan notes. I personally don't think Sam realised it himself until it was staring him in the face. Sam really had no other choice but to sanction the dilution of his shares.

Over the next year, even when results seemed to go from bad to worse, I felt the media; especially the local media were backing Ridsdale no matter what. It seemed that even when we should have strengthened the squad after Sam went and we were in a good position for promotion to the Premier League, they never had a bad word to say about him or Dave Jones the manager. Then, when 2007-08 season came along, the local media still backed both of them and yet the results in the first couple of months were diabolical. All that the fans kept reading in the media was that there's no money available but we are still going forward.

Peter Ridsdale had gambled on 2007-08 season, in my opinion. We had sold our top scorer Michael Chopra for a reported £5million, released Neil Alexander on a free to Ipswich who has now signed for Glasgow Rangers after outstanding performances for Ipswich and Ridsdale brought in Robbie Fowler, reported to be on £20,000 a week, Jimmy Floyd Hasselbaink on £15,000 a week and Trevor Sinclair and Gavin Rae from Rangers also thought to both be on over £6,000 a week each. I will be honest when I heard that we had signed these players, especially Robbie Fowler, I did feel great about it that City were having all these star players playing for us and I did not moan at the time. Nearly 19,000 fans turned up for the first game against Stoke which we narrowly lost 1-0. City played some good football over the next few months but there seemed to be something dramatically lacking. By November 10th 2007, we were languishing in 20th position and we had only won two home League games in the last seven months. I thought that the fans had been very patient with the team and the new board of directors.

I had met Ridsdale only briefly on a couple of occasions; once at Reading away and once when he did a speech in the Marriot hotel so I can only really base my opinions on his past and what I have read in the newspapers since he joined Cardiff. Sam had invited me out a couple of times to meet him but, like I said before, over the last few years I had distanced myself a lot from Sam. Back towards the end of September 2007, I received a text from Peter Ridsdale which read, "I've seen the shit that is being peddled. The club should get Sam back, it would be insolvent b4 xmas and no new stadium" (received 9:22pm, 20/09/2007).

I had a feeling he had sent it to me only after I had sent a text to Terry Phillips which had been sent to me from a lad called Leighton from the Valleys. The text I had sent had said 'no passion, no commitment, bring back Sam'.

I replied to Ridsdale saying that I hadn't written this but I agreed with it. To be fair, Ridsdale immediately rang me and for 50 minutes, we had a friendly debate and, by the end of it, he had me believe we still had a future.

I invited Peter Ridsdale around my house the following week for tea, which he quite happily accepted the invitation. The day before he was due to visit, Suzanne from the Commercial department rang me saying "Peter is still coming for tea and just cook him Scampi and chips," I laughed and said no problem.

The following night when he arrived, I put my dogs in the back of the car, just in case he was scared of Alsatians, I came out to greet him and shook his hand, he then went to his boot and took out the biggest bouquet of flowers you had ever seen and said these are for your wife, with that he turned back to his boot and brought out three of the most expensive bottles of red wine, "They are for both of you" he said. Ridsdale was always dressed smartly with his usual navy blue suit and shirt; he hardly ever wore a tie, but was always well groomed.

I introduced him to my wife Joanne and offered him a drink, diet coke was all he wanted, even after bringing with him three of the finest red wines. I could see Ridsdale seemed quite nervous and my wife noticed his hand shaking a bit, she joked by saying "Annis won't bite you; I don't know what you've been told about him." Peter smiled and from then on he seemed much more relaxed. We chatted for a good couple of hours and yes I was impressed listening to his stories from when he was at Leeds and he seemed to have real love for them, he said to me "If Leeds had won the Champions League when I was there (lost in the semi final) how things would have been so different," he reminded me that Leeds had crowds of nearly 40,000 each home game whilst he was there, the highest for years. Ridsdale even told me how he once had this woman stalker while he was chairman of Leeds and how mad she was and in the end he had to get the police to sort get her off his back.

We then talked about Cardiff City and his plans for them, like I've said Peter Ridsdale is very convincing and in my opinion can talk better than a politician. I then showed him my football collection that I have collected since I was seven years old, he took a lot of interest in it and whatever my feelings are about Ridsdale he is a football man, maybe not as passionate as Sam but he certainly knows his stuff and has all the right contacts in the football world. After a few hours Ridsdale left and I have to admit I enjoyed his company, his parting words were "We are now going in the right direction."

About a week later Ridsdale phoned me to say he had something for me and asked when it was convenient to call over. The following evening Ridsdale called over and brought with him two signed shirts and handed them to me saying they were a present for my collection. I looked to see whose tops they were and was more than chuffed to find they were Robbie Fowlers and Jimmy Floyd Hasselbaink and both were signed, Ridsdale said they were from City's last home game. I thanked him and I still jokingly said "You will never change mind regarding Sam," he just smiled. We had a coffee and a chat and he kept me updated how things were going at that time.

My friend Julian Jenkins who is the ticket office manager but at that time was the media manager later told me that Ridsdale had a lot of time for me and had personally gone down to the dressing room after the game and asked Fowler and Hasselbaink for them. I actually felt quite honoured by this.

During the next couple of months, Ridsdale popped over to my house where we had quite a few open and frank discussions about Cardiff City and Sam. I said on a number of occasions to Ridsdale that I could never hate Sam as I will never forget Sam after Brussels and also when both my parents died, he was there for me. On the football side, I had totally mixed opinions of Sam. I even have a £50 bet with Ridsdale and Terry Phillips that I believe we won't end up in the top twelve this season; I hope I'm proved wrong. I've also sent him a text that I'd felt Dave Jones should go and that I felt Jones had lost the dressing room. To be fair again to Ridsdale, he never once lost his cool. He always said, "I understand. Stick with us," and also things like, "Believe in us."

By November, the fans had started to turn and some had lost total patience. On November 14th 2007 and with less than forty five minutes' notice, I phoned Ridsdale and asked him if he would like to come to the Municipal Club on City Road and meet an 18 strong group of fans who can be very fiery but passionate. Gwyn Davies and Vince Alm had arranged the meeting to discuss about what would happen if Langston or the club put us into administration and we wanted to speak to Ridsdale about Dave Jones and what was happening on the pitch because the last twelve months had been disastrous. Without hesitation, Ridsdale came to this meeting.

When Ridsdale arrived, you could sense the tension in the room and that certain fans in there were ready to explode on him. We had arranged a top table for him but he just picked up a chair and sat in the middle of us. Ridsdale was probably among some of the most hot-headed fans that City has but at the same time the most devoted fans. Ridsdale answered every question whether we disliked or liked the answers. A couple of the lads did give a bit of abuse at which Ridsdale never avoided the answer. He just asked them to repeat what they had said and then answered them. For over two hours, he answered these questions and I could see that even though he was willing to go on, I said to Vince, fair play to him let's just give him a round of applause for coming which we did. I will state that he hadn't won over this group but he had gained their respect. Only results and some passion on the pitch will win over this hardcore bunch of fans and I do believe Ridsdale left us feeling maybe Jones and the players do need a kick up the backside.

By the end of December, the results had started to get a little better; they couldn't have been any worse. The media were saying that Langston were trying to come to an agreement with Cardiff City while, at the same time, Sam was still denying he was Langston. I asked Peter Ridsdale how it was going and he felt it was finally coming to a conclusion with Langston and that the threat of administration was nearly over. He also stated to me that he didn't know why they were doing this as Langston would get £5m if Cardiff were promoted and that they 'believed' Langston was Middle East businessmen. Ridsdale concluded by saying that we were winning in the battle with Langston. I felt good in one way hearing that but I had Sam telling me the opposite. My head was telling me that Langston had no other choice but to settle this and stop the court case.

Just as everything seemed to calm down with the court case, Sam issued a writ against the club for his loss of wages of around £70,000 which, compared to Langston claim for £35m, this was a drop in the ocean. Sam's claim for payment from the club arose from the agreement struck when he left. City had agreed to pay £200,000 upfront plus £100,000 for the next three years to Sam's company Rudgwick. I rang Ridsdale on the 20th December about this and he agreed that they owed Sam the money but he said, "How would it look if I pay him his wages to sue me; I would look like a prat!" He then said, "Eventually the club would just pay him off." By the way Ridsdale spoke to me I felt that they were just playing Sam at his own game but in a smaller way.

The team seemed to be just getting back on track and Ridsdale was finally winning over the doubters including myself when suddenly one of our future stars Chris Gunter was sold to Tottenham for a reported £1.1m down with add on payments which will amount to nearly £2m. Here we go again I thought and so did thousands of City fans. We also heard that Chris Gunter was himself shocked and was in tears about leaving. Yet the club was saying it was good business and that they couldn't stand in his way. The night I heard Gunter was being sold, I rang Terry Phillips and I told him the club were out of order. He replied with, "I've had over twenty phone calls, all having a go about it." I said, "Print what they've said." Terry said that it was too late and that they would do so later on. I fell out with Terry over this. I felt he was backing the club too much on this issue. To me, if you keep on selling your future stars, what signal are you sending out to the fans?

In the period from November to December 2007, Ridsdale and Jones were getting abusive phone calls and even some so called fans had gone as far as death threats to Dave Jones. This is going way too far. Ridsdale did have one fan arrested and, after I'd managed to speak to the fan, he eventually apologised, Ridsdale agreed to drop the charges and hopefully that's the end of the matter. Then the South Wales Echo chief sports writer made a statement in the Echo replying to Sam in a statement he had made through me.

'I genuinely feel for Sam Hammam that he should be revered; instead his reputation among City supporters has nose-dived. If he can still have a word with Langston, Hammam could still come out with his reputation in South Wales enhanced if he could persuade then to call a halt to the court action and agree a payment plan on the monies owed.'

My answer to that is that Sam has stated to me and the South Wales Echo that Langston don't listen to him anymore and had lost patience with him. Sam is saying it's not down to him anymore. I'm not sure who or if anybody believes that. I also think that all this bad press was affecting the crowds at home games. It felt everything coming out of the club was negative.

So let's just get back to what is happening on the pitch and that's what I said to Ridsdale one day. He agreed. I felt that this court case was tiresome to him. The more I came to know Peter Ridsdale, the more I came to believe in him. Even if we disagreed on some of the things that were happening at the club, he will always speak to you, yes like Sam, but the difference is he will really let you have your say and not just shout you down, which I felt Sam sometimes did. I continually reminded Ridsdale that I would never turn my back on Sam and that he will always be my friend, his reply was "I am not trying to turn you against him, I am just reminding you that if Sam had stayed on you would not have a football club to support," he repeated this on many occasions and in public meetings with the fans.

The New Year set in and in the League we were just plodding along, when suddenly we started to have a good run in the FA Cup, we had beaten as you would expect Chasetown and Hereford away, then came Wolves at home and we just brushed them aside, if only we could have done this in our League games, but never mind I was enjoying every moment,

Then suddenly there I was watching Cardiff City in the quarter final of the FA Cup as the ball fell to Peter Whittingham, his Ronaldinho football movement mesmerised the Boro defence, before he calmly slotted the ball into the top corner passing the helpless Mark Schwarzer. If Thierry Henry or David Beckham had scored this goal, it would have graced every television station in the world. Suddenly, in the twenty seventh minute, the mercurial Peter Whittingham delivered a pinpoint cross with the accuracy of an arrow to the diving header of hero Roger Johnson which sent nearly four thousand Cardiff fans delirious with the vision of walking down Wembley Way. In the back of my mind, I was always worried that, once again, City would burst their own bubble. Maybe I didn't give them enough credit. This was potentially the greatest all round performance that I have ever witnessed. Who could have blamed me for thinking otherwise due to the sins of the past?

After we had beaten Middlesbrough away 2-0, the scenes of jubilation of City finally going to Wembley left grown men crying. I was thinking, is this possible? Can this really be happening to us? Cardiff City, where dreams never come true? We've done it. We really have, the club, the team and the ones who count most, the fans are on their way to Wembley. No, No. I am dreaming this. Well, if I am then I don't want to wake up as all we ever hear is the club could go bust, we have no money and now Peter Ridsdale is in court against Langston on the very day of his birthday and if we lose, not only do we go bust, we lose ten points. Ridsdale tells me he has prepared one hell of a case and he says he is confident that we will win the case.

Yes, our dreams really have come true and the whole of Wales has erupted into a frenzy. Wales rugby has won four on the trot but no one cares. Cardiff City had gone one better and is going to Wembley for the first time in over 81 years.

Steve Borley, our vice chairman and a true Bluebird posted a message out to us all via the internet
9th March 2008 :

Just got back from Boro, what an amazing day and amazing result. The chaps at the FA will raise a few eyebrows with us coming to town and this could be the first 'bubble' game at Wembley if the Met have their way. Great scenes, grown men crying, fans cheering and great performance from the team. The fans played a great part today and should be applauded for silencing a big Boro crowd.

WE'RE THE FAMOUS CARDIFF CITY AND WE'RE GOING TO WEMBERLEE,
WEMBERLEE.
MADE AN OLD MAN HAPPY TODAY AND BIG BREAK FROM ALL THE CRAP.

The following day while we are still all in dreamland, we are drawn against Barnsley in the semi-final of the FA Cup at Wembley and my family and I will be there along with 35,000 other Bluebirds who will constantly pinch themselves through the duration of this historic game.

Can McPhail, Loovens, Ramsey, Ledley and Co fail the ghosts of the past, Keenor, Davies, Curtis and Ferguson and bring the Cup once more across the bridge. Who knows but we can only dream.

So March 2008 became a great month for the Bluebirds not only had we secured our first visit to Wembley since 1927 but also Peter Ridsdale, who had worked tirelessly preparing the case against Langston in the High Court and at the same time trying to keep our club afloat with no money, won the first battle in court by stopping Langston getting an immediate repayment of £31 million. If he had not have won, it would have put us immediately into administration, so Ridsdale says. The bad news is that it's still not over with Langston but, after speaking to Ridsdale, Ridsdale has told me that Langston and Sam seem prepared now to sit down and reach a mutually amicable resolution to the dispute.

I also asked him if he was excited about Wembley and he replied, "I am very nervous and all I want to do is succeed with Cardiff City." The irony of the whole situation was typified to me recently when our fierce arch rivals, Bristol City, were chanting, "There's only one Sam Hammam" to rub our noses in the financial mess that this, once upon a time, much loved character seems to have left us in. But he, who laughs last, laughs longest, as Peter Whittingham smashed the ball into the Robins net and sealed a memorable 2-1 Severnside derby victory which, in reply, the Bluebirds fans sang, "There's only one Peter Ridsdale."

Whilst I'm on the subject of our club nearly going bust and now performing miracles, I would like to mention Aldershot Football Club who I watched at Ninian Park in March 1992 play their last ever League game and which we won 2-0 with goals by Nathan Blake. Their few hundred loyal fans who made the trip sang, "We'll support you ever more," from the beginning to the end of the game. They have risen from Division 3 of the Diadora Isthmian League to the Football League again. The reason that I mention them is because they went totally bust for a mere £120,000 and had to wait 16 years to come back. We are going to Wembley with debts of over £30 million and have this threat of bankruptcy hanging over us every day. Little clubs like Aldershot and AFC Wimbledon who are on the rise again and are also back in the Football league, should remind us that our beloved clubs would never die as long as the fans stay with them and believe in dreams. So congratulations, Aldershot and AFC Wimbledon. I have followed your progress through the years.

Our Dreams had finally arrived. It was Sunday, April 6th 2008. We were on our way to Wembley. The journey east along the M4 towards London was punctuated by the heavy snow showers that further enhanced a scene that grew every increasingly wintry on the approach to the English capital. None of this appeared real.

What was going through my head on the momentous journey to North West London? Well, it wasn't the many soccer battles that had been fought out over a century previously on the old site. Of course, old monochromic television clips had always made me aware of England's 4-2 victory against Germany to lift the World Cup in 1966 and Manchester United winning the European Cup at the legendary site two years later. My club Cardiff City had snatched the FA Cup in 1927 with that 1-0 triumph at Arsenal's expense and had taken the trophy out of England. But this was vivid reality, the convoys of coaches, minibuses and cars; all draped in the Bluebirds' colours brought a huge lump to my throat. It felt like the whole of Wales was invading England.

As we walked the Wembley Way and I saw a sea of blue; only then was it starting to sink in. My belief congealed as my family and I entered Wembley about an hour before the 4:00pm kick-off. A biting wind cut through the arena yet my heart was warmed with the sound of my fellow countrymen's Welsh voices; ordinary working class, entrepreneurs, unemployed and professionals, laden with so much expectancy. This was the day that we were going to show the rest of the planet what Cardiff City, albeit a team of promising talent and scared journeymen, was all about.

Barnsley made a promising start which had all us Bluebird fans on the edge of our seats. Any worries that we may have had soon disappeared when Joe Ledley hooked a loose ball into the Tykes net inside the opening ten minutes. From that minute to the end of the game, I was making every tackle and so was probably every Cardiff fan that had made the Wembley trip. Later, when Barnsley striker, Kayode Odejayi, made a horrendous miss on the Cardiff goal, the 34,000 Bluebirds fans greeted every tackle with a roar and then Men of Harlech and many other Ninian Park favourites were sung with a deafening sound around the Wembley arena. The rest, if I was honest, is a gigantic multicoloured haze. Our May 17th FA Cup Final date with Premiership team, Portsmouth, was for me confirmed and almost 24 hours later, a recording of the Sky TV match encapsulated my joy. Yes, there were tears but these were tears of happiness as I will be going back to Wembley, this time for the final of probably the biggest club competition in the world and with my club Cardiff City. Who said dreams don't come true.

That famous day, I heard from Sam Hammam who said he was so pleased for the Cardiff fans and that he sent his love to every one of them. I asked him where he was. He was in the mountains in Lebanon. Yes, some of these players were Sam's babes and had come through his academy. One being the hero of the day, Joe Ledley who, as a Cardiff born lad, scoring the winner must have made all his dreams come true.

Peter Ridsdale deserves a pat on the back. Through all the problems off the field, he stayed strong and on many occasions, said to me that we will achieve something this season. We have. Thank you, Peter. This will go down in history. Wemberleeee, Wemberleeeee !!!!

This is not a dream anymore. This is a fairytale come true. Now we are going to be on nearly every person's television set, not only in Great Britain but around the world and everyone is now going to know who my club is. This summer, when the diehard Bluebirds fans and myself all go on our summer holidays, we will all wear our tops knowing that everyone will be looking at us and finally recognising that Cardiff is not only the capital of Wales but has a football club that had finally come out of a coma.

THE SLEEPING GIANT HAS FINALLY AWOKEN.

April 7th 2008

The front page of the Daily Mirror today declared Cardiff City's Players the *'Princes of Wales'*.
It was just one example of the praise lavished by the national press on the team that is now the pride of the nation after they yesterday completed an historic victory at Wembley. The Mirror called the win *'FA Cup miracle'* and wrote on its front page: *'Dave Jones led skint Cardiff into the FA Cup Final and insisted it was his greatest achievement in football'*. The paper called Joe Ledley's goal *'stunning'* and said, *"Ledley strikes as Bluebirds heroes soar into the final."* Every City fan would agree that Ledley's goal was spot on, along with the Daily Express who called him a *'hero'*. Meanwhile, the Sun shouted, *"You're next, Harry,"* saying the Cardiff boss vowed to punch a hole in Harry Redknapp's dream.

Saturday May 17th, 2008. Once again we walked Wembley Way. In our thousands we came. Our Dream was still going, I don't know why but somehow the atmosphere was not there like it was in the semi-final and in my opinion we had as much chance as Pompey on the day, our fans and team did not seem to be up for it. Maybe we were just happy to be in the final and the occasion just took over the day. As Kanu scored for Pompey, the air of resignation took over and the FA Cup became a distant dream again. Let's hope it's not another 81 years before the Bluebirds fly again. Reality checks in once the season has finished and you think to yourself we're still a Championship club, but a dream did come true not once, but twice going to Wembley in such a short space of time and Cardiff City were now on the map, but not for fighting on the terraces or financial problems this time, but for once being up there with the best.

CHAPTER TWENTY FOUR

TRYING TO BUY A FOOTBALL CLUB AND MARCHING AGAINST CCFC

I had written a book called from Shattered Dreams to Wembley Way; there is a long story to how and why I had ended up writing it, I won't go through the whole story, but it was thanks to a Kilmarnock fan called George Calder who I had met whilst on holiday in Majorca and I had told him of my many adventures/tales with Sam Hammam, my problem was I could not type and my father used to say to me that typing was for girls, as back in his day that was probably true and remember my father was still old fashioned right up to the day he passed away. So after many weeks of George texting and ringing me and telling me the book would be worth writing, I finally decided to start the book and seven months later, after hand writing the book five times and persuading my wife Joanne to type it all up, the book was finished and launched on my wife's birthday Saturday June 28th 2008. Peter Ridsdale had kindly let me use the main function room at Ninian Park, free of charge and he even drove down from the North of England to attend the book launch and along with ex-Cardiff City legends Phil Dwyer and Scott Young, they met and signed my book for the 500 fans that turned up. I have to say a big thank you to the fans and Phil and Scott for that and especially Ridsdale for helping make it such a successful day for me with my first book, as I had been very nervous about the whole event.

During the next three years I published five more books, three Soul Crew books and Cardiff City fans through the years and the Rise and Fall of the Cardiff City Valley Rams by Gwyn Davies, I helped produce that book for him, which to be honest Gwyn is a far better writer than me and knows how to tell a story, with a humorous slant throughout. My first Soul Crew book, The Diary of the Real Soul Crew was launched in a bar called Bar M, Macs old bar in the City Centre of Cardiff. Over 700 lads turned up, our main spotter Simon Insole stood opposite watching and he said it was the biggest football turnout he had ever heard of for a football lad's book launch. To be fair to Simon, that day the police had wanted to put a dozen or so police outside, which would have probably caused aggravation and Simon knew that and with him just being there to monitor it, the day passed by totally peacefully, with the three pubs in that street being packed to the rafters. Lads from all over the Country came down for the launch, Pat (Chelsea), Dave (C. Palace) and Gilly (Wolves) just to name three of them and at another book launch with Diary of the Soul Crew 2, Pat came down again but this time he was joined by Cass Pennant, Ginger Bob (Millwall), Mike and Danny (Plymouth), Marc and Neil Blackmore (Bristol C), Sooty (Jason) and some other Birmingham City lads and even a couple of Forest lads.

A couple of months later Danny from Plymouth invited me down to Plymouth to launch my Soul Crew books, they had a pub all set up for me and about sixty of their lads turned out and every one of them made me feel welcome, fair play to them, what a great bunch of lads, and remember through the years Plymouth and Cardiff have had many a battle, but to this day there is plenty of respect for each other. When you think about it, all these different lads from all over the country coming together to have a drink, you have to laugh to yourself, as not so long ago we were all fighting each other and were supposed to have pure hatred for each other, that's if you were to believe what the media prints.

In 2008, I also tried to go one further than I did when I tried to buy in to Cardiff City eight years ago. I tried to buy a football club outright. I had always had a soft spot for Merthyr Tydfil and over the years I had watched many a game at Penydarren Park when Cardiff were not playing. Merthyr had a great history and a ground which reminded me of a mini Ninian Park, with a lot of character. In the Eighties they regularly had crowds of 4,000 and even went as high as 10,000, actually bringing shame to Cardiff's crowds. The last few years had seen Merthyr drop down the leagues and of course with that the crowds had gone down to around the 400 mark. A Merthyr Councillor called Adam Brown who supported both Merthyr and Cardiff told me about how bad things were. I enquired about them and even took my wife and children up to watch them and sponsored a few games for them. I eventually spoke to a couple of wealthy friends Dave Bennett and Steve Day about whether they would be interested, they were and we all put a business plan together for them. At first I got nowhere with the owner, but eventually he just let them go in to administration and so I dealt with Robert and Sharon Parker who were really helpful and brilliant to work with. All was going well until I had to deal with their Trust, who in fairness had worked really hard to keep their club going but this was where it all went wrong. I wanted total control of the Club, if Dave, Steve and I were putting all the money in and working on the ground to bring it up to Conference League standard. I was also putting the majority of the time and money in to the Club so I did not want to answer to a Committee. For weeks we tried to get somewhere, but it was never going anywhere and I felt they did not want outsiders controlling their club, in a lot of ways I fully understand, but that's not the way I work. I asked Sam Hammam's advice and he told me in no uncertain terms Merthyr was not for me. But Sam told me to ask myself the following questions regarding buying Merthyr football club.

1. Can you to treat Merthyr Football club like it was your own child?
2. Money to lose? As you do not make money out of a football club.
3. Love Merthyr like you love Cardiff City?
4.Can you take the strain of fans slagging you off, turning on you, even after you have put your own money in, given thousands of hours of your time, given the club promotion and the minute your club is not successful, are you prepared for this flak?

Sam said "I have experienced all of this; if you cannot do these four things then Merthyr is not for you."

So Merthyr was not to be and maybe it was for the best. I still look out for their results and one day who knows what will happen.

But going back to my club Cardiff City they had now sold Glenn Loovens and Aaron Ramsey, but the transfer deadline was coming to a close, it was the 31st August 2008, transfer deadline day and our fans including myself were fearing losing another player, Joe Ledley to Stoke City, it was rumoured that Stoke were willing to pay £6 million for him and Ledley had gone up there to sign. The deadline time that day was midnight and at about 11'o'clock that night, everyone was saying the deal had been done. So I rang Ridsdale and asked him straight, was he sold. Ridsdale said "Stoke were willing to pay £6 Million but since we had now sold Loovens and Ramsey, we did not need to sell anyone else." I did say to him that the fans would not put up with another star player being sold, but Ridsdale reassured me "Ledley was going nowhere." True to his word the following morning the papers confirmed that Ridsdale had turned down a last minute bid of £6 Million by Stoke for Ledley.

I really can't describe how low I felt after the last ever season at Ninian Park, it was sad, bad ending, whatever you want to call it being the last ever football season there, I had been watching the City there since the early Seventies, but to turn up on the last ever game there on the 25th April 2009 and watch our team get absolutely slaughtered by Ipswich Town 3-0, who had nothing to really play for, to me that is one of my lowest ever times of visiting Ninian in nearly 1,000 games that I had attended there. Ninian Park was packed to the rafters, the atmosphere was very emotional but electric at the same time, but the players in my opinion, were gutless, no care in the world and did not seem to even want to be out there, what a disgraceful send off they gave Ninian Park. Then when the final whistle went they just walked off the pitch and then returned twenty minutes later in an all-white strip to do a lap of honour, WHAT THE HELL WAS THAT ALL ABOUT?

Going in to the final four games of the season we were in the top 6 of the Championship, but then a 6-0 hammering at Preston, followed by a last minute equaliser at Charlton(2-2), then as I have just said one of the most embarrassing games I have ever witnessed at Ninian Park the 3-0 home defeat to Ipswich, which then followed with a 1-0 defeat at Sheffield Wednesday, yet even at that stage we could have still made the top 6, with just a draw, but we could not even do that. In my mind there was no way back for Dave Jones as it showed to me he could only put a team of bottlers and a bunch of individual prima donnas together. Dave Jones to me had no plan B when we went one nil down. I believe the statistics show when he finally left years later, when one nil down, we only managed to come back and win something like 10 out of 120 games. So my last memories of watching Cardiff City play at Ninian Park will always be remembered as a complete and utter shambles.

On a brighter note, the book launch that I will remember more than any of the others was the launch of Cardiff City fans through the years and the Valley Rams book, which were both launched on the same date. Saturday 6th June 2009 will always be remembered by me as it was the last official function ever held at the grand old lady 'Ninian Park'. This came about due to a bit of cheekiness by me, during the Ninian Park days I was able to walk in and out of the main part of the club freely and would often wander up to the boardroom and pop in and see Peter Ridsdale or our vice chairman Steve Borley who to be fair to them both always had time for a chat. I would also visit my good friend Julian Jenkins, head of the media department and manager of the ticket office. Ridsdale would ring down to Julian and ask him all the latest news or what were the latest ticket sales and of course I would then be first to hear everything. I would look through Julian's diary in front of him and that's where my cheekiness came about as I asked Julian, "What was the final date of Ninian Park actually being totally closed down, offices and all?," he told me, so I immediately opened the diary to Saturday 6th June and said nothing is happening then, Julian said "The beer pumps might be gone and all the carpets in the function room" I replied "Leave it with me." I rang Peter Ridsdale there and then and said "This date is available, can I have it for my book launch and will you attend?" without hesitation he said "Yes." Once again I can't fault Ridsdale on this, as he had again gone out of his way for me. I would often go in the dressing rooms, show my children behind the scenes of my great Club, Ninian Park really did feel like my second home.

So the launch went ahead and was built up as the last ever function at Ninian Park, ex-City legends Phil Dwyer and Scott Young turned up along with Peter Ridsdale, Steve Borley, the media and over 800 fans, I could not have asked for a better launch. The fans bought a book and sat in the Canton stand seats with a pint, which was a first. My children and my wife Joanne came along, with Joanne selling the books for me and making it a day to remember. Ridsdale, when it came to me asking for any help to do with the football club, nothing was too much trouble for him, but that still did not change my mind on how he was running my club financially and on that I had to be straight about it and over time, tell him my honest feelings and opinions, even if it would upset him and lead to us falling out.

Come August/September 2009, Ridsdale was now frantically looking for new investors as our debts were still mounting. Many fans from the Valleys had approached me and asked if Ridsdale could come up and meet them. I asked Ridsdale if he would and he had no hesitation in saying yes. So I contacted my mate Geraint Handley (Cheggers) who owned a pub called the Brunswick in Merthyr (about 25 miles from Cardiff) if I could hold a meeting there, he was chuffed to bits and said "Any night that suits you." So on the 7th September 2009, a Monday night, Cardiff City chairman Peter Ridsdale, fresh from his business trip to Malaysia, after looking for investment on the clubs behalf, met with 250 fans at The Brunswick public house, Merthyr. Ridsdale rang me whilst he was parking up outside the pub and I went out and met him and then took him in to where Cheggers and another friend of mine Greg Davies had set up a table and chair for him. Greg was also there to write up everything that was said that evening.

The following is just some of the things Ridsdale said to the 250 City fans, who stood there hoping for good news .Ridsdale stated the clubs current debt stands at £25 million. He said they owe £15 million to Langston and £9 million to PMG for the stadium build. The other debt is from future transfer fees and from the day to day running of the club.

The Langston debt was considerably higher, but, through negotiations, he'd managed to get it down to £15 million. Ridsdale also said he gets calls from a 'certain someone we all know' about when the Langston debt will be repaid. Ridsdale also believes that he can further reduce the Langston debt through ongoing discussions with Sam Hammam.

Whilst he's looking into the Far East for investment to help pay the debt, the door hasn't been closed on any deal in the States. He touched on his trip to the US in the summer, saying he had an indicative offer from banks in the US to discuss the debt and the possibility of taking over the clubs debt. At the time, the figures quoted were unacceptable to the club but they are still in talks, and Keith Harris who works for our club, was in the States on behalf of the club whilst Ridsdale was in Malaysia.

Ridsdale said that the club, although still in debt, is in a healthy position and has more assets than liabilities on the balance sheet, which is a long way away from where we were when he came to the club when on the Friday before the second game of his spell, against Gillingham, he had to go to the tax office and persuade them not to put the club into administration. That's how close we were. He said James Collins, Danny Gabbidon and Jobi McAnuff were all sold just to pay the tax man.

He believed the deal in Malaysia became bigger than he imagined and is part of the solution to pay the debt, Ridsdale also said that he'd be willing to discuss with anyone about eradicating the debt at the club as one single strand (Malaysia) will not solve everything.

The possibility of a deal came about when a businessman from the Far East was trying to secure a trial for his son at a club in the English League Pyramid West Ham. Most clubs laughed off the possibility but Cardiff City took him on trial, and although the trial was somewhat curtailed due to the bad weather (snow) that happened at the time, the businessman was impressed by the way the club treated his son, and with what he saw when he came to watch City versus Nottingham Forest. He and Ridsdale have kept in contact since via email, and Ridsdale received an email inviting him to Malaysia to discuss business.

Peter Ridsdale thanked the Cardiff City fans for their loyalty, and said it was a privilege to be chairman of the club. He said over the last 3-4 years, the supporters have taken the club forward. They have been outstanding and perhaps don't get the credit they deserve. He said his proudest moment in football was when the CCFC fans stayed behind at Wembley to watch Portsmouth lift the FA Cup and that on that day,

Cardiff City fans gave the FA Cup back to the fans where it belongs, and we received worldwide praise for it. Ridsdale had won the fans over with his speech. I then walked him backed to his car and thanked him personally for coming up there; his answer was "Not a problem, my pleasure."

On the 22nd October 2009, Joanne and I had another baby girl, growing up I had always wanted a boy, but the closeness and love I already have with Annaise and Alexandra is second to none and I don't think a boy would have ever have given me the love my girls give to me, so I am more than happy that I have now got three girls. As we've decided not to have any more children, we have called our new baby girl Tilly-Annis Abraham, so Tilly is the nearest I will ever get to having a boy. So in my house, I am well outnumbered by girls, four to one, it looks like I've got an expensive future with all their weddings.

After the meeting that I had arranged in Merthyr with City fans and Peter Ridsdale, many City fans in Cardiff then asked if I could arrange a meeting locally, so once again I asked Ridsdale and fair play he was quite happy to do so. This meeting was arranged in the Municipal club in Cardiff on Monday evening the 30th November 2009. Ridsdale had previously visited the Municipal club in mid-November 2007. On that occasion, he faced the wrath of a group of eighteen angry fans, myself included, who were upset about the team's woeful form at the time. In Ridsdale's book, United We Fall, the Chairman wrote a brief account of that particular meeting. He described the Muni meeting as "not a place for the faint-hearted or thin-skinned," and said walking into it was
"Like entering the lion's den."

Going into this meeting we had just lost our last three league games, to Swansea, Barnsley and now Ipswich with two late goals, which may have eased the pressure on the Ipswich manager, Roy Keane, but they had the opposite effect on his Cardiff City counterpart, Dave Jones, who was booed by fans after his side again slipped up when they appeared to have the points in the bag. Unlike the team on Sunday afternoon, Cardiff City Chairman Peter Ridsdale was in fine form on Monday evening upon his return to the Municipal Club. The Bluebirds Chairman answered questions for almost two hours from a crowd of well over three hundred fans who had gathered at the dingy venue on City Road in order to express their concerns about the club's current fortunes. Whether you love him or loathe him, and whether you believe the answers he provides or not, you cannot help but admire the way in which Ridsdale handles himself in situations like these. He is an excellent public speaker who is extremely adept at dealing with large groups of people, and he has the ability to make supporters feel positive about their club regardless of the team's results or any alleged troubles behind the scenes. Many fans apparently arrived at the meeting determined to have a go at the Chairman, but he easily rode the storm and eventually left the stage to a generous round of applause. Once again, he had managed to win over a large percentage of the doubters, which speaks volumes about the man's PR skills.

But what was definitely going to come back and haunt Ridsdale was the fact he said to us all at this meeting, that these Malaysian Businessmen had already given a few million pounds to Cardiff City and more was to follow.

On December 15th 2009 Peter Ridsdale announced the Golden Season Ticket for the City fans in a bid to raise £3million for team strengthening in January and was described as an 'Ideal Christmas gift' by the club. Supporters were urged to take the offer by the deadline of December 31st and in return of raising £3million for new players, the fans would be rewarded with their money back if we got promoted and also a five year price freeze on season tickets as a 'Thank You'. I was asked by the club to help promote the offer on the message board and along with Carl Curtis and Gwyn Davies we did exactly that. The fans did not need much encouraging as they bought the 10,000 tickets that were on offer by the end of year deadline. Players were going to be bought to help the manager and the team to deliver the hope of Premier League football. Manager Dave Jones came out and said "Back us and we will strengthen. Back me. Back the team. Back your football club."

Despite Families being hard up due to tough economic times and coupled with the fact it was just two weeks until Christmas, the City fans got behind the scheme and bought the 10,000 available Golden Tickets, believing that the money was going to be spent on new players as the club had no money available itself to spend on squad strengthening. There were sceptics who claimed that the club was close to financial meltdown and our money from the season ticket sales would be swallowed up by the club's debts, but Ridsdale kept denying those claims and stated on January 6th that *"We will be bringing in new players this month, I can guarantee that. I would go as far as to say that, come January 31st, we will be holding a press conference to parade the players brought in during this month."*

Despite the reassurances from Ridsdale there was still talk amongst fans and media that maybe all is not right as we faced a second winding up order on February 10th, if the club failed to pay an outstanding tax bill of £2.7 million owed to Her Majesty's Revenue and Customs. Ridsdale made assurances earlier that month that the club was "trading as normal" and there was "no immediate threat" to the future of the club.

And asked on January 8th if the money from the season ticket initiative, known as the "Golden Ticket," would be used to pay off the debt, he said: "No, there is money to pay for that."

Over the Christmas period and into January the team were struggling, we hadn't managed a win in five games, we needed new players to give fresh impetus to the squad but there were no new players yet and we were quickly running out of time before the January transfer window slammed shut. It became apparent that there were to be no new players and some of us felt we had been conned and duped by Ridsdale.

We were hurting, families had given up their hard earned money at the very time they needed it most. We were furious and on the message board, the members of our forum wanted something done, they wanted Ridsdale out.

They wanted to demonstrate against Ridsdale, some were seeking legal advice after the promises given by Ridsdale, but some were still clinging to the hope that there were a few days left of the transfer window and we may just get some new players in, I knew that there would be no players and I felt that we had been done.

It got to January 26th and we were playing Bristol City away in the league on a Tuesday night, Myself, Geraint Handley (Cheggers), Robert Barrett (Baz), Thomas Fish and Greg Davies decided we were going to make our thoughts known and we took banners to Ashton Gate saying 'RIDSDALE OUT' and 'WHERE'S OUR MONEY GONE?'

At Bristol City, we were told, Ridsdale had instructed the Cardiff City stewards, who travel to away games with us, to remove the banners, we argued with the stewards that we had a right to show our feelings but eventually the police were called to intervene and even though they asked us to take down our banners they did sympathise with us. We emphatically won the game 6-0, we were ecstatic that we annihilated our rivals on their own patch; many of their fans were leaving after just thirty minutes. At the end of the game we celebrated together with the rest of the City fans and we held up our banners again as the players and management looked over but to my surprise, some of our fellow fans did not believe in what we were doing and started to boo us and some even abused us and shouted over "You don't know what you're on about."

I believed that we had done the right thing that night and it was backed up the following day when a statement was published on Cardiff City's website saying no new players would be bought. On the 28th Peter Ridsdale held a press conference where he said *"It's saying to our supporters, if I misled you - and clearly you feel I did - I apologise."*

"We undoubtedly have some short-term challenges and these challenges will be addressed fairly and squarely, and it would not have been appropriate to add to our overheads by bringing in players until they've been resolved."

The fans on the message board went mental; our fears had turned into reality. Now they wanted a full demonstration and they wanted it at the next game, Doncaster Rovers at home on January 30th. Carl set about organising the demonstration on the message board with a place and a time for the demonstration to start. It would be at 5pm outside the main entrance doors to the Grandstand. We wanted to make sure that the protests were after the game and not before, so that everyone could concentrate on supporting the team during the game.

I had a dilemma that day, my two daughters Annaise and Alexandra were chosen to be mascots for this game and as much as I wanted to be involved with the demonstration there was no way I was going to let my family down. It was an amazing day for the kids, my friend Warren Feeney (Cardiff City player) took my daughters around to meet each player and to have their photographs taken with every one of the players. The girls were then taken out onto the pitch and I went out with them, but I couldn't help but notice I was being watched; everywhere I walked there were people seemingly following me.

We were fortunate enough to be in the dressing room when Dave Jones gave his team talk and whilst he was doing so, Jay Bothroyd sat there with headphones on, eyes shut, bopping his head to the sounds. Dave Jones shouted "Jay, Jay!" Chopra banged Bothroyd's arm and then he finally took off the headphones, I actually think Dave Jones was embarrassed and Bothroyd was not bothered by it.

As we were leaving the dressing room so the girls could lead the team out onto the pitch, I bumped into Peter Ridsdale in the corridor, "Hi Annis, everything ok?" "Yes and don't worry Peter they have not got 'RIDSDALE OUT' t-shirts on!" I replied. "I know you wouldn't do that Annis," but as I walked off I noticed again that I had security watching me.

Annaise walked out onto the pitch with Michael Chopra and Alexandra held the hand of Jay Bothroyd, I took my seat in the new grandstand, the first time I had been in there, and sat with my wife Joanne and Warren's wife Katy. We won the game 2-1 and it was really a proud moment to watch my daughters lead out the Cardiff City team. We went into the players bar at half-time and I was told by a member of the bar staff who I knew, that the club had brought in more security today and she was told that it was because they thought I would start a demonstration on the pitch or in the grandstand. I would never have done anything like that as this day was to be special for my daughters.

At the end of the game I made my way to the players' lounge and looking through the windows at the front of the stand to see the demonstration, there was approximately 400 hundred fans gathered and were holding up banners and chanting "We want Ridsdale out, we want Ridsdale out!" The players came over to the windows to look at the scenes too; I really wanted to be out there with Carl, with his daughter Angharad on his shoulders, his brother Jamie (Jam), Nathan Millichip (Milly) and his brother Adam Millichip (Chippy), Baz, Big Sam, Corky, Peter Morgan, Fish, Steff and Cheggers and many others who I knew.

I knew in my heart what I was going to do next; I decided I was going to call for the resignation of Peter Ridsdale at the upcoming EGM. I spoke with some friends over the coming weeks and asked them what their views were about my decision to ask

Peter Ridsdale to resign as Chairman of our club. I spoke with Sam Murphy (Big Sam), Carl, Robbie and Mike Roderick and they all agreed that I should do so. The EGM was held at the stadium on Wednesday February 24th. Days before the EGM I was in the car with Carl and I decided to ring Steve Borley and tell him that I was planning to put a vote of no confidence forward of the Chairman. As I was on a hands free kit, Carl heard the full conversation between Steve and me.

Steve said "We need to get him out of the club Annis, we need the fans to get him out," I asked Steve "Why couldn't the director's do it if that is what you feel?" Borley replied that "He has got allies on the board Annis that is why it has got to be the fans." I told Borley again that I would ask Ridsdale to resign and Borley said "Annis I would cut my right arm off for his resignation!"

Carl and I chatted when the phone call ended and we felt that the demonstrations were having an effect and now we knew the feelings of Steve Borley and how much he wanted Ridsdale out then it justified the actions of the protests, some of Ridsdale's fellow directors wanted him gone for the good from Cardiff City, I was certain in my mind that I was going to call for the vote of no confidence in him.

The morning of the EGM I was nervous, I will be honest. I walked into the meeting and there were 80 shareholders in attendance. Peter Ridsdale was on fine form again and spoke at length about how far the club had come forward and he certainly tried to paint a rosy picture of the club at this time, as opposed to the one he came into. Ridsdale is a showman there is no doubt about it; he can stand there amongst any audience and make you feel positive about something when you feel the angriest. Ridsdale gave his explanation as to why the club was facing the cash flow problems and despite being Chairman none of it was his fault. The problem, according to Ridsdale, was that certain players that the club anticipated selling were not sold and investment of millions, that the directors thought was coming into the club had not materialised.

The moment had arrived, I stood up and put forward a vote of no confidence in the Chairman, it was seconded immediately by Big Sam and Tim Wegner, Mike Roderick, Robbie and a few others stood up and supported it. Ridsdale looked at me, he had expected it I was certain, he said that if any shareholder wishes to stage a vote of no confidence in either him or any other board member, they need to call a General Meeting for that specific purpose and obtain the backing of at least 5% of the company's shareholders. Ridsdale had dodged the bullet and used the company's constitution to do so. I turned to Steve Borley and asked him "Do you back us Steve?" Borley paused for a moment and replied "What are you trying to achieve Annis?" "You know what we are trying to achieve Steve and I am asking, do you and the other directors back the Chairman? Borley paused for a few seconds, then Borley's response stunned me "I support the Chairman."

I was dumbstruck, after the conversations between Steve Borley and I and how he told me that it was down to the fans to get Ridsdale out and the stuff about cutting his right arm off to get Ridsdale's resignation, all this was racing through my mind. I had failed in my attempt to force Ridsdale to stand down but despite all the emotion I was feeling at the time I also felt proud, proud that I had stuck to my belief and I could hold my head high. I couldn't smile to a person's face and then when their back is turned be stabbing them in the back. I speak my mind but you will always know that I am honest, whether people like it or not. Whilst mulling over what had just happened, the remainder of the EGM passed by very quickly for me and when the end of the meeting was called, I faced criticism from someone else in the room, Steve Borley's wife, Christine.

Christine came over to me and was obviously angry, which I understand, and shouted at me "What do you think you were playing at?" I was still thinking about the meeting, when Christine came charging over to me and the only response I could give her was "I thought Steve felt the same as me." She walked back to the group she had been with and I am glad to say since the EGM, Steve, Christine and I have made up. When I left the EGM and was outside the stadium there were reporters waiting to speak with the shareholders, Sky news, ITV and BBC, I was asked a couple of questions and I told the waiting reporters "This is not the end of it, the fans will march!"

I thought about the EGM a lot on the way home and I was questioning myself, I was asking myself had I done the right thing? It kept going round in my mind. Yes I did do right, I am a supporter and the chairman had let us down. For the next few days I chatted with friends, who were supportive of my actions, but the main topic was that fans wanted action; they wanted to show Peter Ridsdale how they were feeling and that they had felt they had been deceived. Men and women of all ages kept repeating the same feelings, they were angry, they wanted Ridsdale out.

It was time for me to take action and bring all these people together as one. It was decided that we would not wait any longer and that we would march against the chairman and we would do so on March 6th 2010 before our home game against Middlesbrough. The members of the message board were behind it and despite it being a successful forum it was still in its infancy, I needed to raise awareness. I took out a full page colour advert in the South Wales Echo, a local newspaper, to publicise the march and the reasons behind it. The Echo gave me a special price because of the nature of the advert. The day the advert went out; I started to receive hundreds of messages supporting the march, whether it be via text, phone calls, message board or people of all ages coming up to me in the streets, many were giving their support.

I was contacted by South Wales Police and was told that they wanted the organisers of the march to attend a meeting with them. Carl was unable to attend the meeting due to work commitments, so Gwyn Davies and I went along and met with Simon Insole and Wayne Palmer, two of Cardiff City's football intelligence officers. Gwyn and I were told that what we were planning was actually illegal as we had not had permission off the Council for such a protest and that we should have permission to have roads closed etc. But they knew we would still go ahead with the march, so it's better to work together. The police were helpful and said they would work with us, but we must be aware that if any trouble occurs then the organisers of the protest could be in trouble as a result. I told them that this would be a peaceful demonstration and there was no intention of creating trouble.

It was a hectic ten days before the march and on the eve of the event, Steve Borley came on the message board and said that the march was detrimental to proposed investment from Malaysia and told us to not go ahead with it, as in his words "What would the Malaysians think?," Borley was ridiculed by other members on the forum for saying this. Peter Ridsdale pulled what I can only call a stunt, to disrupt the march and try and put doubt into the fans minds. At 16.30 on the Friday afternoon a day before the march, through the club's official website, he released a statement. As part of the statement Ridsdale wrote "Anyone thinking of joining this march should look themselves in the mirror and ask if they really care about Cardiff City Football Club and its future. If the answer is yes, then come straight to the ground, enjoy the match and support the Club. If the answer is no, then join the march."

Books off City shop's shelves after vote call

Saturday, 27 February, 2010 **South Wales Echo**

Simon Gaskell
simon.gaskell@walesonline.co.uk

BOOKS written by a Cardiff City shareholder have been taken off the club shop shelves after he called for a vote of no confidence against club chairman Peter Ridsdale.

Annis Abraham has written and published four books which have been sold by Cardiff City's club shop for more than two years.

A day after Mr Abraham stood up to propose a vote of no confidence in the chairman at the EGM, he was told his books would no longer be sold.

The club shop asked Mr Abraham to pick his books up by 10am yesterday along with a cheque for money owed to him.

Mr Abraham says when he went to collect the books, which were bundled into sacks, he was told he would have to wait for the cheque because Mr Ridsdale had not signed it.

Mr Abraham, a property developer and season ticket holder for 37 years, said: "Surely, as a fan, if I don't think my club is being run right, I have a right to have a say."

Mr Ridsdale said he had no say about what was or wasn't sold in the club shop.

He told the *Echo*: "I don't agree with every single item in the club shop but the shop doesn't report directly to me.

"I have no personal problem with Annis Abraham nor have I since I walked into Cardiff.

"As I made it clear at the EGM, whoever gets the requis-

ite number of votes can table a resolution for a vote of no confidence. I am merely a servant of the shareholders."

The club shop said it had not been given a reason to take the books down, it was just told to pull them.

The books include From Shattered dreams to Wembley Way, Cardiff City Fans through the Ages and The Rise and Fall of Cardiff City Valley Rams.

They are stocked by Waterstones, HMV and Cardiff Airport and have sold 48,000 copies in three years.

Mr Abraham said: "They have

been very successful, the club have done well out of it.

"The club were making £5.50-£9 for each book, I was making £1-£1.50.

"They lose an income stream where they didn't have to."

Fans come from far and wide to buy the books.

Geraint Hinbley, 25, from Merthyr Tydfil, was hoping to buy two books for his uncle's birthday. He said: "I am a season ticket holder and I regularly see the books in the club shop and then I go down there and all of a sudden they have disappeared."

■ Author and City shareholder Annis Abraham outside Cardiff City Stadium   PICTURE: Richard Swingler ©

249

CARDIFF CITY STATEMENT
Fri 05 Mar 2010

Cardiff City Football Club Limited.

Adverts have been taken out by Annis Abraham in the local media asking for our supporters to march prior to this coming Saturday's home match against Middlesbrough. In this advert he is asking the Club to answer questions with regard to the Club's finances.

Annis has a small number of shares and attended last week's EGM. Following the EGM, a presentation was made which addressed each of those questions. Annis already has the answers.

Maybe the true reason that Annis wants our supporters to march is so that you can destabilise the Club. Then what? Are you prepared for the consequences?

We are currently seeking external investment. Will a march against the current management or the Club assist that? The answer is simple. No.

This Club has made tremendous progress over the last five years. A new stadium, an FA Cup Final appearance, the highest league finish since 1971 and positive net assets for the first time for many years.

We have short-term cash challenges like many football clubs. Over the last five years we have had to be self sufficient. We have not had external investment topping up the football club's financial needs. Now we have the new stadium and with positive net assets we have a chance to attract external investment. This will not be forthcoming if they see our supporters demonstrating in the streets, you will merely drive such investors away. Then what?

If anyone agitates for change they have to have an alternative. Annis has no alternative. If he has or if anyone else has, then let them come to put such proposals to us. My door is always open.

It is now time for all Cardiff City supporters to decide whether they want this Club to thrive and move forward or to throw away everything that has been achieved over the last five years. On many occasions Annis has made it clear to me personally that he never wanted to leave Ninian Park. Maybe we have a different vision for the future of this football club.

Anyone who wants to have constructive dialogue can meet with me or my colleagues at any time. We only have the best interests of Cardiff City at heart. I hope that this is a mutually shared objective.

Anyone thinking of joining this march should look themselves in the mirror and ask if they really care about Cardiff City Football Club and its future. If the answer is yes, then come straight to the ground, enjoy the match and support the Club. If the answer is NO, then join the march.

Peter Ridsdale, Chairman.

5th March 2010.

8 March, 2010

The protest was led by organiser Annis Abraham, right

FOOT BAWL: Cardiff City Fans protest loudly over the handling of the club by chairman Peter Ridsdale

WALES on SUNDAY

Fans say: We're deadly serious!

By ANTHONY O'CONNELL

I immediately received calls from friends and fans, they were livid about the statement our chairman had put out. How dare Ridsdale claim that if a fan joins the march then they do not care about Cardiff City Football Club? This is the exact reason we were going to march because we cared and loved the club and under his stewardship we were at the brink of going under. For a chairman to come out and release a statement like this was one of the biggest mistakes he could have made and either he was told or he realised his error as within forty minutes of releasing it, the statement was promptly taken down.

I travelled to the meeting point of the march, which was at the back of the Admiral Napier pub in Canton, with my friend Lyndon and met with Carl, two of his children Cameron and Angharad and his brother Jamie along with his son Josh. Carl had bought a megaphone to help organise the fans and control the crowd. Jamie was carrying a full size coffin with the words 'RIP CCFC'. When we entered the car park of the pub at 13.00 there were around 200 fans waiting. Carl and I chatted and thought that the numbers were not going to be as big as we thought. Hundreds of people had been telling us they were joining the march but on the early indications of that day, we thought that we were going to fail. There were reporters from the National press, television cameras from Sky and the BBC.

I was called aside by a Chief Inspector of South Wales Police and he told me that the police would keep a distance but would monitor the events; he said that Simon Insole would walk along the route with you; again I must say the police were very helpful. It did cross my mind that I was working with the police and for the first time.

Every ten minutes that passed between one and two o'clock, more and more were turning up. Gwyn took hold of the megaphone and instructed everyone that this was a peaceful march and that we were going to do ourselves proud and keep it that way. When the march started I was not sure of how many had actually turned up. We set off from the pub and made our way through Canton and walked along the main road and past the Canton Cross pub, as were walking and chanting "We want Ridsdale out, we want Ridsdale out" fans were joining us along the route. We were walking too fast and quickly we arrived outside the Ninian Park pub, where fans were coming out to either clap us or to join the march themselves, it was at this point I could look back along the main road and see how many had supported the march. I was ecstatic there were at least 2,000 who were united as one. Simon Insole spoke to me and said the pace is too fast; to have more affect, you need to slow down. Gwyn was on the megaphone again and calling for everyone to walk at a pace of a funeral march.

We turned the corner onto Sloper road, the stadium was in sight but I knew we were too early, we had only been marching for ten minutes, and Gwyn turned and started chanting "If you hate Ridsdale sit down" everyone young and old sat down on Sloper road, covering it. There were now at least 2,500, I was so proud. I saw friends of old

like Steve Day, along with his daughters, holding up giant £10 notes with Peter
Ridsdale's face on them, which appeared in the News of the World the following day.
Claire Jeremy with her son Joseph, who wore a t-shirt emblazoned with a slogan
"Who will we watch?" A lad called Paul (Rhooster) was at the front alongside
Cheggers and I, Paul had helped immensely behind the scenes in promoting this
march. Hundreds of fans were wearing specially designed t-Shirts and others were
wearing scarves with the original colours of brown and yellow, of Cardiff City, known
originally as Riverside FC. This march was not just lads, this was about families, all
backgrounds, and all were coming together as one.

We made our way into the stadium car parks and walked up to the main entrance
outside the Grandstand. The chanting was at its loudest and it was non-stop as it had
been from the minute we started to march. When we got outside the stadium we were
greeted by a team of security, stewards and police. Carl, Gwyn and I stood between
the fans and the stewards. We chanted and made our feelings known for over ten
minutes. The television cameras were filming from all angles. The three of us thanked
the fans for turning up and supporting the march and urged everyone to go into the
ground and get right behind the team, who had been on another run of poor results. On
the way to my seat I was thanked by many fans for organising the march and I know
Gwyn and Carl were too, on their way through to the family stand where they sit.

When we went in the stadium that day there was something different about the
atmosphere, it had an edge to it that I was yet to experience in the new stadium. It was
electric in there and we beat 'Boro 1-0 that day. I don't know if it was because of the
fans that marched that day, that the atmosphere inside was something special and
much more lively, but everyone who I have spoken with have said they felt exactly the
same.

Even the press reports of the game suggested we should march every week going on
the atmosphere and the performance that followed it. Here is part of an article written
by Paul Abbandonato, Wales on Sunday

*"Perhaps Bluebirds fans should demonstrate outside the ground at every match because
something they do seems to galvanise the Cardiff City players.*

*The last time an anti-Peter Ridsdale protest was staged; Dave Jones' Bluebirds beat Doncaster
2-1. Yesterday, the 2,000-strong march to the stadium was followed by 90 minutes full of pride,
passion, commitment, defensive resilience*

*The fans have a right to let their voices be heard and they certainly did yesterday, young, old,
female and male marching to the stadium. Various banners bearing anti-Ridsdale messages
were displayed, including 'Leeds, Barnsley but not Cardiff please', 'Where's our money gone?'
and 'Stand up if you hate the Riddler'.*

The message was loud and clear, but fans' leader and march organiser Annis Abraham insisted that once the demonstration was over, the fans would disperse, walk to their seats inside the stadium and back the team to the rafters. That they most certainly did, with a vengeance. I'm not saying this was down to the fans, but two game-tilting decisions went the way of the Bluebirds, the sort of thing we used to see in a passion-filled Ninian Park."

Did we achieve anything with the march? Yes we did. We got the voice of the fans heard, not just outside the stadium or on the streets of Cardiff but around the whole Country. We were on all the major news channels and that evening we were featured on the BBC's Football League show. The following day's press all had images of the march and the reasons behind it. We had gained the exposure and showed the rest of Country what Peter Ridsdale had done to our fans. We showed together that Cardiff fans had strength and when we need too we come together. We had pride; everyone who marched that day can feel proud of what they did. Cardiff City fans showed that day we still had fight in us.

We were told days later that the Malaysians had not been put off at all by the demonstration, but in fact they liked the passion and feeling that we showed and they were impressed with the peaceful nature of the protest. In a little over eight weeks later I was part of a group that went to Cardiff City stadium and were filmed and interviewed for Malaysian press to show our appreciation for the investment of £6million that, Tan Sri Vincent Tan and Dato Chan Tien Ghee, had saved our club from going under in April. Carl received an email from TG to thank the fans for our support and that they appreciated what we had done.

I would like to thank each and every fan who supported the march and congratulate you on helping the march remain peaceful and at the same time sending a powerful message to the then chairman Peter Ridsdale, that we are Cardiff City and we have a voice.

CHAPTER TWENTY FIVE

A RETURN TO WEMBLEY, FOLLOWED BY GOODBYE PETER RIDSDALE

In my opinion, the march and the demonstrations during February and March 2010 were worthwhile as they brought many of the club's fans closer together. They also indicated that Cardiff supporters can show solidarity when it's needed. The demonstrations reminded me of the way our fans used to be in the Eighties and Nineties. I reckon the supporters who took part should feel proud of themselves as we made our feelings known about how the club was being run without causing any trouble.

The media reacted positively to the demonstrations and some local journalists began labelling Peter Ridsdale as 'The Riddler' after we'd produced t-shirts bearing that name along with fake ten pound notes with pictures of his face on them instead of the Queen's.

At that stage, the club was in a strange position. On the one hand, the team was in the top six of the Championship and challenging for promotion; on the other, it was in the High Court with a serious threat of being wound up by the HMRC over an unpaid tax bill. Some fans feared that City would go into administration and get a ten-point penalty, but with the Revenue's barristers telling the Judge the club was clearly insolvent, it looked just as likely that it would go into liquidation. It was a very worrying time for the supporters and the staff.

Some of the stories in the press were shocking. Every other day there seemed to be more unpaid creditors coming out of the woodwork and it became clear that the club still owed lots of local firms money for work they had done on the new stadium. Also, the players' wages weren't being paid on time and some of the directors had to dip into their own pockets to meet the costs.

Peter Ridsdale had been very quiet since the protest march and it was Steve Borley who travelled over to Malaysia to try and negotiate the takeover deal with Dato Chan Tien Ghee (TG) and Vincent Tan. I believe the Malaysians had almost given up on the club when they found out what a mess the finances were in, but Borley was able to get them back on board. He was becoming more involved in the running of the club, as was Paul Guy, who was one of the major creditors.

During that period, Sam Hammam was ringing me from Lebanon almost every day to see how things were going at the club. He kept saying that he wished he could get involved again, but he had decided to stay quiet while he was in temporary exile. However, he told me that one day he will walk back into the club with me, Carl Curtis and Gwyn Davies alongside him as we have always backed him no matter what the situation has been.

Personally, I believe Sam still loves Cardiff City Football Club. We all know he made mistakes during his time in South Wales and some of them were huge, but I will never forget the fact that we were in the Football League's dungeon division when he arrived here. Nobody else wanted the club at that time and it desperately needed someone like to Sam to step in and take it forward. He had the vision and passion needed to take us up two divisions, build us an academy and get us planning permission for the new stadium. Those things were all just pipe dreams before Sam strolled into town. I only wish he had been able to continue on the rollercoaster ride with us and take us all the way up to the Premiership. That was his dream when he first came here and he would have loved it, but it was not to be. Nevertheless, I'll always be very grateful for what he did for my football club.

On the pitch, City had become a Jekyll and Hyde team – great one minute but poor the next. We played away at Coventry in mid-March and it was a vital game, because if we had lost it we would have dropped out of the play-off positions for the first time in months. We went 1-0 down to a Clinton Morrison goal midway through the first half and most of us thought that was it, as our record under Dave Jones of coming back to win after conceding the first goal was terrible. However, the team battled back well on this occasion. Jay Bothroyd equalised just before half-time and then winger Peter Whittingham scored a penalty in stoppage time to give the Bluebirds a vital three points.

From that night onwards the team went from strength to strength, winning six and drawing three of the final ten games. That run included a thrilling victory over our old friends Swansea at the Cardiff City Stadium. Michael Chopra scored the winning goal in injury time and over 23,000 Bluebirds celebrated like we'd won the league. The visiting fans had been taunting us by signing 'you'll never beat the Jacks' for most of the game, but they were very quiet after Chopra's late winner. Swansea never managed to recover from that defeat. They ended up finishing seventh and missing out on the play-offs by one point, which made a lot of Cardiff fans very happy!

City's great run of form meant we finished in fourth place and faced Leicester in the play-off semi-final. The first leg was at the Walkers Stadium with a Sunday lunchtime kick-off and our lads did us proud as they fought their way to a hard-earned 1-0 win. Around 3,000 Bluebirds supporters travelled to the game and went home happy thanks to superb free-kick by Peter Whittingham.

The second leg was an amazing match that was played in front of a sell-out crowd of 26,033 – Cardiff's biggest attendance since the mid-Seventies. Michael Chopra put City 1-0 up after twenty minutes to make the score 2-0 on aggregate, but Leicester battled back brilliantly. Shortly after half-time they went 3-1 up on the night and 3-2 on aggregate and many of us thought our Wembley dream was over, but Chopra was fouled in the area with twenty minutes to go and Whittingham scored the penalty to make it 3-3 on aggregate and take the game into extra time.

The extra period ended goalless, so the game went to penalties, with Leicester taking theirs first. The atmosphere inside the stadium was electric and both sides scored their first three penalties before a French player called Yann Kermorgant stepped up for Leicester. He tried to be clever and chip the ball over our keeper David Marshall, but it was a pathetic attempt and Marshall easily saved it. Left-back Mark Kennedy kept his cool and scored the next penalty for Cardiff before Marshall brilliantly saved the final kick from Martyn Waghorn to send City to Wembley.

The reaction of the supporters inside the stadium was unbelievable. The celebrations when we beat Swansea a month earlier were fantastic, but this was on another level. Hundreds of Cardiff fans invaded the pitch but it was purely to celebrate the win, so the media couldn't twist things like they had when we beat Leeds in the FA Cup at Ninian Park in 2002. This time around the only scenes to be witnessed were those of sheer joy at reaching the play-off final. I must admit I felt a little sorry for the Leicester players and their supporters. The team had put up a great battle and their fans had helped to create an incredible atmosphere, so it must have been heartbreaking to lose on penalties, but I believe that overall City just about deserved the victory.

One of the first things I did was text Sam and asked him to come to Wembley with me, as I felt he should be part of it, he replied "Annis thanks a million .You know 100% how I feel and how much you all and the club mean to me and how central in my life the dream is. I dedicate my life to achieve what we all set out to do. However, emotionally it is very distressing for me to come to the big day. Since I was forced into temporary exile I have never spoken publicly to the media and haven't attended a live game. I consider that this is still my club and therefore find it painful to come to my own home which is under occupation. You are FAMILY so I can tell you this. The fat lady has not sung for me yet but she might be singing in the not too distant future, for me. However I am being tempted to come with over 10 messages today asking me to come. Let us talk tomorrow. Much love Sam." I was never able to persuade him and I understood his reasons why.

We faced Blackpool in the play-off final and were strong favourites to beat a team who had surprised everyone by getting that far. It felt amazing to be going back to Wembley for the third time in two years. Although I'd always dreamt about going there, I didn't think we'd ever get anywhere near the place during all those years we spent in the bottom two divisions in the Eighties and Nineties. But now we were going back to Wembley again and were on the verge of getting promoted to the top flight for the first time in almost fifty years.

My good friends Cheggers and Carl Curtis organised three coaches for the lads who use my internet forum. So in May 2010, almost 40,000 City fans went to the game and beforehand I firmly believed we'd secure promotion to the Promised Land of the Premiership, but the day developed into a massive anti-climax.

Michael Chopra put the Bluebirds 1-0 up early on and I thought we were on our way, but Blackpool came back strongly and by the end of an unbelievable first half they were 3-2 up. City had lost Jay Bothroyd to injury not long after Chopra's goal and they couldn't find a way back during the second period, but to be fair I feel Blackpool deserved their victory. Their players seemed to want it a little more than some of ours and their manager, Ian Holloway, beat Dave Jones in the tactical battle. Holloway put three players in the centre of the park but Jones stuck with his usual 4-4-2 formation and City's midfield just couldn't cope. During the game Warren Feeney text me from the City dug out, "Some of our team have no balls mate, we're soft centred" that just summed it up for me and reading that text hurt me.

Losing at Wembley to Portsmouth in the FA Cup final in 2008 was tough enough, but it didn't even compare to the hurt I felt after losing to Blackpool. After many years of watching City play the likes of Rochdale, Darlington and Hartlepool, I honestly believed I was finally going to see us play Manchester United, Arsenal and Liverpool during the 2010/11 season, but I suppose I should have known better because the Bluebirds have a habit of kicking you in the teeth. Still, that's football I suppose and now we just have to forget about the defeat look forward to next season in the Championship, which is still a great league to be in. Blackpool spent decades in the lower divisions like us and we played them on many occasions, so I know exactly what it must mean to their fans to get promoted to the Premiership. I wish them good luck in the top flight and I reckon they are going to need it!

I felt very low for a few days after the final, but within a week we had the shareholders' General Meeting at the new stadium where the deal involving the Malaysians taking a 30% stake in the club would be rubber-stamped. An hour or so before the meeting, I met up with a few other shareholders such as Big Sam Murphy, Mike Roderick and Keith Morgan, who was there representing the Supporters' Trust. My friend Nathan Millichip (Milly) also came along and while we ate breakfast we discussed how we would react if Peter Ridsdale made any long speeches.

I'd had a long conversation with Sam Hammam the night before the meeting. He said there were plenty of questions he would have liked to ask the outgoing chairman if he had the chance, but he warned me to stay calm on the day. Sam said he understood the fans' frustrations over issues like the season ticket fiasco and the unpaid tax bills, but he reckoned we needed to bite the bullet and make sure everything went smoothly so that the Malaysians would come onboard.

To my amazement, Peter Ridsdale didn't make any grand speeches during the meeting. In fact, the whole thing was over and done with in just sixteen minutes. Ridsdale quickly conducted the formal business of the day by getting the necessary resolutions passed so that the investment could take place. Then he handed the meeting over to new chairman TG, who made an upbeat speech about the club's prospects next season. He said he felt honoured to be Cardiff's chairman and was aiming for automatic promotion next time around, TG Said, he never wanted to do the play-offs again, it has to be automatic promotion next season, although he did warn that the club needed to be run like a proper business from now on. His words were very convincing and he made me feel a lot happier despite what had happened at Wembley a few days earlier.

After TG's brief speech had finished, a shareholder got up and proposed a vote of thanks to Peter Ridsdale for the work he did during his time at the club. There was plenty of applause from the shareholders, more than I thought there would be, but I didn't join in and neither did some of those around me. I couldn't help but notice that Steve Borley, who was up on the stage, hardly put his hands together.

Ridsdale then brought the meeting to a close. After briefly chatting to a couple of shareholders, he left the stage and headed straight towards me. I though he was going to have a go at me for the criticism I'd given him on my website and at the previous General Meeting, plus of course the march and the demonstrations, but instead he held his hand out and said "Mr Abraham, I'd like to wish you and your family the best of luck for the future."

I was left with no option but to shake his hand, I finally felt the battle was over and we could both move on, although to be fair I thought he deserved a little respect for the way he had conducted himself during the meeting. A couple of the other lads said the same thing. Ridsdale hadn't tried to blow his own trumpet like we thought he was going to do and had instead simply got the business of the day done and dusted before handing the stage over to TG.

In my opinion, Peter Ridsdale is a man with many faults but I have to admit he was always a gentleman whenever I dealt with him face to face, and for that I must give him some respect. I had no respect whatsoever for the way he handled the finances at our club, but that's another matter. As a person, I must be honest and say I actually quite liked him. But as to running our club financially, my belief is that Peter Ridsdale was not the right man for Cardiff City on that side of things but that's just my opinion, as to knowing his football and having plenty of contacts in the football world, you cannot take that away from him. What a lot of Cardiff City fans and myself will be looking to with plenty of interest, is a criminal court case that has been brought against Peter Ridsdale by Cardiff City Council regarding the 'Golden Ticket' scheme. On the 5th May 2011 at Cardiff Magistrates Peter Ridsdale was charged on three counts, one of them was that he committed fraud in that he dishonestly made a false representation, namely the sale of the season tickets intending to make gain, namely using revenue to purchase new players, which never happened, contrary to sections 1 and 2 of the Fraud Act 2006. No charges were brought against Cardiff City as a club. The Council has indicated for this court case to be dealt with in the Crown Courts. Peter Ridsdale's lawyers indicated he would be pleading not guilty. Over the last year Ridsdale has been working with Plymouth Argyle, who have since had 10 points deducted and have been relegated.

Ridsdale on fraud charge over season tickets offer

Friday, 6 May 2011

FORMER CARDIFF CITY BOSS APPEARS IN COURT

FORMER Cardiff City Football Club chairman Peter Ridsdale yesterday appeared in court to face charges connected with a special season ticket offer made to fans.

He faces two charges under the Consumer Protection from Unfair Trading Regulations 2008 and one under the Fraud Act 2006.

The criminal charges have been brought against Ridsdale, who stood down as Cardiff City chairman in May 2010, by Cardiff council's trading standards department.

Ridsdale appeared at Cardiff Magistrates' Court to confirm his full name – Robert Peter Ridsdale – and address.

It was indicated he would plead not guilty. He was represented by David Williams QC of Fulcrum Chambers.

Following his court appearance Ridsdale, who is currently acting chairman of Plymouth Argyle, said: "I can confirm that I was present and that I will be vigorously rebutting the charges."

The so-called "Golden Ticket" scheme was announced in December 2009, offering Cardiff City fans who buy season tickets early a full refund in the event of promotion to the Premier League.

NEWS OF THE WORLD, March 21, 2010

Meanwhile, fans will step up their bid to oust Ridsdale at today's home clash against Watford.

Anti-Ridsdale T-shirts will be sold outside the ground while a petition containing more than 2,000 signatures will be handed to the Bluebirds chairman before kick-off.

Earlier this month more than 2,000 fans staged a protest march before the home game against Middlesbrough to protest about Ridsdale's handling of the club.

ON SALE – protest shirt

CHAPTER TWENTY SIX

OUR NEIGHBOURS FROM DOWN WEST

I've been to every Derby match that has been played against the Jacks (Swansea) in the last thirty years, I've even gone down there when we have been banned on two occasions, the first time just as I was about to go through the turnstiles I was collared by the old bill and told "not on this occasion Annis," and as I walked away from the ground there were lads from the Valleys standing outside shouting to each other "Everyone do the ayatollah." On the other occasion so many of us managed to get in that eventually 400 of us were put into the empty away end behind the goal.

I have also been there on many occasions when we have swamped the town centre and taken over virtually every pub, well I suppose those days are well and truly gone but they were great days and any true honest Jack should admit it, Cardiff in the Eighties would well and truly take over Swansea.

When the fixture list came out for the 2008/09 season every fan in Wales was looking for the fixture dates of the Cardiff v Jacks games, as it had been ten years since we had played them in the league and even more interesting was that we would be going to their new stadium.

So we knew we had them away in November on a Sunday morning and at home in April 2009, but it was soon announced that they would both be bubble trips but that didn't matter to the lads and fans from Cardiff as they were going no matter what. So in the meantime we had Birmingham, The Wurzels and Sheffield United to play. Before the season had even started there was trouble at Swindon away and Ajax at home in pre-season friendlies. At Doncaster away and Southampton home, Cardiff fans were involved in scuffles and about thirty Southampton lads took a right pasting in the suburbs of Cardiff (Grangetown).

On Saturday August 30th I went up to Sheffield Utd with all the Bridgend lads, a great bunch of lads to be with, yes they like a good piss up and have a good laugh at the same time. They don't go looking for trouble but if trouble came their way, man for man they would match any mob that is around today. A mate of mine Dibs (Wayne Anderson) runs a coach to every away game from the Bridgend area and goes out of his way to pick me up at every game. I started travelling with Dibs' lot in the last two seasons, one because they are a good bunch of lads who don't backstab and second like I say Dibs is a good friend of mine and I have always been good friends with the Bridgend lads over the years through another lad called Jaffa (Alun Griffiths).

Anyway back to Sheffield United away, we stopped off in Rotherham Town Centre on the way and just after we had got off the coach we were greeted by hundreds of other Cardiff lads celebrating like we had just won the cup, but in fact it had just been announced we had drawn the Jacks away in the 3rd round of the Carling cup. At first the old bill thought they were going to be attacked when everyone came running out of the pubs and the old bill retreated onto the main road, until they realised and were told by Simon Insole (our police spotter) that we were just celebrating drawing the Jacks in the cup. For the rest of the day and night that was all that was on everyone's minds and was the main conversation of the day. There was trouble at Sheffield that day and was mostly caused by their overzealous police force who seem to love whacking Cardiff fans with their batons even though United's lads had put windows through one of our buses, but that's a story for another day.

So for the next few weeks all that was on everyone's lips was how many tickets were we going to get to go to Jack land, we all knew that the away end held 3,000. Different rumours were coming out of the club, yes we could have the full allocation because it was the cup, the next minute it was being said that the police were against it, then the police said they were staying out of it and that the 500 police that would be on duty for the game could handle whatever we brought down to Jackland. Then Sky TV wanted to televise it live, which then gave the Jacks the chance to reduce our away support as they said the car park at the away end could hold no more than 28 coaches due to Sky and their Lorries setting up on it. The Jacks at one point offered us 1,100 tickets but eventually City agreed on 1,457; to me we were sold short. The fans offered to take double decker buses and the club then announced that the police were against it, but the police to this day insist it was the clubs decision, yet again will we ever know the truth?

So 1,457 Cardiff fans was the final allocation, the tickets were like gold dust and this upset and hurt a lot of the lads and fans. A number of lads did buy tickets in the Jack end but they knew the days of showing themselves had gone, not because of the fear of any of the Jacks, but of the courts and banning orders for just being in the wrong end.

The night before the game, my phone rang and it was Sam Hammam who was ringing to wish us luck and said he wished he could be there himself. He was still in Lebanon and said he kept up to date with everything that was happening at the club. He reminded me that the cup wasn't important and beating the Jacks wasn't everything, but promotion to the Promised Land was more important. He finished off with his usual words of love to every Cardiff fan and to my family; sometimes I wish he was still our chairman.

Well the day finally arrived and I drove down to Bryncethin near Bridgend to a pub called the Royal Oak, with my brother in law Jamie and a good mate of mine Simon. We got there nearly 5 hours before kick-off and on arrival nearly all the Bridgend lads were already down there, downing the ale as usual. Dibs had got a 70 seated bus so it meant we had a good group of lads. We then had to go all the way back on ourselves to meet the other coaches at Ninian Park, where we were met by over sixty old bill including some of our spotters and the usual video cameras were out in full swing, I thought to myself, what's the point of all this as we were forty odd miles from Jackland and yet the police were already in our faces. These police were going to travel down with us to make sure no one accidentally took the wrong turning. We were the last coach to arrive as usual, so we were the last to leave Ninian Park.

Soon we were back on the motorway, 28 coaches all in a line holding the M4 virtually to a standstill and the chants soon went up as we past Bridgend the place we originally left from. The buzz on the coach was unbelievable and the slow 40mph journey was broken up by laughter and cheers when a Valley lad got himself on top of one of the coaches and sat himself down as it moved along the motorway. As we passed through the outskirts of Port Talbot and Neath there were some amazing sights, only a few miles from Jackland and many houses had Cardiff flags hanging out their windows and the bridges above us on the motorway, banners were hanging over with Cardiff City and Bluebirds on them, it was a sight to be seen. Cars drove past, hooting their horns and people cheering us on as they passed and I will repeat again; this was on the door step of Jackland and 30 odd miles from the heart of Cardiff, "BLUEBIRDS."

The journey went quickly, until we were taken past the outskirts of Jackland into a quiet trading estate and yet again as we were one of the last coaches to pull in it meant that we would be at least an hour waiting by the side of the road as the police took about 8 coaches at a time to the Liberty Stadium. The problem for us was there wasn't even a toilet on the coach and tempers soon started to flare up as the lads asked for a piss to only be refused time and time again by the police. Every coach had at least five old bill standing outside the door in the middle of an empty trading estate, what was that all about? I tell you that's how trouble can soon start. We were all sweating as the air conditioning didn't work, (thanks Dibs) and the driver was told the doors had to be kept shut, illegal immigrants are treated better, but just as tempers were about to boil over, a Sergeant saw this and allowed us one at a time to have a piss by the side of the coach, hooray common sense prevails.

Eventually we were off to finish our last few miles of the trip and the chants went up again and as we passed any man and his dog, up went the chant "You Jack bastards." We were all getting phone calls saying that the first few coaches had been attacked by flares and rockets. As we drove nearer the ground on the right hand side by a pub called Coopers Arms, there looked like 600 Jacks all being kept back by riot police, dogs and horses. The Jacks looked a mixture of all sorts from lads to hundreds of kids and even women shouting abuse, well you can imagine the noise on our coaches .We were eventually put into a specially erected steel caged area (built in the last 2 weeks prior to the match especially for us). As we got off the coaches I looked around me and beside our coach of lads you had Big Sam, Ketty and Mogs' coach full of monsters and then you had Mac's lot even the Ely Trendies had brought their own coach led by my old mate Mikey Dye. Everyone tried to stand outside, but the police with cameras in our faces had opened double doors to the stadium, no turnstiles were used we were just pushed in, tickets weren't even checked.

Once inside, the bar was absolutely packed, I was shocked to see them selling alcohol as most places we go to, alcohol is banned to Cardiff fans, yet Swansea, of all places were allowing us to drink, they must be desperate for money.

Jamie and I went upstairs to have a look; we had been here once before a few seasons ago to see Wales play their first ever match at the Liberty stadium. About 100 of us had travelled down there in cars and that evening, we didn't see a Jack lad all the way to the ground or in the ground that night. The crowd had been a paltry 10,000 for the first ever Welsh game in the Jack stadium, there wasn't an atmosphere full stop. Anyway back to today's events as we entered the seats I was stunned, there was just an arena of hate all around us and virtually the whole ground was just pointing and singing hatred songs against us from pensioners, women, to school kids they were all doing the stupid "swim away," one idiot had the full costume on with a rubber ring around him. The hatred on their faces was unbelievable, now yes we hate them but they're not the be all and end all, but you could see by their actions how much they hated us, jealously maybe, we are the Capital, all the money comes to Cardiff, everyone has heard of Cardiff throughout the world and even Cardiff's lads "The Soul Crew" are known throughout Europe, I suppose you could say, what is Swansea known for? Not once did the crowd stop for breath, like I'd said earlier I'd been to their old ground the Vetch field and yes the North bank had been loud and always had a mouth at us but this was different all three sides of the ground were filled with sheer hatred.

The police had positioned themselves so that we could not move left or right or enter the seats down below, there were three lines of police and stewards between us and rows of empty seats and on top of that black sheets had been placed across rows of empty seats. How times have changed, none of this would have happened ten years ago. As the match started the atmosphere got worse and their fans seemed to go into overdrive with their hate filled songs and they had actually managed to drown our singing which to be fair I've never witnessed before, I suppose there were 15,500 of them and only 1,400 of us. The atmosphere reminded me of when we played Leeds in the great giant killing FA Cup win at Ninian Park, this time the roles were reversed.

What I did notice was that the Jacks didn't have hundreds of lads, as most were just kids that were either side of us. On the left hand side I noticed Ledley getting continually abused, it was Toozey and his cronies sat in the front rows by the halfway line, well done to Ledley anyway the more stick they gave him the more he kissed his badge.

To the right of us the Jacks had no more than 100 lads, probably only 50 good ones at that; they had hundreds of wannabe kid fighters. I knew if there had been a proper outbreak of trouble at least 400 amongst the Cardiff contingent were proper old school game lads.

Most of the first half was just abuse going back and forth and the odd coins and rubbish thrown at our players as they took the throw-ins. We had played well for the first twenty minutes but when they scored, from that moment the game went downhill and the longer the game went on the more it looked like they would score again. At half time and one nil down I went under the stand, bars were packed once again, everyone was wound up but felt we were like in a prison camp.

During the second half a lot of our lads stayed down in the bar. Our end got quieter and quieter as we were continually drowned out every time we tried to sing, so most gave up just like our team, you could say. In the last ten minutes a lot of our younger Cardiff lads tried to push through the police lines only to be quickly sent flying back. For the whole game the police had cameras in our faces.

Whilst the game had been going on about 100 lads who follow Cardiff had sat themselves down in Port Talbot waiting to see if any Jacks came back after the game, they had originally wanted to meet in Neath nearer Jackland, but every pub had been banned from showing the match and many of the lads pubs had been closed down for the night. Five van loads of old bill sat there all evening monitoring the Neath and Port Talbot lads.

When the final whistle blew, I really felt that the Jacks had deserved to win as their players had more desire to win than ours and it felt like our team never really bothered to turn up on the night, maybe Dave Jones hadn't wound them up enough of what the game meant to us. We were told we had to remain in our seats for thirty minutes. Well for the next half hour, thousands of Jacks stayed in as well taunting us, at one stage a group of thirty older Cardiff nearly got over to them, the Jacks on the right of us, for about ten minutes fought with the police to get to us, but the ones on the left just sang their stupid song, the police just let them stay in the stadium, it would never happen at Ninian park in the year 2008. Toozie's little firm had already left the stadium by now.

The old bill had moved in closer to us not allowing us any space, we were sitting ducks with missiles continually flying our way and the old bill were more concerned with watching us. So Cardiff decided to try and leave and everyone steamed out the back, a few lads from the Rhondda managed to get up a fire exit left open by the police when they had dragged a fan out, a small charge occurred up the stairs with the Jacks retreating but the police soon got to the area.

As I stood in the coach car park, a hail of stones and bottles rained down on us, we were sitting ducks just like in the ground, Cardiff fans had had enough of it and it wasn't just the lads, everyone near the fences tried to tear the fencing down, which did come down by the Sky TV lorries but this only led to the main steel cages which got the old bill steaming towards the Cardiff fans. For a good 40 minutes Cardiff refused to go onto the coaches and at one stage a lot of Cardiff fans decided to sit down on the floor as we were totally surrounded by police and steel cages. They eventually forced the Cardiff fans onto the coaches. While this had been going on (I've seen the videos of the following on ITV Wales and on the internet) about 800 Jacks and I mean mainly kids had running battles with the police, which later led to twenty of them having their mugs put in the local papers.

Finally the coaches were on their way, I thought we might be one of the first coaches out as we were one of the last in but we were about eighth and as we came out hundreds of Jacks tried to attack the first two coaches, everyone tried to get out of the fire doors but as the coaches drove out, the police in their dozens were having to run by the side of each coach, whilst the rest of the police were chasing the Jacks back into their slums. Rockets and flares were fired once again by them.

The journey home was fast and the police let us go straight back to Bridgend (hooray) and not take us back to Cardiff first, the Jacks never did go back to Port Talbot or Neath.

All in all I have to say even though not a punch was thrown by either side, the Jacks had got the message over to us, and they hate us with vengeance and are jealous as fuck of us. What this did show was that the hatred has never gone away and that if it wasn't for the CCTV, also handheld cameras by the old bill, black plastic sheets across rows of empty seats between us, a steel compound put up just for us, no freedom of movement outside the ground, every single supporter vetted before they got a ticket, bubbled in, surrounded by mass ranks of police and weeks of police gathering intelligence, there would have been fighting all over the ground and probably on every street corner. So the Eighties feelings are still there amongst the fans and have never really gone away and if it wasn't for this mass operation by the police a guaranteed riot would have happened.

I've written just a short story on our league game down there, we were once again in our usual bubble. But this time the lads had to get up at 6am and report to Ninian Park for 7.30am, for a journey by car that would have taken only forty minutes. The league game at the Liberty stadium at 11.15 am on Sunday November 30th 2008 had a larger police presence again and the atmosphere wasn't as bad, but the day still had its incidents. Cardiff were allowed a couple more hundred fans this time, the Jacks did their 'swim away' again including one of their players Pratley, when he scored in the 19th minute, he ran past the Cardiff fans doing the 'swim away', you could say that was inciting violence in itself, oh my mistake it's alright he's a player and can get away with it.

Trundle and Tate once wore t-shirts in the Millennium stadium with derogatory comments on them and held a Welsh flag up with 'Fuck off Cardiff' on it. Are they all obsessed with us or what? At the end of the game the Jacks did their pretend charge at the police, while a lone Cardiff fan stood next to them doing the Ayatollah and was smacked a bit and fell down the seats and into the arms of one of our spotters, probably the highlight of the day. The good news was he was put back in the Cardiff end. After the game the Jack kids did their usual stone throwing and then it was off home after a great match ending 2-2.

I have continued to go to our local derby games even though the forty minute trips have continued to be about three hours long due to them still being full bubble trips. The arrest figures have got less on each occasion and the atmosphere, in my opinion, at our new stadium is even dying on these derby games. At the Liberty stadium there still seems to be as much hostility towards us as ever and even at the Liberty on Sunday 6th February 2011(1pm kick off, coaches left at 9.30am) quite a few of them tried to tear up the netting between us and them, even though if they had got through that, there was still two lines of police to then get past. Our lot just stood there laughing at them and thinking you've got to be mugs to still think you can still do all that in this day and age. I still believe there is more hatred from them towards us than us towards them and they still have jealousy about us being their Capital. Even when they won promotion to the Premiership this season, their manager talked about us on the day they celebrated it, surely he should have been more interested in talking about Manchester Utd, Chelsea and the Arsenal?

CHAPTER TWENTY SEVEN

RIVALRY, CHELSEA/CARDIFF & THE OLD FIRM

CHELSEA V CARDIFF CITY – FA CUP, 13TH FEBRUARY 2010

We had Chelsea away in the cup, the team that many Cardiff fans dreamt of. Apart from West Ham, Spurs and Millwall, I think Chelsea also dreamt of playing us. Cardiff fans were rubbing their hands together and so were Chelsea's lot. My old mate Pat Dolan rang me and said, "Look, Annis, me and you are the best mates of all time but I think its best I stay in the house for this one. I love Cardiff and I love Chelsea." I said "I understand my old friend, but I won't be coming up as it's my daughter Annaise's birthday that day and I have well and truly moved on from those types of days."

Pat went on to say, "I've never known so many Chelsea fans think of Cardiff as their dream of dreams." "It's also the same for many Cardiff fans" I replied. When the draw was made for this game, I received about 40-50 texts from people saying they couldn't believe it! Chelsea was my second team in the Eighties, as well as little Bury from where my mother is from. I've been to many Chelsea games and I've got lots of friends there too. I felt that Chelsea fans were very similar to Cardiff's, but from the year 2000 onwards they had become a different type of fan.

For the game with Cardiff, the entire old firm Chelsea would be turning up. Surely the police would know this? There was no way you could let these two sets of fans mix together. Surely they could see the writing was on the wall for this one? They gave us 6,000 tickets but we could have sold 10,000. When you give Cardiff 6,000 tickets they are going to get into the wrong hands. It doesn't matter whether you are a member or not, people are going to pass them on. There were probably a lot of fans that didn't want to go because of the anticipated violence, so they were happy to sell them on. Also, because it was London, a lot of banned fans travelled. The logistics of London as an area means you have a loophole around the banning order restrictions, and as long as the banned person stayed a certain distance away from Stamford Bridge they were free to travel to other parts of the City, quite a few putting themselves up in Shepherd's Bush for the day.

The police made it a 12.30pm kick-off, closing all the pubs before the game. I think the whole of the West London police must have been there. The following is what I have been told and not just from one person that was there that day.

Before the game, Chelsea tried bullyboy tactics. Like I've said, Cardiff have never been organised and have never pinpointed people. Cardiff fans knew this was the 'big one' and knew it would be the Chelsea of old. You name them they'd be there, all the names of the past, all the major faces of Chelsea and Cardiff were going to be at this one. It would be a real nightmare game for the police.

Cardiff fans were arriving in groups of twenty, thirty and forty. They were all rushing to get to the ground as the traffic was making everyone run late. Chelsea fans were hanging around in their hundreds on the streets of Fulham Broadway. They were trying to use bullyboy tactics, calling Cardiff on, and Cardiff were just laughing at them. The police were pushing Cardiff on and there were lots of handbags before the game, with Chelsea doing most of the mouthing. Chelsea tried to put the fear into Cardiff, using the old exaggerated cockney voices to intimidate. They didn't realise that Cardiff have grown up since those days. They aren't kids anymore.
Chelsea probably were the governors in those days, but the Cardiff lads were now older and more active. Cardiff had no fear for this fixture – no fear whatsoever. They actually believed they could turn Chelsea over. They knew Chelsea would be big, but nobody thought, Oh God, its Chelsea!

Inside the ground the atmosphere was like a library with the Chelsea fans. It wasn't like the days I remembered, with the noise and the roars in the west and east stands, and fights breaking out everywhere. The Cardiff fans didn't stop singing. It was a good game and the team tried their best, but they were never going to outclass a team like Chelsea. We got well defeated on the day, 4-1.

Can you believe it? They let both sets of fans out at exactly the same time. Surely the police should have known better? Even our spotter said he asked them to keep Cardiff in the ground for half an hour after the game.
On the way out of the ground you had 6,000 Cardiff fans, and out of those you'd probably got 1000-2000 looking for trouble or trying to arrange it. As Cardiff came out onto the streets there were around 700 Chelsea, all the old faces and names from the past. The fans from the Valleys have no fear of the police, so Cardiff just went straight through the lines. Nobody was going to stop them, and the Chelsea faces were dumbstruck with shock and horror. They thought they were going to bounce around and torment Cardiff, but while Chelsea were doing all this Cardiff just came forward. In the end it was more like Cardiff fighting the Metropolitan Police than Chelsea. It went on for quite a few minutes.

As this was going on, Chelsea apparently had a massive mob along the King's Road as well, including a lot of the old faces. About 100 of Cardiff's younger lads, aged between 18 and 30, went off alone down the lanes and had a toe-to-toe head on with about 150 Chelsea old heads, just like it was in the Eighties. One of our spotters said, "I've been a police spotter for 15 years and that was full on!" He said he'd feared for his life. "For four or five minutes it was horrific. I've never seen so much violence. Nobody was giving way. Chelsea and Cardiff were going at each other and beyond –

way beyond!" Chelsea also showed that when it really matters they can still pull big numbers of all their old heads.

And where could all this be seen taking place? On CCTV, of course. When the police turned up there were just bodies all over the floor. Both sets of fans said, "Nobody ran and nobody backed down." They also said it was some of the worst violence they'd been involved in for many a year. Cardiff had a few battles with faces from the past: you had your infamous well known old-school Chelsea firm. They'd all turned out for this one, and I think you'll find a few of them had broken noses and were knocked around a bit.

What Cardiff couldn't understand, why was there were 20 of the Wolves firm there outside the ground with Chelsea? And what were five Stoke faces doing with them? Ten-fifteen QPR? Actually, the ones who did have a go at Cardiff outside were Wolves and QPR. Cardiff were shocked, because they were by themselves and couldn't understand why Chelsea needed all these others. Apparently, they were mates of mates and people from all over London had come to have a look at what was going on. But did Chelsea really need all of them?

It brought back memories of the Eighties. This was not the Soul Crew, the Soul Crew was formed in 1982 (as I told the true story earlier), by the 1990's it was finished. There is no Soul Crew, just youngsters have tried to carry the name on through the years, but the original lads all gave it up by the time the Nineties came around. Since then, on Sky TV and the BBC they have been asking the public to name about forty-fifty photos they have of Cardiff and Chelsea fans. In total nearly 100 Cardiff/Chelsea fans have now been arrested and many have since been sent to prison for what happened that day. A lad called Stefan Davies (from Merthyr) was later arrested for the incidents after this game, he pleaded guilty due to being with the crowd that had had a fight with Chelsea, he never threw a punch, never kicked anyone or never even threw anything at any Chelsea fans, but he was there during the incident. Stefan at the time was 24 years old, had worked since he left school and had a good job working for Lloyds bank as a mortgage advisor, was settled down with his fiancé, but most of all he had never been in trouble in his life before, in fact Stefan had never even had a parking ticket. That day he admits he got caught up in it and when he appeared in court he pleaded guilty. Stefan was sent to prison for 16 months, banned from football for 6 years, where by every time Wales play football Stefan will have to report to the police station and hand his passport into them for the next 6 years, plus banned from parts of Cardiff City centre on match days, yet the incident happened in London. In my mind, the sentence was ludicrous and outrageous; Stefan was just one of many other Cardiff fans who received the same kind of sentences for the Chelsea/Cardiff game. I know people reading this might think I am biased, but just think of the sentences drug dealers/paedophiles/burglars and people who carry knives get and compare them. But I will say this, to anyone who thinks fighting at football is just a laugh, it really is not worth it nowadays and Stefan has since lost his job and is basically watched over now for the next 6 years. Football has changed totally from the

Eighties and has really moved on and what has happened to Stefan and the other Cardiff/Chelsea really tells you, IT'S JUST NOT WORTH GETTING INVOLVED.

Celtic/Rangers (The Old Firm) 4th May 2010.

A good friend of mine Warren Feeney who played for Bournemouth and Luton before he signed for Cardiff asked me if I fancied going up to watch Rangers with him at Celtic. Now Warren who also plays for Northern Ireland is a staunch Rangers fan and is very open about his views regarding what goes on over in Northern Ireland and believes strongly about Northern Ireland staying part of Britain. Warren was born in Linfield and both his father and grandfather played for Northern Ireland and were living in the area during the troubles with the Loyalists and IRA. Warren's time at Cardiff City never went well for him under Dave Jones and I felt for him, as he might not have been the most gifted player around, but you were guaranteed 110% commitment. After signing for us, a few weeks later we signed Robbie Fowler and Jimmy Floyd Hasselbaink, so Warren was never really going to get a chance and was sent out on loan to our neighbours Swansea, who after a very successful spell there, tried to sign him, but Cardiff said no. Also something that needs clearing up, many Cardiff fans gave Warren stick as they were told he kissed the Jack badge when he scored for them, first Warren would only ever kiss one badge and that's Northern Irelands and secondly the only thing he ever kisses when he scores a goal is his wedding ring.

The following season, Warren was loaned out to Dundee Utd for a whole season where he had another successful spell. Dundee Utd also wanted to sign him, but Dundee Utd could not afford Warrens wages. Warren had scored against his beloved Rangers whilst playing for Dundee Utd, but he never celebrated the goal and when he played against Celtic the Celtic fans taunted him for 90 minutes with vile/evil songs. Warren returned to Cardiff and gave his all in training, but realised he never figured in Jones plans so asked if he could go, but Warren tells me Jones would not let him leave, as Jones said he needed every player. Maybe Warren was not good enough for the Championship, but surely he deserved a run in the side and lets be honest we had no battlers in our team and during many of our games that's where we were lacking. He was given six starts in three and a half years, what a waste of those years for him and what a waste of our money by us.

During his time down here, we spent many a good night out with our families. We even went up in to the Neath Valley and bought a Husky each and called them Santa and Snowy, well the children called them that. He has a young son called George, who I tried to get to support Cardiff, but he remained loyal to his Dad and Rangers was his team. Warren always went out of his way for the fans and would stop and chat to everyone who approached him. After the home night games, Warren would sometimes meet up with quite a few of us and chat with us over a curry, the lads loved to hear his stories. Warren even came down to watch Cardiff v Swansea with us after he had left the club.

So one of the funniest, strangest times I had with Warren was when I went up to Scotland to watch Rangers with him, Warren sorted the tickets for Celtic v Rangers and booked the accommodation. Rangers had just won the Scottish league, so playing at Celtic just after winning it, was definitely going to stoke up the atmosphere. I had been to many Scottish games over the years but never to an Old Firm match, so I was really looking forward to it, as so many people had said this was one of the biggest games in the world that you would ever see for atmosphere. I had been to Parkhead when Cardiff were playing in Scotland, about 100 of us popped over to watch Celtic v Palma, the day before our game, Gwyn Davies had organised it, but a lot of us left by half-time including myself as we were fed up of all the anti-British songs, it was supposed to have been a bloody football game not used for politics.

The Celtic/Rangers game was on a Tuesday night, the 4th May 2010, the good news for Warren was that Wednesday the following day was usually the players' day off, so we could fly back on the Wednesday morning. Originally Chris Burke and Ross McCormack were supposed to be coming with us, but that changed nearer to the day of the game. On the Monday the day before the game, Dave Jones, out the blue, decided the players would come into training on the Wednesday, not the Thursday, which is still a mystery as to why it was changed. Lucky enough the flight back would arrive in Bristol at about 9am on the Wednesday and training was scheduled for about 10.30am, so everyone was still up for it.

But then things were about to get even worse, airports were cancelling flights by the dozen due to the volcanic ash cloud, but our flight to Scotland was still flying. I rang Warren and said, I understand if you want to cancel, he said he would see if he had a chance of playing on Saturday, if he did, then he would cancel. After training on the Tuesday, Warren rang me to say let's still go as Jones has no intentions of picking me, Chris Burke and Ross McCormack had pulled out as there was a good chance both would be playing. I rushed up to Warrens and we both set of for the afternoon flight to Glasgow from Bristol airport.

We already had our boarding cards so it was all straight forward, but we were both still a bit worried as. As we were waiting for our flight, more and more flights were still being cancelled. Warren rang Chris Burke who told Warren even if our flight was cancelled there was another airline with a flight back in the morning. We both stood in the airport bar and fair play to Warren he never had an alcoholic drink in the bar or on the plane just water, that's one thing about Warren you could not fault, whilst a football season was being played he always kept himself as fit as a player who was playing week in week out and never turned to alcohol or gambling like many other City players had been renowned to do.

We were met at Glasgow airport by a mate of Warrens called Derek Holmes who plays for Queen of the South (ex-Shrewsbury player), Derek seemed a good laugh from the start and drove us to our hotel and then we only had to walk over to where a lot of Rangers fans were meeting up in a pub. We went in and Warren was immediately surrounded by Rangers fans all wanting to say hello to him and shake his hand, you could see he was thought of in high regards by them. After about an hour of chatting, another mate of Warrens had two double decker buses outside ready to take us all to Parkhead. Now this is where I was a bit taken back as there were no police outside, no one was going to escort us to Parkhead, yet at a Cardiff/Swansea game we would by now have been surrounded by police filming us and all our fans would have had to have been in the football grounds car park at least four hours before the kick-off to then be escorted to the other teams ground on official transport vetted by the clubs. Seeing as Rangers and Celtic hate each other so much, I was more than surprised by the totally relaxed travel arrangements. We all jumped on the double decker buses and made the short journey to Parkhead, the closer we got, the heavier the traffic got and we were now hardly moving along, you could actually walk faster. Along the sides of the roads were hundreds of Celtic fans, chanting and gesturing to us but then two seconds later, they would just hurry along to the ground. At a Cardiff/Swansea game only two years ago, rockets were fired at our coaches and hundreds of Swansea fans tried to get at us and in return Cardiff fans were even climbing on top of the coach roof and this was all happening whilst mounted police and dozens of police vans were all around us. Maybe we are still living in the dark ages in South Wales as our fans would never be allowed to walk the same streets as Swansea and it shows how bad it still is, even at Wales's games, you will hardly ever see a Swansea fan there.

The person who was organising these buses decided it was best if we all get off as the traffic was now at a standstill, with that the buses emptied; everyone just seemed to split up. I walked along with Warren and Derek and personally, I felt that outside the ground was no different than being at a Premiership game in England. Outside the away end was a bit different, there were barriers erected everywhere and there was a large contingent of police, many on horseback and a number of them with police dogs. Anyone who appeared drunk was immediately refused entry, they were then left out on the road side singing Rangers songs to any passing Celtic fan. When we got in the ground, I have to admit, the atmosphere was electric and the shear hatred between them both was heard in every song they sang. Most songs were about the Protestants and the Catholics, hardly any songs relating to the actual match we were watching. Police were now on either side filming both sets of fans but there was no areas left empty like there are at the Welsh derby game. The singing was non-stop and Rangers may only have had 8,000 of the 50,000 crowd but they certainly made their presence felt. Just before half-time my mate Carl Curtis rang me to tell me that all airports were now closed in the UK, due to the ash clouds. I turned to Warren and you could see how gutted he was, because now our problems had started, how do we get home for his training tomorrow at 10.30am? I rang my wife Joanne and asked her to see about car hire and times of trains/buses back to Bristol; Carl was also looking it all up for us at the same time. Joanne and Carl both rang back saying there was a train at about 11.20pm, but we probably would not get back to Bristol train station until about 10am the following day due to changing trains etc. I won't go in to detail but we spent the next half an hour under the stands finding out that it seemed quite impossible to get home on time and also the car hire places were also all shut now.

We were now getting depressed and so left the ground just after half-time to get a taxi back to our hotel, now that was a mission in itself, we finally got one and I enquired how much back to Bristol airport and was told £800 (they all knew of course, that there were no planes flying). In the meantime my mate Cheggers offered to either drive all the way to Crewe train station to pick us up or was also willing to drive to Carlisle (that's what you call a real mate). We checked out of our hotel and sat in the bar for ten minutes thinking what to do, I could see how worried Warren was, as he had never been late in his life for football training and was definitely not going to give Dave Jones the chance to have a go at him. We decided to get a train and get Cheggers to pick us up at Crewe train station at 6am. So we got a taxi to the train station, as we were driving along I asked this driver the price to Bristol to see if it was any different, he offered it to us at £600, we said no, but then he said he had a mate who could do it for £400. He rang his mate, but there was no answer, so he said forget it, if you don't mind going in my own car, a fiesta, I will take you for £300, but we will have to go back to the Gorbals where I live (apparently one of the toughest and roughest places in Glasgow). We said "No problem sounds great to us." On our way to the Gorbals his mate rang back and said "Sorry for not answering I am on my way to the vet's because my dog has eaten a box full of sleeping pills," when the driver repeated it to Warren and I, we couldn't believe how mad an evening we were having. But the mad tales kept on coming.

Warren jumped in the back to have some kip, whilst I sat listening to this taxi driver, shall we say fantasy stories about the amount of women he had had sex with in his taxi and the amount who had seduced him and even how two women dragged him in the back of his taxi and stripped him naked. I just kept nodding my head and looking at this 5' foot 2," 50 odd year old, thinking, in your dreams. After we had filled up with petrol at Carlisle services Warren woke up, I got the taxi driver to tell the same stories to Warren, Warren told him I was writing a book and that I would put it in there for him, his face was a picture and he said don't put my name in will you as the wife doesn't know, we just burst out laughing, well I have put a part of his story in, the rest would make this book a triple X rating, but as promised I have not put his name in.

Celtic beat Rangers 2-1, but it didn't really matter as Rangers were still Champions. The driver was driving at a constant 90 odd miles an hour and with the motorways virtually empty, we were able to finally relax. By now Warren and I had both nodded off to sleep and were woken up at Bristol airport at 3.30am, Warren said "amazing," I was chuffed for him. We paid and thanked our fantasy story telling taxi driver and by 4.15am I was fast asleep at Warren's house.

The following morning Warren made sure he was the first in for training, he later told me he could see on Dave Jones face he was shocked to see him and Warren honestly believed he knew. It could have all been so different, but thankfully it all ended well, even though we didn't get to see most of the second half of the game, I would definitely go back up to see a Rangers/Celtic game, I can see the passion and hatred they both have for each other and luckily now it does not spill over on to the terraces like it used to.

CHAPTER TWENTY EIGHT

MEETING UP WITH SAM HAMMAM AGAIN

Throughout the years since Sam Hammam was forced out of Cardiff City he has always remained in contact with myself and a number of other fans. Sam has continued to follow the progress of City and will follow each game from his home in Lebanon using the BBC ticker. Sam had never gone away and would send me texts saying things like "I am just behind the door" and "You may not see me but I am still here."

Sam always told me that one day he would tell the whole story of how he was forced out and by whom. It was May 2010 and Sam was on the phone again, he wanted a meeting; he wanted to talk to a group of our fans and tell us what had gone on and how the situation could be resolved. Sam was to fly into London and asked me to arrange a group of fans to come and meet him, fans that he could trust and fans who would remain silent on anything that was spoken in the upcoming meeting.

Sam spoke with Vince Alm, Gwyn Davies, Peter Morgan and Carl Curtis and invited each one of them along with myself to come to London for a meeting on June 21^{st,} all agreed. When it came to the time Carl, of Neath, offered to drive the rest of us to London and back, I arranged for us all to be picked up at my home. Unfortunately due to the funeral taking place of Stereophonics drummer Stuart Cable, Gwyn and Mogs were unable to make the meeting so it eventually left the meeting with Sam, Vince, Carl and myself.

We arranged to pick Sam up at Heathrow Terminal 3; we did not wait long until Sam was striding toward us with a huge grin on his face looking happy and healthy. After exchanges of handshakes and hugs we got back in the car and Sam directed Carl to the venue of the meeting. None of us travelling knew where the meeting would take place, I suspected it would be held in a hotel in the capital but I was wrong, Sam was taking us to his London home in St Johns Wood. Along the route Sam was like a tour guide showing us landmarks such as Abbey road, and it's still full with Japanese tourists and everyone wanting a photo on the famous Beatles site.

We pulled up in his drive and when his neighbours saw a car pull into the drive they were out to greet him, Sam was still popular! We went inside and sat in the lounge of this huge London property and I must say we were treated superbly. Sam was eager to talk and said we have much to talk about and amongst us we have important decisions to make. I cannot go into what was spoken about on that day as there are on-going discussions between Sam Hammam and the club over loan notes that have yet to be resolved.

For the first time ever Sam Hammam was telling his side of the story and it is a very different story to that portrayed by the club under the Chairmanship of Peter Ridsdale. Sam wanted back and he showed us the proposals that he was offering the Malaysians, who he was due to meet soon afterwards, to give the club opportunities to either settle the debt fully or other ways in which it would benefit the club if they did not wish to settle. There were four options that Sam was to propose to the Malaysians and we saw them all.

Sam's maid catered for us for the first few hours we were there, she prepared us Lebanese food, like we ate with Sam in the old days. Sam's daughter, Summer, came home and she was as hospitable as you could possibly imagine. She told us whilst her Father was not present how much he loved Cardiff and how he always talks about them and is constantly keeping an eye on the progress of the team and how he is a fan of the club. There was an endless run of drinks, food and snacks, the Lebanese certainly know how to look after their guests. We had chatted for seven hours in the lounge and over the dinner table, it was tiring but Sam did not want to stop.

Sam was talking and telling us everything that had remained silent for so many years, there was no stopping the man. The last time I had seen Sam was when he was forced out of Cardiff City three and a half years previously, he was a broken man, a shadow of the lovable, funny and eccentric character I had first got to know in 2000. But here he was again, back and on fire.

Sam was energised, he wanted action and he had his ideas, the three of us in the meeting all agreed to give Sam our backing and support and that we would do what was necessary to help him. Sam was giving me belief that he could come back, he sparked that fire inside of me and was making me believe again that the club I love could have a leader back at the helm, a leader which we were sadly missing greatly.

We had snacks again and then told Sam that we have to get back home, Carl and Vince were back in work the following morning and it was now seven o'clock and we got a three hour journey home. Sam said you cannot leave yet I have not bought you a drink. Sam took us for a walk like in the old days, this time it was over a place called Primrose hill, it felt like a new adventure was beginning all over again. As we walked, we chatted and I could see that the way he was speaking that the fire and enthusiasm was back in Sam, he had got his energy back and you could feel all that passion Sam had for Cardiff had by no means gone away. Listening to Sam, I realised that yes we had our club Cardiff City, but in my opinion our club was missing a leader at the helm, yes we have the Malaysians, but, in my opinion, they have no idea how to run a football club and they have left our club in the hands of a new chief executive called Gethin Jenkins, whose previous jobs were all rugby related.

We walked for half an hour and stopped off in a pub for a drink and some more food. Whilst walking back to Sam's house, we all agreed that what was said that evening would be kept between us. The hours had flown past as we had now been chatting to Sam for at least nine hours. We said our goodbyes and Sam said he would let us know how his meeting with the Malaysians went. On the way back home Vince, Carl and myself felt Sam still loved Cardiff City, but the chances of him coming back at this stage were remote, I think even Sam thought that, at this moment in time.

Sam attended meetings with the Malaysians in September 2010, the Malaysians were made aware of Sam's friendship amongst the fans and Sam told us that he would not tell us what had been said in the meetings with the Malaysians as he had given his word to them that everything said in their meetings stayed in their meetings.

Sam was being honourable to the Malaysians, he would keep us informed of meetings and he would tell us how his feelings of the meetings were but he would not disclose any details. Details of these meetings were still getting out and to either me or Carl. I know where I was hearing it from and it certainly was not Sam, the same can be said for Carl as we would speak with each other and discuss anything we had been told. We both felt that somebody within the meeting was putting out information to try and discredit Sam to the Malaysians. I phoned Sam and told him of things that were said in this meeting and Sam knew exactly who was blabbing.

For the following months there were numerous phone calls, sometimes hours at a time, where Sam would be telling me that we must keep faith and keep our dignity throughout. But the one thing he kept telling me over and over was that, if he comes back he will come back through the widest front door and not through a back door, he would tell me constantly that I have an important role to play and if the day comes that Sam returns to the club then he wanted this group to walk through with him.

Sam wanted another meeting with us again but this time he would come to us. I asked Sam where he wanted to go for the meeting I thought he would want to go to a hotel or somewhere like that but he said "No it has to be more private," I offered that, it take place at my home. The date was November 11th 2010, remembrance day, it is a day I will never forget as Sam was back in Cardiff for the first time since he was forced out of the club.

Carl and his wife Alison were the first to arrive at my home, closely followed by Gwyn, then shortly after Vince arrived. We sat and chatted while we waited for Sam to arrive. The evening was quickly moving on and there was no sign of Sam, I rang him and when he answered he sounded quite agitated, I said "Sam, what's wrong and where are you?"

"I have been driving for five and a half fucking hours, I got lost. I took the wrong turning out of my home (London) and when I saw the turn off for Derby I knew I was heading in the wrong direction and on the wrong motorway!" I put the phone down when Sam said he was less than five minutes away but again 25 minutes passed and he rang I cannot find your house, I passed the phone to Carl to explain to Sam how to get here, the next thing Carl is setting off from my drive to escort Sam in, he had driven passed my turn off on the M4 and was now nearly in Bridgend.

Finally Sam arrived, he looked exhausted and he apologised explaining to everyone what he had done and how tired he now was. We went into my Lounge while Joanne continued to prepare the Lebanese food she had bought for Sam's arrival. Joanne had made a huge effort preparing the food and was a perfect hostess to our guests. We sat down and Sam got straight into the meeting, we were already aware that an agreement between Cardiff City and Langston, who were represented by Sam, had a date of December 31st 2010 to settle a loan note at a reduced rate, it was agreed in the previous meeting by all of us who attended that we felt Langston would not receive the money by the end of the year. Sam promised that he would tell us far more than we previously knew it was about to be an explosive meeting or so I thought.

We paused for a while whilst Joanne and Alison along with Alexandra my 5 year old daughter, brought through the food and more drinks, everyone started tucking in the buffet except Sam, he was intent on talking, he had driven for many hours, I guess he did not wish to waste any more time by eating! Sam went through the history of how the debt and subsequent loan to Cardiff City came about; he told us which members of the board that had worked during his time had let him down. He began to tell us about how Peter Ridsdale had approached Sam to come up with a settlement figure for the loan on behalf of Langston to enable a better chance of the club receiving investment from the Malaysians and possibly a takeover. Most of this we had heard before, Sam has a habit of going over and over a story so he makes sure you understand it.

There we were all listening intently to what Sam has got to say and he is building up to the real reason he wanted the meeting and then out of the blue Vince, in a raised voice said to Sam "Bullshit! What you are saying is not true" Sam looked stunned, I think we all were, Sam said "What do you mean Vince?"

"I am saying I can smell a rat, none of it is adding up" Sam looked at Vince puzzled; this outburst came from nowhere and changed the tone of the meeting and the evening all together. I believe what Sam had come to tell us that evening never got told, because of what Vince had said, I looked at Sam and each time I did I sensed that he was hurt and deeply so. He loves Vince and he said to me the following day, he had never seen Vince like that before and what was wrong with him? I told Sam that I didn't know what it was about.

I will be honest and say I was left disappointed with how the meeting panned out and as far as I am aware so were the others, but there was nothing that could be done, Sam left my home looking confused by what had transpired. I spoke to Vince over the next couple of days and he felt bad about what he said that night and Vince said he just wanted this finally settled and was fed up of it going on and on, like the never ending story. Vince and Sam then spoke to each other and made up. I know Vince deep down had a lot of time for Sam and I know for a fact Vince loves the man and knows if it was not for Sam this club was going nowhere and those are Vince's words, which he echoed to me over the next few weeks.

I had been telling Sam for months that I did not think the club would settle its debt with Langston before the season was over but Sam disagreed with me and kept saying "Annis, they will pay by December 31st 2010 as they are honourable people and if they don't by then, then we have to allow the time for them to do so, I do not want to hurt or threaten my club."

December 31st 2010 came and went and Sam was back on the phone early in the New Year, he told me that the Malaysians wanted to meet Sam over the next few days and get the matter sorted. I was delighted for Sam but still had strong doubts as to whether it would happen; he was upbeat and confident that they were going to settle the debt; I was sceptical but did my best to be happy for Sam. Days and weeks went by and still there was no settlement, Sam was being pulled along as if on a string but I kept thinking to myself, if we go up to the Premiership then they will pay the debt off and Sam will no longer have any ties to the club. But if we did not make the Premiership then they would want Sam back to help them.

My thoughts were backed up, I felt by the fact TG had got in contact with Sam during a time when our fans were calling for the manager's sacking, results were not going the way the manager had promised and now TG was on the phone to Sam seeking advice. Sam would ring me and tell me "I have been helping out TG with football matters"; he said to me that he had told TG that the club had to keep hold of their best players like Jay Bothroyd to give the club the best possible chance of promotion.

Sam came back to Britain and again he asked if I could bring the group back to meet him to discuss where things were at and he wanted our advice. Sam came over and would spend a family holiday initially, with his children and grandchildren, and then he would meet us. The meeting this time would be held at the Exclusive Wyndham Grand in Chelsea Harbour, London's only 5 star all-suite hotel, on the evening of Tuesday 19th April 2011. This time the group that went to the meeting would be Carl, Gwyn, Corky (Paul Corkrey) and Mogs (Peter Morgan) and of course myself. When we arrived at the hotel Sam paid for Carl's car to be valet parked and we were invited up to his suite. We followed Sam up to his suite. Again Sam was looking and sounding very confident, with each meeting I could see that Sam was physically and mentally stronger on each occasion and I felt Sam was raring to go and wanted to be given another chance of trying to make Cardiff a Premier League club.

Sam ordered Champagne, beer and snacks from room service before the meeting began. He was cracking jokes and was very relaxed. Sam told us that the time was near for the Malaysians to make a decision on Langston. He said he believed that the club has a real chance of promotion and that he would not do anything nor would Langston to hamper the club's chances so until the season is over Langston and himself would remain patient as they had done for the previous few years.

But this time Sam was clear once the season ended, no matter what the outcome may be, then he on behalf of Langston, would be waiting no longer, but would be taking the necessary action to put an end to the on-going situation. Sam was given the full backing by everyone in the room, we all felt it was right that because the club owed money to Langston then they should pay the money or deal with Langston and not postpone the dealings any longer. Just to let everyone know, Sam went through every detail of who Langston really were and they were a type of hedge fund, where wealthy people who Sam knew had invested money and had let Sam sort of be in charge, I had, I admit I thought Sam was really Langston all along with his brother Ned as partner, listening to Sam now and I do believe him, Langston is a number of wealthy people who have invested into them and he was very clear and decisive on this. Sam told us that he was also still waiting on his offer to the Malaysians, that if they did not want to pay Langston off they could run our club on a 50-50 basis with Sam. Sam would totally run the football side, as that's what Sam knew best and they could totally run the business side of our club and in return he would make sure that Langston would be dealt with and the debt the club owed to them would no longer be. I said to Sam, "If we go up, I feel they will just pay off the debt," " Fine" Sam said," I added "and if we don't go up, they might then offer you a place back at the club," "Fine, I will do whatever is the best for our club" Sam replied.

We sat in the suite with Sam and continued to chat for over three hours, before we went downstairs and had a meal. Around the table we laughed with Sam as he was telling us some tales of his from some of his days involved with football. Sam was asked by Mogs if he will be coming back to the club, Sam said if that is what it takes to settle the Langston loan note then that may have to be the case. Just by his enthusiasm and confidence I could see that everyone on the table was buzzing at the thought of it. I repeated to Sam what I had said in the last few months regarding the lack of atmosphere at our new stadium and that if you were caught three times standing up, you would either get a letter in the post warning you that you will be banned if you continue to do so or they would just stop your season ticket card being able to be used again, Sam replied "If I returned I would ban anyone who was not standing up during the match," we all burst out laughing, what a character. Sam was also telling us how well he had done in New York and Lebanon business wise, during the years he had spent away from our club.

We left Sam to make our journey back home and for the trip back there was a general feeling amongst us that unless the club pay Langston then the likelihood of Sam returning is becoming greater each day that passes.

Going into the final few games of the season Sam would ring all of us, sometimes on a daily basis and just talk football and go through the tactics of what Dave Jones should be doing at Cardiff City, Sam like myself really felt with the players Dave Jones had at his disposal, there was no way we should fail and as long as we had a leader on the pitch such as Craig Bellamy, without a doubt our club should be promoted.

CHAPTER TWENTY NINE

FOOTBALL IS NOT EVERYTHING

During the year 2010, I still seemed as busy as ever when it came to Cardiff City, the BBC and directors of TV documentaries contacted me on a number of occasions asking me if I wanted to do a documentary called 'My friend Sam', they even came down from London to discuss it with me. My answer to it was, lets see how the future develops with Sam and Cardiff City.

I also had meetings with club officials regarding improving the atmosphere in our new stadium, they wanted all our fans who like to stand and sing to go in one area of the ground, the Canton Stand, it sounded good at first, but after consulting many fans who sit by me in the Ninian Stand, they were happy where they were and many felt the club were trying to bit by bit get rid of the old fans from the Ninian Park days. So I told Julian Jenkins who works for the club and is a friend of mine that we were happy where we were and that the atmosphere should come from all parts of the ground and that the club should not try and isolate us from the rest of the supporters.

I also felt strongly about the lack of local youth players that were now coming through our system and I felt that the club over the last few years had let it go downhill. So Carl Curtis, Gwyn Davies, Clive Sedgebeer and myself started a fund for the youth development and named it "Young Guns" after a local player called Scott Young who works with our youngsters, we felt that this department of our club needed helping more than anything.

On our away trips we did raffles, in the Ninian Park pub collections were held before the games, we started a membership scheme and monthly donations are now donated to the fund. Gwyn and Carl organised a bucket collection around our stadium before the QPR home game in April 2010. Since we started the fund we have been joined by Paul Corkrey, Ian Hallam (Bakedalaska), Nathan (Milly), Jamie Curtis, Claire Mallon and Baz who have contributed massively and helped out on all our fund raising ideas. Also I have to thank the club as they have allowed us to have many meetings at the club with Scott Young and his staff regarding the raising of the funds. 'Young Guns' has been a success with thousands of pounds being raised.

The last two seasons has also seen our internet forum which Carl Curtis, Owain Davies, Gwyn Davies and myself set up, organise its own Supporters club and become officially affiliated to Cardiff City, once again how times have certainly changed for me. For every away game we run at least one or two coaches and through this I have made a lot of new friends and had some real laughs on the trips and at the same time, the police have given us no hassle at all, even my daughters Annaise and Alexandra come on the coaches.

As for what happened on the pitch, the writing was on the wall once again for the sixth season running, as when it really mattered in the last few league games we got hammered at home to mid table Middlesbrough 3-0 and incidentally, some of our players were seen out drinking and some even drunk, in our town centre the night before leading up to the match, Dave Jones said it would be dealt with severely, but we never ever heard if anything did happen to those certain players. But still when it came to our last away league at Burnley, 3,500 Cardiff fans travelled the long journey north, even though we had now lost automatic promotion and were already in the play-offs, all that was to play for now was who would end up higher in the league us or Swansea.

I had travelled on one of our Forum buses with over a hundred of our members, including my eldest daughter Annaise, Carl and his daughter Angharad and a mate of mine called Lyndon and his daughter Laura who is Annaise's best friend in school. My good friend Cheggers who had stopped going as much now as he was now playing rugby, a sport I detest, but who could blame him playing for his home town Merthyr and being Captain as well had also come along for this trip as the rugby season was now over. Oh how times have really changed for me, gone were the days of the lads and myself going to these away games, now I was more than happy to go to these games in a family, fun atmosphere and not even have a local police officer look our way. The girls were all covered in face paints like Smurfs and half our coach was dressed up like that, sorry but I wasn't able to bring myself to do that, but I could see they were all having fun and that's all that mattered. Carl and Lyndon, who is a printer, had made up 50 masks and when I stepped on to the coach, Carl shouted "Now" to everyone and 40 of my mates all put on face masks with my face on it, but Lyndon had gone one better and made 10 of Carl, to the surprise of Carl, my face well, I just went red and cringed with embarrassment, I did see the funny side of it, the whole coach just burst into laughter including my daughter Annaise and her friends Angharad and Laura who were loving every minute of it, but every time I got up for a chat, many of them would put the masks on, I was speechless and I can tell you that's not like me.

We arrived in Burnley well in time for the early 12.45pm kick off, all you could see were Cardiff fans in fancy dress and doing the Ayatollah, the occasion was like a party atmosphere, but come the match that was a different occasion. Cardiff struggled to get a 1-1 draw with Craig Bellamy equalising in the final minute, which let our rivals Swansea finish above us for the first time in 18 years. At the end of the game my frustration took over me and I was able to get to the side of the players tunnel, as Dave Jones trudged off looking like he didn't have a care in the world, I shouted loudly to Jones and he looked straight at me, for six seasons I had said nothing, but this time I told him he should do the right thing and leave our club this season, he just shrugged his shoulders and wandered down the tunnel. Once again the players hardly acknowledged us at the end of the game, other than Bellamy who threw his top into the 3,500 Cardiff fans behind the goal, who had sung their hearts out for 90 minutes. All season I felt Dave Jones and his players had never ever really acknowledged our fantastic support and there was no rapport between us, Dave Jones and his players, that hurt me and many other City fans who I have spoken to felt the same.

So we were in the play-offs for the second season running, having to now play Reading away first and then home to them in the second leg. Once again we travelled in our thousands including our forum buses. City played well and fought for 90 minutes, even after Bellamy went off injured and we earned a 0-0 draw. Within a few days the return game at home was upon us and with nearly 24,000 City fans cheering our team on, surely we could not fail, but in my mind I never felt positive at all, one we had no leader on the pitch as Bellamy was still injured and two I had no belief in Dave Jones being able to do it when it really mattered and sadly my feelings were right, but worse than right, as Reading hammered us 3-0 at home, another heartbreaking end to the season, I don't think I or thousands of other City fans could take another season of Dave Jones, and these in my opinion gutless/passionless and clueless players being here next season, The funny thing is about ten of them won't be anyway, as Jones had built most of our team up with loan players, I felt Jones hadn't built a team for the future, just a team for today and I would have loved local lads playing for their hometown team, but that's not Jones' style.

To people who are not football fans they might find my comments about the last four years a bit dramatic, but every City fan will understand what I mean. Four years, four heartbreaking endings, under Dave Jones it's becoming a familiar ending. You all know now the history of the past few years, last year it was a narrow defeat in the play-off final against Blackpool. The year before, one point from the last twelve available to us and a 6-0 hammering by Preston, followed by another hammering in our final ever league game at Ninian Park by Ipswich Town 3-0,which meant we could not even reach the play-offs. In 2008, FA Cup final defeat and this season with probably our best ever squad in our history and even Dave Jones saying he expected automatic promotion, we ended up finishing fourth place, with two out of the three teams above us on a playing budget nearly half the size of ours, followed by a comprehensive play-off defeat at home to Reading, who had finished below us in the league table. To add to our wounds our bitter rivals Swansea made it to Wembley on a shoe string budget, it just seems that Dave Jones' teams cannot make it over that final hurdle and that will only ever bring agony to Cardiff City's loyal supporters.

Continual comments by Dave Jones, about our supporters never helped, like "We live in a part of a world where everyone thinks they can do better," this part of the world was mentioned on numerous occasion, after we had just lost a game, if he did not like this part of the World, no one forced him to stay here for over six years. Remember this part of the world gave Dave Jones a 'Five star luxury life' with a wage higher than nearly any other manager has ever been paid in the league we are in. So to me Dave

Jones had to step down as manager now and give us a new start. Our support has been fantastic at home with average crowds of over 23,000 and away with regular support of over 2,000 City fans travelling the length and breadth of the country. Surely after fifty one years of not playing in the top Division, Cardiff City fans finally deserve that prize.

I spoke to Steve Borley, Cardiff City's vice chairman the day after the shambles of the Reading game, I could feel he was hurting badly, remember even though Steve was the vice chairman of our club, he too was a supporter like us. Steve had cancelled his planned holidays to Majorca as he felt there was now a lot of planning to do regarding the future of Cardiff City.

Life is so weird and the unexpected things can happen, when you least expect it, Sam asked if I was willing to speak to Peter Ridsdale, I said yes, but he probably won't speak to me. Well I rang Ridsdale and within minutes he returned my call. I immediately said to him that I never expected him to ring me back, but fair play to him once again, he said "I shook your hand on the day I resigned and wished you and your family all the best, I had no bad feelings to you then and I don't have now, you had your beliefs and I had mine." Ridsdale also went on to say "If the Malaysians had put the millions in before Christmas when I was there, then things would have been totally different." I then told him why I was ringing and wanted him to answer what his opinion was regarding the money owed to Sam/Langston as he was the person who had made the new contracts up with them, Ridsdale's answer was "That the money was now owed to them and should be paid and that Sam/Langston would win in court." I thanked Ridsdale for speaking to me and verifying the answers that Sam had already told me. The following day it was announced that Ridsdale was the new owner of Plymouth Football Club.

On Monday the 30th May 2011, I was one minute on a high, but by evening one of the worst things that could happen to us happened. First the great news I had been waiting for, for at least the last four years I have personally wanted this day to come, Dave Jones was given his notice, now that to me was music to my ears. But by 5pm that day the Jacks had done what we have failed to do in the last 51 years and won promotion to the Premier League by beating Reading 4-2 at Wembley and if I am really honest they deserved promotion as they had been man managed and played like a team and not a bunch of overpaid individuals. Yes it hurts, especially seeing them on national news celebrating, but that's life and we must just get on with it and with nearly 18,000 season ticket holders for next season our club must continue to be ambitious and go for promotion once again, our fans in my opinion at least deserve that.

Then on Tuesday the 31st May 2011, our club made a statement through chief executive Gethin Jenkins that there would be no return for Sam Hammam while the Malaysians were in charge and they were going to go one step further and have forensic accounting done on the loans Sam took out with the club. My personal opinion on this and I mean my personal opinion, what a load of bollocks, for the last year they have been talking to Sam and have been on very friendly terms with him and have made him feel everything would be sorted and to me, this is just another delaying tactic, but the truth will come out in the end, it always does. Sam told me, he now has no other choice but to take legal proceedings, which he really did not want to happen, which could be the beginning of probably another long drawn out court case. All I want is what is best for Cardiff City; this has to be finally sorted for the future and good of our club.

On the plus side the Malaysians also announced that they are committed to Cardiff City and will be challenging for promotion next season, let's hope so. On the 17th June 2011 our club introduced our new manager Malky Mackay, an up and coming manager from Watford, the weeks leading up to his arrival, we were linked with Alan Shearer, Chris Hughton, Roberto Di Matteo and even Robbie Fowler, at some point they all had some contact with our club. Our fans need to give Mackay time and get behind him from the start and that includes me. I am honestly excited by the appointment of Mackay and the feel good factor has returned throughout South Wales.

No doubt the next few years will be another rollercoaster ride, but that's always the way life is when you follow the Bluebirds. Being a Cardiff City fan guarantees you'll experience many ups and downs but it's very rarely dull!

Football and working in nightclubs was once everything to me, that's all I used to want and probably the only things I knew in life, but in the last few years being with my daughters and wife has brought me so much happiness. Thanks to my wife Joanne helping to teach acting and dancing to my daughters, Annaise (aged 10) and Alexandra are now real little stars, as Annaise has now appeared on stage, well over a hundred times with stars like John Barrowman (in Robin Hood) and Tommy Steele (in Scrooge, West End production), appearing in the Millennium Centre, New Theatre, River Front Theatre and many other theatres all over South Wales and Alexandra still only five, already has appeared on stage in the New Theatre Cardiff and in Barry. I have more excitement and joy watching my little girls grow up, than football has ever brought me and with our baby girl Tilly Annis needing plenty of attention and love, football will certainly now more than ever, definitely have to take a back seat.

So many people ask how I personally made my money in life, well as you have just read I worked in nightclubs/pubs/hotels/shops from the age of 12 to 36 years old, never having a weekend off not even Christmas or New Year's eve, whilst my mates were out drinking and socialising, I would save every penny of my wages other than the money I spent following football and especially my club Cardiff City. I bought through those years properties on fifteen to twenty year mortgages and rented them all out, whilst I worked in the other businesses. I was prepared to sacrifice going out and to me my vice was just going to football, thankfully it has all paid off and my children will have a good start in life. I enjoy my home life and being with my family each and every day and evening. I am a humble man who has not forgotten my roots; I am comfortable being in the company of all kinds of people and still do everything for myself and my family. I take care of the chores around the house, I have never been a snob or consider myself upper class, you will not find gardeners or cleaners in my home, I have followed my father's roots regarding work and taking care of things yourself, and I am hopefully a rock to my children like my mother was to me. The values my parents taught me are handed down to my children as I know they are good old fashioned morals built on principal.

I would like to finish by saying that I don't regret anything I've done in the past and I don't feel the need to apologise to anyone either, as I believe I have always been straight and honest whenever I've been dealing with people. I hope I have followed in my father's footsteps in that respect, as that's the way he always lived his life.

My only regret is that my mother never got to meet my lovely wife and my beautiful daughters, as I know they would have meant the world to her, as they do to me. It's also a shame that Joanne and the children were never able to see my father while he was at his strongest. Unfortunately, he was frail and weak by the time he met Jo and Annaise. I idolised my father and had a massive amount of respect for him, so I would have loved for him and my mother to have been able share in the joy that raising my children is bringing me. On Sunday June 19th 2011on Father's day my family and I went to the cemetery to pay our respects to my parents and their grandparents, whilst we were sitting there by the grave looking at the photos of my parents on the gravestones, Alexandra my 5 year old said "Is that you Daddy? " "No" I said, "that's your Granddad, when he was getting married to your Grandmother." Alexandra's words brought a smile to my face and I loved it that she actually saw my father in me.

I feel I have matured considerably in recent years as a result of my relationships with Joanne and my daughters Annaise, Alexandra and Tilly. I'm very much a family man these days and I believe I am a better person for it. Cardiff City is obviously still hugely important to me, but my wife and children always come first. Nevertheless, I have met some very good mates over the years through football and I continue to make more friends with each new season. I would like to take this opportunity to thank each and every one of them for their friendship. It means a great deal to me.

I would again like to thank Carl Curtis for helping me with this book.

The day before this book went to print, Wales played England at Wembley on Tuesday September 6th 2011, one of my closest friends Mikey Dye tragically lost his life after he was attacked outside the turnstiles when he was entering the stadium.

Mikey you were a friend I will never forget, may you rest in peace my old mate.

Other Books by Annis Abraham Jnr

"From Shattered Dreams to Wembley Way"

"Diary of the Real Soul Crew"

"Diary of the Soul Crew 2"

"Cardiff City Fans Through the Years"

"The Chronicles of the Real Soul Crew"

Plus Published by Annis

"The Rise and Fall of the Cardiff City Valley Rams" by Gwyn Davies

All Available at

www.annisabraham.co.uk

www.cardiffcityforum.co.uk

Amazon

Waterstones